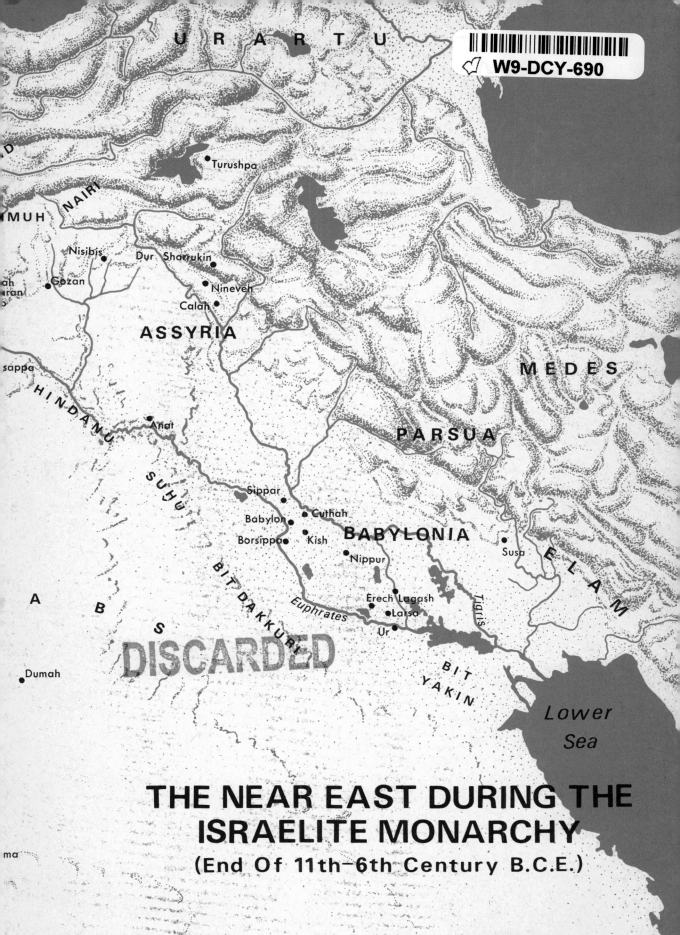

U R A R T U

•Turushpa

NAIRI

MUH

Nisibis•

Dur Sharrukin•

Gozan•

•Nineveh

Calah•

ASSYRIA

MEDES

sappa

HINDANU

PARSUA

SUHU

•Anat

Sippar•

BIT DAKKURI

Babylon•

•Cuthah

Borsippa•

Kish•

BABYLONIA

Susa•

E L A M

Nippur•

A

B

S

Erech •Lagash

Euphrates

•Larsa

Tigris

Ur•

•Dumah

BIT
YAKIN

Lower
Sea

ma

THE NEAR EAST DURING THE
ISRAELITE MONARCHY
(End Of 11th–6th Century B.C.E.)

THE AGE OF THE MONARCHIES: CULTURE AND SOCIETY

THE WORLD HISTORY OF THE JEWISH PEOPLE

FIRST SERIES: ANCIENT TIMES

GENERAL EDITOR

BENJAMIN MAZAR

MANAGING EDITOR

ALEXANDER PELI

JEWISH HISTORY PUBLICATIONS (ISRAEL–1961) LTD.

THE AGE OF THE MONARCHIES: CULTURE AND SOCIETY

VOLUME FOUR - II

EDITOR

ABRAHAM MALAMAT

ASSOCIATE EDITOR

ISRAEL EPH'AL

MASSADA PRESS LTD., JERUSALEM, 1979

PUBLISHED IN ISRAEL
BY JEWISH HISTORY PUBLICATIONS (ISRAEL – 1961) LTD.

PRINTED IN ISRAEL

CONTENTS

CHAPTER IX

CHAPTER X

PUBLISHER'S NOTE

The present book in the First Series of the World History of the Jewish People is a direct continuation of THE AGE OF THE MONARCHIES: POLITICAL HISTORY. The period covered by these two volumes is, in effect, one unit with inter-connected themes throughout.

Professor Abraham Malamat's introduction to the previous volume is, therefore, also relevant as an introduction to this volume.

AUTHORS

ILLUSTRATIONS

DRAWINGS

ABBREVIATIONS FOR BIBLICAL BOOKS

Gen.	Genesis	Hab.	Habakkuk
Ex.	Exodus	Zeph.	Zephaniah
Lev.	Leviticus	Hag.	Haggai
Num.	Numbers	Zech.	Zechariah
Deut.	Deuteronomy	Mal.	Malachi
Josh.	Joshua	Ps.	Psalms
Jud.	Judges	Prov.	Proverbs
I Sam.	I Samuel	Cant.	Canticles (Song of Songs)
II Sam.	II Samuel	Lam.	Lamentations
Isa.	Isaiah	Eccl.	Ecclesiastes
Jer.	Jeremiah	Dan.	Daniel
Ezek.	Ezekiel	Neh.	Nehemiah
Hos.	Hosea	I Chron.	I Chronicles
Ob.	Obadiah	II Chron.	II Chronicles

ABBREVIATIONS FOR JOURNALS
AND SCIENTIFIC LITERATURE

AASOR	—*Annual of the American Schools of Oriental Research*
ABL	—R. F. Harper, *Assyrian and Babylonian Letters*, vols. I–IV, Chicago, 1892–1914
ADAJ	—*Annual of the Department of Antiquities of Jordan*
AfO	—*Archiv für Orientforschung*
AHw	—W. von Soden, *Akkadisches Handwörterbuch*, Wiesbaden, 1965 ff.
Ain Shems	—E. Grant, G. E. Wright, *Ain Shems Excavations*, I–V, Haverford, 1939.
AJA	—*American Journal of Archaeology*
AJSL	—*American Journal of Semitic Languages and Literatures*
Alt, *Kleine Schriften*	—A. Alt, *Kleine Schriften zur Geschichte des Volkes Israel*, vols. I–III, München, 1953–1959
Amiran, *Pottery*	—R. Amiran, *Ancient Pottery of the Holy Land*, Jerusalem, 1969.
Ancient Gaza	—W. M. F. Petrie, *Ancient Gaza*, I–IV, London, 1931–1934.
ANEP	—J. B. Pritchard, *The Ancient Near East in Pictures*, Princeton, 1954; 2nd edition, 1969.
ANET	—J. B. Pritchard (ed.), *Ancient Near Eastern Texts Relating to the Old Testament*, Princeton, 1950; 3rd edition, 1969.
AO	—*Der Alte Orient*
APEF	—*Annual of the Palestine Exploration Fund*
BAr	—*The Biblical Archaeologist*
BASOR	—*Bulletin of the American Schools of Oriental Research*
Beer-sheba, I	—Y. Aharoni (ed.), *Beer-sheba*, I Excavations at Tel Beer-sheba, 1969–1971 seasons, Tel Aviv, 1973
BIES	—*Bulletin of the Israel Exploration Society* (1951–1962) (continuation of *BJPES*)
BJPES	—*Bulletin of the Jewish Palestine Exploration Society* (1933–1950)
BJRL	—*Bulletin of the John Rylands Library*
BiOr	—*Bibliotheca Orientalis*
BZAW	—*Beihefte zur Zeitschrift für die alttestamentliche Wissenschaft*
CAD	—*The (Chicago) Assyrian Dictionary*
Enc. Miqr.	—*Encyclopaedia Miqra'it*
Gezer	—R. A. S. Macalister, *The Excavation of Gezer*, I–III, London, 1912
Hazor	—Y. Yadin *et alii*, *Hazor*, I–IV, Jerusalem, 1959–1964
HT, I	—C. Singer, E. J. Holmyard, A. R. Hall (eds.), *History of Technology*, I, Oxford, 1956
HTR	—*Harvard Theological Review*

HUCA	—*Hebrew Union College Annual*
IEJ	—*Israel Exploration Journal*
IOS	—*Israel Oriental Studies*
JAOS	—*Journal of the American Oriental Society*
JBL	—*Journal of Biblical Literature*
JCS	—*Journal of Cuneiform Studies*
JEA	—*Journal of Egyptian Archaeology*
Jericho	—K. M. Kenyon, *Excavations at Jericho*, I–II, London, 1960–1965
JESHO	—*Journal of Economic and Social History of the Orient*
JNES	—*Journal of Near Eastern Studies*
JSS	—*Journal of Semitic Studies*
JThS	—*Journal of Theological Studies*
Judges	—*The World History of the Jewish People*, vol. III, Judges, ed. B. Mazar, Tel-Aviv, 1970
KAI	—H. Donner-W. Röllig, *Kanaanäische und Aramäische Inschriften*, vols. I–III, Wiesbaden, 1966
Kaufmann, *Tol^edot*	—Y. Kaufmann, *Tol^edot ha-Emunah ha-Yisre'elit*, vols. I–IV, Tel Aviv, 1937–1956 (Hebrew)
KUB	—*Keilschrifturkunden aus Boghazköi*, Berlin, 1921–
Lachish, II–IV	—O. Tufnell *et alii*, *Lachish*, II–IV, Oxford, 1940–1958
MAB	—A. Barrois, *Manuel d'archéologie biblique*, vols. I–II, Paris, 1939–1953
Megiddo, I	—R. S. Lamon, G. M. Shipton, *Megiddo*, I, Chicago, 1939
OLZ	—*Orientalistische Literaturzeitung*
OTS	—*Oudtestamentische Studiën*
Patriarchs	—*The World History of the Jewish People*, vol. II, The Patriarchs, ed. B. Mazar, Tel-Aviv, 1970
PEQ	—*Palestine Exploration Quarterly*
PEF QST	—*Palestine Exploration Fund*, Quarterly Statement
QDAP	—*Quarterly of the Department of Antiquities in Palestine*
RB	—*Revue biblique*
Samaria	—J. W. Crowfoot *et alii*, *The Buildings at Samaria*, London, 1924
Samaria, Harvard	—G. A. Reisner *et alii*, *Harvard Excavations at Samaria*, I–II, Cambridge, Mass., 1924
Shechem	—G. E. Wright, *Shechem, The Biography of a Biblical City*, New York, 1965
Tell en-Nasbeh	—C. C. McCown, *Tell en-Nasbeh*, I–II, Berkeley, 1947
ThWAT	—*Theologisches Wörterbuch zum Alten Testament*, 1970 ff.
ThZ	—*Theologische Zeitschrift*
UT	—C. H. Gordon, *Ugaritic Textbook*, Roma, 1966
VT	—*Vetus Testamentum*
VTS	—*Vetus Testamentum*, Supplement
WO	—*Welt des Orients*
Yediot	—Continuation of *BIES* (1962–1967)

ZA   —*Zeitschrift für Assyriologie und verwandte Gebiete*
ZAW   —*Zeitschrift für die Alttestamentliche Wissenschaft*
ZDMG   —*Zeitschrift der deutschen morgenländischen Gesellschaft*
ZDPV   —*Zeitschrift des deutschen Palästina-Vereins*
ZThK   —*Zeitschrift für Theologie und Kirche*

HEBREW-ENGLISH TRANSLITERATION

1. All Hebrew names found in the Bible are given as they appear in the English translation of the Holy Scriptures by the Jewish Publication Society of America, Philadelphia, 1955.

2. Those names that are familiar to the English reader are rendered in their customary, accepted spelling (e.g., Caesarea).

3. All other Hebrew names and words are transliterated as follows:

א	Not noted at beginning or end of word; otherwise by ', e.g. Mē'ir (מֵאִיר).
בּ	b
ב	v
גּ	g
ג	g
דּ	d
ד	d
ה	h (unless consonantal, ה at the end of the word is not transliterated)
ו	w
ז	z
ח	ḥ
ט	t
י	y
כּ	k
כ	ḵ
ל	l
מ	m
נ	n
ס	s
ע	'
פּ	p
פ	f
צ	ṣ
ק	q
ר	r
שׁ	š, sh
שׂ	s, ś
תּ	t
ת	t (except in the word בית —beth)

a) The *dagesh lene* is not indicated, save in the letters ב and פ . *Dagesh forte* is indicated by doubling the letter.

b) The Hebrew definite article is indicated by *ha* or *he* followed by a hyphen, but without the next letter doubled, e.g. *ha-shana*, not *ha-shshana*.

ˉ	a	ֶ	e
ֲ	ă	ֱ	ĕ
ָ	ā	וּ	ū
ָ	o	וֹ	ō
ֳָ	ŏ	ֻ	u
ֵ	ē	ִ	i
ֵ	ē, ēi	ִי	ī

Sheva mobile (שוא נע) is indicated thus: ^e or ^ĕ. Neither long vowels nor *sheva mobile* are indicated in proper names.

ARABIC-ENGLISH TRANSLITERATION

ء	— ' (not indicated at the beginning of a word)	ض	— ḍ
ب	— b	ط	— ṭ
ت	— t	ظ	— ẓ
ث	— th	ع	— '
ج	— j	غ	— gh
ح	— ḥ	ف	— f
خ	— kh	ق	— q
د	— d	ك	— k
ذ	— dh	ل	— l
ر	— r	م	— m
ز	— z	ن	— n
س	— s	ه	— h
ش	— sh	و	— w
ص	— ṣ	ى	— y

The *lām* of the definite article ال is assimilated before a solar letter. Proper names familiar to the English reader are rendered in their customary spelling.

THE AGE OF THE MONARCHIES: CULTURE AND SOCIETY

CHAPTER I

KINGSHIP AND THE IDEOLOGY OF THE STATE

by S. Talmon

A. The Sources

A S WITH most matters of belief and social thought, the Bible deals with monarchy not systematically but primarily by observing actual events. Exceptions to this rule are the "Law of the King" (*miṣvat ha-meleḵ;* Deut. 17:14–20),[1] the "Statute of the King" (*mišpaṭ ha-meleḵ;* I Sam. 8:10–17), Nathan's prophecy (II Sam. 7:4–17),[2] Gideon's declaration (Judg. 8:22–23), and perhaps Jotham's fable (*ibid.* 9:7–20). The biblical concept of monarchy must therefore be dealt with as an idea and as a social organization, by framing fragmentary information which the scholar extracts from the text, explains, and tries to synthesize into one system of thought. It is by no means to be expected that by connecting one clue or one fragment to another it will be possible to present a comprehensive view of monarchy in the biblical period or of the political ideology from which it sprang. The discussion must perforce remain fragmentary.[3]

Moreover, the bits of information to be gleaned from the biblical texts do not always tally. Sources might even contradict one another, and this is not at all surprising. The biblical literature developed over the course of centuries. It therefore reflects concepts of the monarchy at various stages of its development, the diverse reactions and changing attitudes toward it of generations of scribes, and echoes of contrasting opinions about it which were entertained in Israel at any one point in time as well as at various periods.

The problem presented by the heterogeneity of sources concerning the concept of monarchy is compounded by the difficulty of dating them. Most biblical statements, whether pro- or anti-monarchy, bear no signs which would enable them to be dated, especially when they are contained in literary anthologies such as the book of Psalms, which crystallized progressively over a lengthy period. The same holds true for the historiographical and prophetic literature, our principal source for understanding the concept and nature of monarchy in the biblical period. Even where a superscription specifies the date of writing a book, there is no way of telling when specific individual passages concerning the monarchy were composed or committed to writing. A precise presentation of the development of political thought or of the view of the monarchy in the Bible is therefore impossible. This is especially difficult in surveying the time when the monarchy actually sprang into being between the period of the Judges and the days of Samuel.

Despite these limitations, the biblical sources still remain the major basis for every study of the concept of monarchy. We have no extra-biblical evidence which directly illuminates the ideological foundations of the monarchy in Israel or informs us of the ways in which royal power was exercised. Extra-biblical sources, by way of comparison, can serve to fill out the picture which emerges from the biblical account by pointing out similar or identical characteristics in the Israelite kingdom and ancient Near Eastern kingdoms, and by highlighting what was peculiar to Israel in contrast to the monarchical regimes of surrounding nations. With regard to the early monarchical period, we depend especially on the relatively meager information concerning the ethno-political entities in Transjordania whose social structure at that time was similar to that of Israel: Edom, Moab, and Ammon. For the period of the United Kingdom—when the Israelite monarchy was at the height of its development—we have at our disposal the more numerous references to the monarchical regimes in the Cisjordanian Canaanite city states of Syria, Tyre, Sidon, and Ugarit, as well as sources from the Mesopotamian empires. It should be remembered, however, as Frankfort said, that the elements of Israelite culture which supposedly were drawn from neighboring civilizations, or whose like can be found there as well, are less important threads in the fabric.[4] Similar or even identical terms and phrases in the literatures of different peoples can express differing conceptual loads. The exact meaning of biblical phrases and terms dealing with monarchy should therefore be derived from their own linguistic context and the immediate contextual matter and are not to be defined on the basis of the socio-political vocabulary of other ancient Near-Eastern peoples.[5]

B. THE IDEA OF THE STATE IN THE BIBLICAL PERIOD

The concept of the state results from Israel's viewing its own place in history and the place of the surrounding peoples as a reflection of the principles upon which the world was created—a set of concentric circles. The political system is considered the historical embodiment of the complex of relationships between men, established by God at the creation of the world: on the international plane in defining the relations between Israel and her neighbors, and on the intranational in delineating the functions and stipulating the rights which govern the relations between the deliverer-ruler (*mōšīa'-nāgīd*) and the community he leads. Ideally, the laws of creation permeated the foundations of the Israelite historical-national existence which, for the biblical writers, reached its fullest expression in the United Monarchy. There is practically no definition of the political sphere which is not conceived of and couched in terms of monarchy, because only under the monarchy did Israel crystallize as a people with a common faith and consciousness of a common origin and establish a national territorial framework on a basis of political sovereignty. The idea of state[6] and the concept of monarchy are one.

In identifying the concept of state with that of monarchy, Israel was no different from most ancient Near-Eastern peoples. The biblical traditions concerning these peoples also speak of them in terms and imagery of monarchy.[7] Similarly, both Israel and her neighbors conceived of divine rule as monarchical.[8] Such epithets and definitions applied to mortal kings as *nāgīd, mōšīa', sār, šōfēṭ,* etc. also apply to the heavenly kingdom, especially with respect to two types of imagery drawn from the life of society: military leadership[9] and legislation.[10]

It does not concern us here whether the terminology of political monarchy was derived from the image of the god-king or whether notions of government on the terrestrial plane were transferred to the celestial sphere. A single world of concepts permeated Israel's historical existence, from its beginning after the Exodus unto the "later days:" when it was a self-contained political entity, and when it was integrated into the general political structure of the ancient Near-Eastern nations; in terrestrial reality and in relation to the celestial realm. The parallelism of terms of government common to all aspects of Israel's existence, actual-political and ideal-religious alike, correctly reflects a basic conceptual principle of socio-political leadership which remained constant. In the biblical period Israel viewed monarchy as the quintessence of social life.

Biblical Israel viewed the socio-political order not as static but as a developing, changing mechanism. This is also true of the monarchy, which by a historical process gradually grew out of the confluence of internal social factors and external political pressures, and was influenced in its variations by the types of monarchical government prevalent among the nations with which Israel maintained mutual relations from the time of the conquest of Canaan until the ultimate loss of political sovereignty. In other words, the monarchical regime was not perpetuated in the form in which it emerged in the time of Saul. From the very beginning, elements and principles inherent in it found expression in historical reality in executive agencies which constantly changed form. This dynamism which marks the history of Israelite government from the outset should guide any discussion of the idea of state and the concept of the monarchy in the biblical period.

C. A Kingdom of Priests and a Holy Nation[11]

The essence of Israel's special status is defined in a programmatic divine statement in the book of Exodus: "Now then, if you will obey Me faithfully and keep My covenant, you shall be My treasured (or special) possession[12] among all the peoples. Indeed, all the earth is Mine, but you shall be to Me a priestly kingdom and a holy nation"[13] (Ex. 19:5–6; cf. Deut. 7:6, 14:2, 26:18). Israel's social existence was founded on the premise of being distinct from all peoples by virtue of divine election. The election is meant to be realized in historical actuality in the political framework of the kingdom to be founded after the Conquest of Canaan, when the geo-political conditions are conducive to its realization. The biblical writer viewed the independent national kingdom in the Promised Land as the embodiment of an ancient vision. The definition of Israel as a priestly kingdom and a holy nation therefore reflects the ideological principles which are the foundation of monarchy.[14] Israel's covenant with God elevates the political national existence to the rank of a social-religious experience based on the mutually complementary cooperation of people and king under divine supervision.[15] The territorial and political sovereignty and the idea of religious submission are the warp and woof of the Israelite monarchy.

The Covenant of Sinai bridges the divine promise of royalty to Abraham— the father of the Hebrews—and the future covenant with King David and his descendants. The blessing of Abraham uses phrases and historical-conceptual motifs which parallel the statement in Ex. 19:5–6, and which refer to Israel as God's chosen people, marked by the political-territorial quality of a monarchy in the land of Canaan: ". . . and I will make nations out of you, and kings shall come forth from you. And I will establish My covenant between Me and you and your descendants after you throughout the generations for an everlasting covenant, to be God unto you and to your descendants after you. I will give to you, and to your descendants after you, the land of your sojournings, all the land of Canaan, as an everlasting possession; and I will be their God"[16] (Gen. 17:6ff; cf. *ibid.* 16 and 35:11). Similar language and imagery appear in Nathan's prophecy (II Sam. 7), and in a more concise form in the Royal Psalm 110:3–4: "Your people offer themselves willingly in the day of thy warfare; in adornments of holiness . . . The Lord hath sworn and will not change his purpose: You are a priest for ever after the manner of Melchizedek." Notwithstanding the uncertain meaning of the passage, the four words ʿamkā, qādōš, kohēn, malkī (ṣedeq) evidently paraphrase Ex. 19:6 with the intent of applying the formula of the covenant between God and His people to this covenant with the Davidic dynasty which, for the poet, represented the essence of Israel's nationhood.

The similarity in language and motif which, on the one hand, apply to the ethnic and national entity, and on the other to the monarchy, indicates the centrality of kingship in biblical political thought. Israel from its very beginning was destined to become a kingdom, just as monarchy was destined for Israel. All pre-monarchical social institutions were considered merely introduction to and preparation for the sublime gift of royal splendor. Israel's history throughout the biblical period unfolds under the banner of kingship.

D. THE SAVIOR

Socio-political leadership, in any form, is viewed in the Bible as a function of God's divine Covenant with Israel. In the period of Israel's political self-crystallization—between the Conquest of Canaan and the Settlement to the beginning of the Monarchy—the Covenant centered around the military and political experience and was concretized in the "savior," the divinely appointed emissary who brought his people deliverance from their enemies.

At first the savior is appointed *ad hoc*. The term of his appointment is commensurate with the duration of the danger. His mission consists of fulfilling a specific task. The delineation of his mission accords with the nature of the peril and guarantees that the power given him will remain temporary. Since the appointment answers a specific need, it ends when that need is satisfied. In theory, therefore, Israel required no formal limitations of the rights and obligations inherent in the mission because they were determined by the task itself. In practice, however, the divine spirit was never removed from a leader, from Moses to Samuel. All biblical traditions concerning saviors report the leader's death (Judg. 3:11), usually at a ripe age (*ibid.* 8:32).[17] Even when no mention is made of his death, it is understood from the text that he died while still "in power" (*ibid.* 3:30, 5:31). This clearly indicates that when divine inspiration alighted upon a chosen person, it stayed with him all his life (*ibid.* 16:31; I Sam. 7:15).

His mission to save Israel from its enemies determined the savior's position among his compatriots. Along with the spirit of God came some of the divine authority and the people obeyed him in socio-political matters because his power derived from God's sovereignty.[18] Being delivered by the savior obliges the people to bear his yoke as well. As the one who crystallizes the covenantal promise in the historical realm, he has the right to limit the freedom of his people, just as has the Covenant.

The establishment of the Covenant is subject to Israel's agreement to enter into it (Ex. 24:7; Deut. 5:24). Similarly, for the concept to be translated into action, the savior's mission must be sanctioned by the people. Just as there can be various forms of divinely appointed leadership, so there can be various forms of the people's acceptance: by acclamation after the fact—as with Moses, Gideon, or David—or by *a priori* agreement—as with Jephthah and Saul;[19] by all the people (*'īš Yisrā'ēl, bᵉnei Yisrā'ēl*) or by the people's representatives (*ha-zᵉqēnīm, ziqnei Yisrā'ēl*)—as with Moses, Joshua, and Gideon—or by part of the people— as with Deborah, Jephthah, David, Rehoboam, and Jehu. Just as the bestowal of the divine spirit upon a person is understood to be *ad hoc*, so is Israel's readiness to accept the authority of such a person, for the immediate purpose of helping him carry out his specific mission. The people, however, generally gave the savior consent for life. There is not a single example of a pre-monarchical savior being ousted by the people or its representatives.

Because the savior's course of action and the relationship between him and the people were pragmatically determined *ad hoc* and were not governed by any institutionalized patterns, some scholars have defined the Israelite type of government as "primitive democracy."[20] This definition, however, does not satisfactorily express the essence of political leadership in Israel from the days of Joshua, and perhaps even of Moses, to the days of Solomon. The Bible describes the patriarchal age as essentially peaceful and tranquil, but after the Exodus and especially after the invasion into Transjordania, the situation changed drastically. The biblical traditions realistically depict the internal-social and the external-political conditions which determined the concept of leadership and the image of the savior in this crucial period. Historical vicissitudes confined him to the military sphere. His holy enthusiasm, stemming from divine inspiration, propelled him to only one goal: the holy war to save Israel from its enemies. The historiographical books again and again reiterate the same motif: Israel's cries which induced the Lord to send a savior to rescue His people from its plight. Joshua and the Judges, Saul and David attained power because of their military prowess. Their achievements in battle gave legitimacy to their divine mission.

The savior's success in accomplishing his mission depended on the cooperation of the people's army. As long as there were no mercenaries in Israel until David introduced them, the hero-savior's power of action derived directly from Israel's military might. This made him dependent on popular sanction, and enabled the people to control his activities. The democratic elements in the pre-monarchical Israelite society resulted from the prevailing give-and-take relationship between leader and led in the military sphere which was then the focus of sociol-political life. This reciprocity, though lacking constitutional definition, marked the social system of Israel from Joshua to David as a *de facto* "military democracy."

E. THE FOUNDING OF THE MONARCHY

A dominant element in Israel's socio-political thought prior to the reign of David is the principle that appointment to leadership by divine inspiration and popular consent is always *ad personam* and non-transferable, either by inheritance or, after the days of Moses and Joshua, even by designation. The outgoing ruler never appointed his successor. This principle of discontinuity in the chain of leadership resulted in interregnal gaps between saviors. These were periods of decline in Israel's political ascendancy. The shortcomings inherent in the non-continuous rule of divine emissaries were felt in the fate of the people in the Conquest period, when Israel was forced to battle with the autochthonous population of Canaan for possession of agricultural (Jos. 17:14–18; Judg. 1:19, 34–35; 18:1–31) and pasture lands (I Chron. 4:39–43; 5:9–10; 7:20, 8:13), and for political supremacy in the area. The ups and downs of the prolonged military struggle led to the recognition that, for the people to exist as an independent political entity, a centralized government and predetermined procedures of succession were essential prerequisites. This was not recognized at once, but only after an extended, multiphased historical process. Its effects were first felt in Israel's offer to Gideon, which contains a capsule definition of the change needed in the governmental institutions: "Rule[21] over us, both you and your son, and your son's son also" (Judg. 8:22). However, the implementation of the demand to replace the sporadic rule of the judge-savior by instituting a monarchy was delayed until the middle of the eleventh century B.C.E. when ecological-economic and socio-organizational factors combined with external political circumstances finally tipped the scales in favor of a more centralized and continuous form of government.

Saul's rise to power was not different from that of the Judges. As the *šōfēṭ* (judge) in his time, Saul was inspired by the strength of the fervor which seized him. He drew his authority from the inspiration that qualified him to stand at the head of the community. Like the saviors who preceded him, Saul received popular sanction to act. Thus the monarchy was not created *ex nihilo* as a revolutionary eruption of a new form of government without roots in the preceding social system. On the contrary, the nascent monarchy was imbued with the same values which had been basic to the social leadership in Israel from its very beginning: a charismatic, authoritative mission based on a pragmatic military democracy.

The founding of the monarchy was accompanied by criticism and attempts to block its emergence. It is widely held that traces of the struggle against it are reflected primarily in Gideon's refusal to accept hereditary rule (Judg. 8:23), Jotham's fable (Judg 9:8–15),[22] Samuel's address which precedes the Statute of the King (I Sam. 8:4–22), and his speech after Saul's coronation (*ibid.* 12:16–24).

The opposition was many-faceted. Jotham's oration was directed specifically against Abimelech's kingship, and cannot be deemed a statement of principle.[23] It therefore recommends no alternative form of government. Gideon, however, posited the prophetic ideal "the Lord will rule over you" (Judg. 8:23)[24] as a principle opposed to any form of human overlordship perpetuated by dynastic succession.[25] Similarly, Samuel was concerned lest the concept of divine rule be at stake when the people demanded that he appoint a king (I Sam. 8:7, 10:19), and therefore proclaimed "the Lord is your King" (I Sam. 12:12, cf. *ibid.* 19–20 and Obad. 21). In the long run, however, the attempts to prevent the implementation of the monarchy were abortive. Once the idea of terrestrial kingship had taken root it grew and gathered strength, and Israel was never to abandon it. From the time of its inception, the monarchy withstood every internal crisis, until it was abolished by external adversaries. If there remained any opposition to the monarchy during its historical existence, as is claimed, this resulted not from negative experiences with monarchical government, but rather had its roots in the pre-monarchical period. From the days of David, the anti-monarchical sentiment that existed, was merely the echo of historic memory and had no real influence on the life of society. No proof to the contrary can be derived from the solitary statement in Hosea (13:10–11): "Where now is your king to save you from all your enemies,[26] and your saviors of whom you said—'Give me a king and prince.' I have given you kings in my anger and I have taken them away in my wrath," which some wish to interpret as a relatively late negation of monarchy as such. If these verses indeed refer to the earthly king, and not to foreign cults of the Moloch type (cf. *ibid.* 7 ff.), they are but a reflex of the polemic from the days of Saul and Samuel, as can be gathered from the literary and topical similarity with I Sam. 8, 10, 11, 12.[27]

The traditions about the emergence of the monarchy in the days of Samuel[28] contain an element which has no traces in the preceding polemic nor in the later prophetic rebuke of the kings: "Give us a king *like all the nations . . .* and we too will be *like all the nations . . .*" (*ibid.* 8:5, 20). Similar language is found in the Law of the King in Deut. 17:4: "I will put a king over me *like all the nations around me.*" It appears that Samuel took absolutely no exception to the people's wish to be like the other nations in the matter of monarchy,[29] implying tacit acceptance like that of the author of the Law of the King (Deut. 17:1). It is reasonable to assume that in this matter the Bible accurately reflects Israel's history. At the time of the founding of the Israelite monarchy, Israel was socially and politically similar to the nations of Canaan, especially the Transjordanian nations, and above all Edom.[30] Because of this affinity, the Bible pays special attention to Edomite history. Genesis 36 (cf. I Chron. 1:35–54) contains a capsule account of the history of Esau-Edom which parallels in its scope the more expanded presentation of the history of Jacob-Israel covered in Gen. 29—I Sam. 12. Genesis 36 gives a concise survey of the story of the eponym-hero Esau and his descendants who became tribes, their settlement in the Seir region, and the founding of their national state, ending with a list of "kings who ruled in the land of Edom before a king reigned in Israel" (Gen. 36:31 ff., cf. I Chron. 1:43 ff.).[31]

The Edomite chronicle does not reflect a dynastic system but, rather, records the names of eight rulers, no two of whom are father and son, and not one of whom ruled in the city of his predecessor. It reflects, therefore, a socio-political situation similar to that mirrored in the book of Judges. The biblical writer was obviously aware of parallels between the forms of government which obtained in Israel and Edom in the period between Moses and the establishment of monarchy: a national leadership of kings-judges with no permanent seat of centralized administration and no institutionalized transfer of power.

The same parallelism can be discerned in the later phases of the history of government in the two states. The first possible reference to dynastic rule in Edom comes in a fragmentary retrospective note from the days of Solomon which speaks about Hadad the Edomite of royal descent who fled to Egypt when David and Joab made war against Edom, and who returned to his land in the time of Solomon. It can be surmised that he is Hadar—the last in the Edomite King-List—or his son or grandson, if that Hadad actually lived in the days of Saul. In any case, by combining all these bits of information, one reaches the conclusion that at approximately the same time—in the second half of the tenth century B.C.E.—the Edomite and Israelite systems of government underwent a period of crisis, and in both states dynastic monarchies began to emerge.

Neither biblical nor external sources inform us as to the type of government in Moab and Ammon before the period of Saul. An anonymous king of Ammon is mentioned in the Jephthah episode (Judg. 11:12 ff.). The traditions about Saul and David mention Nahash king of Ammon (I Sam. 11:1–2; 12:12). Only from the time of David is mention made of a dynastic monarchy in Ammon: Nahash's son Hanun succeeded his father in the capital Rabbath-Ammon (II Sam. 10:2; I Chron. 19:1–2)[32]

A chronistic comment in Numbers 21:26 refers to the first king of Moab without giving his name (cf. *ibid*, 20:14). Shortly after mention is made of Balak son of Zippor, king of Moab,[33] who was allied with Balaam son of Beor. The book of Judges mentions Eglon king of Moab (13:12 ff., cf. 12:9). In I Samuel 22:4 a Moabite king, a contemporary of Saul and David, is mentioned. However, the first reference to dynastic monarchy in Moab appears in the Mesha inscription[34] (mid-9th century B.C.E.), in which Mesha claims that his father reigned before him in Moab for thirty years.[35]

Although there is no decisive proof, we may perhaps conjecture that the socio-political development of Moab and Ammon was similar to that of Israel and Edom: a non-continuous government from the time of their settlement in Transjordania in the thirteenth century B.C.E. and the establishment of national states. Dynastic monarchy centered in a capital began at the end of the tenth or the beginning of the ninth century.[36] It would follow that at the time of the emergence of monarchy, Israel shared in the socio-political culture of the Trans-jordanian ethnic groups which, like Israel, were in a stage of transition to permanent settlement based on a mixed economy of cattle-breeding and agriculture and in the process of national and political solidification.

Against this background one must study the biblical documents which were meant to set normative guidelines for the monarchy in Israel: the Law of the King (Deut. 17:14–20) and the Statute of the King (I Sam. 8:11–16).

F. *Mišpaṭ ha-mᵉlūḵāh* (THE LAW AND STATUTE OF THE KING)

The Law of the King and the Statute of the King probably preserve parts of a social contract which laid down quasi-constitutionally the rights and duties of the king. This is the *mišpaṭ ha-mᵉlūḵāh* (the Law and Statute of the King) which Samuel proclaimed and committed to writing subsequent to Saul's coronation (I Sam. 10:25) as attesting the covenant between the king and the people before God.[37] Of this document only a selection of prescriptive and proscriptive ordinances which apply to the king have been preserved in the Bible. Some of these have been transmitted in a circumstantial formulation in Deuteronomy[38] and some seem to underly the polemic formulation in which Samuel presented the Law and Statute of the King to the people who came to ask for a king to be appointed. These details do not complete the picture. The exact stipulations of the covenant between king and populace remain unknown, as do the punishments to be dealt to a violator, customarily found in similar legal documents both in the Bible and in the ancient Near East. The reason might be sought in the fact that the Bible preserved only a selection of these matters, i.e. those which are directly applicable to the socio-political situation at the time of the birth of Saul's monarchy.[39] It stands to reason that in the course of time there developed further statutes, possibly transmitted orally, which were no less binding than the Law and Statute of the King.[40]

Parallels in content and style as well as similarities between the structure of the Law of the King and the order of events connected with the founding of the monarchy in the days of Saul attest to the connection between these two issues. The Law of the King consists of three parts: an introit (Deut. 17:14–15) and an epilogue (vv. 18–20) of a theoretical basic nature which frame a cluster of specific prohibitions and instructions (vv. 16–17). Similarly three parts can be discerned in the account of Saul's coronation: an introduction (I Sam. 8:4–9) and an epilogue (*ibid.* 10:25; 12:13–14, 24–25) dealing with the bases of the monarchy, and between them a series of matters which bear upon the actual arrangements of the monarchical government (*ibid.* 8:11–17).

The conclusion of the Law of the King contains references to the threefold covenant between the king and the people before God: the king is commanded to write for himself "a copy of the [King's] Law", *et mišneh ha-Tōrāh ha-zōt*, the wording of this specific pericope, so that he may learn to fear God, observe and act in accord with the prescribed ordinances (Deut. 17:18–19). Similarly, Saul's coronation concludes with the writing of the Law and Statute of the King— although by Samuel and not by the king (I Sam. 10:25)—and in Samuel's exhortation to the people and its king to obey the Lord and serve Him faithfully (*ibid.* 12:13–25).

On the basis of this comparison it may be conjectured that the Law and Statute of the King which Samuel wrote down and placed before the Lord,[41] i.e., most certainly placed in the hands of the priests of Mizpah (cf. Judg. 20:1, I Sam. 7:5–13), was of the *mišneh ha-Tōrāh* (copy of the [King's] Law) type referred to in the Law of the King pericope (Deut. 17:18).

We should bear in mind that the preserved text of the Statute of the King has been distorted because of the polemical tone in which it was presented. However, we can still reconstruct from it two basic issues without which there would be no continuity in a monarchy or in any type of government that concentrates in its hands the administration of the state. Both of these were considered fundamental to the monarchy in ancient Near-Eastern states such as Ugarit and Alalakh.[42] They are the organization of the army and the administration of the realm, each demanding that taxes be levied.

1. Establishing an army, training soldiers and officers, furnishing arms, and organizing cavalry and chariotry are dealt with in the following passages which, somewhat freely translated, read: "He will take (of) your sons, and appoint them charioteers, and runners before his chariot" (I Sam. 8:11, cf. I Kings 9:22); "(and) he will appoint them captains of thousands, and captains of fifties" (cf. I Sam. 22:7); " . . . and to make weapons and the furnishings of his chariots" (*ibid.* 8:12). In actually granting authority to the king to draft people for the army, there is no difference between the king and the "savior" of old. However, the king's role is not confined to calling up the army in time of emergency as it had been under the Judges. This method was adequate in its own day when Israel's wars were waged against nomadic tribes such as Midian and Amalek, or against the East Jordanian peoples whose military organization and equipment were similar to those of Israel. The descriptions of these wars make no mention

of chariots and horsemen.[43] Most "savior" traditions, such as those about Ehud, Gideon, Jephthah, and Samson, speak exclusively about infantry battles. An exception is the war of Deborah and Barak against Sisera (Judg. 4–5), the first to transfer the Israelites' war effort from Transjordania and the mountains of Cisjordania to the coastal plain and the great valleys whose inhabitants threatened Israel "because they had iron chariots" (Josh. 11:16, 18, Judg. 1:19, 4:3, etc.).

The introduction of cavalry and a chariot force is a distinct function of the monarchical regime.[44] The chariot must be operated by a unit and not by an individual and entails training teams and tactically co-ordinating several units. The charioteers and horsemen had to be available for drills and manoeuvers. Chariots and horses meant establishing stables and provision centers. By their very nature, cavalry and chariot corps are professional units which cannot be organized and mobilized by clans and tribes. Because of all this, in Israel and probably elsewhere, a central government, like the monarchy, was indispensable for the introduction of chariots and cavalry. It is for this reason that the matter was taken up in the Law of the King in Deut. 17, and was given even more emphasis in the Law of the King in I Sam. 8. True, in Saul's days, plans for the development of mounted forces were not yet implemented.[45] because he was still struggling with primary problems of organizing and arming the infantry (I Sam. 13:19–22). Nevertheless, the delays in implementation do not contradict the traditions about Saul's election, which stated that military considerations, especially the demand to strengthen the Israelite army by cavalry and chariots, were an important or even decisive factor in the people's demand to establish a monarchy. The ideal king was conceived by the Hebrews in that period as a warrior-king and savior who would effectively lead the Israelite army in battle— "who didst lead out and bring in Israel" (II Sam. 5:2).

2. It was the king's responsibility to provide for the full-time military and administrative personnel who had left their previous occupations and means of livelihood. In a period, like David's, of military victories and conquests, these expenditures would be at least partially covered by booty and tribute collected from vanquished enemies. However, under Saul, at a time of defensive wars, such means were expected to come from the people by tithes imposed on produce and livestock, and by conscription to the royal labor force. The authority invested in the king to levy taxes and to impose corvée duties is reflected in the following verses: "He will take your men-servants and your maid-servants, and your best young men,[46] and your asses and put them to his work" (I Sam. 8:16), "and he will take your daughters to be perfumers, and to be cooks and bakers" (*ibid.* 13), "and you will be for him servants (or slaves)."[47] "He will tithe your flocks (*ibid.* 7), your seeds [probably produce],[48] and your vineyards

(and give to his officers and to his servants);"[49] "and he will take your fields, and your vineyards, and your best olive yards, and give them to his servants" (ibid. 14–15; cf. ibid. 22:7). Taxing the people either for *ad hoc* requirements (II Kings. 15:19–20; 23:35) or permanently (Amos. 7:1) was recognized in the biblical period as a legitimate right of the monarchy.[50] According to biblical tradition, general taxation supervised by a royal officer—'ăšer 'al ha-mas—was introduced in Israel only in the days of Solomon within the administrative framework of the realm which he developed (I Kings 4–5, especially 4:6; cf. *ibid.* 12:18 = I Chron. 10:18). The biblical term *mas* is to be understood as an apocopated form of *mas 'ōvēd* i.e., corvée, and usually refers to imposed labor obligations.[51] But it stands to reason that the term also refers to taxes in the form of tithes levied from agricultural produce and from livestock. Probably the foundations of taxation were laid by David, possibly even by Saul. An indirect allusion to taxation may be found in Saul's promise to whomever would vanquish Goliath that "his family will be free (*ḥofšī*) in Israel" (I Sam. 17:25), which presumably means "free from tax." As long as the tax remained within reasonable limits and was spent on recognized public requirements, it was accepted by the people as a necessary evil. No protest was raised until the burden of taxation became too heavy, as was the case under Solomon (I Kings 12:3–16).

The preceding analysis shows that the Statute of the King reflects the technical military and socio-economic situation of the Israelites from the days of the Judges to the time of David and Solomon. It bears the imprint of generations not yet actually experienced in institutionalized government. Historically and logically this "Law" finds its place in the dynamic development of the biblical society from the discontinuous leadership of the "saviors," who had no national machinery or organization, to the structured multi-faceted network of royal administration.

There is no reason to doubt the essential historicity of the biblical account of the founding of the monarchy in Samuel's time. Saul, Israel's first king, was elected in the wake of negotiations between the elders representing the people and the charismatic, divinely-appointed Samuel, who were partners in the national leadership of that time. The pragmatic formulation of the people's demands as expressed by the elders—"give us a king to save [rather than 'to judge'] us"—and their insistence even in the face of Samuel's objections indicate that the negotiations were conducted on the basis of clear knowledge of the obligations and privileges that went with the monarchy. The people were willing to limit individual as well as tribal-local freedom in order to enjoy the military and political benefits expected from a continuous rule of kings. At the time of its foundation Israel did not look upon the monarchy as a social ideal but saw it rather as a pragmatic solution to the problems of the day.[52] This attitude is clearly reflected in the words of the elders at the conclusion of their negotiations with Saul: "There shall be a king over us; that we also may be like all the nations; and that our king may rule us, and lead us, and fight our battles" (I Sam. 8:19–20). Because of its inherent military character, the monarchy preserved the democratic characteristics of the regime of the savior-judges. Without the cooperation of the people, the king was incapable of carrying out his principal task—to save Israel from its enemies. The monarchy came into being on the basis of a freely contracted covenant—the Law and Statute of the King—which was intended to preserve the balance between the ruler's power of action and the people's right to consent or refuse. By virtue of these criteria, the rule of the kings in biblical Israel may be defined as "participatory monarchy,"[53] a monarchy based on the participation of the people and their representatives in executing the political and administrative activities directed by the king.

G. THE INSTITUTIONALIZED MONARCHY

Saul's kingdom marks the watershed between the period of the Judges and the institutionalized monarchy. Through it, certain principles which characterized the leadership of savior-emissaries were fused into the monarchical model which developed under David and Solomon and even in the times of the divided monarchy. This is shown in the terminology, imagery, and motifs pertaining to the monarchical government,[54] which are but variations of terms and concepts marking the premonarchical government. Titles such as šōfēṭ,[55] mōšēl, nāśī',[56] and mōšīaʿ[57] apply to the king just as they applied to pre-monarchical rulers. To these were added new designations such as nāgīd.[58] Despite etymological differences, the use of these terms in *parallelismus membrorum* and their interchangeability in parallel passages indicates that they were considered synonymous during, as well as preceding, the monarchy. At the same time, however, the social life of Israel changed. Internal factors which affected social development clothed themselves in new ideologies and terminologies, and crystallized in forms of political organization resembling those of neighboring peoples.

The transition from the rule of the saviors, whom the people obeyed because they were divine emissaries who proved their claims to leadership by successful action, to the rule of kings with power inherited (but still rooted in the idea of a personal mission) led to an ideological crisis which permeated the biblical traditions concerning the beginnings of the institutionalized monarchy. By its very nature, the institutionalized monarchy is dynastic. In contrast to previous forms of social leadership which stood on the principle of discontinuity and appointment *ad personam*, the transfer of office from father to son was accepted as basic to monarchical government. Indeed, from the days of Saul the right of succession within the royal family was considered the norm (I Sam. 13:13–14). Saul certainly intended to pass on his power to his son Jonathan and considered David a threat to the establishment of his dynasty: "Then Saul's anger was kindled against Jonathan and he said unto him . . . 'as long as the son of Jesse liveth upon the earth, thou shalt not be established, nor thy kingdom'" (I Sam. 20:30–31). After the death in battle of Saul and Jonathan, Abner unhesitatingly made Saul's son Ishbaal king over Israel (II Sam. 2:9), as a matter of course. The dynastic principle received its full ideological, systematic expression in Nathan's prophecy bringing God's promise to David: "Thy house and thy kingdom shall be made sure forever before thee [read: 'before me']; thy throne shall be established forever" (*ibid.* 7:16; cf. 13, 25–26, 29; I Kings 3:6; 5:19; Ezek. 37:23–28; II Chron. 13:5–7). Whenever this prophecy was composed, a matter widely discussed in scholarly circles,[59] there can be little doubt that it contains thoughts and sentiments from the period of David. This is confirmed by the fact that David's sons Absalom, Adonijah, and Solomon saw themselves as prospective successors to the throne, and that this was undisputed by the king's entourage and all Israel alike. However, at that time, no definite system of succession had been agreed upon. This caused the wars of succession among David's sons, each of whom attempted to capture the monarchy, backed by courtiers and faithful supporters from among the populace. The issue was decided by David, who designated Solomon heir and successor over his older brother Adonijah (I Kings 1:32–35; cf. II Sam. 3:4; 5:15). Similarly, Rehoboam appointed Abijah in preference to his older brothers (II Chron. 11:22). With Solomon's enthronement the dynastic principle was established. After Solomon's death, no one contested Rehoboam's right to succeed his father (I Kings 11:43—12:1), even though the people demanded that Solomon's taxes be alleviated (*ibid.* 12:4–17).

The same principle applied not only in Judah but also in Ephraim. Ahijah the Shilonite who appointed Jeroboam king over the northern tribes promised him everlasting kingship, just as Nathan had promised David: "And I will take thee,[60] and thou shalt reign over all that thy soul desireth, and shalt be king over Israel. (And it shall be) if thou wilt hearken unto all that I command thee, and wilt walk in My ways, and do that which is right in Mine eyes, to keep My statutes and My commandments, as David My servant did, then I will be with thee and will build thee a sure house, as I built for David, and will give Israel unto thee" (I Kings 11:37–38; cf. I Sam. 13:13). However, since Jeroboam did not live up to the conditions of his covenant with God, the promise of a dynasty for all generations as given by Ahijah (I Kings 14:7–14; cf. II Kings 9:9) was revoked, just as Saul's kingdom was taken from him by Samuel who had appointed him in the first place (I Sam. 13:14; 15:10–28), and just as the rule over the ten northern tribes was denied to the Davidic house (I Kings 11:7–13, 29–36). Similarly, the often repeated reference to "Baasha and his house" (I Kings 16:3, 7, 11, 12) implies that Baasha's rule had been intended to be dynastic. And indeed, he was succeeded by his son Elah, but, Zimri's conspiracy put an end to Baasha's line (ibid. 16:9 ff.). Also, the chronistic summary of Jehu's reign indicates that initially he had been promised an enduring dynasty by the prophet who appointed him, though this is not expressly mentioned (I Kings 9:1–10), but forfeited the pledge because of subsequent wrongdoings and was granted a line of four generations only: "And the Lord said unto Jehu, 'Because thou hast done well in executing that which is right in Mine eyes, and has done unto the house of Ahab according to all that was in My heart, thy sons to the fourth generation shall sit on the throne of Israel'" (ibid. 10:30–31). There is therefore no basis to A. Alt's contention that the court revolutions, more frequent in Ephraim than in Judah, constitute evidence that the ideology of a disjunctive rule by saviors from the period of the Judges was prepetuated in the North also after the establishment of the monarchy.[61] It follows that even though for the larger part of its history, Ephraim's royal rule was non-dynastic, kings often being dethroned and replaced, this should not be taken as evidence that a different concept of monarchy prevailed in the North, but rather as a sign of the internal weakness of the monarchy, the causes of which should be sought in the social structure or in external political circumstances. Conceptually, the dynastic monarchy was as firmly rooted in Ephraim as it was in Judah.

The paucity of our sources does not permit any final decision regarding the laws of succession. The Bible usually uses the neutral statement "and his son ruled after him." It is reasonable to assume that in the course of time primogeniture was accepted in Israel as, presumably, it was among the neighboring nations. Primogeniture is expressly mentioned in the tradition about Jehoshaphat: "And their father gave them great gifts, of silver, gold and precious things, with fortified cities in Judah; but the kingdom gave he to Jehoram, because he was the first born" (II Chron. 21:3). Nevertheless, we encounter in Israel, as in other nations,[62] younger sons who were preferred over the elder, either because a king loved the mother of the son designated as his successor, or because of a court cabal (II Kings 23:30; cf. ibid. v. 36), because of foreign intervention.

The internal consolidation of the dynastic concept was strengthened by the increasing contact between Israel and her neighbors. As stated, there is reason to believe that dynastic monarchy, which was customary in the Canaanite city-states, took root among the Transjordanian peoples at the same time that it was adopted in Israel, i.e. in the period of David and Solomon. At that juncture, we observe a clearly discernible trend towards centralization in that area of the ancient Near East. Capital cities became focal points of the royal administrative network spanning the country. Next to the royal palace, central temples sprang up, symbolizing the stability of the monarchy.[63] The king, who often served as a priest or assumed the title of priest, took overall charge of the cult.[64] The peoples in the area maintained close political and economic contact. They were all subject to Mesopotamian culture influence[65] which by its very nature was open to the absorption of foreign elements. The situation was conducive to the integration of the kingdom of Israel in the political and cultural fabric of the Syro-Palestinian sphere. The belligerent expansion under David and Solomon's economic enterprises opened a window for Israel to the world of ideas of the neighboring peoples and their socio-political ideologies.[66] The parallel social development, language affinities with the immediate neighbors, and the existence of a *lingua franca*—Akkadian or Aramaic—facilitated assimilation. From the days of the United Monarchy, an unprecedentedly distinct trend towards Canaanite-Mesopotamian acculturation characterized biblical Israel. The literature of the monarchical period—the Former and Latter Prophets, and especially the book of Psalms—contains a plethora of images and motifs familiar to us from Ugaritic literature and from North-West Semitic inscriptions. They testify to the continually increasing participation of Israel in the surrounding world of beliefs and ideas.

Under the influence of the court style which typifies the literature of neighboring monarchies, the idea of the savior-king, God's elect, evoked imagery and phraseology which brought the king and his office within the heavenly sphere. The king was cloaked in a sanctity never bestowed upon the savior-judges: whosoever harms the king will not go unpunished (I Sam. 26:23; II Sam. 1:14, etc.); to curse the king was considered a capital offense (*ibid.* 19:22), like cursing God (I Kings 21:10 cf. Ex. 22:27); one would call upon the king to witness, as one called upon God (I Sam. 12:3), and people would take an oath by his name (I Sam. 15:21). The king sheltered his people (*ibid.* 21:17; Lam. 4:20) just as God gave protection to Israel. The identity of metaphors applied to the king and to the Diety eventually led to the depiction of the king as the first-born son of God (Ps. 2:7–9; 89:27–28),[67] probably borrowed from Near-Eastern mythic-religious terminology. The image obviously does not imply an actual biological father-son relationship, as is sometimes maintained,[68] but rather an adoption formula to provide the king with a special place among those enjoying God's protection.

At first sight, the cultural affinities of Israel with her neighbors, appear to have resulted from the intercourse of an élite stratum with their peers in other nations. However, a closer look reveals a somewhat more purposeful and structured relationship. We seem not to be dealing solely with processes of unplanned acculturation but with intentional assimilation on the part of the Israelite kings and royalist courtiers. For them, the cultures of Canaan and Mesopotamia provided welcome models of government and socio-political ideologies which focused on the image of the king.[69]

In contradistinction to the historical conception of monarchy lacking any ideological dimension, which was the original Israelite view,[70] other Near-Eastern peoples considered the monarchy a basic element of creation.[71] Kings had ruled the world from the beginning of time. The sanctity of primordiality permeated the institution of monarchy and the person of the king. From this world of ideas, Israel derived concepts and motifs out of which it wove an ideology of monarchy principally based on the Davidic house, but also leaving its impressions on Ephraimite concepts. The monarchistic ideology set out to make the Davidic dynasty transcend the realm of historic singularity and implant it in primeval antiquity: "Thou Bethlehem Ephrathah, which art smallest (youngest) among the clans of Judah, out of thee shall one come forth a ruler of Israel whose roots are in the distant past, in days gone by (or possibly: in the days of creation)" (Micah 5:1). The Davidic line is like the people of Israel whose political and territorial existence is also rooted in the dawn of history: "When the Most High gave to the nations their inheritance, when He separated men, He set the borders of the peoples according to the number of the children of Israel" (Deut. 32:8). The survival of the Davidic kingdom and that of the people of Israel are both compared to the eternality of the laws of creation: just as these laws will never be annulled, so God will never cast away His chosen people nor the seed of His servant David (Jer. 33:25–26; cf. *ibid.* 31:35–36; Ezek. 37:23–28; Ps. 89:3–5, 29–30; 110:3, etc.).

The monarchical ideology sought to free the government of kings from the polemics in which it had been embroiled at its inception and to invest it with ideological justification. The elevation of the monarchy beyond mundane history upset the balance between the power of action granted to the king and the controlling power of consent invested in the people on which the smooth working of the participatory monarchy was based. There was a definite danger that kings might develop a tendency towards an autocracy deriving its power from its own unlimited and unconditional sanctity, as was true of ancient Near-Eastern monarchies. In opposition to such trends, tempering lines of thought emerged and crystallized; in them can be discerned variations on concepts which had determined the political structure of Israel at the time of the savior. The two forces which had interacted in the founding of the monarchy—the prophet, representing the divine, and the people—now forged new principles and institutions which would contend with the monarchy over the definition of its place in the socio-political fabric, within the framework of the Covenant between Israel and God and between the king and the people.

H. Changes in the Relations of King and People

The boundaries of Saul's kingdom were identical with the area settled by the Israelites. Saul's wars were primarily defensive and preventive and were not aimed at territorial expansion and annexation. Conquered territories were not incorporated into the Israelite political system (I Sam. 14:47–48). Foreign populations, such as the inhabitants of the Canaanite cities, remained outside the political framework of the national state, or else were assimilated into the Israelite ethnic fabric, like the Kenites and Gibeonites, thus completely losing their national identity.[72]

This situation changed radically in David's time. Conquered states were absorbed into the political framework of the empire at different levels of incorporation, without losing their national and ethnic identity. In Solomon's day there even developed a rather liberal socio-religious outlook (not to be mistaken for syncretism)[73] which provided an ideological basis for the ethnic and religious pluralism of the citizenry.[74] Concurrently the diverse components of the realm evinced a variety of attitudes towards the king of Israel, the "king of kings." The concept of Israel as a "priestly kingdom and a holy nation" (i.e., a holy state) was lost on the non-Israelite ethnic elements. Similarly meaningless for them was the concept of the king's mission as savior of Israel, which was a function of God's covenant with His people. A rationalist political conception of kingship replaced the image of the king as God's emissary.

The politicization of the image of the king, which probably emanated from ethnically foreign elements in the population, brought with it significant changes in the relationship of the Israelite citizens to their monarch. The growth of the one-nation state of Saul's time to the multi-national empire under David was accompanied by a process of socio-economic and cultural-religious differentiation in the Israelite stratum of the population. Signs of this transformation can be discerned in the changing character of the army, which had been the backbone of the pragmatic democracy of the period of the saviors. David conscripted an army of mercenaries partly from the foreign conquered populations, such as the Cherethites and Pelethites (II Sam. 8:18; 20:23). As a result, the importance of the people's army dwindled and its influence in matters of state waned. At the same time, the king's status and tasks changed and his role in the body politic was redefined. Toward the end of David's reign, the image of the king as Israel's military leader which had brought the people to choose him as their ruler (*ibid.* 5:1–3) began to fade. His participation in military matters became symbolic, as is evidenced by his merely ceremonial conquest of Rabbath-ammon (*ibid.* 12:27–31; cf. *ibid.* 21:15–17).[75] Professional officers like Joab, Abner, and Benaiah replaced the savior-king at the head of Israel's army. The gap between the king and the people in one of the vital areas of political life could not be bridged even by the increasing royal participation in other areas such as the judicial (*ibid.* 14:1–11; 15:2–6), in which the saviors of old had not been involved.

Solomon's reign, which was entirely peaceful, was marked by a total loss of the close relationship between people and king which had characterized the period of the great war-leaders. Nothing remained of the former image of the savior-king envisioned by the people in Samuel's day: "And he shall go out before us and fight our wars" (I Sam. 8:20). In contrast, Solomon is depicted as inexperienced in military matters, a mere youngster who could not lead an army into battle (I Kings 3:7). The military expansion of David's days gave way to Solomon's tendency to stabilize existing borders and develop a system of static defense which demanded massive building projects (*ibid.* 5:1–8; 9:15–19; 11:26–28). The means were provided by taxing the population (*ibid.* 4:7 ff.; 5:2–3, 7–8, 27–32), collecting duties from transit trade passing through Israelite territory (*ibid.* 10:14–15), and developing independent economic enterprises as a monopoly of the crown (*ibid.* 9:26–28; 10:22). These projects necessitated creating a ramified administration (*ibid.* 4:2–19; 9:23) and establishing channels of communication between the king and his subjects. There emerged a stratum of royal officers and courtiers between the king and the people (*ibid.* 12:6–7), who represented the king vis-à-vis the populace. This development reached a peak in the days of Rehoboam, the first generation when the idea of a hereditary monarchy was properly realized. The negotiations between Rehoboam and the people who were to confirm his kingship, if Solomon's corvée were alleviated, reveal first signs of formal implementation of participatory government. In order to reach a decision, Rehoboam consulted with a "royal council" which, according to the biblical sources, was first established under Solomon (*ibid.* 12:1–15). Scripture does not enlighten us about the nature of this council[76] nor indicate the composition of the group negotiating on behalf of the people. The results, however, prove its real power: for the first time in its history, the socio-political leadership in Israel deposed its ruler. It is of interest to note that, despite his increased power, the king was more vulnerable than any previous type of leader. Not one of the pre-monarchical saviors had been removed from office by the people, even though some encountered antagonism and even open opposition (Num. 17; Judg. 8:1–3; 12:1–6 and perhaps 15:9–13, etc.). On the other hand, with the institutionalization of the monarchy, the political system was recurrently rocked by internal rebellion and political upheaval (II Sam. 15–18; I Kings 11:26 ff.). Assassination of kings by rebels was common not only in Ephraim (*ibid.* 15:27–28; 16:8–12; II Kings 9–10; 15:10, 14, 25) where hereditary monarchy did not take firm root, but even in Judah where the Davidic dynasty became well-established (*ibid.* 11:1, 16; 12:21; 14:19; 21:23). Even though it cannot be proved, in most cases the rebels probably came from the army hierarchy or from the royal retinue who opposed the king because he failed in his task as military leader.[77]

These developments disclose the diminishing immunity of political leadership in Israel which was intended to, and in actual fact did, counterbalance the increased power which the kings derived from dynastic continuity. It seems that there developed intuitively non-institutionalized means of socio-political checks and balances which succeeded in renewing the balance of power between the king and the people, and helped to perpetuate even in the institutionalized monarchy certain principles from the time of the saviors.

I. The Political Function of Divine Inspiration

In the pre-monarchical age, the divine Spirit was exclusively revealed in Israel in the person of the savior. The savior's unique charisma afforded him a special position in his society. Because Covenantal promises were embodied in him alone, no one could criticize him on behalf of the Covenant and in the name of its giver. From the beginning of the monarchical period there was a bifurcation of the divine Spirit in Israel. The Spirit revealed itself in two types of social functionaries: the king-savior and the messenger-prophet, each of whom claimed precedence over the other. Appointment as a ruler (*nāgîd*) no longer came directly to the man selected, as with Moses and the Judges, but was transmitted by a man of God (*'îš 'ĕlōhîm*).[78] The anointing of Saul and David by the prophet Samuel became the prototype for future generations.

The bifurcation of the divine Spirit is discernible in the appreciation given to the kings in biblical literature. The deeds of the savior-judges were evaluated by only one criterion: their success in accomplishing their military mission. Saul was initially measured by the same yardstick. After he had defeated Ammon in a holy war, no one dared any longer to oppose his leadership (I Sam. 11:12–15; cf. 10:26–27). However, his later achievements in the political arena, the victory over Amalek and over all his enemies, were judged by religious-ideological standards, unrelated to historical reality. Prophetic inspiration appointed itself judge over the king and his actions. Starting out by hailing Saul's political achievements, that he "fought against all his enemies everywhere, against Moab, Ammon, Edom, the kings of Zobah and the Philistines," the report then incongruously continues: "and wherever he turned he failed" (*ibid.* 14:47; cf. 15:10–28). Similarly, Scripture reports negatively about Jeroboam that "he did that which was evil in the sight of the Lord," and then continues by praising him: "He restored the border of Israel from Lebo-hamath unto the sea of the Arabah, and (God) saved them (Israel) by the hand of Jeroboam the son of Joash . . . The rest of the acts of Jeroboam, and all that he did, and his might, how he warred and how he recovered Damascus and Hamath, . . . they are written in the book of chronicles of the kings of Israel" (II Kings 14:24–28).

Prior to the monarchy, divine inspiration was never removed from a man who had been revealed a savior, even if he went wrong. Samson's marriage to a Philistine woman indeed angered his parents (Judg. 14:3; cf. Gen. 26:34–35; 27:46), but the Bible justified his action "for he looked for a pretext [to fight] against the Philistines" (Judg. 14:4), and the Spirit remained upon him (*ibid.* 14:6). Gideon, by erecting the Ephod in his city Ophrah, sinned, and caused others to do so: "And all Israel went astray after it . . . and it became a snare unto Gideon and to his house" (*ibid.* 8:27). Even so, his mission was not terminated.

In the monarchical period, however, the very mission of the savior-king could be voided because of his failings. The first king was also the first leader to be deposed. Samuel who crowned Saul also dethroned him (I Sam. 13:13–14; 15:26–28). Because of Solomon's sin in marrying foreign wives (as Samson had done) and building high places (like Gideon's at Ephod), the rule over ten tribes was divested from his son Rehoboam (I Kings 11:1–13) and assigned to Jeroboam (*ibid.* 29–39). Ahab's transgression led to his son's being deprived of the throne and Jehu was anointed king over Israel by the emissary of Elisha the prophet (II Kings 9).

The very possibility that the rule of a king could be terminated *de jure* for religious and doctrinal considerations, and not only *de facto* after revolts, differentiated the Israelite monarchy from that of neighboring nations, and curbed the development of absolutism characteristic of monarchical governments at all times. The threat that the king's mission could be revoked should he not comply with the statutes of the divine Covenant and the social contract with the people, as interpreted by the prophet, meant that even the institutionalized dynastic monarchy in Israel retained the principle that continuity of leadership was not automatic, neither in the lifetime of a king, nor from generation to generation.

Against the background of these changes in political ideas and practice, the significance of anointing with oil must be examined. The practice was obviously an innovation of the monarchical regime, and unheard of in the era of the saviors. Anointing, though, is known from biblical sources in such contexts, as reference to the High Priest (Ex. 28:41; 29:7, 36; 40:13–15; Lev. 8:10–12; Num. 3:3; 35:25, etc.), who was called the "anointed priest" (Lev. 4:3, 5, 16; 6:15), to a prophet (I Kings 19:16; cf. Ps. 105:15), or to cultic implements (Gen. 31:13; Ex. 30:26; 40:9–11; Num. 7:10, 84, 88, etc.). Extra-biblical sources show that the practise of anointing kings was common to many ancient Near-Eastern monarchies including the Canaanite city-states. However, *māšiaḥ* (= "the anointed one"), the title applied to the king, has thus far been attested only in the Bible, where it always occurs in either the construct form—*m^{e}šiaḥ YHWH* (I Sam. 24:6, 10; 26:9, 11, 16, 23, etc.), *m^{e}šiaḥ 'ĕlohēi Ya'aqōv* (II Sam. 23:1), or with a possessive suffix—*m^{e}šīḥī* (I Sam. 2:35; Ps. 132:17), *m^{e}šīḥekā* (Hab. 3:13; Ps. 84:10; 132:10 etc.), *m^{e}šīḥō* (I Sam. 2:10; 12:3, 5; Isa. 45:1, etc.), *m^{e}šīḥāi* (Ps. 105:15). The Bible mentions explicitly anointing only certain kings: David (I Sam. 2:4; 5:3; Ps. 89:21), Solomon (I Kings 1:39), Jehu (II Kings 9:1 ff.), Joash (*ibid.* 11:12) and Jehoahaz (*ibid.* 23:30). The Jewish sages deduced from this that a king was anointed only if he had founded a new line. A king coming to the throne in dynastic succession was anointed only if his rights had been contested (Yer. Sheqalim 49, 3; Horayot 47, 3). However, the recurring use of the term "anoint as king" (*māšaḥ l^{e}melek*: Judg. 9:8, 15, etc.; II Sam. 2:4; I Kings 19:15, etc), to mean "enthrone," and the often employed term *m^{e}šiaḥ YHWH* indicate that anointing was fairly widespread, and that possibly every king in Judah and Ephraim was anointed, although our sources are silent about the fact.

The anointing was done by the High Priest (I Kings 1:39; II Chron. 33:11), apparently with the "holy oil" kept in the Tabernacle and later in the Temple (Ex. 25:6; 37:29; Lev. 8:2; I Kings 1:39), or by a prophet (II Kings 9:6 ff; cf. I Kings 19:15–16) on divine command. The Bible also mentions anointing by the people. Such was the case with Solomon. According to I Chron. 29:22, the people acclaimed him king by anointing him at the customary coronation banquet.[79] Similarly with Joash: "and they made him king, and anointed him; and they clapped their hands, and said 'Long live the King'" (II Kings 11:12),[80] and with Jehoahaz: "And the *'am ha-'āreṣ* took Jehoahaz the son of Josiah, and they anointed him (the last phrase is missing in II Chron. 36:1) and made him king in his father's stead" (II Kings 23:30).[81]

The above analysis suggests that in Israel anointing was not a purely sacred act but also a socio-political one.[82] It gave formal expression of approval of the king by the representatives of the people or by the prophet or priest as representatives of the religio-cultic dimension, or by both. Even though conceptually the act of anointing lent the king immunity through sanctity (I Sam. 24:6, 10; 26:9, 11, 16, 23; II Sam. 1:14–16; Ps. 105 = I Chron. 16:22), factually it gave expression to the king's dependency on his constituents, symbolizing the people's control over the monarch. In historical reality, the act of anointing was a ceremonial manifestation of the checks and balances inherent in the basic conditions of the covenant of monarchy which the participatory monarchy imposed upon the king.

The image of the anointed king, scion of a dynastic line, as realized in the

Davidic house, contained two essentially contradictory principles: the concept of inspired leadership deriving its power from personal charisma, which by definition is non-consecutive, coalesced with the idea of an automatically continuous government drawing its strength from an institutionalized charisma of office.[83] The principle of election by the divine spirit was grafted on to the system of dynastic government, which in essence is void of any religious and ideological dimension. This unexpected amalgam of seemingly contradictory concepts raised the dynastic monarchy to the level of a basic principle of biblical ideology. Nathan's prophecy and related traditions (II Sam. 7; I Kings 8:22–26; I Chron. 28:4–7; II Chron. 6:16–17; 13:5, etc.), in which the House of David was assured of God's everlasting benevolence and support, produced in biblical literature the image of an ideal king who became a sign and symbol for all generations: a king blessed with understanding and wisdom, on whom the spirit of the Lord rests; a righteous king and savior under whose leadership Judah and Ephraim would be reunited to overcome their enemies: "Behold the days are coming, says the Lord, when I will raise up for David a righteous shoot, and he shall reign as king and deal wisely, and shall execute justice and righteousness in the land. In his days Judah will be saved, and Israel will dwell safely. And this is his name by which he will be called, 'The Lord is our righteousness'"[84] (Jer. 23:5–6; cf. Isa. 11:1–10; Jer. 22:1–4; Hos. 3:4–5; Amos 9:11–15; Micah 5:1–8; Hag. 3:20–23, etc.).

The biblical writers conceived of the monarchy as the pillar of national existence and the pivot of Israel's historical experience. A deep-seated pious hope for Redemption was implanted in the monarchy and in the anointed king of the Davidic line. Generation after generation lived with the expectation that in their day the ideal anointed king would reveal himself and would realize the divine promise affirmed and reaffirmed in God's Covenant with the patriarchs, with Israel at Sinai, and with David. The hope did not focus on the image of a unique Messiah but was kept alive by the vision of a dynasty of anointed kings. The belief received its fullest expression in the prophetic vision of "the latter days" (*'aḥărīt ha-yāmīm*), which draws most of its ideas and images from the historical experience of national life, from the splendor of the Davidic and Solomonic realm. In the period of the United Kingdom, Israel had realized its desire to live as a nation in its own land, secure and thriving, its social fabric firmly established to a degree never experienced, in any period of Israelite history.

Israel's political ideology in the biblical period, to all intents and purposes, must be identified with the idea of monarchy. The Books of Samuel and Kings, and the passages in the Pentateuch, the Latter Prophets, and the Psalms, which reflect the institution of the monarchy and its ideological foundations, essentially constitute the *politeia* of Israel in the biblical period.[85]

CHAPTER II

LITERARY CREATIVITY

by M. Weinfeld

E VERY STUDY of the literature of the monarchical period must distinguish between works which, although written down during the period of the Monarchy, deal with earlier ages (the pentateuchal literature, Joshua–Judges, I Samuel 1–12, Ruth) and works which deal with and were written down during the monarchical period itself (I Samuel 13 ff., Kings, Psalms, Proverbs, Job, and perhaps Canticles). As regards the latter group, there is no doubt that even their early stages, such as those of oral traditions (e.g. the prophetic narratives) and underlying documentary material (chronicles, lists, etc.), belong to the monarchical period, but there is a duality in the nature of the former. On the one hand, it is clear that these works contain material—some of it even in fixed form—from early ages; on the other hand, it is apparent that the compositions in their present form did not reach literary formulation before the time of the First Temple. Admittedly, part of the literature dealing with the First Temple period was edited after the Destruction of the Temple and this presents certain difficulties. Nonetheless, everyone agrees that the bulk of this literature originated in the pre-exilic period and that the exilic and post-exilic period is principally discernible in the editorial strata (the Deuteronomic redaction of the Former Prophets) and in some parts of Psalms and Proverbs.

Similarly, it should be realized that the existing familiar division into books does not indicate the development of the ancient Israelite literature. The appearance of any particular passage in one book or another is no indication of its authenticity, its date, or its background composition, etc. Every text must be examined individually and categorized in accordance with its own pecularities and in the light of its own literary context. So, for example, the story cycle about the period of the Judges does not terminate in the book of Judges but continues into I Samuel 12, which contains the farewell address of the last of the judges. In the same way, the stories about David's court do not come to an end with the last chapter of the book of Samuel but continue into I Kings 2. On the other hand, a seemingly unified literary source may contain passages of varying literary types, such as poems, lists, laws, etc., which reflect different literary types as well as various life settings. Two factors must therefore guide us in defining a biblical literary unit: (a) the literary type to which a certain pericope belongs; (b) the source or the cycle in which the pericope or the small literary unit is incorporated.

A. Pentateuchal Literature

We shall start with the pentateuchal literature, dealing with the Patriarchal age and the Mosaic period. This is the "classical" period of Israelite history, during which God revealed Himself to the national forefathers and to the entire people and established Covenants with them. It is not surprising, therefore, that this period occupies the foremost position in Israelite literature. It was described in different versions, as the parallel sources incorporated in the Pentateuch make clear. These sources themselves contain various literary types: folk tales, legends, poetry, laws, cultic instructions, and lists of various types. Therefore, in keeping with the above-mentioned principles, when we analyze the literary character of the Pentateuch we must pay attention both to the various literary types which it embraces and to the sources and larger units into which these various types have been woven. First, however, a few words must be said about the historical setting of the pentateuchal literature.

The pentateuchal literature in its present form is not older than the Monarchy. Various hints of this are scattered throughout the Torah, such as Gen. 36:31 (a king in Israel), Ex. 15:17 (temple), and Num. 24:7 (Agag, cf. *ibid.* vv. 17 ff). The final two allusions are of added significance since they occur in poetic works considered more ancient than the prose compositions. Moreover, the sources in the Pentateuch and Former Prophets cite poetic passages from ancient sources: the book of the Wars of YHWH (Num. 21:31), the book of Jashar (Josh. 10:13, II Sam. 7:18, cf. also LXX I Kings 8:13). Even though these "books" seem to have contained poems from the periods of the Conquest and the Judges, they, too, apparently were not crystallized before the monarchical period. The book of Jashar, apparently similar in nature to the book of the Wars of YHWH—and perhaps even identical with it—was clearly not edited before the monarchical period, for it seems to have included David's lamentation for Saul and Jonathan (II Sam. 1:18) as well as the poem recited by Solomon at the dedication of the Temple (I Kings 8:13) (in the LXX version). We should therefore assume that the traditions underlying the pentateuchal literature, even though they were first formulated either as orally transmitted stories or as written epics during the period of the Judges, were not finally formulated before the monarchical period.

1. THE SOURCES

The prevailing view in biblical scholarship is that the literature of the Pentateuch is composed of four main sources: J(= Jahwist), E(= Elohist), P(= Priestly), and D(=Deuteronomy). This division is founded upon literary criticism based on material, linguistic, and stylistic criteria. The separation of J from E is based primarily on the varying use of the divine name in the two strata: the Tetragrammaton (J[= Y]HWH) in J and *Elohim* in E. The use of different names is not only a formal difference, but goes hand in hand with variant concepts of the development of Israelite religion. According to J, YHWH, the God of Israel, was already known and worshipped in the days of Enosh (Gen. 4:26), while in E's view the Tetragrammaton, which is the Israelite God's true name, was first revealed to Moses at the Burning Bush (Ex. 3:6 ff.). P, who has a similar view, expressed the difference explicitly: "I appeared to Abraham, Isaac, and Jacob as El Shaddai, but I did not make Myself known to them by My name YHWH" (Ex. 6:3). The debate about whether monotheism started at the time of Moses or was a direct continuation of the Patriarchal religion seems then to exist, in embryonic form, in the pentateuchal literature. J sees religious continuity starting from the days of Enosh and carrying on through the Patriarchal period up to the time of Moses. In contrast, E and P, although admitting that the God who revealed Himself to the Patriarchs is the same God who revealed Himself to Moses, are of the opinion that the Patriarchs did not know Him by His true name, and certainly this ignorance is theologically significant. Furthermore, P, who most strongly emphasizes the religious discrepancy between the Patriarchal and the Mosaic ages, sees no possibility of regular divine worship (sacrifice) prior to the revelation at the time of Moses.

J and E: J and E are most readily separable in the book of Genesis where the division into sources is based on the striking external feature of J's use of YHWH as opposed to E's use of *Elohim*. It is more difficult to differentiate in the following books of the Torah, because after the revelation of the Burning Bush the name of YHWH is used by E as well. For this reason, it is customary to speak of JE, thereby avoiding the problem of uncertain division. The differentiation between J and E in Genesis helps explain such contradictions and repetitions as: two flights of Hagar (chap. 16; 21:9–21); two abductions of Sarah (12:10–20; chap. 20); Jacob's wealth covered by his own cunning on the one hand (30:25–43) and by the advice of an angel in a dream on the other (31:9, 11 ff.); the rescue of Joseph by Reuben by being thrown into a pit and pulled out by the Midianites, on the one hand (37:22–24, 28a, 29–30), and his being saved by Judah by selling him to the Ishmaelites, on the other (37:25–27, 28b); Reuben's offering surety for Benjamin (42:37), against Judah's identical offer (43:9), and so on.

The division into sources is supported both by the varying use of divine epithets and the employment of different names for Jacob (Jacob as opposed to Israel). Similarly, the two sources can be recognized by their different religious ideologies. While J presents direct contact between God and the Patriarchs, E tends to soften and refine this contact by introducing a dream or an angel as intermediaries (20:3 ff.; 28:12; 21:11–13, etc.), even though this difference is not to be viewed as absolute and decisive.[1] The difficulties encountered in separating the sources stem from the fact that the redactor who combined them attempted to smooth out rough spots and create uniformity, errating the impression that we are dealing not with two independent sources but only with one (J), which was simply supplemented by a later source (E).

Priestly Source (= *P*): This source is much more unusual in character than J or E and is marked by a style and peculiar linguistic features which greatly facilitate its identification, for example *tol^{e}dōt* "the (genealogical) line of" *prh vrbh* "be fertile and increase," *be'eṣem ha-yōm ha-ze* "on that very day," *le dōrōt* "throughout the generations," *m^{e}gūrīm* "(the land of) sojourn," *'ăhuzzāh* "possession/inheritance," *q^{e}hal gōyīm* "assembly of nations," *bēn ha-'arbāyim* "at twilight," *b^{e}kol moš^{e}vōtēkem* "in all your settlements," etc.[2] The passages attributed to P are Gen. 1:1–2, 3; 5; 6:9–22; 7:6–9, 13–16a; 8:14–19; 9:1–17; 11:10–27; 17; 25:1–18; 28:1–9; 35:9–13, 22b–29; 36; 46:6–27; 47:7–11; 48:3–6; 49:28–33; 50:12–13; Ex. 6:2–7, 13; 12:1–20; 43–51; 16*; 25–31; 35–40; the book of Leviticus; Num. 1:1–10:28; 13–14*, 15–16*, 17–19, 26–36.[3]

This source is marked by a systematic religious and ideological outlook not found in JE. As we have said, it is P who explicitly states the idea that God did not reveal Himself in His true name prior to Moses (Ex. 6 ff.), and according to this source the God of Israel designated the tabernacle erected by Moses as His abode, the only place where sacrifices could be offered (cf. Lev. 17). In accordance with this view the Priestly source describes the Patriarchal period as devoid of divine worship through sacrifice. Consequently, the Priestly stratum in the Flood story makes no distinction between unclean and clean animals (Gen. 6: 9–22; 7:6–9), as does J.[4] In contrast, this source clearly cares about Israelite lineal purity (cf. Gen. 27:46 ff.), as is seen from the genealogical lists so characteristic of P. Circumcision and the Sabbath occupy significant positions in this source (Gen. 1; 17; Ex. 12:44, 48; 16:12–17; 35:1–3, and others). It is only natural that priestly circles should be highly concerned about these matters, which give external-physical expression to Israel's uniqueness. Furthermore, circumcision and the Sabbath, along with the rainbow (Gen. 9:1–17), are, in accordance with the Priestly source, parts of the complex of signs symbolizing the Covenants made by God with mankind and with the Israelite forefathers.[5]

Actually, the Priestly material in Genesis has the sole purpose of serving the Priestly-sacred tendency which emphasizes the element of holiness in Israel and institutions, the purpose served also by the priestly passages in Exodus, Leviticus, and Numbers.

Central to the world of the Priestly source is the Temple and all that it entails. This is so important in the Priestly work that it supersedes even such a crucial matter as the Sinaitic Covenant. In contrast to JE and D, the Priestly source says nothing about the Revelation when giving the Law at Sinai. It describes instead a theophany at the time of the dedication of the Tabernacle, when fire comes forth from before YHWH and consumes the burnt offering and the fats on the altar (Lev. 9:24), symbolizing the establishment of Divine Presence in Israel.

The material in the Priestly source deals primarily with such matters of holiness and cult as sacrifices (Lev. 1–10), impurity and purity (11–16), abstinence for the sake of holiness, pertaining to the Israelites (Lev. 18; 20) and the priests (chaps. 21, 22), holy seasons (Lev. 23; Num. 28–29), Sabbatical and Jubilee Years as the land's observance of the Sabbath of the Lord (Lev. 25), etc. Even when recounting a past event—the creation (Gen. 1:1–2:3), the Covenants with Noah and Abraham (Gen. 9:1–17; 17), or the Exodus from Egypt— interest is still centered in the sacred institutions of Israel like the Sabbath, circumcision, the prohibition against eating blood, or the Paschal offering. The laws in this source concerning such familial or civil matters as the laws of incest in Lev. chaps. 18, 20 or the law of inheritance in Num. chaps. 27; 36 are not primarily interested in presenting legal matters from the realm of familial or inheritance laws—as we find in Deuteronomy (21–22)—but in emphasizing the sanctity of the family and the land.[6]

Deuteronomy (= D): Another source, contained in one book of the Pentateuch and literally an organic composition, is Deuteronomy. It is fashioned as a farewell address of Moses (delivered in the Plains of Moab), is written in an autobiographical fashion (Deut. 1–31), and is characterized by its unique style and expressions. Both by its ideas and its linguistic peculiarities it influenced the redactor of the books of the Former Prophets, especially the editor of Kings, and also the book of Jeremiah.[7]

This book was fundamental for the determination of the dates of the pentateuchal sources in general. De Wette in 1805[8] established the still-accepted premise that Deuteronomy reflects, in both content and form, the period of Hezekiah-Josiah. Thus he paved the way for the historical-chronological sequence of the pentateuchal sources whose actual existence was already recognized in the eighteenth century.[9] De Wette looked for a historical anchor for the formation of the Pentateuch and found it in the account of the discovery of a book of the Law in II Kings 22–23. The story of the book's discovery and the description of its contents and the activity which it stimulated indicate that the book found was the book of Deuteronomy.[10]

The most important proof is the centralization of cult in Jerusalem: according to the information in the book of Kings the first king to unify the cult in Jerusalem was Hezekiah (II Kings 18:3); before him this idea had occurred to no one. On the contrary, Elijah sees the destruction of altars to the God of Israel as a sin (I Kings 19:10, 14). We also know that in the Pentateuch the only law which demands unity of worship is found in Deuteronomy (cf. chap. 12 and the other laws there based on the idea of centralization).[11] We can therefore assume that this law started to develop in the time of Hezekiah and was already fully formed and had achieved literary expression in the days of Josiah. The criterion of cult unification in dating D is supplemented by two other criteria: (a) style of a sort that does not appear before Josiah's time, but afterward spread rapidly and dominated biblical literature (Kings, Jeremiah, and the books of latter Prophets); (b) the book of Deuteronomy, which is structured along the lines of a covenantal document (historical introduction [chaps. 1–11], stipulations [12:1–26; 15], commitments [26:16–19; 27:9–10], blessings and curses [28]), contains a wealth of literary forms and modes of expression known to us from contemporary Assyrian literature (eighth and seventh centuries B.C.E.), especially from treaties between the Assyrian kings and their vassals.[12]

The Date of the Sources. The date of the book of Deuteronomy serves as a point of departure for determining the dates of the remaining pentateuchal sources. Those assuming the existence of non-centralized worship (such as Ex. 20:21–23) clearly belong to the pre-Hezekiah-Josianic age, while those demanding centralized worship come from a later period. Accordingly, it is clear that JE is earlier than D; as for P, there is still debate. In the view of Wellhausen,[13] who contended that P was written during the Babylonian Exile, this source takes unification of the cult for granted. Kaufmann,[14] in contrast, refutes his claims and convincingly proves that P does not assume unification of the cult and that the Priestly laws reflect a stage prior to centralization. The decisive factors in dating P are the time of the cultic institutions described and the style of the source. Wellhausen's claims do not stand up to either of these tests. Documents from the ancient Near East show us over and over again that institutions such as those found in P were known throughout the ancient Near East centuries before Israel even entered its land.[15] On the other hand the Priestly style has no features which would indicate lateness.[16] D seems therefore to be the last pentateuchal source and is preceded by JE and P. D is related in ideas and language to JE and not to P because, in contrast to P which developed among Priestly circles—and therefore represents a Priestly view—D as well as JE are popular sources.

Paradoxically, although D was the last source to crystallize, it was the first to become "canonical." In the time of Josiah a covenant was established on the basis of the book of Deuteronomy (II Kings 23:1-3) and became a binding law,[17] and only at the time of Ezra was D supplemented by the traditions of the first four books of the Torah, the whole complex becoming the canonical five books of Moses.

In contrast to D, which reached final formulation in the seventh century B.C.E., it is most difficult to date JE and P. These sources clearly did not crystallize before the monarchical age, although they undoubtedly contain older traditions and laws. As for JE it seems, especially in Genesis, that its background is one of national political prominence. The promises to the Patriarchs which unify this work speak not only of the gift of progeny and land but also about victories over enemies, subjugation of peoples, and "a great nation" (gōi gadōl)[18] which rules the territory from the Euphrates to the Brook of Egypt (Gen. 15:18-21; cf. Ex. 23:21). These signs may indicate that the period of the United Monarchy was the time of the formation of this source.[19]

P also contains indications of a period of political greatness, such as the promises that the Patriarchs will bear kings and form an assembly of peoples (qᵉhal gōyīm) (Gen. 17:4-6; 28:3; 35:11; 48:3), and therefore it also seems to reflect the days of the United Monarchy. Even so, we must consider Speiser's opinion[20] that this composition is the cumulative work of Priestly circles working over a period of centuries, thus making it most difficult to determine the final date, which is, in any case, before the time of the composition of D during the seventh century B.C.E.

2. THE LITERARY TYPES

The material under study contains, as indicated, ancient literary material of various genres. We find narrative, poetry, law, cultic instructions, lists of various types, prayers, speeches, etc. It is of interest that each source individually and independently selects the material most suited to its views and purposes. JE has a preference for poetry and narrative prose, P for laws, lists, and cultic instruction, and D, although including both story and law, for the form of rhetorical oration.

Let us briefly survey this literary material according to its various types.

The Narrative

The story in pentateuchal literature, in contrast to that in the Former Prophets, is largely of legendary nature and not historical. Even though the stories in the Torah reflect some kind of authenticity, their main purpose is not to record history as such—as is the case in the book of Kings—but to tell a tale. Under the influence of Gunkel it is now common to classify the biblical stories into the same groups as folk literature:[21] Myth, *Märchen* (fairy tale), Saga, Legend, Anecdote, and Novella. The confines of these literary genres are not strictly defined, but the principle of the division is reasonable and can be employed in studying biblical literature.

The Myth, which is most common in ancient literature, is a story about the gods. Myths developed against a polytheistic background where the divine realm is described anthropomorphically. The gods eat, drink, have sexual intercourse, give birth, fight, etc. Israelite religion, which knows only one God who transcends nature and is not subservient to its laws, gradually eliminated the myth. To the extent that myth is actually found in biblical literature, it is expressed in two characteristic manners: (1) Accounts of God in His relationship to man by means of revelation, speaking, etc. This type contains, for instance, the story of God's descent to Mt. Sinai in Ex. 19; the story of the descent of the "Sons of God" and their copulating with the daughters of men in Genesis (6:1–4); Jacob's struggle with the angel of God (32:25 ff.), etc. (2) Remnants in poetic literature of accounts of God's struggle with Tanin, Rahab, Leviathan, i.e., primeval monsters who rebelled against God's dominion (see, e.g., Ps. 74:13–14; 89:10–11; Job 26:12–13; Isa. 51:9).[22]

In this area, Israelite literature drew upon myths of ancient Near-Eastern peoples in which the motive of theomachy (wars of gods) prevails. However, in contrast to the pagan myths, God—in the biblical narrative—does not battle with enemy competitors but with His own rebellious creations.[23]

The Fairy Tale (Märchen) is divorced from any concrete realistic background and tells of a wondrous human event which could take place anywhere, at any time. This type is exemplified by the tales of the ass which speaks to Balaam (Num. 22:22–35), the ravens which feed Elijah (I Kings 17:14; II Kings 4:1–7), the fish which swallows Jonah, etc.

The Saga is a miraculous story about a specific personality or an extraordinary phenomenon which grows out of a concrete geographical and historical situation. Distinction is generally made between the saga chronicling the origin of an unusual natural phenomenon like the destruction of Sodom and Gemorrah (Gen. 19), and that concentrating on a people or tribe, such as the origin of Canaan (Gen. 9:20–27), Ishmael (Gen. 16:4–15; 21:8–21), Edom (25:21–26), Ammon, and Moab (19:30–38). Sagas also deal with the lives of heroes and leaders (Moses, Joshua, Samuel, and others).

The Legend usually intends to explain the origin of holy places, and is exemplified by the story of Jacob's dream at Bethel (Gen. 28:10–22), the story of the appearance of an angel of God at the threshing floor of Araunah the Jebusite

(II Sam. 24:16, cf. I Chron. 21:16 ff.), and so on. It can also tell about the commissioning of a prophet or a spiritual leader as it does in the revelation to Moses at the Burning Bush (Ex. 3:1–15, the appearance of an angel to Gideon in Ophrah (Judg. 6:11 ff.), and the appearance of an angel to Samson's mother (Judg. 13:2 ff.).

The Anecdote describes unusual or supernatural acts of heroism like those in the story of Samson and the foxes (Judg. 15:4–5), his ripping down the gates of Gaza with his hands (*ibid.* 16:3), and the exploits of David's warriors described in II Sam. 23:8–23.

The Novella contrasts with the above-mentioned literary types, which concentrate upon a wondrous act, by describing the natural experience of daily life, involving a chain of events and the appearance of many characters. The Joseph stories represent a novella typical of this definition.

3. LAW

Biblical law, too, consists of different literary types, indicating varying backgrounds of formation. In the oldest Israelite law corpus, entitled the book of the Covenant (Ex. 21–23), we can recognize three types of laws: civil (21:1–22:16), moral-social (22:17–23:9),[24] and cultic ordinances (23:10–19).[25] However, this distinction blurs in the later law corpora of P and D, where the laws mingle and blend, leaving little possibility of distinguishing between the various types. Furthermore, the civil laws which account for over half the book of the Covenant (21:1–22:16) and which make up the larger portions of Mesopotamian law codes, gradually diminish and disappear in the later law codes because the religious legislator in Israel is no longer concerned about them.

This blurring of borders between types of laws is also discernible in the form and formulation of the laws. While in the book of the Covenant the civil laws use a style known as casuistic (if . . . should), predominant in the ancient Near Eastern law corpora, and the cultic and moral-ethical laws use primarily an absolute apodictic style (you shall, you shall not . . . do not . . . etc.),[26] in the collections of P and D the styles are completely mixed. A law commencing casuistically switches in midstream to the apodictic and no distinction can be made between them (see e.g., Lev. 22:18–20, Deut. 22:23–24).

Another important difference between the ancient book of the Covenant and the Priestly and Deuteronomic law codes appears in the scarcity of motive-supplying clauses in the former—as in other ancient Near Eastern legal codes—and their abundance in the latter, especially in Deuteronomy.[27] Furthermore, the Deuteronomic Code, which is the most recent, slowly frees itself of its legalistic character, and turns into humanistic sermonizing and rhetoric. Most enlightening in this respect is a comparison between the law of slaves in Ex. 21: 1–11 and its parallel in Deut. 15:12–18. While the statue in the book of the Covenant is formulated in a totally dry casuistic style and defines the master's rights in contrast to those of the slave, the corresponding law in the Deutero-nomic Code, which is stylized as didactic rhetoric, disregards the rights of the master and instead turns to him in the second person and urges him to furnish his emancipated slave generously and send him away good-naturedly, none of which is mentioned in the earlier code. Such a sentence as "When you do set him free, do not feel aggrieved" cannot even be imagined in the older legis-lation or even in modern law, which is also true of a sentence like the one in the Holiness Code (incorporated into P): "You shall not hate your kinsman in your heart . . . Love your neighbor as yourself" (Lev. 19:17–18). Such words are directed to a man's heart and, although they can be recommended, they cannot be legislated.

The historical gap between early and late law is most apparent in the law of seething a kid in its mother's milk. In Ex. 23:19 and the parallel verse Ex. 34:26, the law appears in a cultic context connected with the seasonal holidays, giving the impression that the custom was part of certain Canaanite fertility rites opposed in the verse.[28] In D, however, the injunction appears in the context of forbidden foods (Deut. 14:21), indicating that the Deuteronomic author, no longer aware of the law's true origin, placed it among the dietary laws (as it was subsequently understood by late Judaism), even though the law itself speaks about seething and not eating.

Another point emphasizing the ancient background of the book of the Covenant is the warning about cursing God and the *nāsī* (chieftain) (Ex. 22:27). During the monarchical period we hear about cursing God and King (I Kings 21:10, Isa. 8:21, cf. Prov. 24:21), and in the book of the Covenant about God and chieftain, showing that these laws were formulated against the background of tribal rule, which preceded the Israelite Monarchy.[29]

4. CULTIC INSTRUCTION

This literary genre is most prevalent in the Priestly source, its most notice-able hallmark the formula, "Speak to the Children of Israel and say unto them," when the instructions are intended for the Israelites, and "Speak unto Aaron and unto his sons," when they are for the priests. These instructions deal mostly with sacrificial procedure (Lev. 1–7), preserving purity (11–15), observing holi-days (23), guarding the temple (Num. 3–4), rites for the putative unfaithful wife and for the Nazirite (Num. 5–6), and holiday and seasonal sacrifices (Num.

28–29, cf. Lev. 23 and others). This literary type is found among the Hittites and the Assyrians[30] and in documents from Ugarit.[31]

5. LISTS

Much pentateuchal literature, especially in the Priestly source, is concerned with various types of lists. There are genealogical lists of several types: antediluvian patriarchs (Gen. 5; cf. 4:17–26), post-diluvian patriarchs (Gen. 11: 10–26), nations and tribes somehow related to the family of Hebrews (Gen. 22: 20–24; 25:1–18; 36:1–14), the nations and their sub-branches (Gen. 10:1–32), genealogies of the Israelite tribes (Gen. 46:8–27; Num. 26:1–65), and also a genealogy of the Israelite priestly houses (Ex. 6:14–25). We also find census lists of Israel and the tribes (Num. 1; 26), of the tribal chieftains ($N^e\acute{s}\bar{\imath}\ \bar{\imath}m$) (Num. 1:5–16; 13:4–15:34:16–29), and even of the chieftains and kings of the Edomites (Gen. 36:15–43). Another type of list is the geographic-historical, such as the border lists (Num. 34:1–15, cf. Josh. 13–19), itinerary lists (Num. 33: 1–49; Deut. 10:6–7), and lists of gifts and contributions for building the Tabernacle (Ex. 35:21–29) and for its initiation rites (Num. 7).

This genre was well-known to the peoples of the ancient Near East. We find in the Mesopotamian tradition[32] a list of antediluvian kings reminiscent of that in Gen. 5; Malamat found in the genealogical stock of an "ancestral tree" of the ancient Babylonian and Assyrian kings a parallel to the patriarchal genealogy in Gen. 11:10–26.[33] He showed, furthermore, that if we extend the list in Gen. 11 through the three patriarchs Abraham, Isaac, and Jacob and go through Judah down to David (cf. the list in Ruth 4:18–22, I Chron. 2:5, 8–15), we find a structure entirely concurrent with the family tree of the kings of Babylonia and Assyria: (1) genealogical stock—a basically fictitious substratum; (2) determinative line—i.e., the specific descent of a people or dynasty (compare Abraham, Isaac, Jacob, Judah); (3) a list of ancestors which is the actual pedigree of a concrete historical line or dynasty. The fictitious substratum and the ancestor list contain ten generations equivalent to the corresponding portions of the Mesopotamian lists. Perhaps this equivalence means that the table in Gen. 11:10–26 is intended as a prologue to the Davidic line and, if so, was compiled by scribes of the United Monarchy.

Most of the lists apparently served administrative needs during the Monarchy (especially in the time of David) and were anachronistically incorporated into the Torah, just as lists of cities and borders were incorporated into the book of Joshua (see below).

B. HISTORIOGRAPHY IN THE FORMER PROPHETS

While the historical literature of the Pentateuch has come down in three parallel versions, in other words, from three compilers, the Former Prophets discloses only one editor, although it is not to be ruled out that parts were edited by earlier writers.[34] The material now before us, however, shows signs of a single editor and is known as Deuteronomistic because of the recognizable influences of the book of Deuteronomy. The editor, or editors, of this school gathered such various material as legends and sagas, historical narratives, court stories, excerpts from royal chronicles, temple archives, historical-geographical lists, etc., and gave them a framework. This is based on a division of Israel's history in its own land into the three major periods of the Conquest, the Judges, and the Monarchy. The editor summarizes and typifies each period by placing an oration in the mouth of the leading figure of the time or by making a summary statement himself. In this way the period of the Conquest is brought to a close by Joshua's farewell address (Josh. 23),[35] the period of the Judges by Samuel's valedictory address (I Sam. 12), the period of the Israelite Monarchy by an editorial in II Kings 17:7–23, and the period of the Judean Monarchy in II Kings 21:11–16.[36] Similar discourses mark the beginnings of periods. Thus Josh. 1 is a prophetic discourse introducing us to the events of the conquest, Judges 2:11–3:3 a preamble to the period of the Judges, and David's speech in I Kings 2:3–4 a sort of prologue to the period of the Monarchy.

Besides the introductions and conclusions in which the Deuteronomic style is easily recognized,[37] we find the editor's words in evaluatory passages interspersed among the various judges in the book of Judges ("The Children of Israel did that which was evil in the eyes of the Lord, etc."), and among the kings in the book of Kings ("He did that which was evil in the eyes of the Lord" or "He did righteously in the eyes of the Lord"). Similarly, we find editorial additions to the speeches of kings and prophets. These expansions actually reflect the outlook of the editor, but put in the mouths of national leaders they derive added authority.[38] The words of the prophets are usually supplemented by the editor with a rebuke for breaking the Covenant (I Kings 14:7 ff.; 21:21 ff., etc.), while the long prayer put into the mouth of Solomon reflects the editor's special view of the function of the Temple (I Kings 8:31 ff.).[39]

Apart from these additions the editor makes no changes in the traditions[40] presented to us, but delivers them as he has received them and lets them speak for themselves. Thus for instance, Elijah at Mount Horeb (I Kings 19:10, 19) expresses ideas not congruent with the principle of cult centralization used by the editor as a yardstick for evaluating kings, but nothing is deleted or changed because the editor venerated the tradition.

It is difficult to date the editorial work of the Former Prophets. A certain focal point can be found in II Kings 25:27–30, which mentions the release of Jehoiachin from prison, an event that took place in 560 B.C.E., thus making it impossible for the book of Kings in its present form to have been written before this date. This reference, however, which gives the impression of an appendix, may have been added after the book finally crystallized. In any case, the edition of the books Joshua–Kings, and especially of the book of Kings itself, was not finally crystallized before the Destruction of the Temple, which occurrence is reflected in various rebukes throughout the work (II Kings 17:19; 21:12 ff.; 22:20; 23:26; 24:3. Cf. Josh. 23:15 ff.). The redaction of the material in the books of Joshua–Samuel could have been accomplished before the Destruction of Jerusalem, but not before 622 B.C.E., i.e., the year of the discovery of the book of Deuteronomy, whose style and views permeate the entire editorial strand of the Former Prophets.

1. The Literary Types Found in the Former Prophets

The literary material incorporated into the books of the Former Prophets varies in character from unit to unit. The literature dealing with the Conquest period, described in the book of Joshua, abounds with national legends. The book of Judges hosts mainly stories of the heroism of the national "saviors." The literature from the monarchical period is full of authentic historical descriptions based on written documents taken primarily from the royal archives. Below we will review this literary material and its various types.

The Traditions in the Book of Joshua

a. *The Conquest Narrative in Joshua* 2–12: In this unit miraculous legendary tales, such as the account of the crossing of the Jordan (Josh. 3–4) and the fall of the walls of Jericho (chap. 6), are juxtaposed with stories of a historical nature, like the war with the southern kings, the battle in the north, and the conquest of Hazor.[41] The unifying motive is Gilgal, central point of these traditions (cf. esp. Josh. 3–5), which, according to these stories, served as a military base from which the warriors set out and to which they returned after the forays (5:10; 9:6; 10:6, 9, 15, 43). It is therefore altogether reasonable to assume that the sanctuary at Gilgal was the place of origin of the legends in this unit. This sanctuary, located within the territory of Benjamin, could well have nourished these traditions, which generally deal with the settlements in the Benjamin area (Gilgal, Jericho, Ai, Gibeon). The period best suited to the development of such a cycle of traditions is that of Saul, the first king of Benjamite origin, who was crowned in Gilgal (and also in Mizpah) (I Sam. 11:14–15) and functioned actively at the Gilgal Shrine (13:8–12; 15:12, 21, 33). Furthermore, only after the unification of the Israelite tribes into a kingdom could the desire have arisen to create a kind of national epic of the Conquest of the Land by a single leader.

The image of zealous King Saul scheming against the indigenous Amorites (II Sam. 21:2 ff.) fits the idea of the *herem* (ban) in the story of the conquest of Jericho and the Achan incident (Josh. 7). Another unifying feature is their noticeable aetiological tendency, which uses the stories to explain strange phenomena and such unusual and prominent objects as the ruins of Jericho (Josh. 6), the stone pillars at Gilgal (Josh. 3–4), a pile of stones in the valley of Achor (Josh. 7:26), the Gibeonites serving in the temple (9:27), or the cave at Makkedah with its nearby trees (10:27). This does not mean, however, that the stories were invented solely for aetiological purposes, as Gressmann, Alt, and Noth have claimed,[42] since the aetiological factor was neither primary nor creative, but generally attached to an independent historical tradition.[43]

b. *Lists of Cities and Borders in Josh.* 13–21: This section presents a detailed description of the tribes, borders, and cities. As Alt has already shown,[44] we must distinguish both materially and literally between the lists of tribal borders which have come down almost in their entirety and the lists of cities which include only the southern tribes Judah and Simeon, Benjamin and Dan, and some of the tribes of Galilee. In Alt's opinion, the lists of cities, and especially those of the southern tribes with their regional divisions, reflect the administrative division of Josiah's kingdom, since only under his reign did Judah achieve the size depicted in these lists. Alt's view has recently been reinforced both by the archaeological find in Meṣad Ḥashavyahu,[45] showing that Josiah controlled the Ekron area (cf. Josh. 15:45–46), and the En-gedi excavations, showing that the city of En-gedi was not founded before Josiah's time.[46] All this makes it clear that the editor of Joshua employed lists of cities of his own period to describe the geographical situation at the time of the Conquest. As for the lists of the borders of the tribes, as well as the lists of Levitical cities and cities of refuge, it is reasonable to assume that all reflect the period of the United Monarchy.[47] This assumption is based on the overlap between the tribal borders and the borders of the land in the period of the United Monarchy (see esp. II Sam. 24:5–8; cf. I Kings 4:7–20).

c. *The Narratives in the Book of Judges:*[48] In the book of Judges, as in the book of Joshua, we find historical descriptions along with tales of national heroes, even though the legendary thrust is much weaker than that in the book of Joshua. The Samson stories, with their anecdotal and personal character, are exceptions, Samson is not presented as a national savior to the degree that the other judges are, but more as an adventurer who reacts when personally affronted.[49] Closer in their historiographical nature to the type of story found in Samuel and Kings are the chapters about Gideon, Abimelech, and Jephthah (chaps. 8–9, 11–12) and the brief biographical sections about the minor judges (Judg. 10:1–5, 12:8–15) which are fitted in around the Jephthah pericope. These periods, times of stabilization of rule after the defeat of great enemies (Midian[50] and Ammon), seemed conducive to writing chronicles, an activity that might have commenced in the time of Gideon, who assumed some of the attributes of royalty (Judg. 8:27, 29) and whose government boasted certain features of monarchy.[51] As with Saul, who united the kingdom after defeating the Ammonites (I Sam. 11), kingship was offered to Gideon after he conquered Midian (Judg. 8:22–23); Scripture testifies that he turned it down. His son Abimelech, in any case, pretended to the throne and the protest against his enthronement, sharply expressed in the fable of Jotham (Judg. 9:7–20), contains an anti-monarchical polemic[52] reminiscent of that found in the stories about Saul's coronation (I Sam. 8; 10:17 ff.; 12).

In the appendix to the book (chaps. 17–21) are stories based on historical reality which are somewhat blemished by their polemical tendency (the opposition to the Dan Temple and the hatred toward Benjamin and the people of Jabesh-gilead). The refrain in these stories, "In those days there was no king in Israel, everyone did that which was right in his own eyes" (17:6; 21:25; cf. 18:1; 19:1), displays the tendentiousness of the section. The editor who arranged these stories and placed them where they are at present wanted them to illustrate the anarchy rampant at the end of the period of the Judges which, in his opinion, made monarchy unavoidable.

The Historiography of the Monarchical Period

The distinguishing feature of the works of Samuel and Kings is their basis in written documents. The book of Kings makes explicit reference to its written sources: "The book of Chronicles of the kings of Israel," "The book of Chronicles of the kings of Judah," "The Chronicles of Solomon." Other signs also indicate that Samuel and Kings derive from written sources, like lists of the staff of David and Solomon (II Sam. 8:16–18; 20:23–26; I Kings 4:2–6) and a list of Solomon's governors and their districts (I Kings 4:7–19; cf. I Chron. 27), details certainly not transmitted orally but taken from documents in the royal archives. This is true also of the court narratives in II Sam. 9–I Kings 2, written approximately when they occurred, as we shall see below, and of royal chronicles incorporated in both the books of Samuel and Kings. We will start with the court from the time of the United Monarchy.

a. *Court Narratives:* From II Sam. 9 until I Kings 2 (excluding the appendix in II Sam. 21–24),[53] we find historical tales of events in David's court after he set up the monarchy in Jerusalem. The stories are written superbly and are the world's first history (about 500 years before Herodotus). Their unifying theme is, in the opinion of most scholars,[54] the struggle for succession. II Sam. 9 tells about the last remnant of the house of Saul. Immediately afterwards comes a chapter describing the war with Ammon, which sets the background for the birth of Solomon, who is to inherit the throne. Then begins the main plot about the actual struggle among the sons for the right to succeed to the throne. The firstborn Amnon is removed by Absalom's scheming, rebellious Absalom meets a tragic end, the rebellion of Sheba ben Bikri follows the rebellion of Absalom, and finally the struggle between Solomon and Adonijah brings the epic to its conclusion.

Even though the chain of events presented supports the common supposition, we are nevertheless not certain that it was really so. The story probably intends to illustrate by way of this arrangement of events the fulfillment of Nathan's prophecy that on account of the sin with Bathsheba, David's house would be plagued with bloodshed (II Sam. 12:10). If so, the drama actually starts in chapter 13 rather than in chapter 9. The preceding chapters in I and II Samuel, and especially those describing the struggle with Saul, represent from the literary point of view a similar tradition. The more picturesque nature of the chapters in II Sam. 9 ff. can be explained by the fact that the writers had actually witnessed the incidents described but had apparently learned from oral tradition about the events of David's youth.[55] That the stories about David constitute a unified literary creation of one writer or circle of writers can be seen from recurring expressions like "Chariot and horses/riders and fifty men running before him" (II Sam. 15:1; I Kings 1:5: Absalom and Adonijah); "His father had not grieved him all his life" (I Kings 1:6; II Sam. 13:21 in Septuagint); "When the tidings came" (II Sam. 13:30; I Kings 2:28); "As the Lord lives who has redeemed my soul out of every adversity" (II Sam. 4:9, I Kings 1:29); "As blameless in my sight as an angel of God" (I Sam. 29:9; cf. II Sam. 14:17, 19:28— all referring to David); "If I am guilty slay me" (I Sam. 20:8; II Sam. 14:32). Most enlightening also is the theological outlook of this writer or group of writers. Even though there is no mention of divine involvement in the action, some passages nonetheless indicate that the writer was aware of a hidden hand guiding the events. Thus David says in response to Abishai's desire to behead Shimei, "because the Lord has said to him 'Curse David'" (II Sam. 16:10); this is also true of the verse about YHWH confounding Ahithophel's counsel (II Sam. 17:14), and Adonijah's remarks about Solomon's kingship, "for it was his from the Lord" (I Kings 2:15).

We must point out the objectivity and restraint demonstrated by the recorder of these stories. In contrast to the Deuteronomic editor who passes judgment and evaluates positively or negatively every royal personality, this narrator offers not a word of evaluation or criticism, permitting the reader to concentrate on the events themselves. Even concerning David's treatment of his sons, as in "his father had not grieved him all his life," referring to Adonijah (and also about Amnon in II Sam. 13:21), we cannot tell whether David's laxity is considered worthy of praise or blame.

Various hypotheses about the author's identity—Abiathar, Ahimaaz the priest, or Jehoshaphat the *mazkīr* (II Sam. 8:16; 20:24; I Kings 4:3)—are purely guesswork, making speculation futile.[56]

b. *Royal Historical Documents:* This literary genre derives from royal accounts usually dealing with building projects and military campaigns. In the ancient Near East and in Mesopotamia in particular we find three major types of these accounts:

a) Memorial stelae usually erected at the site of a victory, recording its details (cf. the Mesha Inscription);

b) Annals chronologically listing the king's enterprises. These were written down by the king's scribes and preserved in various editions as a result of having to be brought up to date to include the latest events;

c) Chronicles with brief notices about royal activities of long duration.

Clearly the stelae and the annals were closer to the actual events than were the chronicles, which recorded the happenings of centuries. The stelae and annals are usually written in the first person, i.e., the king tells about himself—although in Egypt third-person diaries are attested—while the chronicles are formulated in the third person.

Egyptian and Mesopotamian historical documents have been discovered in the original, but in Israel only second- or even third-hand evidence has been preserved (cf. "the Chronicles of the kings of Judah and Israel" quoted by the author of Kings), and it is therefore difficult to trace the formation of this literature. In any case, the Bible contains no document in which the king tells about himself. Possibly this was a matter of principle (avoidance of absolute power), but more probably it results from reporting information second-hand. It is interesting that first-person history is found in the memoirs of Ezra-Nehemiah. The concluding verses of Nehemiah's memoirs, "Remember me, O my God, for good" (Neh. 13:31; cf. 14:22), give the memoirs a certain annalistic flavor, since the annals, like the memorial stelae, are types of "reports to the gods."[57] Despite the difficulty of reconstructing the sources on the basis of extant secondary and tertiary material, it does seem that the three types of historical writing were known in Israel as well.

a) Memorial Stelae—The Pentateuch tells us that Moses was commanded to write a "reminder in a document" (*zikārōn bᵉsēfer*)[58] about the victory over

Amalek, and it is perhaps more than coincidental that Saul, after he defeated the Amalekites, also set up a monument (*yād*) (I Sam. 15:12).[59] When he returned from vanquishing Edom in the Valley of Salt, David made a "name" (*šem*) which also designated a memorial pillar (II Sam. 8:13, 56). It might perhaps be claimed that this was a blank uninscribed slab, but considering the fact that neighboring peoples were accustomed to record their victories on a stele and dedicate it to their god, there is no reason why an Israelite king might not engrave his thanks to his God on the monument he set up.

b) Annals—These are factual accounts of wars and royal building projects from the time of the Monarchy. The material that seems to belong to this literary genre is: I Sam. 11:1–13; 13–14; 31; II Sam. 5:4–9, 17–25; 8:1–14; 10; 12, 26–31; I Kings 5:15–8:8, 62–66; 9:10–10:29; 11:14–28, 40–43; 12:25–33; 14:25–31; 15:17–22; 20; 22:1–38; II Kings 3:4–27; 6:24–7:20; 8:25–10; 27; 11:1–20; 12:5–17; 14:8–14; 16:7–18; 18:14–16; 22:3–20; 23:1–20. Unlike the Mesopotamian annals, which are schematic and stereotyped, the style here is narrative and picturesque, similar to Egyptian historical texts[60] and probably influenced by them. That these annals were composed when the events occurred is clear from technical details which could not possibly have been preserved in the memories of subsequent generations. There is a question about whether the annals of the court scribes existed along with those of the Temple scribes. Thus, for instance, it has been claimed that the description of the Temple buildings in I Kings 6–7 and the account of the repair of the Temple in II Kings 12 and of the reform of Josiah in II Kings 22–23 are products of Temple scribes. However, considering that the Temple was a royal sanctuary and shared with the palace a common lot (tribute to foreign kings was paid both from the Temple and palace treasuries, cf. I Kings 14:26; 15:18; II Kings 12:19; 18:15, etc.), and that Assyrian annals are also concerned with the temples, this is not necessarily true. But stories dealing with the sanctity of a site or an object, like the one about the altar in Aravnah's threshing floor (II Sam. 24), or about the wanderings of the Ark from Shiloh to Kiriath Jearim (4:1–7:2) and its transfer to the City of David (II Sam. 6), or about the sacred vessels transferred to Solomon's Temple (I Kings 8:1–13) are of a different type. They certainly developed in Priestly circles, even though they might have been recorded later by royal scribes.

c) Chronicles—In contrast to the annuals, royal chronicles are schematic and have a dry, statistical flavor. The constantly repeated details in the schematic skeleton include the year of the king's ascent to power, along with the date synchronizing him with the neighboring kingdom (Judah/Israel), the central events of his reign (wars and building projects), the number of years of his reign, the year of death, and place of burial. Remarks attached to this framework are usually from the pen of the editor but the chronicles themselves seem to be independent creations which the editor has incorporated into his own work. There is great similarity between the chronicles of the book of Kings and the Babylonian Chronicles, a similarity also expressed in the use of synchronistic chronology (Judah in comparison ·to Israel, Assyria in comparison to Babylonia).[61]

c. *Prophetic Narratives:* These stories center round Samuel, Ahijah the Shilonite, Elijah, Elisha, Isaiah and others comprise a considerable portion of the books of Samuel and Kings; I Sam. 1–13; 7–16, I Kings 11:29 ff.; 13; 14:1 ff.; 17–22; II Kings 1–10, 18–19. In order to avoid any misunderstanding it must be pointed out that not every story dealing with a prophet or prophets belongs to the category of prophetic narrative. For example, I Kings 20, which deals at length with prophets, or II Kings 3, where Elisha makes an appearance, or II Kings 9:1–10:25 about Jehu's rebellion, carried out under Elisha's inspiration, were actually recorded by court scribes. On account of the prophet's active role in the events, however, the stories seem to have originated in prophetic circles. Because the prophets performed a vital task in battle campaigns in Israel and the surrounding ancient Near East, it is no surprise to encounter them in stories about the kings. The true prophetic narratives are those whose main purpose is to glorify the image of the prophet, usually by emphasizing his miracles and wonders, like the Elijah-Elisha cycles in I Kings 17–19; II Kings 1–2; 4:1–6; 7; 13:20–21. These legends undoubtedly originated among prophetic disciples who revered their masters and told miraculous tales about them.[62]

Some of the Elijah and Elisha legends are repeated, such as the resurrection of the child (I Kings 17:17–24; II Kings 4:18–37) and the cruse of oil which does not run dry (I Kings 17:8–16; II Kings 4:1–7), miracles which appear in conjunction in both the Elijah and the Elisha cycles. The majority of critics believe that these stories originated in the Elisha cycle and were only later transplanted by prophetic disciples to the Elijah cycle. This is likely, since most of the miraculous stories, told for their own sake[63] without other motive, were woven around the image of Elisha, while the miracles associated with Elijah usually have a national-religious-moral background.[64]

C. THE PROPHETIC LITERATURE

Classical prophecy, which started with Amos, is distinguished from the popular prophecy which preceded it by the fact that it was written down. Classical prophecy encompasses prophetic speeches delivered by the prophet and subsequently recorded, in contrast to the legacy left us about popular prophecy which contains not the actual words and orations of the prophets but stories *about* them, as they were written down by disciples.

Writing down the prophecies is not to be considered a merely technical activity but an integral part of the prophetic mission. A prophetic word written upon a sheet (Isa. 8:1), a tablet (Isa. 30:8, Hab. 2:2), or a scroll (Isa. 30:8; Jer. 25:13; 30; 36:2, 4, 10 ff.; Ezek. 2:9; cf. 37:15 ff.) is like a check waiting to be cashed. The fulfillment of a prophecy was a *post factum* certification of the pending divine word and legitimized the prophet in the eyes of the people. The written prophecy served as a document which was at times drawn up in the presence of reliable witnesses (Isa. 8:7) and even signed and sealed (*ibid.* 8:16), just as legal documents were folded and tied with string (cf. Job 14:17). It was opened and read at the time of fulfillment and its truth proven.

The process of writing down prophetic testimony is first encountered in the Pentateuch. Moses' rebuke before he died, which is styled as a prophetic poem (Deut. 32:1–43), is seen as a *witness* to the Israelites about the future: "When . . . the many evils and troubles befall them—then this poem shall confront them as a *witness*" (Deut. 31:21; cf. 19). According to Deuteronomy,[65] not only the Song but the entire book was written and deposited at the side of the Ark of the Covenant as testimony in the event of any future rebellion: " . . . let it remain there as a witness against you. Well I know how defiant and stiff-necked you are, etc." (*ibid.*, 26–27). Similarly Isaiah speaks about his prophecies: "Now go, write it before them on a tablet, and inscribe it in a book, that it may be for the time to come as a witness for ever. For they are a rebellious people . . . who refuse to hear the teaching of the Lord" (30:8–9). At the outset of his prophetic career, Isaiah writes down the prophecy about the fall of Damascus and Samaria on "a large sheet" (*gillāyōn gādōl*) and arranges for reliable witness (8:1 ff.). The chapter goes on to speak about binding up the prophecy in a document and sealing it (16 ff.), and in this connection the prophet says that he will wait and hope for God Who in the meantime is hiding His face (cf. Deut. 31:18). Similarly in Hab. 2:2 ff.:

> And the Lord answered me:
> "Write the vision;
>   make it plain upon the tablets,
>   so he may run who reads it.
> For a vision is a witness [reading '*ēd*]
>   for the season and a testimony[66] for the time—
>   it will not lie.
> If it seem slow, wait for it;
>   it will surely come, it will not delay,"

a prophecy interpreted in various ways in the book of Daniel (10:14; 11:27, 35). The sealed prophecy was a secret which only a true prophet could know, as we learn from the words of Isaiah who complains about the prophets whose eyes God has shut and who are incapable of knowing a sealed vision (29:11). Secret and cryptic prophecies also appear in Mesopotamian literature, like for instance, Ashurbanipal's boast that he has checked the sealed and obscure stone inscriptions from before the flood,[67] and their secret lore of divination.[68] In this connection we should mention Daniel 12:4: "But, you, Daniel, shut up the words, and seal the book, even to the time of the end," continuing, "for the words are shut up and sealed . . . but they that are wise shall understand" (*ibid.* 12:9–10), and similarly the *pᵉšārīm* of the Qumran literature, actual attempts to penetrate the secrets of the prophecy.[69] Ancient visions with hidden secrets which must be deciphered and interpreted are found in the Sibylline oracles in Rome. In Israelite prophecy the "oracles concerning the nations," which contain hazy visions from bygone days (see below), represent a similar phenomenon.[70]

The important function of a written scroll in prophecy is clearly illustrated in the story in Jer. 36. In the fourth year of Jehoiakim king of Judah, during the first year of Nebuchadnezzar king of Babylon (605/4 B.C.E.), Jeremiah was commanded to write on a scroll all that the Lord had said to him from when he first began to prophesy, in the thirteenth year of Josiah (cf. Jer. 25:3). The timing for writing down the prophecies was dictated by the historical circumstances. For twenty-three years Jeremiah had prophesied about "the foe from the north" coming down upon the land but it was not known which nation this was or whether the prophecy would be fulfilled. With Nebuchadnezzar's rise to power, the identity of the nation was clear and the fulfillment of the prophecy seemed to be at hand. The time was now ripe to write down the prophecy to testify to the truth of Jeremiah's mission.

Jeremiah was also commanded to write down the prophecies of consolation in chapters 30–31 (cf. Jer. 30:1–2), so that the generation returning from Exile would know that the Return had been prophesied many years before the event (*ibid.* 3). The collections of prophecies about the kings of Judah (21:11–23:8) and about the prophets (23:9–40) had apparently also been written on a scroll.

In Ezekiel, prophecy in writing is self-understood, since at the time of his commission he was required to eat the scroll offered to him by the hand of God as a symbol that the word of the Lord was placed in his mouth (see Jer. 1:9; cf. Deut. 18:18).

1. Basic Patterns in Prophetic Literature

In prophetic literature, we find a few basic patterns or literary forms which the prophets utilized and apparently inherited from earlier tradition. In the following survey we shall attempt to present the major ones.

a. *The Lawsuit (Rīv)*: In the speeches modeled after this pattern the prophet voices to the people[71] God's complaint that Israel has rejected Him. The complaint is formulated like a legal suit (Isa. 1:1–20; cf. 3:13–15; 43:22–28; Jer. 2: 4–4:4;[72] Ezek. 16; 20; Hos. 2:3 ff.; Mic. 6:1 ff.; cf. Amos 4:4 ff., etc.)[73] and presented as though before witnesses (heaven and earth, mountains and hills).[74] It describes Israel's unfaithfulness to God, Who has fulfilled His promises despite their ingratitude. The pattern appears in the old poetry (Deut. 32:1–43) and in the Psalms (50, 81, 95), and seems to have originated in the popular religion or, in the opinion of a few scholars,[75] in the popular prophetic circles often called "cultic prophets." The "rebukes" in the Former Prophets (Judg. 2: 1–3; 6:8–10; 10:11–15; I Sam. 7:3; 12:6 ff.) also reflect the lawsuit pattern discussed here.

The relationship between God and His people is described in this speech as that of a father and son (Isa. 1:2; cf. Deut. 32:5; Isa. 30:8) or of a husband and wife (Hos. 2:4 ff.; Jer. 3:1 ff.; cf. Ezek. 16),[76] and had been used in the context of the Convenant established between God and Israel at the time of the Exodus (see Ex. 4:22–23; 19:4, to be compared with Deut. 32:11; Deut. 1:31; Jer. 2:2; Ezek. 16:8; Hos. 2:17; 11:1; etc.). The sins mentioned in the "lawsuit" are usually idolatry (Hos. 2:10, 15; Jer. 2:7 ff.; Ezek. 16:15 ff.) and transgressions of morality (Hos. 4:1 ff.; Isa. 1:15 ff.; cf. Jer. 7:9), two subjects central to the Decalogue. The "lawsuit" in Hos. 4:2 (cf. Jer. 7:9) refers clearly to the Ten Commandments.[77] In Psalms 50 and 81, which, as we have seen, employ the lawsuit pattern, we find quotations from the Decalogue: "I am Elohim your God" (Ps. 50:7).[78] "There shall no strange god bè in you; neither shall you worship any foreign god. I am the Lord your God Who brought you up out of the land of Egypt" (Ps. 81:10–11).[79] Psalm 50 tells about making a covenant by sacrifice, familar to us from the Mount Sinai pericope (Ex. 24: 3–8), while the rebuke in vv. 17 ff. refers to moral transgressions prohibited in the Ten Commandments: theft, adultery, and false testimony.

b. *The Primacy of Morality*: By mentioning violation of morality in the "lawsuit," the prophets are struggling with the popular illusion that sacrifice and prayer, in other words, standard, routine divine wρrship, will satisfy God. We therefore find in the lawsuit orations conveying the idea that cult is worthless in comparison to observing moral statutes and covenant righteousness (Isa. 1: 11–17; Micah 6:6–8; Jer. 6:20; Amos 5:21–25; Hos. 6;6; Ps. 50:18 ff.). This idea is usually presented as a rhetorical question: "What to Me is the multitude of your sacrifices" (Isa. 1:11), "To what purpose is it to Me the frankincense that comes from Sheba?" (Jer. 6:20), "Shall I come before Him with burnt offerings, with calves a year old? Will the Lord be pleased with thousands of rams . . ." (Micah 6:6–7). Also in Amos 5:25, "Did you bring to Me sacrifices and offerings the forty years in the wilderness, O house of Israel," and in Ps. 50: 13 ff., "Do I eat the flesh of bulls, or drink the blood of goats?"

Accordingly, the prophet sometimes condemns Festivals and seasonal convocations (Isa. 1:14; Amos 5:21; cf. Isa. 58), making it likely that rebukes of this kind were actually delivered in the Temple when the people assembled for Festivals. This is perhaps suggested in Psalm 81, where the rebuke is made immediately after the song is announced and the trumpet blast of the holiday sounded (4), and in Psalm 95, whose rebuke (8 ff.) comes after the announcement of a pilgrimage to the Temple, with shouting and song (1–6).

The idea that morality supersedes cult is attested in Israelite wisdom literature (cf., e.g., Prov. 15:8; 21:3, 27) and in Egyptian literature as well. So, for instance, in the story of the Shipwrecked Sailor the god responds to the sailor's suggested offer of sacrifices and incense: "I am the Prince of Punt, myrrh belongs to me . . . place my good reputation in your town, this is all I ask from you."[80] In the Instruction to King Merikare we read that the god desires a righteous man's offering (=loaf of bread) more than the ox of a wicked man,[81] and in the admonition of the Egyptian sage Ipuwer we read: "All the carvings (amulets) insufficient and meaningless. Is it by sacrifice . . .by libating to the god Ptah? . . . it does not suffice for him . . ."[82] It is interesting that this Egyptian rebuke resembles the questions above because it is also phrased as a rhetorical question.

As for the moral rebuke itself, it must be admitted that in spite of its elevated nature similar ideas occur in the literature of surrounding nations, particularly Mesopotamia. Thus we read in the inscriptions of Esharhaddon that the destruction of Babylon resulted from the breakdown of social morality:[83] "The people living in it [Babylon] answered each other yes but [in their hearts]: No . . .[84] . . . They were oppressing the poor and putting them in the power of the mighty; there was oppression and acceptance of bribe within the city,[85] daily without ceasing, they were robbing each other's property, the son was cursing his father in the street . . . then the god [Enlil/Marduk] became angry,[86] he planned to overwhelm the land and to destroy its people."

This reminds us especially of the prophecy of Micah 7:1 ff. As a consequence, we cannot accept Kaufmann's thesis that the classical prophets were the first to see in moral decadence the determining factor in the national destiny.[87]

c. *Prophecies about the Day of the Lord:* The prophets speak much about the approaching day[88] when God will appear before Israel and the nations. This awaited day is sometimes one of vengeance on the foreign nations (Isa. 34: 1–17; 63:1–6; Jer. 46:10) and sometimes one of disaster for Israel (Ezek. 7; Amos 5:18–20) or for the whole world and its inhabitants (Ezek. 30:1 ff.; 39:13; Joel 3:4; Mal. 3:23, etc.) On the other hand, this day, which is one of divine self-manifestation, has certain aspects of salvation, since the very obliteration of evil in itself brings redemption nearer.

The idea of a time when God will appear in order to judge the world is found in the hymnic literature and therefore shows us that the eschatological aspirations found in prophecy is ancient. So for example we read in Psalm 75:3 ff.:

> At the time I choose
>   I will give judgment equitably.
> Earth and all its inhabitants dissolve.
>   To wanton men I say:
> "Do not be wicked;
>   Do not lift up your horns,"
> For God it isWho gives judgment;
>   One man He brings down
> Another He lifts up.
>   There is a cup in God's hand
> With foaming wine fully mixed,
>   From this He pours;
> All the wicked of the earth drink,
>   Draining it to the very dregs.[89]

In this passage we find the natural upheavals which accompany divine theophanies (both in the Bible and in ancient Near Eastern literature; see below), the humbling of the haughty on the day of God's appearance, a concept characteristic of Day of the Lord prophecies in Isaiah (2:12 ff.; 13), and finally the cup which God gives all the nations to drink, a theme in Jer. 25:15 ff. and also in Isa. 51:21–23.

The motifs accompanying descriptions of theophanies in the Day of the Lord prophecies are identical with those marking theophanies in hymnic literature, in the account of divine revelation at Mount Sinai, and in theophanic descriptions from ancient Near Eastern literature.[90]

So, for instance, in Psalm 18, which describes God's coming to save Israel from her enemies, we find earthquake, fire and smoke, cloud and darkness, thunder and lightning (8–15), all elements to be found in the Day of the Lord prophecies, in the Sinai pericope (Ex. 19), and in God's appearance to save Israel in the time of Deborah (Judg. 5), as well as in the ancient Near Eastern theophanic descriptions.[91]

Most enlightening in this respect is the account of the appearance of the goddess Inanna (=Ishtar) in Mesopotamian literature:[92]

"When mankind comes before you in fear and trembling at [your] tempestuous radiance,[93] they receive from you their just desserts... In the van of battle everything is struck down by you... with a roaring storm you roar, with thunder you continually thunder... The great gods, fluttering like bats, fly off from before you to the clefts, they who dare not walk in your terrible glance, who dare not proceed before your terrible countenance."

Isaiah's Day of the Lord prophecy contains a similar description: "On that day men shall cast forth their idols of silver... to the bats to enter the caverns of the rocks and the clefts of the cliffs from before the terror of the Lord and from the glory of His majesty when He rises to terrify the earth" (2:20–21; cf. *ibid.* 10, 19). Hiding oneself in a rock from a divine appearance occurs in Ex. 34:20 ff.,[94] and the idea of the haughty hiding himself in earth before the glorious terrifying appearance of God is found explicitly in Job 40:10 ff.

In the wake of God's awesome, terrifying appearance and working of judgment follows the heartening idea that righteousness is restored. It is said, for instance, in Ps. 96:11–13 (cf. 98:7–9): "Let the heaven be glad and let the earth rejoice... let the field exult... then shall all the trees of the wood sing for joy before the Lord, for the comes... to judge the earth" (cf. Isa. 35:1 ff., etc.).

The duality concerning divine appearance is characteristic of Mesopotamian literature as well. In the hymn to Inanna, a section of which we quoted above, we find: "When you roar at the earth like thunder, no vegetation can stand up to you" (line 10) (cf. Amos 1:2: "The Lord roars from Zion... the pastures of the shepherds mourn, and the top of Carmel withers"), while in a hymn to Adad we read: "At your voice mountains are joyous, fields are jubilant."[95]

d. *Prophecies of Consolation:* In the prophecies of redemption of the classical prophets one can uncover two sets of motifs, one spiritual and the other physical. The first set paints a picture of spiritual, religious redemption, with future salvation a repetition of the salvation of the Exodus from Egypt.

The motifs in the spiritual redemption pattern are:

(1) A new Exodus (Hos. 2:16 ff.; Isa. 11:15–16; 43:18; 48:20–21; Jer. 23:7–8 [16:13–14]; Ezek. 20:34; Micah 7:14 ff.).

(2) Wandering in the Desert (Hos. 2:16; Isa. 35:7 ff.; 43:19–20; 48:21; 49:10–13; Ezek. 20:35–38).

(3) Crossing sea and river (Isa. 11:15; 43:16; 51:10).

(4) Purification and forgiving of sins (Hos. 2:19; Jer. 31:28; 33:8; Ezek. 36:25; cf. 11:17–20; Micah 7:18–19).

(5) A new Covenant based on knowledge of God planted in the heart (Jer. 31:30–33; Hos. 2:21–22; Ezek. 11:19; 18:30–31; 36:25–28; Micah 7:20; Isa. 11:9).

This set of motives understandably draws sustenance from the Exodus tradition known in ancient Israel.

The second set presents a picture of physical redemption which includes the following motifs:

(1) The emergence from the house of David of a savior-king who will unite the kingdoms (Hos. 2:2; 3:5; Amos 9:11; Isa. 11:1 ff.; *ibid.* 13; Jer. 3:18; 23:1–6; 33:14 ff.; Ezek. 37:15 ff.; 34:23).

(2) The establishment of justice (Hos. 2:11; Isa. 11:1 ff.; 32:16–17; cf. 9:6; 16:5; Jer. 23:5; 33:15).

(3) Ingathering of the dispersed (Isa. 11:11; Jer. 23:4; 32:37; 3:14–15, 18; Ezek. 34:13).

(4) Fertility of the land (Hos. 2:23–24; Amos 9:13 ff.; Jer. 31:6; 31:26–27; Ezek. 34:2, 6 ff.; 36:29; Micah 7:14).

(5) Peace and tranquillity (Hos. 2:20; Amos 9:15; Isa. 32:17 ff.; Jer. 23:6; 33:16; Ezek. 34:25).

Although the first set of motives was nurtured by an ancient national tradition, the second set, of physical aspirations, is known to us from ancient Near Eastern prophecies and can therefore be viewed as a pattern common to all ancient Near Eastern peoples. So, for example, we read in a Mesopotamian prophecy from the first half of the second millennium B.C.E.:[96]

"A King of Babylon will arise . . . he will establish justice in Babylon . . . he will enjoy the favor of the god . . . he will prolong his days . . . he will gather the dispersed . . . he will feed his people from the fruit of the land . . . the fields will be abundant with crop, the produce of the summer will last to the winter and the produce of the winter will last to the summer . . . [97] men will love each other, son will revere his father, mother will live in peace with her daughter, a prince will rule over the lands, people will dwell securely, evil will be removed . . ."

Similar predictions can be found in the Egyptian prophecy of Neferti, also from the beginning of the second millennium B.C.E.:[98]

"A king will arise . . . he will assume the white crown, the people of his reign will rejoice . . . right will come to its place again and wrong will be thrust aside."

These tidings come after a series of prophecies of disasters which remind us of the prophecies of doom of the classical prophets, where we read:

"The sun is veiled and does not shine (cf. Isa. 24:23; Joel 3:4; Zech. 14: 6 ff.); men will take weapons and the land will live in confusion . . . one man will kill the other, the son turns an enemy, the brother a foe . . . the weak now possesses strength, men salute one who saluted, the lower becomes upper."

These descriptions of catastrophes strongly remind us of the oracles of doom in Isaiah (3:11–12; 9:12 ff.), especially chap. 24, which tells about confusion and disorder in the land (1–6) and the eclipse of the heavenly luminaries (21–22). In the above-cited Mesopotamian prophecies similar descriptions of disaster come before words of hope. It is therefore likely that in Israel, too, prophecies of doom should be seen as harbingers of redemption.

e. *Oracles of Cosmic Redemption:* Just as the prophecies of national consolation draw upon the Exodus tradition, so the oracles about the redemption of the world are rooted in the ancient cosmogonic tradition, the accounts of creation. The God who defeated the forces of evil and destruction (Rahab, Leviathan, etc.) at the time of creation, will vanquish the powers of wickedness (Isa. 27:1; 51:9) and create a new heaven and earth (Isa. 65:17).

In the new world described by the prophets there will be on the one hand an end to idolatry which symbolizes human pride and self-worship (Isa. 2:12 ff.; 17:7–8; 45:14–17), and on the other an end to war among nations and the establishment of peace (Isa. 2:1–4; Micah 4:1–4). So also enmity between man and beast will cease (Hos. 2:20; Isa. 11:6–9; 65:25).

It should be pointed out that the idea of obliterating idolatry and returning the gentiles to the God of Israel is suggested by many classical prophets (Jer. 3:17; 16:19–21; Isa. 45:20–25; 56:1–8; Zeph. 3:9; Zech. 2:15; 8:20–23, etc.), but the idea of universal peace is unique to Isaiah. This is in character with his overall prophecy, which foretells no revenge[99] and which dilates against the subjugation of peoples and foreign lands.[100] Isaiah's picture of cosmic peace and an end to idolatry draws upon the ancient Garden of Eden tradition of a period before man and snake were enemies and before mankind's division into different religions and peoples.[101] The ancient Sumerian description of life in paradise offers a nice parallel to Isaiah's vision in chapter 11: "Once upon a time there was no snake, there was no scorpion, there was no hyena, there was no lion . . . no wolf . . . the whole universe, the people in unison, to Enlil in one tongue [did obeisance].[102]

f. *Jerusalem as the Spiritual-Religious Center of the World:* In the visions of the end of idolatry and international peace Jerusalem occupies a central position. The nations turn toward Jerusalem to receive religious and political guidance, but the concept of Jerusalem as a cosmopolitan metropolis is not in itself an innovation of classical prophecy.

The idea also appears in the hymnic literature (Ps. 48:3; 68:30; 72:10 ff.; 76:12–13) and really originates in the ancient Near Eastern tradition about central holy cities. For example, it is said about Nippur the city of Enlil (= the head of the Sumerian pantheon), called *du(dur)-an-ki* (= the link between heaven and earth), that all the lands bow down to it, offering gifts, sacrifices, prayers, etc.[103] Similar claims are made for Babylon,[104] which inherited Nippur's tradition.[105]

It was mainly the prophets of the Restoration who developed the traditional motif of Jerusalem as a cosmopolitan metropolis to which the nations bring their gifts and even their silver and gold (Isa. 60:5 ff.; 66:19 ff.; Hag. 2:7–9), although this grew out of their enthusiasm for the God and the people of Israel. Specific to classical prophecy in this matter, however, is the abandonment of idolatry following the pilgrimage to Zion (e.g., Isa. 45:14–16; Jer. 3:17; 16: 19–21), and the establishment of peace among nations, characteristic of First Isaiah (2:1–4; 19:23–25; 25:6–9).

The vision about the end of idolatry and the return of the gentiles to the God of Israel reaches the height of its development in Deutero-Isaiah. This anonymous prophet turns to the people of the world in a concrete way and asks them to abandon their idolatry and convert to the faith of one God: "Assemble yourselves and come . . . you survivors of the nations . . . who carry about their wooden idols and keep on praying to a god that cannot save . . . Turn to me and be saved all the ends of the earth! For I am God, and there is no other (Isa. 45: 20–22).

In another passage he promises the foreigners who accept the religion of Israel full acceptance into the Israelite community (56:1–8). He also develops the anti-idolatry polemic and bitterly mocks the gentile faith and cult (see, e.g., 44:9–20). Similarly, by means of his prophecies about "the former and the new things," he lauds the truth of the prophecies of the God of Israel in contrast to the futile ones of the false deities (Isa. 40–48).[106]

2. PROPHETIC UNIVERSALISM AND ITS BACKGROUND

Classical prophecy arose in the middle of the eighth century B.C.E. along with the rise of the Assyrian Empire. This is no mere coincidence; we might in fact claim that Assyrian imperialism was a prerequisite for the emergence of classical prophecy. The ascent to power of Tiglath-pileser III was a turning-point in the history of mankind, where for the first time a superpower swallowed up smaller nations, terminating their aspirations, struggles, and hopes. Significance no longer accrued to the small nation and its unique goals. All the nations which had combatted each other for position and status now stood helpless in the face of the lion which destroys nations (cf. Jer. 4:7).

Until now, Israel—like the other peoples—struggled not only to exist but to strengthen national pride and aspiration. National success increased confidence in their God, Who proved Himself by keeping His promises of a land for His people and defeat for their enemies. The God Who is a great King over all the earth is the One who leads peoples and nations under Israel's feet and thereby assures the pride of Jacob whom He loves (Ps. 47:3–5) (cf. on the other hand,

Amos 6:8: "I abhor the pride of Jacob and hate his strongholds"). In a prophetic message to David, when giving him status as an adopted son, God promises to make nations his inheritance and the ends of the earth his possession (Ps. 2: 7–8; 89:26–28;[107] cf. 72:8; 80:12). The destiny of Israel, like that of other nations, was determined on the battlefield, where the prophets were predicting victory in the name of the God of Israel and encouraging the destruction of the enemy, the foe of Israel and her God (cf. I Sam. 15; I Kings 20:22; II Kings 3). (This is the origin of the oracles about the nations which preserve material from the pre-classical period.) With the rise of the Assyrian Empire these aspirations ceased to exist. From now on the entire world was subservient to one empire which it was foolish even to attempt to defeat, national considerations no longer existed, and all nations shared a common lot.

This then is the political-historical background for the emergence of classical prophecy. The great prophets arose at a period fateful for world history. Amos prophesied at the eve of the rise of Tiglath-pileser III, Isaiah at the peak of the Assyrian Empire (Sargonic Dynasty), and Jeremiah at the rise of the Babylonian Empire. Isaiah developed the concept of Assyria "the staff of God's wrath" (10:5), Jeremiah went to the point of calling Nebuchadnezzar "God's servant" (25:9, 27:6), and Second Isaiah was daring enough to call Cyrus "YHWH's anointed one" (45:1).

The new reality, therefore, shaped the outlook of the classical prophets, who in turn expressed the new circumstances in their prophecies. They were the first in human history to ask about the meaning of the phenomenon of world dominance by a great power, and they provided an answer. The question: To what is God reacting in this new mode of global catastrophe? The answer: Only that He has decided to punish not Israel alone but the entire world. The Assyrian or Babylonian emperor is a merely divine emissary for executing the punishments.

This global view of the events and their causes is already attested in Amos, the first classical prophet. He begins with a series of oracles against the nations, in which he predicts the destruction and burning of the capital cities of the nations in the area (an Assyrian custom during their campaigns) because of their disregard of human and social morality. The oracles about the nations are transferred by Amos from the national soil of their origin, to the international. As well as Israel and Judah, all nations are to be punished for their moral neglect. The gentiles will suffer for such gross offences as ripping open pregnant women, threshing with iron sledges, exiling peaceful populations, and desecration of the dead (1:3–2:3); Israel will suffer for oppressing the poor and violating morality (2:6 ff.). God, in a sense, declares war on mankind, which has become corrupt and overstepped its bounds: "For the Lord of hosts has a day against all that is proud and lofty . . . And the haughtiness of men shall be humbled and the pride of men shall be brought low" (Isa. 2:12 ff.). While it once had been customary to speak about a day when God would appear in all His magnificence and glory to defeat the enemy (Judg. 5:4 ff.; Ps. 18:8 ff.; II Sam. 22:8 ff.; Ps. 97:2 ff.), now God is the adversary of mankind (Zeph. 1:17) and all fear His coming (Amos 5:18 ff.; Isa. 2:12 ff., etc.).

The change in God's management of the world means that man must drastically alter his conduct. God does not want to be worshipped in the accustomed perfunctory manner. He demands a new way. Such accepted religious norms as sacrifice, holidays, dependence upon the Temple, reliance on the Covenant, and Election are unimportant to God because they have obscured what is really significant: the direct unmediated union with God through righteousness—justice, steadfast love, and mercy (Hos. 2:21 ff.; Isa. 11:9; Jer. 31–33).

3. Conflict with Tradition

The prophets reject the accepted mode of formal divine worship which has become heartless, "a commandment of men learned by rote" (Isa. 29:13). They speak sarcastically and cynically about the conventional institutions of divine worship and to the people this seems sacrilegious. Thus Amos mocks Bethel and Gilgal, saying, "Gilgal shall surely go into exile and Bethel shall come to nought" (5:5), and even dares to say that the very service in these temples is a crime (4:4). Amos and Isaiah stand in the Temple courts when the people gather for holiday celebrations and declare that God hates and despises these feasts (Amos 5:21; Isa. 1:13). Under similar circumstances Jeremiah says that God never even commanded them to bring sacrifices (7:21–22). The most daring diatribes against Israel's sacred institutions are those of Jeremiah and his predecessor Micah, who said that the Temple, their utmost hope, would be destroyed and in ruins (Jer. 7:14; 26:6, 9; Micah 3:12). The people's confidence in God Who dwells in Zion, a confidence expressed over and over again in various Psalms (see, e.g., 46:6: "God is in the midst of her, she shall not be moved;" 125:1: "Mount Zion which cannot be moved but abides for ever," etc.), is called false by Jeremiah: "Do not trust in these deceptive words: 'This is the Temple of the Lord, the Temple of the Lord, the Temple of the Lord'" (7:4). It is therefore no wonder that the people considered these declarations blasphemous and that the priests and prophets demanded that Jeremiah be sentenced to death for his utterances (Jer. 26).

4. THE METAMORPHOSIS OF THE TRADITION

The classical prophets, however, did not abandon the national values but gave them instead a new universal meaning. Zion and its Temple, once the symbol of the religious and national immunity of the kingdom of Judah (Ps. 2:6 ff.; 48; 76; 110, etc.), became in the eyes of the classical prophets symbols of universal significance. Jerusalem became a center not only for Israelite pilgrims but for all nations (Isa. 2:2–4; Micah 4:1–3; Jer. 3:17; Isa. 60, etc.), and its teaching was universal in character. First Isaiah sees Jerusalem as a center for world peace, while Deutero-Isaiah calls the Temple of Jerusalem "a house of prayer for all the peoples" (56:7). The Davidic dynasty is no longer merely a provincial royal house which rules Judah but a symbol for the establishment of peace and righteousness among all nations of the earth (Isa. 11:1–10; 55:3–5), and dominion is no longer exercised with an iron staff (cf. 2:8–9; 110, etc.), but by the rod of the king's mouth (Isa. 11:3).

The classical prophets of the First Temple period spoke little about the election of Israel for fear that such an idea would increase the national confidence and pride against which the prophets were trying to fight. This specific national value, however, received a universalistic interpretation by Deutero-Isaiah. Like Deuteronomy, he uses the term 'election' (*bḥr*) but totally changes its meaning. Deuteronomy uses election to explain Israel's uniqueness and supremacy (7: 5–6; 14: 15–21: 26: 18–19), but the anonymous prophet uses it as an instrument to advance universal goals. The people of Israel were created and selected by YHWH to deliver the message of the God of Israel to the nations of the world (43:10; 49:6–7) and to be a light unto the nations (42:6; 49:6; 60, etc.).

These outlooks, whose point of departure is not Israel, but the entire world, originated in the profound changes that accompanied the rise of the great empires of Assyria, Babylonia, and Persia. The prophets translated the Israelite ideals into the language of the new reality: a world under a single leadership is given by the one God, the God of Israel, to an empire, whose purpose thereafter is to advance His plans not only for Israel but for the entire world. Both tragedy and consolation take on universal proportions. The catastrophe is total because it is fomented by a world-power which, by the same token and at the same time, bring about world-wide redemption. Isaiah dreams of a time when there will be a highway from Egypt to Assyria via Israel, Egypt will be subject to Assyria, and Israel will be a third partner in Assyrian-Egyptian alliance which will be a blessing to the world (Isa. 19:23–25).. This prophecy, once considered late and unauthentic, has recently been elucidated by an Assyrian text from the time of Sargon: "I opened the closed harbor of Egypt and let the Assyrians and Egyptians mix freely and engage in trade with each other."[108]

We can therefore assume that Isaiah's hopes, as expressed in the preceding prophecy, were based on political reality. Sargon's liberal foreign policy opened the door for a wish formulated in a most daring manner in the passage already cited: "Blessed be Egypt my people, and Assyria the work of my hands, and Israel my heritage" (Isa. 19:25). It is unimaginable (as some scholars claim) that a Second Temple period scribe would invent such a statement, which puts Assyria and Egypt on a level with Israel, effectively cancelling the importance of Election. "My people," and "the work of My hands" are titles reserved for Israel (for "work of My hands" cf. Isa. 60:21), and only an original visionary like Isaiah would have been capable of assigning them to Egypt and Assyria as well. We should point out that Isaiah was the only prophet to envision "world peace" (see above). an idea that seems directly connected with the special circumstances of his period.

D. Psalmodic and Wisdom Literature

1. Psalmodic Literature

Sumerian writings provide us with a wide variety of liturgical literature. We find seven kinds of religious poetry: hymns to gods, hymns to temples, prayers, royal hymns, historical meditations, and religious meditations.[109] H. Gunkel, whose work did much to advance the study of Psalms, divided the biblical psalms into types strongly reminiscent of this categorization of Sumerian religious poetry.[110] He tried to determine what circumstances might have engendered each type: communal disaster gave rise to communal prayer, personal tragedy to personal petitions, national salvation or personal redemption to hymns of thanksgiving, mourning to lamentation, and routine divine worship to hymns. Even though Gunkel's assumptions are reasonable, we must not feel compelled to categorize each psalm specifically. Most psalms are heterogeneous in character, only rarely occupied in the entirety by themes of praise, lament, or thanksgiving. They include a variety of themes, and this tells us something about the nature of liturgy. Before a request is made to the god one must offer words of praise, a process that naturally gives rise to the mixture of themes in the liturgy. We therefore come across many lamentations which include passages of praise (44:2–9; 77:12–17; 89:2–19, etc.) and even prayers of thanksgiving which partake of lamentation, since they retell the troubles of the past (30:9–11; 56:2–10; 118:4–13, etc.). It is therefore often impossible to decide whether a particular psalm is a lament or a thanksgiving.

Definite determination of a psalm's type is difficult from other standpoints as well. Every psalm is an independent literary creation and, like all individual work, has a certain uniqueness of character, structure, and idea, which is why no two are identical.[111] About a specific type of psalm we can say only that an overall similarity of ideas and formulae characterize all the psalms of the particular group. Furthermore, we can neither pinpoint the exact situation (*Sitz im Leben*) for which the psalm was composed nor identify the author. Thus, for example, Gunkel made a sharp distinction between public and private psalms and established different criteria for private as opposed to public petitions, as well as for private and public songs of thanksgiving. Although private and public types were undoubtedly found side by side, we must admit that we have no objective criteria for determining the public or private nature of each individual work. A prayer written in the first person singular is not necessarily a private prayer, since the nation itself can speak as an individual, at times a community leader or a king expresses himself in the singular, although he prays on behalf of the entire nation. An example is Ps. 56:2–3: "Have mercy on me, O God, for men persecute me; all day long my adversary oppresses me. My watchful foes persecute me all day long; many are my adversaries, O exalted One." The petitioner is certainly the leader of the community or the king facing his enemies in battles.

We shall try to characterize the various types of psalms which, although usually found in the Book of Psalms, are scattered through other books as well.

a. *The Hymn*

The hymn usually starts with a call to the community to thank, praise, or bless God, as "give praise" (*halelū*); "give thanks" (*hōdū*); "bless" (*barekū*); "acclaim (*harī'ū*); but the opening invitation is sometimes self-encouraging as in: "let us sing" (*nāšīrāh*); or in singular "bless the Lord my soul" (*barekī-nafšī 'et YHWH*); "I will sing" (*'āšīrāh*); "I will praise" (*'ăhalelāh*); "praise my soul" (*halelī nafšī*). Following the opening, God is praised and His greatness described, manifested in creating the world and controlling the cosmos. The words of praise generally use the present participle: "(who) spreads (*nōṭēh*) the heavens . . . who sets (*meqārēh*) the rafters of his lofts . . . " (104:2 ff.);[112] "makes (*'ōśēh*) heaven and earth . . . secures justice (*'ōśēh mišpaṭ*) for those who are wronged, gives (*nōtēn*) food to the hungry . . . " (146:6 ff.). Such hymns are scattered throughout such biblical books as: I Sam. 2:6 ff.; Amos 4:13; 5:8; 9:5; Isa. 40:28; Job 5:9–10; 9:8–9, and others.

The praise may also dwell on God's exalted attributes, His greatness and heroism. On such occasions, hymn borders on credo: "There is none like you among gods" (18:8); "who is like unto you among the gods" (Ex. 15:11); "Lord, who is like You?" (35:10); "Who is mighty like You, O Lord?" (89:9);

"There is none like You, O Lord. You are great and great is the might of Your name" (Jer. 10:6).

Hymns to gods are known to us from Egypt and Mesopotamia,[113] and even Ugarit has recently yielded one in honor of El.[114] In this hymn, whose language is naturally closer to that of the Israelite psalms than to the Egyptian or Meso-potamian, we find certain elements identical to those in Israelite psalms. Like Psalm 29, which speaks of YHWH Who is ascribed glory (kāvōd) and power by the sons of God and Who sits as King of the Universe (9–10), the Ugaritic psalm tells about El, king of the universe who sits in glory (Ug. yqr = Heb. kāvōd),[115] while his retinue sings praises before him[116] to the accompaniment of instruments (cf. Ps. 68:26 ff.; 81:2–3; 150). Just as Psalm 29 concludes by telling of the strength (‘oz) which YHWH will give His people, so the Ugaritic hymn declares that El's strength and power (‘z, zmrt) will be found in Ugarit. God's strength and power (‘oz, zimrat) are a recurring theme in Israelite poetry Ex. 15:2; Isa. 12:2; Ps. 118:14).

b. *Communal Prayers of Thanksgiving*

Public prayers of thanksgiving are stylistically similar to the hymns but differ by mentioning the salvation and redemption which have occasioned the compo-sition. Immediately after the opening call to praise (’ōlēh, ’āšīrāh, etc.), the reason for it is given: "I will sing to the Lord for He has risen up [in victory]" (Ex. 15:1); "I will praise Your name, for You have done wonders" (Isa. 25:1), "I will exalt You, O Lord, for You have lifted me up" (Ps. 30:2); "I will praise You for You have responded to me and have become my deliverance" (Ps. 118: 21).

These thanksgivings frequently mention the paying of vows: "offerings of thanksgiving" (zivḥei tōdāh) and "cups of salvation" (kōs yᵉšu‘ōt) whose pur-pose is to perpetuate the memory of the event (Ps. 66:13; 116:12 ff., and others). As has already been pointed out, it is difficult to distinguish between public and private prayers of thanksgiving.

c. *Zion Hymns and Temple Hymns*

Mesopotamia presents us with many hymns extolling various temples,[117] their high and lofty places, and their firm foundations, beauty, praiseworthi-ness, and so on. Hymns like this, with similar motives, are found in the book of Psalms: 42, 46, 48, 84, 87, 122. They tell of the beauty of Mount Zion (48:3), the inviolability of the Temple (46), the City of God founded for eternity (48:9), whose praise is until the ends of the earth (*ibid.* 11).[118] In Psalms 42 and 84 we hear the poet's deepest longings for the Temple and all within it. This theme is very nicely paralleled in an Egyptian poetic work from the time of

Ramses III,[119] in which the scribe, far from the Temple of Thebes, expresses his longing for the place of the temple, its sun-bathed courts, etc.

d. *Royal Psalms*

Royal psalms are known to us from Mesopotamia, from the beginning of the second millennium B.C.E.[120] Most of them are written in Sumerian and are principally[121] 1) hymns addressing the god in the name of the king, and 2) hymns in which the poet addresses the king or the king speaks about himself.

The royal hymns in the books of Psalms can be similarly categorized. Psalms 21 and 72, requests to God in the name of the king, belong to the first class. Psalm 45, in which the poet addresses the king, and Psalm 101, in which the king speaks about himself in the first person (cf. II Sam. 23:1–7), belong to the second class. Yet a third type is the prophetic promise and blessing to the king in the name of God, as occurs in Ps. 2:5 ff.; 89:20 ff., and 110, motifs also attested in Mesopotamian psalms.[122]

The themes characterizing royal psalms are: crowning the king and investing him with symbols of royalty (2:6–7; 21:2–5; 45:7; 110:2), the king's beauty and heroism (Ps. 20; 18:34–41; 45:5–6; 110:5; 144:1–2), defeat and subjugation of the enemy (2:9; 18:39; 72:9; 11; 89:23–24; 110:20), supremacy over the nations (18:44; 89:27), universal sovereignty (from "sea to sea") (2:8; 72:8; 89:26), tribute brought to the king from all the lands (72:10, cf. 68:30), and establishment of justice and righteousness (45:5, 7–8; 72:1–7; 101). These motives appear too in Mesopotamian royal psalms.

e. *Communal Petitions*

The communal petition which comes in the wake of threats of pestilence, warfare, or famine (I Kings 8:33; cf. II Chron. 20:8) occurs in Ps. 44, 79, 80, 89:31 ff., as well as in books other than Psalms, such as Ex. 32:11–13; Josh. 7:7–9; Jer. 14:7–9, 19–22, etc. These petitions are typified by complaints: "how long?"; "why do You hide Your face?"; "why do You reject us?"; "why are You angry with Your people?", etc., and by calls for help: "rouse Yourself, why do You sleep, O my Lord?"; "arise and help us"; "rise, O God, judge Your cause." The afflicted and troubled community is made aware that their sins have brought disaster and they have, therefore, no claim against God. The community then requests God to forgive their sins (cf. Num. 14:18 ff., and Jer. 14:20, etc.), but most importantly that God should act not for the sake of the people but for the sake of His great Name, lest it be desecrated among the nations. Therefore we encounter the cries: "Act, O Lord, for the sake of Thy name" (Ps. 109:21; cf. Jer. 14:7; Ps. 25:11), "Why should the nations say: where now is their God" (115:2, compare 79:10, Joel 2:17). Requests

also occur asking God to remember the Covenant with the Patriarchs (Ex. 32:
13; Jer. 14:21; Ps. 77:20, etc.).

f. Psalms of Enthronement

Another type extensively discussed by Mowinckel[123] are the psalms of the
Enthronement of YHWH (47; 93; 96–99). Their origin, in Mowinckel's
opinion, is the New Year Festival, during which the enthronement of YHWH
was celebrated in the Temple by blowing trumpets and rams' horns (47:6;
98:6), similar to the Mesopotamian New Year celebration. There, on this day,
Marduk was enthroned and the creation myth Enūma Eliš, telling of Marduk's
coronation as king of the gods, was read. The name of the New Year zikrōn
tᵉrūʿāh "a sacred occasion commemorated with the sound of the horn" (Lev. 23:24)
or yōm tᵉrūʿāh "a day when the horn is sounded" (Num. 29:1) and the New Year's
liturgy of later Judaism (malkuyōt, zikrōnōt, šōfarōt, Mishnah Rosh ha-Shanah
4:5–6) lend support to this theory.

Like the royal psalms, so in the enthronement psalms the major themes are
universal sovereignty and submission of the nations on the one hand (47:4,
9–10; 96:7 ff.; 99:1–2) and the establishment of justice and righteousness on
the other (96:13; 97:2; 98:9; 99:4), indicating the connection between the
two genres.

g. Psalms of the Individual

Individual Complaints: This type of Psalm makes up the major portion of the
book. The *Sitz im Leben* concerns the troubles which cause the individual to
petition his God. It is difficult to analyze this type of psalm because we cannot
uncover the actual tragedy which has motivated the request. In one psalm illness
is mentioned along with poverty, social discrimination along with violence
and war. We are dealing here, as in the Babylonian petitions, with metaphors
which have come to symbolize every kind of sorrow and calamity.

Study of individual petitions in Mesopotamia help to clarify the development
of this type. Originally the petitioner wrote his request on a figurine, his representative, and placed it in front of the god. The use of statuettes gradually gave
way to letters to the gods recording the petitioner's concrete problem, and
the appeal was finally recited orally by the priests. Because masses of petitioners
had to be served a fixed formula was eventually composed, describing troubles
in a manner general enough to suit all situations.[124]

Typical of these psalms are requests that the god cleanse the suffering man
of the sin which caused his trouble, expressions of confidence that the petition
will be answered, and promises of "thanks" to the god either by sacrifice or,
more commonly, by public thanksgiving.

Individual Thanksgiving (30, 34, 56, 57, 61, 66, 116, 118, 138) is the reverse of the individual lament. We are presented with a man who has been saved from trouble and is therefore thanking his god. This type is represented in the ancient Near East by stelae and monuments erected to gods as tokens of gratitude for salvation.[125] Written evidence of such thanksgiving has come down from all ancient Near Eastern writing and is most frequent in monuments from the Aramean and Phoenician–Punic area, where the monument builder announces that his god heard his voice or that he called upon his god, who answered. This form of thanksgiving is characterized by public advertisement of the miracle and perpetuation of its memory (30:5, 13; 34:4; 56:11; 57:10; 61:9; 66:16; 118:17 ff.). This announcement usually accompanies fulfillment of the vows taken by the supplicant at the time of his distress (56:13; 61:9; 66:13–15; 116:17–19).

The structure of the thanksgiving hymn is usually: (1) announcement of the salvation; (2) address to the community; (3) a description of the transgression and the afflictions it caused; and (4) praise of God (cf. especially Ps. 30). Ginsberg correctly assumes[126] that in Israel too the Thanksgiving psalms were written on memorial pillars and that these are the *miḵtām* psalms (Ps. 56–60, and cf. the *miḵtām* of Hezekiah in Isa. 38:9–20). However, the lower classes, who could not afford to engrave their thanks on stone, apparently recorded them on letters (cf. Ps. 40:8), or proclaimed them before the community in the Temple. The individual thanksgiving hymns and the individual laments thus developed similarly.

Finally we must mention the *historical psalms* (78, 105, 106), the *Tōrāh psalms* (9:8–14; 119), and the *wisdom psalms* (37, 49, 73), which can be viewed as literary creations devoid of cultic connection.[127]

Tradition attributes the composition of psalms to David. Even a superficial survey of the book of Psalms, however, makes this opinion unacceptable. On the one hand, we find psalms which are fundamentally pre-Davidic,[128] and on the other, psalms whose background is clearly the period of the Restoration or even later (cf. Ps. 137, 147, 148, etc.). Nevertheless, this ascription of psalms to David has some truth in it, and a large number are undoubtedly from his time, for various reasons:

(i) The chronicler preserved a tradition that David was the first to establish singers in Jerusalem, an idea supported by such ancient passages as II Sam. 23:1, in which David is called "the sweet Psalmist of Israel;" Amos 6:5, "and like David invent for themselves instrument with music," and the tradition of David the musician in I Sam. 16.

(ii) The royal psalms and Zion psalms reflect the Davidic period, as in the promise of universal reign (Ps. 2:1 ff.) and also the establishment of justice and righteousness in Israel which historiography (II Sam. 8:15) and prophecy (Isa. 9:16; 16:5; Jer. 23:5, etc.) ascribe to David. Psalm 72 is dedicated to Solomon "the son of the king," i.e., the crown prince, and its content suits this king. Psalm 132 fits the occasion of transferring the Ark from Kiriath-jearim to Jerusalem.

(iii) Mesopotamian and Egyptian parallels demonstrate that hymns constituted an important part of Temple worship, which leaves no doubt that David and Solomon, who established the worship of God in Jerusalem, introduced religio-cultic poetry appropriate to the central cultic institution in Israel.

2. WISDOM LITERATURE

This literature includes essentially *didactic wisdom*, i.e., proverbs, aphorisms, and educational instructions (book of Proverbs), and *speculative wisdom*, i.e., reflection about the world order (Job, Ecclesiastes), which is true also of Egyptian and Mesopotamian wisdom literature.[129] In the ancient world, wisdom literature was of an international nature, and especially apparent is the fact that in Israelite wisdom literature, in contrast to all other types of biblical literature, nationalistic values are totally ignored. Not only is there no mention of Israel's Torah and central national historical events, such as the Exodus, the Law, the Covenant, and the Conquest, but even the very name Israel is absent. The Israelite provenance of this literature can be recognized only by its monotheistic nature.

a. *Didactic Wisdom*

Didactic wisdom has two aspects: 1) educational instructions and imperatives given in the second person and directed to the pupil; and 2) proverbs and aphorisms formulated as objective truths, having a moralizing character. Egyptian wisdom literature contains only the first category but both types are represented in Mesopotamian and biblical wisdom literature. In Proverbs we sometimes find a blending of the instruction and aphorism when the latter expresses an experience which supports an instruction stated previously.[130] However, the two genres usually appear in separate collections.

Below we shall survey these collections in Proverbs according to their order and genre.

Chapters 1–9: This collection is essentially imperative, with the instructions addressed to the son or young man, as the opening formulae indicate: "My son," "sons." From Mesopotamian didactic literature we learn that the teacher is called "father" and the student "son,"[131] suggesting that in the Israelite proverbs as well a father is not necessarily teaching a son but a teacher instructing a pupil. It seems that this collection, with its urban background (cf. chap. 7), originated in the schools for aristocratic youth, the only type of adolescent endangered by the enticement of the "foreign" woman so frequently mentioned here.

Chapters 10:1–22:16: In contrast to the first one, this collection consists mainly of observational and reflective proverbs with a popular background. Work (especially working the land) is praised, and slothfulness (12:11 ff.; 27:23 ff.; 20:13, etc.); pursuit of riches, and hoarding of wealth (11:4, 28; 13:11; 28:8) are condemned.

Chapters 22:17–24:22: This collection of imperative statements is attributed, like the Egyptian wisdom works, to "the wise," who were apparently scribes and courtiers. In fact, it opens with a series of proverbs dependent on the Egyptian Instruction of Amenemope.[132]

Chapter 24:23–35: This small collection is also attributed to "the wise" and is of a similar character to the previous one, although it contains observations (30 ff.) as well as instruction.

Chapters 25–29: Like the first two collections, this one is also ascribed to Solomon. However, the additional significant information is given here that the proverbs were copied by the "men of Hezekiah king of Judah." From the prophetic books we learn that at the time of Hezekiah and afterward there was active in Judah a group of wise men who served as court advisers (Isa. 29:14; Jer. 8:8; 18:18; cf. Ezek. 17:26). It can be conjectured that in Israel, as in Mesopotamia and Egypt, the proverbs were written down for use in schools where sons of courtiers were trained for their future positions. Many proverbs in this section are connected by catchwords or assonance,[133] which enhances rote learning. This collection also contains numerous proverbs dealing with the king and the Monarchy (25:2–7; 28:2; 29:5, 14, 25).

The Sixth (chapter 30) and Seventh Collections (31:1–9) are ascribed to foreign (Edomite?) kings, and just as the third collection contained Egyptian wisdom, so these seem to have contained wisdom of Edom (Jer. 49:7; Obad. v. 8) or of the "Sons of the East" (I Kings 5:10). The final section (31:10–31) praises a valorous woman, is arranged as an alphabetic acrostic, and is perhaps intended for use in teaching girls.

The Date of the Collections in Proverbs: As we see in the superscriptions to the various collections, the three largest ones are ascribed to Solomon (1–9; 10:1–22:16; 25–29). Nevertheless, this ascription should not be considered historical fact, any more than is the attribution of the Law to Moses or the Psalms to David. Tradition, however, has correctly identified the initiators of these types of literary creation. Just as Moses was the first legislator and David the originator of psalmic creation in Israel, so Solomon is to be regarded as the one who first nurtured cosmopolitan wisdom in Israel. As already indicated, this literature served the purpose of court education. The period of Solomon, with the building of the Temple and palace, stabilizing the Monarchy, and establishing international relations, demanded schools for courtiers, and is therefore the period best suited to the development of didactic literature. Even so, one should not assume that these collections in their present form actually crystallized in the time of Solomon. Like legal and hymnic literature, wisdom literature grew and developed throughout the period of the Monarchy. In the period of Hezekiah wisdom literature gained momentum, as the book of Proverbs makes clear (25:1).

b. *Speculative Wisdom*

The Sumerians have provided us with a work discussing the problem of a suffering righteous man, a composition dubbed "The Sumerian Job."[134] Extensive literature of this kind appears later, such as the Babylonian work called *Ludlul bēl nēmeqi* ("I Shall Praise the Lord of Wisdom"), which tells of a righteous man who suffers and is finally restored to his former happiness, and the work entitled "Theodicy," which, like Job, presents a dialogue between the sufferer and his friend.[135] Job contains two types of composition somewhat similar to these two Babylonian works: the framework story which tells about Job, his sufferings and his restoration (chaps. 1–2, 42:7–17), and poetic chapters (3:1–42:6), primarily an argument between Job and his friends and God's reply to Job. At the same time we must point out that the Babylonian work *Ludlul bēl nēmeqi* does not entirely overlap the prose narrative in Job, since it is actually a song of praise by the righteous man who has been saved, and not merely a story as in Job. The composition opens with the words "I shall praise the lord of wisdom" and concludes with a long hymn of praise to Marduk for saving the righteous man from his suffering.[136] From this standpoint the work[137] is closer in character to certain individual petitions found in Psalms[138] and in other poems in the Bible.[139] The description of suffering and distress in this is identical to that of the sufferer in Psalms, and to sections of the poetic portion of Job.[140]

The Babylonian "Theodicy" resembles the poetic portion of Job in both structure and content, as certain decisive examples indicate:

1) The sufferer and his friend address each other very courteously as wise men, etc. (Job 12:2; 13:2; 15:2; 32:6 ff.; "Theodicy," lines 1, 23, 45, 67–68, 78, 254).

2) The sufferer points out that the wicked succeed and that his own righteousness had not saved him from distress (*passim*).

3) The friend accuses the sufferer of slighting God and belittling piety (cf. Job 8:2–3; 15:4–6; "Theodicy," lines 78–79, 255).

4) The friend recommends obedience to God and His commandments as a guarantee of success (Job 8:5 ff.; 11:13 ff.; "Theodicy," lines 239 ff.).

5) The friend claims that the ways of God are unfathomable and not to be comprehended:

Job	*"Theodicy"*
Can you fathom the mystery of God?	The plans of God . . . like the
Can you fathom the purpose of Shaddai?	center of heaven (line 82).
It is high as heaven, can you do something?	The divine mind is remote like the center of heaven, knowledge of
It is deeper than Sheol, can you know about it? (11:7–9).	it is difficult (lines 256–257).

6) In neither work are the arguments arranged systematically; they frequently repeat themselves.

The differences between the prose narrative and the poetic body of Job can be illustrated in the following way:

THE FRAMEWORK (1–2; 42:7–17)	THE POEM (3:1–42:6)
1) Prose	Poetry
2) Job suffers silently	Job rebels
3) Folk solution to problem (restoration)	Philosophical solution (no one can understand the ways of God)
4) YHWH	*'El, 'Elō'āh, Shaddai*
5) Sacrifices	No relation to cult
6) Specific suffering (leprosy)	General suffering
7) Personal problem	General problem, and therefore philosophical

The outstanding contradiction between the two sections is that in the framework Job is presented as a pious man who says nothing blasphemous and accepts afflictions with love, whereas in the main poetic portion Job is presented as a rebel who spares no words to prove God's injustice and whose friends try to talk him out of his rebelliousness.

Even though the framework story shows signs of the ancient patriarchal setting and strongly resembles the stories of the Patriarchs, it is impossible to decide whether the poetry or the prose is older. The story is set in the Land of the People of the East (1:3), also the land of origin of the Patriarchs (Gen. 29:1, and cf. Uz in Job 1:1 with Uz in Gen. 22:21). Here, as in the patriarchal stories, wealth is measured by the number of servants and cattle (1:3; 42:12, cf. Gen. 22:16; 32:5); Job's longevity (140 years) and the description of old age (old and full of days [42:16–17] are reminiscent of the patriarchal narratives (Gen. 25:8; 35:28–29; 47:28). Just as Abraham is called "the servant of YHWH" (Gen. 26:24), so Job is called by God "my servant" (1:8; 2:3; 42:8); and just as Abraham, when his faith is tested, withstands the trial (Gen. 22:1, 12), so with Job. The coin $q^e s i \underline{t} \bar{a} h$ is mentioned only in Job and the patriarchal narratives (42:11; Gen. 33:19).[141] There is also a resemblance to Ugaritic literature, especially the Keret Epic[142] (whose family was destroyed and he himself condemned to die and in the end everything was returned),[143] and even between the Job story and the Balaam cycle (7 bulls and 7 rams: Job 42:8; Num. 23:1, 14, 29).

Even though many scholars maintain that the poetic section of the book is post-exilic,[144] there is no real support for such late dating, and the composition might in fact be from the time of the Monarchy.

The Structure of Job 3:1–42:6:

The debate between Job and his friends divides into three rounds:

a) First Round (3–11): Job (3)—Eliphaz (4–5); Job (6–7)—Bildad (8); Job (9–10)—Zophar (11);

b) Second Round (12–20): Job (12–14)—Eliphaz (15); Job (16–17)—Bildad (18); Job (19)—Zophar (20);

c) Third Round (21–26): Job (21)—Eliphaz (22); Job (23–24)—Bildad (25); Job 26.

The third friend (Zophar) is missing in the third round, probably because of a literary accident. The words of Bildad in this round (chap. 25) also seem lacking and cut off. In addition, in chapter 27 a section attributed to Job contains views incongruent with the rest of his argument with his friends because he shows that the evildoer will suffer in the end (see esp. vv. 12 ff.). It is therefore likely that, in this chapter the words of one of the friends were included with those of Job. Ginzberg is of the opinion[145] that chapter 27 has preserved a speech of Job belonging to the prose framework in which "Job spoke rightly" about God (42:7), justifying God's actions in contrast to the condemnation his friends and his wife uttered. According to this view, the friends' caustic remarks were not preserved.

Chapter 28 is an independent literary unit. It is a poem about wisdom, which cannot be achieved by man, and emphasizes that the only wisdom in man's grasp is fear of the Lord.

Chapters 29–31 contain Job's retrospective glance at his glorious past compared to his dismal present (29–30), and a negative confession (31)[146] in which

Job acquits himself by a series of oaths that prove his innocence and moral righteousness.

Chapters 32–37 present the speeches of Elihu who has not previously been mentioned either in the prose narrative or the poem. This seems not to have been an organic part of the debate between Job and his friends but a secondary answer to Job after the other three friends had failed.

In chapters 38:1–42:6 we find God's answer to Job in two phases or in two parallel versions: 38:1–40:5, on the one hand, and 40:6–42:6 on the other.

Even though we have separated the framework from the poetic section for literary reasons, Job, as it is arranged today, still has the unified purpose of emphasizing the value of unquestioning faith. According to the prose narrative, Job remains faithful to his God despite his sufferings; God's answer implies that one should not expect any reward for his deeds; if this is so, then true faith is the one which is independent of material interest.[147]

The Song of Songs (Canticles)

Some of these love poems, which are ascribed to Solomon, are uttered by the lover, others by his beloved. The origin of the book and its date have occasioned much dispute among scholars, some of whom claim that we are dealing with popular wedding songs,[148] an assumption which can be neither proven nor refuted. Many others accept the allegorical interpretation of Canticles—as Second Temple exegesis explained—as symbolizing God's love for His people. This latter opinion is difficult to accept, since, whenever the prophets from Hosea on compared the relationship of God to Israel with that of a man to his wife, they mentioned both the symbol and the symbolized; Song of Songs does not even allude to the symbolized. Furthermore, the physical erotic descriptions of the bodily parts of the two lovers cannot readily be interpreted as descriptions of aspects of the God-Israel relationship.

The solution to the problem lies in the secular love poetry, and especially the Mesopotamian love songs, in the literature of the ancient Near East.[149] We find motives reminiscent of those in Song of Songs,[150] such as (1) longing, (2) spring as a period when love is aroused (2:11 ff.); (3) dance (7:11); (4) lover's garden; (5) description of the beauty of the beloved or the lover; (6) spending the night together; (7) search for the lover and his disappearance (5:4–6); (8) description of love as a fruit (2:3; 4:14, 16; 7:7 ff.); (9) the warning concerning gossipy women who may damage the couple's love (1:5–6; 2:7; 3:5; 5:7 ff.), etc. It is therefore possible to conjecture that, in Israel as in the courts of foreign kings, love poetry was cultivated and in Israel the lover was the king himself. Therefore, King Solomon is not confined to the superscription of the book: his image and age are reflected within the songs themselves (1:5; 3:7; 8:11)[151] and there is even a hint of a contemporary beloved (the Shulamith, or perhaps the Shunamith: 7:1). This composition was apparently included in the canon because the subject of its songs is King Solomon and his love. For the same reason, apparently, a psalm about a royal wedding was included in the book of Psalms (Ps. 45).

Motifs similar to those in Song of Songs are found in Mesopotamian religious poetry associated with the myth of the marriage of Tammuz and Ishtar (Dummuzi and Inanna in the Sumerian tradition), suggesting to some scholars that the Song of Songs originated in this myth and the associated rite.[152] According to this opinion, Israel received the rite through the Canaanites, who had a well-developed system of cultic prostitution. The metaphor of the God-Israel relationship as one of a husband and his wife indeed occurs in Israelite prophecy (Hosea, Jeremiah, Ezekiel) and, according to this opinion, it was nurtured by the myth of the *hieros gamos* (sacred marriage).[153] But the absence of any hint of God and cult in the book itself makes it difficult to accept the theory, especially in view of the abundant parallels to secular love poetry both in Egypt and Mesopotamia. At the same time, however, it must be admitted that secular love lyrics grew out of religious poetry and were eventually severed from it, a familiar phenomenon in the study of human civilization.

The scroll in its present form contains many words and forms (Aramaic) known from the later period: *pardēs* (Iranian word), *apiriōn*, *s^{e}tāv*, *mezeg*, *kotel*, *b^{e}rōtīm* (in place of *b^{e}rōšīm*), *šallama* (1:7), *šeliš^{e}lomo* (3:7) and it is therefore considered a work of the Second Temple period. But this conclusion is not obligatory. The Aramaisms can be explained by a northern provenance of the scroll (cf. the prophetic narratives from the north and especially those dealing with the Aramean wars: *'ēikāh* [II Kings 6:13 cf. Cant. 1:7] instead of *'eifoh*, *miššelānu* [II Kings 6:11], etc., while the foreign words might be *Kulturwörter* which arrived in Israel at an early date. In fact, the geographical-historical setting of the Scroll (Lebanon, Senir and Hermon, Tirzah, Heshbon, and others) hints at the Solomonic period and perhaps even to the northern origin of the work. In any case, even if the literary formulation were not finalized until late, there is no doubt that the main components are extremely ancient.

CHAPTER III

THE EMERGENCE OF CLASSICAL HEBREW

by C. Rabin

WHILE THE ACTUAL origins of Hebrew still are surrounded by some mystery,[1] the nature of the literary idiom of the time of the Judges and of Saul is now quite clear, thanks to the labors of W. F. Albright and a number of his disciples in proving the authenticity of the early poems contained in the Pentateuch and in the books of Judges and Samuel.[2] It is only natural that this language should be set apart from later Hebrew by some archaic features, such as the sparse and irregular use of the definite article or the employment of imperfect ("future"[3]) forms of the verb to denote past events also without the so-called conversive *wāw*. It also contains, however, a number of features which mark it as northern, such as words with a distinctly Aramaic sound[4] and the particle *ša-*, found also in Phoenician, for Classical Hebrew *ăšer*.[5]

Apart from the stories about Caleb and Othniel son of Kenaz in Judges 1–3, all those Judges whose place of activity is indicated belong to the areas north of the great Canaanite corridor which included Jerusalem and separated Judah from the northern tribes. The geographical separation of Judah and its non-participation in the political events affecting the North[6] must also have led to a certain amount of linguistic separatism. How large this gap was, we cannot properly gauge, since we do not possess any literary document of undoubted Judean origin for this period. We may draw conclusions about possible Judean dialect features from observing the elements which entered Hebrew after the unification of all the tribes under David, but this method must be handled with great caution. The main reason for this is that we cannot say whether the language of the early poetry represents the spoken dialect of all or some of the northern tribes or was a literary idiom different from the actual tribal vernaculars. What we know about literary languages in the ancient East points to the second alternative as more probable; but even if we accept that the poems were in the spoken language of some tribes, there must have been some dialect differences in a country so fragmented geographically and divided into distinct tribes politically. There is thus always the possibility that some of the distinctive features of Classical, as opposed to earlier, Hebrew derived from the speech of some northern tribe.

If the language of the early poems was a super-tribal literary idiom, then the entire course of events in the period of the Judges makes it highly probable that its basis was in the central mountain area of Ephraim and Benjamin, where the cultural level was higher, and where practically all of the Judges resided. It might even be argued that such a common language would have been based upon the speech of Shiloh, the place where people from different tribes met, where poems were probably recited, and where lived the priests who guided the people. However, we should learn caution from observing the case of Arabic, where it was not the language of Mecca, the cultic and commercial meeting place of the tribes, which became the language of poetry, but rather the speech of tribes far to the north in the center of the desert. If the song of Deborah was really composed at the time of the events it celebrates, it may well be argued that the local speech of the tribes at the "Canaanite frontier," through the paean on their victory and liberation, became a decisive influence in shaping the language of such poetry.

However, even the tribes of Issachar and Zebulun were located a long way from the boundary of the Aramaeans, and the Aramaic forms in the song of Deborah cannot be explained by the assumption of direct contact with Aramaic speakers. Moreover, the words in question are hardly the kind a language would normally borrow from outside,[7] since they do not denote technical innovations or new ideas. The appearance of such "Aramaisms" in early Hebrew is rather to be accounted for by assuming that they were not taken over from Aramaic, but common to Aramaic and northern Hebrew. It is an acknowledged fact in modern linguistics that dialect features are not distributed in sharply defined areas, but rather each single feature, and in fact every single word in a certain dialect form, has its own distinct area of distribution; the lines drawn around such areas, called "isoglosses," cross and recross each other. Sharp divisions are generally brought about by political events which obliterate the dialects of intermediate areas. There is thus nothing unusual in thinking that certain ones of the phonetic developments which later were characteristic for Aramaic, such as t for original Semitic th and q for the ancient sound represented by Arabic d, extended over part of the northern dialects of Hebrew, as well as over the area of Damascus, which was subsequently to become the focus of the emergence of an Aramaean nation.[8] Some such isoglosses may well have run along the northern edge of the Canaanite corridor of Jerusalem, thus marking off Judah from the northern tribes, but linking the latter to the plain of Damascus. In fact we know of one such isogloss in a period several centuries later. The

Samaria Ostraca contain many times the word for "year" in the form šatt (from an earlier šant), as opposed to the Standard Classical šānāh (from an earlier šanat), but this northern Israelite form is exactly that of Aramaic šattā (with the Aramaic definite article). It is hardly likely that the word for "year" was borrowed from Aramaic; it must have been a local form from the heartland of the Northern Kingdom. The limited number of words and phrases in the Samaria Ostraca, and the lack of other inscriptional material from the northern part of the country, prevent us from getting a clearer idea of the types of language which were spoken there or used for non-literary communication. The book of Hosea, though written in the later literary language common to both South and North, exhibits a number of linguistic peculiarities, some at least of which are likely to represent features typically northern,[9] but our ignorance of the vernacular background prevents us from deciding whether any individual case represents the colloquial, the local northern writing style, slang, fashion,[10] or the exuberant inventions of a great writer. Thus, while we can be quite positive that the language of the early poems was northern (i.e. focused north of the Canaanite corridor of Jerusalem), its exact relationship to the living speech of that area remains a matter of speculation.

The great turning point in the history of the Hebrew language, as in so many other cultural and religious aspects, was the brief spell (about seventy years) during which North and South were united under David and Solomon, and in particular the establishment of the administrative and religious capital in Jerusalem, a city not previously connected with any tribe. After its conquest the city was populated by David with people from different tribes. The cult, which existed in David's time, was carried on by priests from all parts of the country (I Chron. 13:2), and of course even more so once the Temple had been established. David's army, and presumably his administration, and Solomon's more elaborate system of administration, were staffed by men drawn from different tribes. Jerusalem thus became a meeting-place for people speaking different dialects; no doubt, as is invariably the case in such circumstances, dialect mixture took place. It is also likely that the mixed speech of the capital was carried by army personnel and government officials at least into the provincial centers, and that in this way the speech of northerners took on some Judean features and that of the Judeans some northern traits.[11]

The change of the colloquial is a reasonable surmise. The change of the written language is quite visible. The prose books of the pre-exilic period exhibit a language markedly different from that of the early poetry. It is free from Aramaizing forms[12] and very regular in its usage in such matters as the placing of the article, the use of the accusative particle eth, the syntactical distribution of the simple and the consecutive ("inverted") tenses, the regular addition of wāw to the latter, and the overwhelming frequency of clear indication of the logical natural of subordinate clauses by suitable particles, notably *ăšer*, with or without additional prepositions, as opposed to the largely asyndetic subordination of the early poetry. This statement requires some comment. Hebraists are accustomed to attribute these differences to the fact that the one is poetry and the other prose, and that poetry is as a matter of course more archaic and less regular than prose. These differences, therefore, would be due to stylistic level, rather than to any factors of time or dialect. In support of this assumption one can point to the poetry of the time of the Monarchy, which shows to some extent the same archaic features, though less than the early poems, as well as to the "hymnic-epical dialect" of Akkadian[13] or the archaisms in the tense system of the Ugaritic epics as opposed to the administrative texts.[14] However, if we look closer into the examples adduced, we find that the archaism of Akkadian, and probably of Ugaritic poetry[15] is due to the fact that their oral or written composition antedates the prose texts by a long time, and that the poetry is not marked by incomplete application of the grammatical rules of the prose language, but by very strict application of its own laws. It is the prose which is somewhat laxer in structure, and more accessible to the influence of common speech. The difference between the early poetry and the prose-Hebrew of the Monarchy is therefore in all probability not a stylistic matter, but due to a different linguistic basis. Either the latter represents the pure Judean dialect or, more likely, is the result of the desire to use a language comprehensible throughout Israel, and therefore free of extreme dialect features that might impede communication. That this language was so regular, in spite of its composite origin, is a result of its use in official correspondence and royal chronicles by trained scribes. Indeed, we might apply to this language the characterization W. von Soden gives of the legal and epistolary language of the administration of Hammurabi, as being "in part probably the outcome of a conscious language reform."[16]

It seems, however, that the changes we see in the standardized Hebrew prose were not only a by-product of its written and official character, but had deeper significance. As an instance we may consider the particle *ăšer*. *Sa-*, *še-* occur in the Song of Deborah, three times in the story of Gideon in Judges, and in II Kings 6:11 in the mouth of the Aramaean king, otherwise only in the Song of Songs and in post-exilic books: both the prose and the poetry of the time of the Monarchy use only *ăšer*. The latter exists, apart from Hebrew, only in Moabite, and its etymology is uncertain. The reappearance of *še-* in the Second Temple period and in Mishnaic Hebrew shows that it continued to be employed in speech. It seems thus that the consistent use of *ăšer*, perhaps a Judean, southern form, in writing was a conscious effort to use a "Hebrew" form that would clearly set a Hebrew document apart from, say, a document written in Phoenician. We may say the same of the absence of "Aramaic" phonetic developments in Classical prose: while it is quite likely, and indeed made probable by such a case as the one from the Samaria Ostraca discussed above, that such forms continued to be used in speech in some parts of the country, the written language avoids them. This not only implies a certain degree of sophistication, but is indeed characteristic for the emergence of standard national languages. There are numerous cases in language history where features opposed to a neighboring closely related language were consciously developed as part of an emerging national consciousness. Such a desire for clear linguistic differentiation operated with relation to the Phoenicians; the effect of Hiram's neighborly act towards David on Hebrew national consciousness is expressly stated in II Sam. 5:12: "And David realized that the Lord had established him. . . ." But above all it must have operated towards the Aramaic state which emerged about the same time. In 1956, S. Moscati suggested that what we know as Aramaic arose through the radiation of typically "Aramaic" features, especially in phonology, over a wide area from an originally small center, which he placed in northern Mesopotamia.[17] After B. Mazar's demonstration that Damascus was the focus of the Aramaean national idea, we can confidently identify that area also as the focus from which radiated the linguistic features that were subsequently identified as characteristically Aramaic. We may even assume that a certain systematization took place in the official language of the kings of Damascus, so as to differentiate "Aramaic" more clearly from the "Canaanite" to the south. But it was just this emergence of an Aramaic national language that made the Israelites of David's and Solomon's time aware of the fact that their own speech contained "Aramaic" features, which therefore had to be avoided in literary and official Hebrew in favor of typically "Hebrew" phonology and forms. We may perhaps not be wrong in including among these the consistent use of *eth* for the accusative and the regularization of the employment of the consecutive tenses, which Aramaic by then had given up.

While the Hebrew of the Monarchy may well have been born in the chancellery, it soon outgrew its origins and, under the influence of intellectual movements such as the Wisdom schools and Prophetic thought, developed into the rich and sensitive tool of expression which we know it to have been. If we accept the idea of M. D. Cassuto, that the Pentateuchal narratives were originally epics, and were rewritten in prose,[18] then this rewriting must have taken place in the period of the Monarchy. Such a task in itself must have contributed a great deal to making the prose of the period more supple, by incorporating into it the expressiveness of poetic language as well as by facing it with the challenge of saying things not normally couched in an official form of speech.

The cultic and prophetic poetry of this period must have grown out of the official written idiom, since it shares with it some features, e.g. the use of *ăšer* and the absence of *še-*, but it is much less rigid in syntax. This may be because it consciously incorporated some habits of the early poems (or perhaps of the colloquial), such as the use of asyndetic, unmarked subordinate clauses side by side with the syndetic ones. Above all, poetry of this period is marked by its special vocabulary, consisting mainly of synonyms of ordinary prose words.[19] As G. R. Driver has shown, many of these words are commonly used in neighboring Semitic languages,[20] while research has brought to light a large number of pairs of words used in poetic parallelism which also occur in Ugaritic and in other Semitic poetic literatures.[21] It seems that Hebrew poets were not averse to resorting to neighboring literatures to enrich what H. L. Ginsberg has called "the regular stock-in-trade" of the ancient Semitic poet.[22] The poetry most easily accessible was of course that of the as yet unassimilated Canaanites in the midst of the Israelite population, whose poetic tradition was probably similar to that which we meet in Ugarit.[23] The Hebrew literary language, while closing itself to influences from neighboring cultures,[24] was open to contacts with the local Canaanite language.

Because of the great similarity between the two languages[25] we shall probably never know the debt of the language of the period of the Monarchy to the language of the superior urbanized material culture of the Canaanites. One contribution, however, may be suggested. While Hebrew borrowing from Egyptian is small in extent, and the words borrowed all clearly belong either to trade or to well-known Egyptian institutions,[26] Akkadian is represented by a large number of loan-words well established in pre-exilic Hebrew.[27] Many of these refer to the building of houses.[28] It is hardly likely that these words should all date from the contact with the Assyrians in the latter period of the Monarchy; moreover, these contacts were hardly the kind which would have caused the Hebrews to become acquainted with Mesopotamian architectural techniques. The great time of cultural contact was the second millennium B.C.E., with its use of Akkadian as a written language by Canaanites, as documented in the Tell el-Amarna letters. Such terms must thus have been familiar to at least part of the local Canaanite population before the Israelite conquest. They may have passed into the speech of the Hebrews along with other early Canaanite linguistic influences, but it is at least worth considering whether the most likely time for this was not the early Monarchy, with its large-scale building operations and the urbanization of important sections of the Israelite population. Similar criteria could apply to the smaller but still basic body of administrative terms, such as *sēfer*, "letter," or *šōṭĕrīm*, "administrative officers."

After the division of the Monarchy, the literary language established during the time of unity showed a remarkable stability in Judea. For almost three hundred years the grammar and syntax remained unchanged. The Lachish letters and some more recently discovered tablets of official correspondence show that the same standards were also maintained in non-literary writing by educated people or their scribes. This is in itself remarkable, and bears witness to the identification of the people with their language and to the successful establishment of a literary standard. More remarkable, however, is the fact that those northern literary productions which we possess from the period of the Divided Monarchy, are also couched in the same language. The language of Amos is no more different from the writings of Judean prophets than their individual styles are from each other; while the style of Hosea is in some ways exceptional (see above), its grammatical and syntactical basis is identical with Judean Hebrew of his time. There is, to mention just one trait, no instance of *še-*, though *ăšer* occurs ten times. These prophets thus did not write a Hebrew resembling that of the Samaria Ostraca, but followed the standard of language current in the Southern Kingdom. Of course it would be rash to deduce from this that official correspondence or royal chronicles of the Northern Kingdom were in the same idiom. If we assume they were not, then the fact that northern literature was written in a language so closely associated with the rival state becomes all the more remarkable. One might be tempted to argue that Amos and Hosea, being opponents of the local cult of the Northern kings, and adherents of the cult of Jerusalem, also used the language of Jerusalem. However, if they did so, they must have been confident that their public in the Northern Kingdom would understand them, and this would prove a close and constant familiarity in the North with the Judean standard language. However, such an act of linguistic "protest" seems a rather involved and improbable assumption. Much more likely the literary language of the Northern Kingdom (if not also the official administrative language[29]) was at the time more or less identical with that of the South. This means that the Northern Kingdom did not revert to the literary language which had existed in the area before the period of unification. There may have been a sound practical reason for this: the pre-unification language had only been used for poetry, and a new written language would have had to be developed and imposed upon a class of scribes who had been accustomed for seventy years to write Standard Hebrew, and indeed was based on their ability to do so. However, this situation would have led only to a slowing-up of the change, and to a more gradual penetration of the local speech into the written standard language. It seems, therefore, that there was also a loyalty to the standard language initiated by the Davidic dynasty, strong enough to survive the breaking of the connection with that dynasty and with the religion represented by Jerusalem. The language thus represented—to speak in modern terms—an Israelite national identification, as opposed to identification as citizens of one of the two successor states of united Israel. In other words, the administrative language of the time of David and Solomon had in that short time become a national language.

CHAPTER IV

RELIGION: STABILITY AND FERMENT

by M. Greenberg

A. The Sources

THE BIBLICAL SOURCES of our knowledge of Israelite religion during
the monarchy may be divided into two classes: those whose pertinence to
the period may be assumed more or less confidently—such as the primary
materials of the book of Kings and several of the Prophets, and those of dubious
pertinence, such as the Psalms, in which material from the monarchic and other
periods are combined—often, one suspects, indistinguishably.

The book of Kings draws upon the chronicles of the kings of Israel and
Judah; it also contains stories emanating from prophetic circles; the whole is
set in a framework that connects and passes judgment upon kings and reigns.
The final editing occurred between the latest historical datum in the book—
the release of King Jehoiachin from prison in the accession year of Evil-Merodach
of Babylon (561 B.C.E)—and the Restoration, which is beyond its horizon
(538). The hybrid religion ascribed to the Samaritans in II Kings 17:24–41
also indicates a period anterior to the building of the Second Temple, since
at that time the Samaritans were irreproachably YHWH-fearing (otherwise
their idolatry would have been cited in the Jews' rebuff of their participation
in the building of the Temple).

The contemporary material in the book of Kings is of the first importance
for describing the religion of the age. What makes the book problematic is its
tendentious character: it judges the monarchies of Israel and Judah by a late,
absolute standard throughout the history. The editor condemns Judah's worship
at *bāmōt* from the reign of Rehoboam to Ahaz, and the entire official cult in
Israel from its founding by Jeroboam. Now there is no evidence in the primary
sources that such standards obtained throughout the period. The material of
north-Israelite provenience—such as the stories of Elijah and Elisha—does not
display opposition to the official cult so long as it was free from alien influx.
In Judah, no priest or king, be he ever so Godfearing, took exception to the

bāmōt-worship before the reign of Hezekiah (8th century). This contrast between the editing and the primary sources can be explained either as reflecting contemporaneous but divergent values, or (which seems more likely) as reflecting different periods. The affinities of the editorial part of Kings to Deuteronomy, both in ideology and language, indicate that it was inspired by that book. The identity of the editor's standard of judgment with the religious policy of the Judahite kings Hezekiah and Josiah (whom he praises unreservedly) suggests that his ideology, while pertaining indeed to the period of the monarchy, probably cannot be dated much before Hezekiah's time.

The primary sources of Kings give the appearance of reliability, if only because of their freedom from the tendency of editing. Their chief limitation is their narrow purview: excepting the north-Israelite prophetic stories, they deal exclusively with kings. The practices of worship they describe belong to the official cult, founded and maintained by the monarchy. Only in the prophetic stories can one obtain glimpses of popular religion independent of the royal institutions. Thus the book of Kings gives evidence of the royal policies respecting temples and clergy, in the capitals and the country-side, but tells little about the everyday, popular practice and faith. A pervasive tendency stamps the whole with the character of an indictment of the kingdoms of Israel and Judah.[1]

The book of Chronicles contains data on the faith and worship of the monarchic period that do not appear in Kings, but the reliability of these data is dubious. The tendency of Chronicles is plain: it wishes to tell the story of the "Israel" that revived in the Persian province of Judah, putting forth those features that bound present to past (while ignoring discontinuities), and drawing lessons for contemporary faith and practice from the fate of the kingdom. To give expression to his ideology, the Chronicler puts speeches in the mouths of historical characters, composed in a distinctive style that cannot be mistaken for that of the book of Kings. Reports of religious events that accord with his tendency and that are marked by the same style must also be regarded as his inventions (e.g. Manasseh's change of heart, II Chron. 33:12–16). Likewise suspect is his ascription to the early monarchy of institutions known to have existed in Second Temple times, but unattested earlier outside of Chronicles (I Chron. 23–26). Every datum of the Chronicler requires individual evaluation; no blanket generalization is possible. As a working rule, if that which he ascribes to our period is attested elsewhere, his evidence can stand; what is not so attested, had best be left out.[2]

The bulk of the Latter Prophets (Amos, Hosea, Micah, Isaiah [1–37], Nahum, Zephaniah, Habakkuk, Jeremiah) are placed by their date-titles in our period. Precisely when these books were edited is not known; the date of their contents may be conjectured from their historical horizon. By and large, the writings of the prophets of the Neo-Assyrian period (Amos, Hosea, Isaiah, Micah) contain no reference to the rise of the Babylonian kingdom; similarly, the writings of the prophets of the Babylonian period (Nahum, Zephaniah, Habakkuk, Jeremiah) do not refer to the succeeding empire of the Persians. Hence it is to be concluded that the prophetic material was considered sacred close to the time of its publication and was more or less fixed in the period to which it refers. Verses and even chapters were interpolated, not only by the prophets' contemporaries, but by later hands (e.g., Isa. 13 and part of 14), but these are not extensive and are, on the whole, readily identifiable. Testimony concerning the religion of the monarchy may therefore, with due criticism, be gathered from most of the prophetic material.[3]

Unlike the book of Kings, prophecy does not deal only with kings. The prophets embrace all classes in their purview; those to whom they address their reproof are "from the smallest to the greatest" (Jer. 8:10). Hence the picture of a given age as drawn in Kings sometimes differs from that drawn by its contemporary prophets, since many evils denounced by the prophets were not the fault of the kings and therefore go unmentioned in the book of Kings.

The testimony of the prophets is impaired by their tendency to exaggerate and generalize. Their aim was to stir their audience to repentance; to that end, they excoriated sin and sinners without making nice distinctions. Sins of some were attributed to the whole community; they sometimes failed to discriminate past from present sin, bad intentions from actual deeds.[4] Prophetic testimony must be searchingly examined in order to determine the reality underlying their reproofs. The most reliable is the incidental testimony—that which concerns something not at issue but only mentioned in passing.

Criticism has reached the conclusion that the Torah literature was not fixed before the age of the monarchy. Among the indications of this are allusions in the Torah to events from that age, e.g., the struggle between Israel and Edom (Gen. 25:23; 27:40); God's promise to the patriarchs that kings would descend from them, the climax of divine promises to the patriarchs (Gen. 17:6; 35:11). On the other hand, the laws of the Torah virtually ignore the monarchy, its institutions and its values (Deut. 17:14–20 is a notable exception), assuming rather a tribal polity (elders and chiefs) of small farmers and cattle-raisers. The laws do not reflect the economy of merchants and large estate-owners that existed in monarchic times. Tension exists between the wilderness setting of Deuteronomy and its rulings on practices of worship that are not reflected in history before the reigns of Hezekiah and Josiah. It thus appears that while the earliest elements of the Torah literature precede the monarchy, the latest come from its last days. The cultic laws of the Torah are hardest to date. Since they assume a people settled in its land, it is reasonable to date their application to the age of the monarchy. Yet the literature that can most surely be dated to the monarchy makes scant reference to practices regulated by these laws; only in Second Temple literature is the cult law of the Torah clearly reflected. This is explicable in several ways: (1) that the cult laws of the Torah are from late, even post-exilic, times; (2) that the laws existed in the monarchy but were not universally applied until later; (3) that the origin and focus of the datable literature of the monarchy were too remote from the detail of the cult to reflect the laws adequately.

In this quandary, the following rule-of-thumb will be employed: materials of the Torah even partially reflected in literature datable to the monarchic age will be adduced *in toto*; data not even partially reflected will be left out.

There are no criteria for determining the age of the religious ideas and practices of the Psalms, since ideas and terms known from ancient Ugaritic literature are there juxtaposed to patently Israelite material. Only rarely can a specific historical context be plausibly conjectured for a psalm. References to an earthly king (as in Ps. 2) indicate the period of the monarchy; but allusions to the Babylonian exile (Ps. 137) and a widespread diaspora (106:47) point to the inclusion in the collection of later material as well. Here too the abovementioned rule will be used: data found only in psalms whose provenience from monarchic times is doubtful will not be adduced unless they are hinted at in material at least probably datable to the monarchy.[5]

The Bible sets forth the conceptions of the spiritual elite of Israel; popular religion is not expressed in it directly at all. The description of the people's sin is the evaluation of the elite, and exaggerates both its extent (as when acts of a limited circle are attributed to the entire people, like the Baal worship of the northern kingdom) and its heinousness (as when an act is condemned according to a standard that was not contemporaneous with it, like the worship at *bāmōt* before the reforms of Hezekiah). And yet one cannot assume an essential gap between the popular religion and that of the authors of the Bible, for the Bible is wholly concerned with the people; its authors address the people and regard their faith as that of the Israelite people. The elite did not cultivate an esoteric faith, but strove to make the people share in their conceptions. Hence, they portray the popular religion as fundamentally identical with their own, the divergence between the two constituting the people's sin. While such a portrait is of course distorted, the constant orientation of the biblical authors toward the people kept the gap between the two much smaller than, say, the gap separating the religious ideas of the ancient Greek philosophers from those of the Greek masses of their age.

Extra-biblical sources for Israel's religion in the monarchic period are few and of small importance.

The earliest extra-biblical attestation of the name of Israel's God occurs in the 9th-century B.C.E. inscription of King Mesha of Moab. According to the probably correct restoration of lines 17–18, Mesha boasts of "dragging the vessels of YHWH *('[t k]ly yhwh)*" from the (temple of the) captured Israelite town of Nebo "before Chemosh"—that is, into the temple of the Moabite god. The victorious Philistines are said to have done the same with the captured Israelite ark (I Sam. 5:2).

Many of the names in the seals and documents from 8th century Hazor and Samaria and 7–6th century Ophel (Jerusalem), Lachish, and Arad contain the element *yhw/yw*, like the biblical names of the period, and thus attest to belief in YHWH, God of Israel; his epithets *'ēl* and *melek* also appear. [6] There is a noteworthy concentration of names containing the element *ba'al* in the Samaria ostraca (in a ratio of 2:3 to *yhw* names), from the reign of Jeroboam II or Menahem. No such names appear in material of Judahite provenience, hence the supposition that they reflect the imported Baal worship of the northern Omride kings. It is not clear, however, that *ba'al* in these names refers to the Phoenician deity, since the God of Israel probably also bore this title (cf. the names Meribaal, Eshbaal, Baal Perazim from the times of Saul and David), particularly at the time when ties with Phoenicia were strong. [7]

An oath by the life of YHWH and blessings in his name appear in the Lachish letters. [8] In the Arad ostraca a "house of YHWH" appears, and also the names Pashhur, Meremoth, Kerosi—names of priests, Levities and Nethinim, according to the Bible. [9]

The testimony of the Elephantine documents deriving from a 5th century Jewish garrison on the southern border of Egypt is problematic. The faith of the soldiers in this remote outpost is glimpsed in the correspondence about their temple (which was destroyed by Egyptians), a temple of YHW (so spelled), where they offered grain, frankincense and whole offerings; in the mention of Passover and Sabbath; and in many -*ywh* names. The religion of these soldiers was probably similar to that of simple folk in the homeland (the erection of a temple outside of Jerusalem has caused astonishment among some scholars, hardly warranted in the light of the analogous 2nd century B.C.E. Jewish temple at Leontopolis in the Delta). To be sure, no trace of sacred scriptures has been found among the Elephantine documents—perhaps because the last inhabitants of the place took them along when they left it. There are allusions to the association of other gods in the worship of the temple and in oaths, and to intermarriage with local non-Jews. But these are subject to various interpretations; moreover the circumstances of this remote community, surrounded by gentiles, make their religious practice a dubious basis for inferring the state of religion in the kingdom of Judah over a century earlier. Based on the divine epithet *bethel*, found in some names, and the address to Sanballat, governor of

Samaria, of the letters concerning the temple, some have thought that the garrison derived ultimately from the north. But *bethel* is an element of Phoenician and Aramean names, and otherwise too this theory has little to commend it. In sum, no reliance is to be placed on the Elephantine documents as evidence of Israelite religion in biblical times.[10]

In the Arad excavations, a temple from the time of the monarchy, the first such to be laid bare at an ancient Israelite site, was found. The temple has a court, an altar of sacrifice, a holy place, and a raised holy of holies, on the steps to which stood two altars of incense. It thus offers some remarkable parallels to the plan of the Solomonic temple (I Kings 6). In the holy of holies was a painted *maṣṣebah*, and two similar plastered stones. Stones of another altar of sacrifice, including its four "horns," were unearthed in Beersheba, reused in a building of the 8th century B.C.E. On one of the stones the figure of a twisted snake was engraved, recalling the sacred symbol mentioned in Num. 21:8 f., and II Kings 18:4. Indirect evidence of yet another Israelite sanctuary is an 8th-century seal belonging to "[ ]*kryw* priest of Dor." Neither the Arad nor the Dor sanctuary is alluded to in the Bible.[11]

Items apparently having to do with worship from the beginning of the 8th century were found on the Ophel slope: "Two upright stones may have been *massebahs*. On the same site a cave was discovered containing a large hoard of pottery vessels dating from about 800 B.C.E. It may have been a depository for discarded offerings. A square structure, perhaps an altar, was also found there."[12] Diverse cult vessels—not all certainly identified—were found in various excavations, such as the incense altar of Megiddo, and incense ladles from Hazor.

Several types of figurines of naked females have been found in quantity in the land of Israel from the monarchic and other periods. Their relation to known goddesses is problematic, since they often lack specific character. It is commonly assumed that they served as fertility amulets, or as talismans to assure successful child-birth. Very likely they played a role in the popular religion of women (one thinks of the teraphim [housegods?] of Rachel and Michal), but due to the silence of the literary sources our knowledge here is virtually nil.[13]

The sum of testimony outside the Bible regarding Israelite religion during the monarchy does not amount to much. Rather than illuminating, these meager data need themselves to be illuminated. Some confirm the standard belief in YHWH; some indicate "heterodoxy" and perhaps even paganism. At the least, they give color to the biblical condemnations of Israel for deviating from authorized religious practices.

Characteristic of Israelite religion was its dynamic, self-critical component, owing to which it developed a store of ideas and institutions of ultimately universal value. This component flourished in the setting of a popular national religion, whose primary expressions and institutions took shape before the monarchy but like everything spiritual must have changed along with developments in the life of its bearers. Our material, however, does not allow us to follow the shades of change; what comes through is a religious background of considerable stability, which served as the substructure and starting point of ferment in the spiritual elite. From time to time this ferment invaded the substructure and finally worked deep changes in it. In the following sections, the stable and dynamic components of Israelite religion will be, somewhat artificially, distinguished and treated separately for the sake of clarity.

B. Stable Factors: Institutions, Practices and Beliefs

1. Public Religion

The public worship of God—that which was carried on in the name of the community—took place at public installations: at *bāmōt* and at sanctuaries. The *bāmāh*, usually on a height and apparently roofless (cf. "on every high hill, at the top of every mountain, under every green tree, and under every leafy terebinth" Ezek. 6:13; cf. Hos. 4:13) stood in cities too (I Kings 13:32; II Kings 23:8). The term *bēt bāmōt* is altogether obscure, and may well be no more than a pejorative turn of the phrase *bēt miqdāš* ("sanctuary house," Solomon's temple [II Chron. 36:17]), used by the Deuteronomistic narrator to derogate Jeroboam's temples (I Kings 13:32; II Kings 17:29, 32; 23:19). The essence of the *bāmāh* was an altar, alongside which stood a pillar (apparently the sign of God's presence, as appears from the *maṣṣēbōt* in the inner sanctum of the Arad sanctuary; so too outside of Israel),[14] and an asherah—i.e. a tree (or a wooden pole), whose meaning is obscure, but which served it seems, as a sign of local sanctity (I Kings 14:23; II Kings 18:4; according to Deut. 16:21, asherah is any tree alongside an altar).[15]

A description of popular (i.e. non-priestly) sacrifice at a *bāmāh* outside the town of Ramah is given in I Samuel 9. Participants were summoned beforehand, doubtless to purify themselves for the occasion, according to 16:5. After the sacrifice they sat down to the sacred meal in an adjoining chamber. The local prophet uttered a blessing over the meat before they ate, then the meal was served by the cook. Since no priest appears at this *bāmāh*, it is doubtful that a regular, daily sacrificial service was performed there.

Kings erected sanctuaries in Jerusalem (David and Solomon), in Bethel and Dan (Jeroboam), and perhaps also in Samaria (the Omrides); cf. "the calf" and "the 'offense' of (*'šmt*) Samaria" (Hos. 8:5 f.; Amos 8:14; unless Samaria stands for the northern kingdom and the Bethel calf is meant). In other towns, too (e.g. Hebron and Beersheba), sanctuaries stood.

The founding of temples was a privilege reserved for kings in the ancient east, and a sign of their piety.[15a] That is why David took such pains to found a sanctuary, and, when the project had to be put off, labored to collect the materials for it (the hyperbolic account of I Chron. 22:14 is based on II Sam. 8:12). It would seem that sanctuaries were erected at places hallowed by tradition. Those at Hebron and Beersheba could point to legitimation in the time of the patriarchs (e.g. Gen. 13:18; 21:33; 26:23 ff; 46:1). The santuary at Arad was built on a site formerly occupied by a *bāmāh*. Several traditions attached themselves to the site of Jerusalem's sanctuary. The etiological note to the story of Isaac's near-sacrifice on Mount Moriah, calling the place "YHWH *yr'h*" (Gen. 22:14), evokes the first element (*yrw-*) of the name Jerusalem; II Chron. 3:1 expressly identifies the Temple Mount with Mount Moriah. Another tradition identified it with the threshing floor of Arawna the Jebusite, at which an angel revealed himself to David in a plague, and where the plague was halted; by order of the prophet Gad, David then bought the site and erected an altar there to commemorate the deliverance (II Sam. 24:21 ff; II Chron. 3:1).[16]

The maintenance of the Jerusalem sanctuary fell to the Davidides; they supported it, repaired it, altered its appointments, and disposed of its treasures as they wished (I Kings 14:26; 15:15, 18; II Kings 12; 16:10 ff.; 21:4 ff.; 22:3–9; 23:6–9). That northern kings did the same is implied by the designation of the Bethel sanctuary as "the king's temple" (Amos 7:13).

The fact of their being royal sanctuaries did not mean that the populace was excluded from them. On the contrary, crowds filled their courts in festive worship (cf. Amos 5:23, presumably of Bethel). The Jerusalem Temple was specifically designed to be a house of prayer for ordinary persons (I Kings 8:38 ff.), and many psalms testify to the people's attachment to it (e.g., 84; 96:8; 100; 116:18 f).

The Jerusalem Temple, like that of Arad, consisted of a court, a porch, the sanctuary proper and an elevated inner sanctum (the inference of elevation, necessitated by the dimensions given in the text, is now confirmed at Arad). Laity were allowed into the courts, but only consecrated ministers could enter the sanctuary and the inner sanctum (cf. Neh. 6:11, 13). In the court stood a bronze Sea in which the priests washed (II Chron. 4:6), and an altar for whole offerings, around which the festive throngs marched (Ps. 26:6), and before which the oath-ordeal was administered (I Kings 8:31). The most sacred spot in the court was the space between the temple porch and the altar, where priests performed sacred offices in the sight of the crowds (Joel 2:17; cf. the blasphemy of Ezek. 8:16). In the porch stood two pillars (in the Jerusalem Temple they were named Jachin and Boaz); their use is unknown. The "Temple vessels" included a table for shewbread (set out weekly; the loaves were consigned to the priests; I Sam. 21:7; Lev. 24:5 ff.), lamps, an incense altar to perfume the interior, and basins for purification of the priests at their work. In the windowless inner sanctum ("YHWH has decided to dwell in deep darkness," I Kings 8:12) stood the most holy symbol of God's presence: in Jerusalem—the ark of the covenant, over which golden cherubs outspread their wings protectively—replicas of the celestial bearers of "Him who is enthroned upon cherubs" (cf. II Sam. 22:11; Ezek. 10:18 f.). In accordance with its location under the cherubs (symbolizing the divine throne), the ark was called God's "footstool" (I Chron. 28:2),[17] while in Jeremiah 3:16 f. another epithet of the ark is alluded to, "YHWH's throne." In the inner sanctum of the Arad temple, pillars stood; according to Gen. 28:16 ff; 35:14 f., the pillar served to mark God's presence at a site. In the royal sanctuaries of the Northern Kingdom, golden calves took the place of the golden cherubs as pedestals or bearers of God.[18] Hosea's rebuke "they kiss calves" (Hos. 13:2) has given rise to the conjecture that these calves were accessible to the public, perhaps standing, in the courtyard, rather than the inner sanctum; if so, what stood in the inner sanctum of the northern temples is unknown.

The service at the sanctuary consisted of a priestly, sacrificial rite, conducted in the inner area, and a popular accompaniment of song, dance, procession, and sacred meals that went on outside, particularly at festivals. There was an order of daily service: in Jerusalem, "the morning whole offering and the evening oblation" (II Kings 16:16) were brought in the name of the king and on behalf of the people too; the regularity of these offerings made them indicators of the time of day (I Kings 18:29: "till the time of the oblation"). These are apparently the same as the "regular offering" mentioned in the Torah, consisting of one lamb in the morning and one in the evening, with their flour and wine adjuncts (Num. 28:1 ff.). A "regular lamp-lighting" illuminated the temple each night (Lev. 24:1 ff.; cf. I Sam. 3:3); in Jerusalem there were ten lamps in the Temple (I Kings 7:49). A "regular incense offering" was made morning and evening (Exod. 30:7 f.; cf. the reference to this service in Deut. 33:10; I Sam. 2:28),[19] and sets of shewbread appeared weekly on the temple table, to be removed and replaced on the Sabbath by a new set (I Sam. 21:7; Lev. 24:5 ff.). The laity are never mentioned in connection with this regular service; presumably it was the exclusive charge of the priests.

Sacred seasons had two aspects: the sacrificial service and the popular festivity. On the three pilgrimage festivals all males were required to present themselves with gifts before "Lord YHWH" (Lev. 23:17; 34:23)—apparently, that is, at one of the larger temples (as distinct from a local *bāmāh*).[20] The Torah contains several lists of additional offerings meant for the festivals, of which some are individual obligations (so evidently the first sheaf of the reaping [Lev. 23:9] and the loaves made of the firstfruits of grain, [*ibid.*, v. 17]) and others, communal (so evidently the sacrificial animals that accompany the firstfruits [*ibid.* vv. 18 f.] and the whole list of Num. 28–29). The pilgrims brought with them animals for peace-offerings from which they partook in the sacred meal (cf. I. Sam. 1:3 f.). The large numbers of animals in temple cities on festivals was proverbial: "Like the sacred flocks, like the flocks of Jerusalem on its festivals" (Ezek. 36:38).

The festivals occurred during the two critical agricultural seasons: (1) early spring—the time of grain reaping, the seven weeks between the *maṣṣōt* festival (the start of the barley reaping) and the feast of Weeks (the festival of reaping [Ex. 23:16], when the firstfruits of the wheat harvest were offered [34:22]; on the weeks, see Lev. 23:15 f.; Deut. 16:9; Jer. 5:24: "who keeps for our benefit, the weeks appointed for reaping"); (2) autumn—the end of the threshing season and ingathering of fruit (Exod. 23:16, "when you gather in your produce from the fields"), or *sukkōt* "tabernacles" (Lev. 23:39; Deut. 16:13). Sacred seasons clustered around these pivots of the agricultural year: Just before the spring festival of *maṣṣōt*, the *pesaḥ* ("protection"[21]) sacrifice fell; both retain something of the anxiety pertaining to the start of the reaping season, although they were transformed into commemorations of the Exodus.[22] Just before the harvest home festival, "at the outgoing" (or "turn") of the year (Exod. 23:16; 34:22) there occurred two holydays mentioned only in priestly writings. The new moon of the seventh month was "a day of trumpet blasts" (Num. 29:1) or a "commemoration with trumpet blasts" (Lev. 23:24); the tenth of the same month was "a day of atonement" (*ibid.* vv. 26 ff.). "A commemoration with trumpet blasts" recalls on the one hand the blast of horns attending sacrifices "on your days of rejoicing, on your festival days and on your new moon days . . . that they may serve as reminders of you to God" (Num. 10:10). It may be inferred that on the first of the seventh month a supreme effort was made to be remembered for good by God. On the other hand, one recalls the shouts and trumpeting for God so often referred to in psalms describing his kingship (e.g., 47; 95; 98; 100), whence the surmise that this holy day was, like the later Jewish New Year, a celebration of God's kingship and of his deciding the destiny of his creatures.[23] The Day of Atonement, an annual purgation of the sanctuary from its defilement, and atonement for the sins of priests and people, also belongs to the destiny-decision at the turn of the year. The day is described (Lev. 16) as an exclusively priestly celebration, in which the people had no part other than fasting.[24] The seven-day festival of Tabernacles, starting in mid-month, and its contiguous "day of assembly," the joyous harvest-home celebration, culminate this "turn-of-the-year" season. Ps. 81 parallels the new moon day to the full moon day (mid-month) as days of festive horn blowing, alluding perhaps to the autumn festival season, with its "day of trumpet blasts" on the new moon of the seventh month, and the Feast of Tabernacles at mid-month.[25]

New moon days and Sabbaths had additional offerings (Num. 28:9 ff.). Apart from those of the Sabbath, these included whole and sin offerings to atone for the people. New moon and festival sacrifices were accompanied by trumpet blasts, so as "to be remembered by YHWH" (Num. 10:10). The festivals were therefore days of placating God and purgation from sin.

The solemn, and apparently silent, priestly rites were accompanied by joyous popular celebrations. The rejoicing began with the gathering of the pilgrim caravan. "I rejoiced when they said to me: Let us go to the house of YHWH (Ps. 122:1). As it approached the city, flutes were played (Isa. 30:29). The night of the holy day was filled with song (*ibid.*), and on its morrow (the holy day itself), the festive throngs ascended to the temple with shouting and songs of praise" (Ps. 42:5). "First the singers, then the players, amidst maidens drumming" (68:26). Some celebrants walked around the altar, as they told how God dealt wonderfully with them in public fulfilment of their vows of thanksgiving (22:26; 35:18; 40:40). Amos describes the tumult of the singing and the music in the northern sanctuaries (5:23), as well as the merriment of the banqueters there (2:8). Hosea rebukes the licence that sometimes accompanied these occasions (4:13 f.)[26]

Solemn assemblies were held at the sanctuaries in bad times, such as drought or locust plague, as described in Joel 2:15 f.: "Blow the horn in Zion, declare a sacred fast day, proclaim a solemn assembly! Gather the people; order the congregation to sanctify itself. Collect elders; gather children and sucklings. Let the groom come out of his chamber and the bride from her tent. Between the porch and the altar let the priests, the ministers of YHWH, weep . . . ".[27]

The temple had a special role in the administration of justice: when the plaintiff had no witnesses, he might impose an oath ordeal on the defendant. The ordeal was held at the altar, "before YHWH," and there was enough faith in its effectiveness to deter liars and bring justice to light (I Kings 8:31 f., by which Exod. 22:6 ff. is clarified). A reflex of this role is the great vision of Isaiah 2:1 ff., where out of his Temple God adjudicates among all the nations.

Although the Temple was called "the house of YHWH," the sacrifices "his bread" (Num. 25:2), and the altar his "table" (Ezek. 44:16; Mal. 1:7), it does not seem that the service was understood crassly as fulfilling divine need. David's eagerness to establish a proper and honorable abode for God, instead of the tent in which he dwelt, was answered by an oracle to the effect that God did not want it nor had it been his custom from the time of the Exodus to dwell otherwise (II Sam. 7:1 ff.). Nowhere is there so much as a hint that the temple service served a need of God (even in the blunt *quid pro quo* of Malachi 3:10, the food demanded by God is for his temple servitors ["the whole tithe"], not for himself). The people did not give the Temple to God, but he gave it to them (Jer. 7:14). Prophet and audience agreed that "it was not about whole offerings and sacrifice that God commanded Israel when he redeemed them from Egypt" (Jer. 7:22), and that during the forty-year wandering there was no lavish sacrificial service (Amos 5:25). What then did the service mean to Israel?

Altar and sacrifice were the means provided by God to summon his presence to men and bring them his blessings (Ex. 20:24). The priestly conception makes the Temple a "dwelling place" (*miškān*) which God commanded "that I may dwell among the Israelites and be a God for them; and they shall know that I, YHWH, am their God who brought them out of the land of Egypt in order to dwell among them" (Ex. 29:45 f.). The visible sign of his indwelling was "the majesty of *(k^evōd)* YHWH," in appearance like fire enveloped in a cloud. It filled the desert tabernacle on the day it was set up (Ex. 40:35), its cloud appeared over the lid of the ark (Lev. 16:2), and later filled Solomon's Temple on its inauguration day (I Kings 8:10 f.). Dwelling in the sanctuary, God was able to meet there with Moses and give him commands for Israel (Ex. 25:22; 29:42 f.; Lev. 1:1; Num. 7:89). In this priestly conception, the function of the sanctuary as an oracle-site is dominant. The child Samuel heard God's word in the sanctuary (I Sam. 3); at the great *bāmāh* in Gibeon, God appeared to Solomon at night in a dream (I Kings 3:5); Isaiah's vision of the future Zion as the place out of which God's word would go forth to the world is based on the oracular function of the temple. Deuteronomy's analogue to "the indwelling majesty" is God's name: the name of YHWH is "called upon his house," in that he is its owner (cf. I Kings 8:43 with vss. 16, 29, etc.) Hence, "YHWH's eyes are ever open" toward that house, and his ears listen always to prayer offered in it (I Kings 8). Solomon's inaugural prayer (a later composition) lists the uses of the sanctuary: it is a warranty for obtaining justice (through the oath ordeal); a place of public and private prayer (not only for Israelites but for strangers as well); it serves too as a conduit of prayer heavenward from outside the land of Israel. In contrast to the ancient conception of I Kings 8:13, where Solomon calls the temple "a princely house for you, a place for your dwelling forever," the prayer stresses that heaven is God's dwelling place, while the temple is only a means for providing for men. There is no trace of the pagan notion that the temple is a house serving God's needs. More remarkable, this prayer does not even mention sacrifice.[28]

The popular appreciation of sacrifice is far from clear. Even if the sacrifice were not thought of as supplying a need of God—as, say, his food and drink—it was a means of showing him honor and placating him (Prov. 3:9: "Honor YHWH out of your wealth, out of the best of all your produce"), analogous to gifts and tribute presented to a ruler (cf. the scornful rejection of blemished offerings in Mal. 1:8: "Present it to your governor!"). God's "savoring the pleasant odor" of the gift meant he felt goodwill toward the worshiper (Gen. 8:21; I Sam. 26:19). Incense was particularly effective in placating divine wrath and atoning for sin (Num. 17:11). That is why cessation of the sacrificial service might be brandished as a terrible threat—to the people, not to God (Hos. 9:4).[29]

This notion did allow the assessment of sacrifice as a benefit to God, as something done for him. The judgment of God described in Ps. 50:1–14 is directed against such an assessment. It seems to be an inner (priestly?) critique of a popular view from one who (unlike the prophets) does value the service as pleasing to God. God (says the critic) has no complaint against the people concerning their whole and peace offerings—indeed he does not need them. If he did eat and drink (absurd idea!) would he resort to man, when all the world is at his disposal? Away with the misconception that something is done for God by sacrificing! There is however, one kind of sacrifice that God does desire, the thanksgiving adjunct to payment of vows. That sacrifice, acknowledging God's favor and manifesting one's dependence upon him, has no trace of the perverse thought that by sacrifice one is benefiting God. "Call upon me in time of trouble; I will rescue you and you will honor me." To turn to God for help in time of trouble, and when help comes, to praise God by thanksgiving sacrifice in payment of vows—that is true honoring of God. Thanksgiving votive offerings are preferable to all other sacrifices, because with them alone there is no room for mistake as to who is doing for whom. It may be going too far to say that this implies a rejection of all other kinds of sacrifice; explicitly, what is rejected is only the mistaken conception that they do something for God.[30]

The royal sanctuaries were supervised by priests who were appointed by kings. David appointed Zadok—whose pedigree is not given in the oldest sources—as priest, along with Abiathar of ancient lineage (Zadok everywhere takes precedence: II Sam. 15:24, 29, 35; 19:12; 20:25).[31] Solomon expelled Abiathar, leaving Zadok and his family in sole possession of the Jerusalem office, apparently down to the Exile (cf. Ezek. 44:15, and the genealogy of I Chron. 5:34–41). In the northern kingdom too, it was the king who appointed the priests of Bethel and Dan (I Kings 12:31); Amaziah of Bethel staunchly supported his royal patron against Amos (Amos 7:10–13). It is likely that the country priests were also thought of as royal officers; at any rate, when Josiah saw fit, he abolished the *bāmōt* and their priestly offices at a stroke (II Kings 23:8, 20).

Who were qualified to be priests? The sources disagree. On the one hand,

David's sons are said to have been priests (II Sam. 8:18), showing how far the king's right to appoint priests went; on the other, the Torah sources limit the priesthood to one tribe (the Levites in Deuteronomy) or one family (Aaron the Levite, in the priestly writings). Hints of the reality that underlay these divergent norms are few and obscure. Since the northern priests are expressly said not to have been Levites, it is to be inferred that their southern rivals were. The polemically inspired similarity between the golden calf stories of Aaron (Exod. 32) and Jeroboam (I King 12) suggests that the northern priesthood had Aaronite origins; and since in the Exodus story the Levites are opposed to Aaron and the calf-worshipers, perhaps Aaron was once not considered a Levite. In Second Temple times, at any rate, the Jerusalem priesthood did trace its ancestry to Aaron; "sons of Aaron" (not "sons of Zadok") meant legitimacy—in accord with the priestly norm in the Torah. No persuasive historical reconstruction has been offered to account for the conflicts among these fragmentary data. The latest biblical authors, using late priestly traditions, tidied things up through artificial genealogies, deriving all extant lines from Aaron the Levite.

What can be gathered from the evidence is that a definite family-caste crystallization developed. In early times, qualification for sacred office was vague; even laymen might be consecrated (I Sam. 7:1, with which cf. Deut. 10:8a). But even then, Levites were preferred candidates for priesthood (Judges 17:13). The ark sanctuary was in control of a priestly line that traced its origin to Egypt (I Sam. 2:27), probably Levite, if not Aaronite (note the Egyptian name Phinehas, common to Aaronites and Elides). The founding of royal temples led to the appointment of new priesthoods by the kings; it is reasonable to suppose that they too preferred pedigreed families—in the first instance Levites and Aaronites (this pleads against the theory that Zadok was a Jebusite). In the countryside, priestly families also took root in newly formed sanctuaries; they naturally tended to regard their privilege as hereditary. Eventually the priestly caste was crystallized as a monopoly of certain families that sought to exclude further accessions to their ranks. An echo of the struggle over qualification is the story of Korah's revolt, in which non-Aaronite Levites are vehemently excluded from priesthood.[32]

The tasks of the priests are listed in the passage on Levi in "Moses' Blessing" (Deut. 33:8–11),[33] and confirmed elsewhere. "They place incense in your nose and whole offering on your altar" (v. 10) agrees with I Sam 2:28, which states that the Elides were chosen "to ascend onto my altar and offer incense." The altar service was an exclusively priestly domain: it required holiness and ritual purity; service by an unauthorized person was a desecration that imperiled his life.[34] Levi's possession of Urim and Thummim in the Blessing of Moses (v. 8) agrees, again, with the election "to bear the ephod" mentioned in I Samuel

2 (cf. also Exod. 28:6–30); these were instruments of divination reserved for priestly use, to which leaders had recourse in early times for state decisions (e.g., concerning warfare, Num. 27:21; I Sam. 23:9; 30:7). After David's time, the priestly oracle seems to have been replaced by the prophet. "They teach your judgment (*mišpāṭeḵā*) to Jacob, and your instructions (*tōrāteḵā*) to Israel" (Deut. 33:10) refers to priestly instruction concerning what is forbidden and permitted, what is clean and unclean; or, as Lev. 10:10 f. puts it comprehensively "to distinguish between the sacred and the profane, between the unclean and the clean, and to instruct the Israelites in all the laws which YHWH spoke to them through Moses." Basically, *tōrāh* is "instruction" or "direction" for a specific case; thus, for example, "the *tōrāh* of the leper" (Lev. 14:2) was the set of instructions the Israelites were commanded to observe in a case of "leprosy"—"as the Levite-priests order you concerning it" (Deut. 24:8). The priest's role in judgment is set out in Deut. 17:8–13 where priests are included in the tribunal of the central sanctuary-town. Ezekiel lays it down that priests "shall be in charge of judgment in litigations; they shall make rulings in accord with my laws" (44:24). Though the earlier sources are silent about the priestly role in justice, these two passages incline scholars to credit the datum of II Chron. 19:8 that King Jehoshaphat of Judah stationed some of the Levites, the priests and the family heads of Israel in Jerusalem to render God's judgment in litigations.[35] Bearing the main responsibility for maintaining the traditions of civil and ritual law during the monarchy, the priests were called "holders of the *tōrāh*" (Jer.2:8).

The Jerusalem priests supervised the safety of the Temple: the chief priest (*kōhēn hārōš*; the second-in-rank was titled *kōhēn mišneh* [II Kings 25:18]) was in charge of the guards at the gates and entrances to the temple (II Kings 11). The maintenance of the buildings was a priestly responsibility about which we hear only in connection with their failure to discharge it (II Kings 12). Theirs was also to keep in check "every madman who played the prophet" on the sacred premises (Jer. 29:26)—a glimpse of the tension between established and enthusiastic religion.

The priests had servitors to assist them at sacrifice, called (in the Shiloh sanctuary) "the priest's boy" (I Sam. 2:13, 15). The book of Chronicles lists singers as a significant part of the Temple personnel, and credits David with having founded their guild (I Chron. 25). There is no reference to temple singers outside the Chronicles, but Israel's worship can hardly have lacked the musical element known in the other oriental cultures (cf. Amos 5:23). Singers appear in the list of immigrants from Babylon at the Restoration (Ezra 2:41, "Asaphite singers"), and since it is unlikely that such a guild sprang into being after the destruction of the Temple, their existence during the monarchy may safely be assumed. This same argument applies to the other classes of temple personnel listed in Ezra 2: the gatekeepers (v. 44), the Nethinim, and the sons of Solomon's servants (43–58), some of whom bear foreign sounding names (Kiros, Meunim, Barkos, Sisera). Indeed, Ezekiel rebukes the Judahites for having brought aliens into the temple to help in the sacrificial service (Ezek. 44:7). These were presumably descended from captives who were assigned menial tasks in the Temple (cf. the Gibeonite hewers of wood and drawers of water [Josh 9:27]).[36]

The status of Levites during the monarchy is not clear. From passages in Ezekiel (43:19; 44:15), Jeremiah (33:18–22), I Kings (13:31, "Jeroboam made priests . . . who were not Levites") and Deuteronomy (17:9; 18:1, 6 ff.), it appears that all Levites were candidates for priesthood even if not all arrived. The lowly Levites of the laws of Deuteronomy, classed with the resident alien, the orphan, and the widow (14:29; 16:14), are probably the non-priestly sort, who, lacking landholdings, were condemned to penury. If it is assumed that some of these came to serve in temples in inferior capacities, such as gatekeepers and singers, the inferior status of the Levites in the priestly writings of the Torah on the one hand, and the "Levitization" of the originally non-Levite classes of gatekeepers and singers (cf. Ezra 2:41 f. with I Chron. 23:5) can be accounted for.[37]

Portions of the people's sacrifices and dedications were assigned to the priests for their maintenance ("I gave to your father's house all the sacrifices of the Israelites" [I Sam. 2:28]; cf. Num. 18:8–20; Deut. 18:1–5). The sons of Eli wickedly seized their portions indiscriminately and by force, and before the fat (God's portion) was burnt on the altar. The variety of versions of the priests' lawful dues arises perhaps from differences in custom in various times and places, or from divergent sources. The priestly source has indeed a fuller list of perquisites than others: the skin of whole offerings, the flesh of sin and guilt offerings (excepting its "token"), the breast and thigh of peace offerings, the firstfruits, devotions, and firstlings (Lev. 6–7; 27; Num. 18:8–20). In Leviticus 27:30 ff. even the tithes of beasts and produce are claimed for the priests, though in Num. 18:21–24 tithes are the Levites' due.[38]

In theory the priests and the Levites did not obtain any tribal possession in the land; "YHWH is his [Levi's] possession, as he promised him" (Deut. 18:2, referring to Num. 18:20). Their dispersion throughout the country precluded their having a single continuous tribal allotment; but a priest might own fields (I Kings 2:26; Jer. 32:6 ff.), and a city of priests figures in the history (Nob, I Sam. 22:19). Moreover, the priestly source provides the Levites with 48 cities and surrounding fields; in Joshua 21, these cities are listed. This list (not alluded to anywhere else) has features that make it seem utopian to some scholars, though the existence of priestly towns as such is not denied.[39]

2.   PRIVATE RELIGION

Participation in public worship did not exhaust the religious life of the individual. He had many other opportunities to feel the divine presence, to address and be addressed by God: in birth and death, in eating, in sexual relations, and in his daily occupations.

Ordinary slaughter required an altar on which to dispose of the blood; otherwise, the flesh would be "eaten upon the blood," which was sinful, a "defection" from God (I Sam. 14:33). According to Lev. 17:3–7, all slaughter should bear the form of a peace offering; not only the blood but the fat too must be offered up on the altar, to keep the Israelite from sacrificing to the field-demons (the "satyrs"). [40] Both sources agree that wholly profane slaughter did not exist. Centralization of worship eventually entailed the notion of profane slaughter, to allow those far from the single sanctuary to slaughter and eat meat (Deut. 12:15–27). In the laws, the ban on eating dead or torn animals applied to all Israel (Exod. 22:30; Lev. 17:15; Deut. 14:21), though at bottom it belongs to the priesthood only (Lev. 22:8; Ezek. 44:31). The extent of lay punctiliousness about the laws of uncleanness is unknown, though awareness of them is evident: Samson's mother was warned away from all unclean food during her pregnancy (Judg. 13:7, 14). The main care must have been to stay away from contact with the holy when in an unclean state (e.g. Lev. 12:4). Genital issues were defiling, thus "sanctification" meant abstinence from sexual activity (Exod. 19:10, 15; I Sam. 20:26; 21:5 f.). Priestly laws go into much detail on this matter (Lev. 15); evidence for their observance is Bathsheba's washing in order to "sanctify" (i.e. cleanse) herself from her monthly uncleanness (I Sam. 11:4).

Life crises had their religious rites. A male child was circumcised on the eighth day after birth. The reason for circumcision is given in two versions: the main one connects it with God's covenant with Abraham, and calls circumcision "the sign of the covenant" to be kept by Abraham's descendants forever (Gen. 17). An obscure alternative etiology connects circumcision with Moses, and gives it a protective virtue against harmful supernatural attacks (Exod. 4:24 ff). Though circumcision was practiced among some of Israel's neighbors, its Israelite form was sufficiently peculiar and widespread (especially as an infant rite) to make the epithet "uncircumcised" common to all the gentiles (Gen. 34:14; Exod. 12:48; Judg. 14:3; I Sam. 14:6; Jer. 9:25). [41] The male firstborn child was considered God's property and had to be redeemed from a priest at the age of one month (Ex. 13:15; Num. 18:15 f).

Marriage and divorce seem not to have been connected with religious ritual. The earliest Jewish documents touching these (at Elephantine) have no religious reference; certain late passages are alleged to represent marriage as involving a covenant and an oath before God, but this is uncertain.[42] The etiological legend of Gen. 2:21 ff. does not make God party to or ordainer of the union of Adam and Eve, but all happens naturally; God simply provides the man with a woman to end his loneliness. Their union is not blessed or divinely sanctified. To be sure, unchastity was regarded as an offense against God: exile was the punishment for sexual immorality (Lev. 18:20); to remarry one's divorced wife after she had been married to another was to defile the land (Jer. 3:1; Deut. 24:1 ff.).

The sundering of the realm of death from the divine realm in the Bible is astonishing. In ancient Israel, as elsewhere, death must have been associated with mystery and dread-inspired practices and beliefs. The impurity caused by the dead was severe and highly contagious (Num. 19)—in all likelihood a reflection of fear of the corpse. Mourning customs included self-wounding, rending of clothes, and tearing out of hair (Jer. 16:6; 41:5), although these practices were banned in the laws (Deut. 14:1). They probably originated as protection against ghosts, to judge from extra-Israelite analogues. The obligation of burial lay upon the relatives of the dead—presumably because his ghost had no rest until his body was interred.[43] Gifts of food were made to the dead, apparently as an act of piety (Deut. 26:14). But the dead were cut off from God (Ps. 88:11; 115:17); the pre-exilic literature makes no reference either to reward and punishment in the afterlife, or to prayers on behalf of the dead, or to resurrection as in store for them. If, nonetheless, the dead were called 'ĕlōhīm "divine beings" (I Sam. 28:13; Isa. 8:19; and probably Deut. 21:23), one wonders whether the surviving literature has not in fact censored certain popular notions in which the dead played a part in the religious life of the living.[44]

A familial duty embodied in a divine ordinance was the levirate marriage, a means of perpetuating the name of the deceased upon his estate (Deut. 25:5 ff.; Ruth 5:5). A certain reluctance is evidenced concerning the performance of levirate (Gen. 38; Ruth 4), doubtless because of the uncompensated expense it entailed: rearing the "son of the deceased" (really the issue of the levir) and managing his property until he was old enough to take over himself.[45]

Everyday piety expressed itself in invocations of God and in various benedictions, such as greetings: "Come in, you blessed of YHWH; why stand outside?" (Gen. 24:31); "YHWH be with you, brave man!" (Judg. 6:12); "YHWH be with you," and its response, "May YHWH bless you" (Ruth 2:4); "The blessing of YHWH be on you," and the response, "We bless you in the name of YHWH" (Ps. 129:8). Particularly common was the oath in God's name or by his "life" (I Sam. 20:3; Amos 8:14); this was an expression of worship and devotion to him (Deut. 6:13; 10:20; Isa. 65:16; contrast Josh.

23:7). In time of trouble it was customary to take a vow, as did Absalom: "If YHWH will bring me back to Jerusalem, I will worship YHWH" (II Sam. 15:8) Payment was made by the vower's publicly proclaiming the favor God had bestowed on him at a thanksgiving sacrifice and a sacred meal attended by friends (Ps. 22:26 f.; 56:13; 66:13–20; Prov. 7:14). A more refined piety considered the verbal proclamation alone the best form of payment (Ps. 40:7–11; 69:31 f). An attractive conjecture has it that occasionally the thanksgiving was written and deposited as a memorial before God (compare Hezekiah's "letter" upon his arising from his sickbed; Isa. 38:9–20).[46]

Prayer also was a significant expression of popular faith. While public prayers usually were offered in a sanctuary ("before YHWH"), and by the clergy (Joel 2:17), an individual might pray anywhere and without mediation (Gen. 24:12; 32:10–13; Judg. 16:28; Jonah 2:1). Although individual prayers were tailored to the need of the moment, they exhibit fixed forms of supplication, thanksgiving, confession, and the like. Patterning is evident also in psalms of the individual—creations, it seems, of temple singers—through which the common man found a voice. An example of the use of ready-to-hand material is "Hannah's Psalm" (I Sam. 2). Just because this thanksgiving is obviously not tailored to Hannah's case, its attribution to Hannah reflects and thus attests to the custom of utilizing ready-made material by individual worshipers.[47]

The meaning of "detainment before YHWH" (I Sam. 21:5) and of "dwelling" or "sojourning in his Temple," mentioned in the Psalms (23:6; 27:4; 61:5), is obscure. It may refer to retirement to the Temple precinct as a religious exercise or perhaps to dedication to sacred service.

3. The Religious Aspect of Warfare

Between the premonarchic and the monarchic period a change came over the religious aspect of warfare. The popular, voluntary character of the armed force disappeared from the time of Saul and David onward with the establishment of a standing army and the employment of mercenaries. Policy was determined by considerations of state that had little to do with religion. The simple "war of YHWH" (last heard of in Saul's time; I Sam. 18:17), was replaced by war "on behalf of our people and the cities of our God" (in David's time, II Sam. 10:12)—a complex of people, national God, and territory consecrated to him.

Evidently, then, warfare was not altogether separate from religion. God's assurances before and his presence in the camp during the campaign were concerns of the army and its leaders (I Kings 8:44). Saul placated God with sacrifice before going to war (I Sam. 13:9–12), consulted the oracle in its course (14:36

f.), and kept the ark in the camp to guarantee YHWH's presence there (ibid. 14:18). David made no move without first consulting the oracle; e.g., his ascent to Hebron (II Sam. 2:1), or his Philistine wars (5:19, 23). From David's time on, prophetic oracles were regularly requested before and sometimes during military campaigns (I Kings 22; II Kings 3:11 f.; 19), since a campaign launched with divine backing was regarded as a mission of God (I Kings 8:44).[48]

Camp life was marked by religious features. As though consecrated, the soldiers kept away from women (I Sam. 21:6; II Sam. 11:11; cf. Deut. 23:10 f.), which may provide the background for the biblical idiom "to sanctify [i.e., declare] war" (Micah 3:5; Jer. 6:4). The army marched out with sacred vessels (the ark, II Sam. 11:11), a parallel to the gentile custom of bringing idols into the camp (ibid. 5:21). From Solomon's reign on, the ark indeed appears never to have left the inner sanctum of the temple; but the picture in Num. 31:10 of the young priests bearing the sacred vessels to the war with Midian—without the ark—(Num. 31:6) may reflect the custom of monarchic times (cf. the military use of trumpets in the regulation of Num. 10:9; note its setting "in your land"). A late source (II Chron. 13:12, 14; 20:21, 28) describes a battle array including trumpeters and singers.[49] The army was encouraged to believe that YHWH was in the camp, and that he went forth with them into battle (Deut. 20:1–4; 23:10–15; II Sam. 5:24; Ps. 44:60). Since victory was of YHWH (I Sam. 17:47; Ps. 3:9), part of the booty was dedicated to him—i.e., to the temple treasury (II Sam. 8:11). According to Num. 31:25–47, set proportions of booty were reserved for the various clergy; there is no corroboration of this custom from the time of the kingdom, though deposit of choice items of the booty in the temple is mentioned (I Sam. 21; cf. the analogous gentile practice, ibid: 5:3; 31:10).

During the monarchy, the ancient practice of proscribing the enemy (herem) fell into disuse. The last case recorded is from the time of Saul, who was ordered by Samuel to proscribe the Amalekites; it is significant that Saul's army refused to carry out this stern order, apparently out of self-interest (I Sam. 15). Later, when the policy of imperial conquest was inaugurated, proscription would only have been self-defeating; instead, the policy of corvée was instituted (I Kings 9:20 f.). Only the prophets clung to the notion of herem as an expression of zeal for YHWH, even later ones mentioning it as if it were an extant practice (I Kings 20:42; Micah 4:13), when in fact it had long since ceased.[50]

4. PROPHECY

The prophets stood beside the priests as mediators between the people and God; they served both as consultants and as divine messengers. Some of the prophets were men of broad vision, who gave a forward impulse to Israelite religion; these will be described later. Here the role of prophecy as one of the regular means of contact between people and God will be treated (cf. I Sam. 28:6: "[God] did not answer [Saul] either by dreams or by Urim or by prophets").

In Saul's time, there were "bands" (*hevel*, *lahăqăh*) of "prophets" whose role and relation to individual prophetic figures (such as Samuel; cf. I Sam. 19:20) is unclear. They "prophesied" in a group to the sound of music (I Sam. 10:5), an apparent reference to ecstatic raving; susceptible persons might be infected with their enthusiasm and behave like them, "madly" (*ibid.* v. 10; 19:20; 23). Their role is not described; no sermons are ascribed to them.[51] The story of the "prophesying" of the seventy elders of Israel under the impulse of Moses' "spirit" (Num. 11:24 ff.) shows that the phenomenon was considered worthy; this is also implied by Saul's being counted "among the prophets" after his coming under their spell upon being anointed (I Sam. 10:12). At the same time, the antics of the "man-of-spirit" were derided; apparently, then, the attitude toward such ecstatics was ambiguous (cf. Hos. 9:7: "The prophet is a fool; the man-of-spirit, mad"). This group phenomenon persisted throughout the monarchy, though its name changed and signs of ecstasy vanished later. From the time of the Omrides, the "sons of the prophets" appear in the north— groups living together under the aegis of a "master," an individual prophetic figure (II Kings 6:1 ff.). The "master" took care of them (*ibid.* 5:22; 4:38 ff.), and they ran errands for him (*ibid.* 9:1). Such groups appear at times without a master (II Kings 2, in Bethel and Jericho); on occasion, one of their members might be singled out by "a word of YHWH" for a prophetic mission (I Kings 20:35 ff.). The "sons of prophets" were also the objects of derision, presumably on account of their odd behavior (cf. II Kings 9:11). Elisha is the only one of the major figures who resorts to music to induce the prophetic "spirit," thus recalling the practice of "prophetic bands" of earlier times (II Kings 3:15); unlike those, however, Elisha is inspired by the spirit to give an oracle, not to inarticulate transports.

Alongside this "inspired" figure was the prophet-seer proper, also called "man of God" (sometimes, as in the case of Elisha, the two coincided). The variety of epithets indicates that what were originally separate roles may have merged in the figure of the prophet.

The basic sense of the term *nāvī'* "prophet" is "mouth of God" (cf. Ex. 4:16 with 7:1; Jer. 15:19), a divinely designated spokesman (Deut. 18:18). According to I Sam. 9:9, the prophet was formerly (i.e., in Samuel's time) called "seer," apparently meaning clairvoyant (or perhaps visionary; cf. Balaam, "who saw visions of Shadday, fallen but open eyed" [Num. 24:4, 16], or the non-Mosaic prophet of Num. 12:6, to whom God reveals himself in visions or speaks in dreams). The prophets were commonly believed to know hidden things, even when not explicitly told by God (see II Kings 5:26; 6:9, 12, 17 on Elisha's powers), though "standard" biblical doctrine ascribed such knowledge to a divine revelation (cf. esp. II Kings 4:27; similarly I Sam. 16:7; and I Kings 14:5). Such divergence probably reflects different religious levels, the vulgar inclining to a magical conception (the man of God as possessor of a "gift"), the authors of the Bible, to a more "religious" one (the prophet as dependent on the word of God). There is also a middle path—as when the man of God is believed able to issue a decree on his own, with God executing it (Elijah; I Kings 17:1).[52]

Both king and commoner resorted to the prophet. He was appealed to as a healer of man and nature (II Kings 4:22 ff; 2:19 ff; 4:38 ff.); he revealed secrets of the present and the future (e.g., the location of lost asses, I Sam. 9:6; the fate of a sick person, I Kings 14:3; II Kings 8:9). A prophet's reputation depended on his reliability: Samuel was famous from Dan to Beersheba as a prophet of YHWH, because "he did not fail to verify all that he said" (i.e., all his responses to inquiries proved true—cf. I Sam. 9:6). The success of every important public act was determined in advance by a prophetic oracle: a war campaign (see above); policy under siege (Jer. 37:16); building a temple (II Sam. 7:2).

As the intimate and confidant of God (cf. Amos 3:7; Jer. 23:18), the prophet was expected to plead the people's cause before him—whether on behalf of an individual or the community (cf. Gen. 20:7; I Kings 13:6). Interceding for the public good was so essential a part of the prophet's task that to refuse to do it was deemed a sin (I Sam. 12:23). Moses and Samuel served as archetypical prophetic intercessors (Jer. 15:1; cf. Ps. 99:6f; 106:23 with Ezek. 13:5). Many occasions of prophetic prayer on behalf of the people are noted (e.g. II Kings 19:4; Jer. 37:3; 42:2).[53]

In addition to their role as respondents and intercessors, prophets served also as messengers of God, coming unasked with a divine message. The messenger-prophet, an early attested but minor figure among the western Semites,[54] became the chief bearer of the idea of God's rule in Israel and the supervisor of God's covenant with Israel. God's rule was embodied in an unbroken line of prophets, acting and speaking in God's service on royal and national issues. It was the prophets who declared the wars of Israel the means of divine self-revelation (I Kings 20:13 f, 28, 35 ff; II Kings 3:18; 14:25). The misdeeds of kings were exposed and condemned by intrepid messengers of God (Nathan, II Sam. 12; Eliṣah, I Kings 21). In the northern kingdom, where the original principle of the conditional election of kings was maintained, prophets condemned whole dynasties to perdition; they also took part in, and even initiated conspiracies to depose kings (I Kings 11:29 ff; 14:5 ff; 16:2 ff; 21:21 ff; II

Kings 8:12 ff; 9). Theirs was a perilous opposition; the first martyrs for God were prophets of Israel who pursued their anti-monarchic mission to the death (I Kings 18:4, 13; 19:10; II Kings 9:7; Jer. 26). The prophet as messenger and the prophet as respondent are not separate figures; the man who mediated an answer to one who "inquired of YHWH," who did wonders, healed, and told the future, could on occasion be the messenger of God to foretell, warn, or reprove on his behalf. Elijah, eminently God's reproving messenger, champions prophecy's exclusive right to be consulted about the future, condemning Ahaziah's recourse to Baalzebub to learn whether he would recover from his sickness (II Kings 1). Both roles merge in Elisha's meeting with Hazael (II Kings 8:7 ff.). As respondent, the prophet attested to God's power and control of events. The apogee of this testimony is in the story of Naaman's healing: though at first the kings of both Aram and Israel ignore Elisha, in the end he makes it manifest "that there is a prophet [i.e., a spokesman of YHWH] in Israel"; and that "there is no God on earth except in Israel" (II Kings 5). Thus did prophetic interventions express the presence and government of God.

The prophets of the monarchic age mentioned in the Bible were not connected with any institution (Samuel's tie to the Shiloh sanctuary arose from his mother's vow and terminated with the sanctuary's destruction; the priesthood of Jeremiah and Ezekiel was not a factor in their call). How they earned their livelihood is unclear. In exchange for service they received gifts (I Sam. 9:7; I Kings 14:3); mention is once made of firstfruit loaves brought to Elisha (II Kings 4:43). On new moon and Sabbath, visits were paid to the prophet (II Kings 4:23) for reasons unknown; perhaps then too gifts were presented. This practice opened the way to corruption; Micah reproaches "the prophets who mislead my people, who predict prosperity when their mouth is filled; but if one does not put something into their mouths, they declare war against him" (3:5). The later literary prophets are not described as rewarded for service.

There are some indications of temple and court prophets. While still a fugitive from Saul, David had Gad as his prophet; when he became king, Gad was "the king's seer" (II Sam. 24:11). The prophet Nathan, too, appears as a royal advisor. Hundreds of prophets were in the service of the northern kings (I Kings 22:6; II Kings 3:13), and royal officials did not hesitate to instruct them how to prophesy so as to please the king (I Kings 22:13). Like the Baal prophets (I Kings 18:19), these must have "eaten at the king's table," that is, served as royal pensioners.[54a]

A connection of prophets with the temple is suggested by the fixed word pair "priest-prophet" (e.g. Isa. 28:7; Jer. 4:9; 14:18), and by passages placing both in the temple (Jer. 23:11; 26:7; Lam. 2:20). In Jeremiah's time, a temple chamber belonged to "the sons of the man of God" (35:4). The use of the verb "prophesy" for the singing of the temple singers in the book of Chronicles (I 25:1–5) suggests an institution of prophet-musicians that can only have arisen during the monarchy. A lively picture of the work of such a functionary is given in II Chronicles 20:4: after King Jehoshaphat's public prayer in the temple court, a Levite singer was inspired on the spot to deliver a prophecy of victory. The sudden shift from anxious plea to expressions of confidence in several psalms (e.g. 20:7) has been explained by the intervention of a temple prophet with an oracle of deliverance in the course of the prayer.[55]

In Jeremiah's time, prophets were counted among the leading classes, after "kings, officers, priests," and before "the people of the land" (Jer. 8:1; 13:13; 32:32). The "instruction" of priest, the "counsel" of sages, and the "word of YHWH" from the prophet were all state assets (Jer. 18:18; Ezek. 7:26). Prophets participated in shaping policy and advocating it among the people. That is why they were excoriated by the classical prophets in whose writings every "prophet" is of this institutionalized sort.

5. POPULAR BELIEF

Allusions in prophetic literature indicate that the public was generally familiar with tales of God's dealings with the patriarchs, the bondage and the Exodus, the wanderings, the expulsion of the Amorites and the settlement of Canaan. God had singled Israel out of the nations and on the basis of his deliverances, had made a covenant with them, obligating them to serve him alone, and to obey his commandments. His blessing would be with those who obeyed him, his curse on those who defied him (Amos 2:4, 10 f.; Hosea 8:1, 12; 12:4 f., 14; Micah 6:4 f.; Jer. 2; Ezek. 33:24).

The idea of the law collections (in the Torah) is that the obligation to keep the terms of the covenant lay on every single Israelite. A ripe formulation of that idea is Ex. 19:6: "You shall be to me a kingdom of priests and a holy nation"; that is, the entire citizenry must observe a level of holiness and nearness to God that is proper to priests.[56] Note, for example, the formulation in Exodus of the ban on eating torn flesh: "You shall be to me holy men; torn flesh in the field you shall not eat" (Ex. 22:30). In origin, this ban applied to priests only, and was designed to keep them in a constant state of purity—i.e., cultic readiness (Lev. 22:8; Ezek. 44:31). In its Exodus form it applies to all Israelites and thus makes the narrow formulation (in Leviticus and Ezekiel) puzzling to exegetes.[57] The bans on cutting the hair at the corners of the head and gashing oneself for the dead apply to all Israel (Lev. 19:27 f.), though these too properly belonged only to priests (Lev. 21:4 f.; note the grounding of the law in the holiness and sacred service of priests; the language of the ban in Deut. 14:1–2 likewise applies to the whole nation epithets of holiness proper to priests [Lev. 21:6]).

If every man had to fulfil the terms of the covenant, the terms had to be published. Accordingly, tradition had it that the Decalogue was proclaimed in the hearing of all Israel (Exod. 20:18–22; Deut. 5). The rest of the covenantal law collections are set in a narrative framework with Moses proclaiming them to all Israel. The covenant rite described in Exod. 24 includes the public recitation of the terms (the laws) in the hearing of all the people. Deuteronomy provides for the proclamation of the Torah to the assembled people, "men, women, children, and the stranger in your gates," once every seven years, in a re-enactment of the great "day of assembly" at the Sinai lawgiving (Deut. 31:10 ff.; cf. 4:10).

How far this ideal was realized is unknown. The tradition of the Mosaic covenant-making, with the stipulations proclaimed in the hearing of all, evidently served as a model for the covenant rite in the time of Josiah (II Kings 23:2), since it is unlikely (and unreported) that the rite was invented by the king. It must therefore be assumed that the tradition of the covenant in Moses' time was transmitted through the centuries in some established, institutionalized form. The enshrining of traditions of the Exodus in cultic forms—such as the festival of *maṣṣōt* (Ex. 12:25 f.)—suggests the possibility of other regular cultic commemorations of divine interventions in history. Modern scholars have attempted to reconstruct a festival of covenant celebration (or renewal), with the story of the Sinai lawgiving (Ex. 19–24) as its dramatic "script" (or "liturgy"). Verses in Psalm 81, combining trumpet blasts on new moon and at mid-month with verbal reminiscences of the Exodus and lawgiving are taken as evidence for the connection of the period of the autumn festivals (from the new moon of Tishri to the *Sukkōt* festival starting at mid-month) with commemoration of the covenant. Further support is found in the fact that Deuteronomy's septennial assembly for proclamation of the Torah coincides with the *Sukkōt* festival (Deut. 31:10 ff.).[58]

How far did the people as a whole observe the laws of holiness and religion? The biblical histories offer only a few bits of testimony. Saul rigorously enforces among his soldiers the ban of "eating on the blood" (I Sam. 14:32 ff.); this ban is therefore ancient, despite the fact that otherwise it appears only in Leviticus and Ezekiel. Cleansing from menstrual impurity, ordained in Lev. 15, is practiced by Bathsheba and is the occasion of David's great sin (II Sam. 11:4). The requirement of purity for a family sacrifice is alluded to in I Samuel 20:26; cf. Lev. 7:20. That Sabbath and new moon were rest-days in the northern kingdom is proven by Amos' rebuke of merchants impatient for them to be over (Amos 8:5), and by the Shunamite husband's amazement at his wife's visit to the prophet "not on Sabbath or new moon" (II Kings 4:23).

The God of Israel was "the king, YHWH of hosts" (Isa. 6:5); he was hymned as "the king of glory" (Ps. 24:7 ff.), "the great king over all the earth (Ps. 47:3, 8) "the great king" (Ps. 48:3). His throne and seat were in heaven (I Kings 22:19; Isa. 6:1; Ps. 2:4), and he was called "He who sits (or: is enthroned) upon the cherubs," after his cherubic bearers, who apparently were imagined as forming his throne (II Sam. 6:2; Ps. 80:2; 99:1; cf. the lions of Solomon's throne, I Kings 10:19).[59] He had the suite of a great divine king—seraphim, "the hosts of heaven" (I Kings 22:19; Isa. 6:1), "divine beings" (Ps. 29:1), and officers (e.g. "the chief of the army of YHWH" [Josh. 5:14]). The biblical authors distinguished sharply between God and his suite: he alone could be worshiped. The common practice, however, was less discriminating. Ps. 16:3 f. indicates that "holy ones" and "mighty ones" were worshiped "in the land;" in the 7th century several references are made to the worship of the host of heaven (Zeph. 1:5; Jer. 8:2). That the people should have revered them is no wonder, since even the biblical authors ascribed "dominion" to the sun and the moon (Gen. 1:15). Psalm 83 reflects a protest against the entrenched idea that government of the world was parcelled out among the divine beings. Deut. 32:8 f. describes this parcelling: "He [i.e., the Most High] fixed the bounds of the peoples/According to the number of divine beings" (reading *bny 'l[m?]* with a Qumran fragment and the Septuagint). Divine government thus had two levels: a higher, that of the "Gods of gods" (Deut. 10:17), who at the beginning reserved Israel for himself (32:9), and a lower, that of his suite, to whom the rest of the peoples were allocated. Now, if the biblical authors themselves assigned dominions to members of the divine suite, simple folk could hardly be blamed for rendering them homage. The point seems long to have been an issue; note the insistence of Deut. 4:19 that sun, moon, and stars have been allotted to the gentiles and must therefore not be worshiped by Israel.

The named gods of the nations (e.g. Ashtoret, Baal) were regarded equivocally. On the one hand, biblical authors dismiss them as "the empty things of the nations" (Jer. 14:22; cf. Deut. 32:21), as man-made idols, as wood and stone (Isa. 37:19). On the other hand, some acknowledgment of their substantiality existed; when, under Israelite-Edomite siege, Mesha king of Moab publicly sacrificed his child, there was "great wrath upon Israel" (II Kings 3:27)—the reference is most naturally to a baleful emanation of the pagan god's power.[60] To call the heathen gods "demons" (Deut. 32:17, and in the late Ps. 106:37) was also to attribute reality to them.

To what extent did alien customs and beliefs affect Israelite religion? When Israelite kings married foreign women, the wives brought their native cults and planted them on Israel's soil. What the covenant laws warned against in this respect (Exod. 34:15; Deut. 7:3 f.) was realized in the case of kings Solomon

(I Kings 11:1–6) and Ahab (Ib. 16:31 ff.); they were "diverted" from Israel's God by their wives. The intermarriage of commoners must have had similar results, though no direct testimony to this is given. But the exact sense of this "diverting" is unclear: Ahab's sons have names with the theophoric element ya(hu)—Ahaziah, Jehoram—and in all the narratives he himself is depicted as a worshiper of Israel's God. The indictment seems therefore a reflection on his building a temple and an altar to Baal in Samaria (or in a particular "town" [quarter?] nearby the king's seat [cf. II Kings 10:25]); more precisely, on his allowing and maintaining the Baal worship of his Sidonian wife. In all likelihood this was Solomon's case too: the biblical author, who recognized no shades in idolatry, did not discriminate between Solomon's permitting pagan cults on Israelite soil and maintaining them out of the public treasury, and his outright worship of pagan gods.[61] However that may be, the court was for generations a nest of pagan cults imported with foreign wives (cf. also I Kings 15:13).

A Canaanite population, concentrated in the valley of Jezreel and along the coast, was absorbed into the kingdom of Israel when it expanded during the reign of David and Solomon (I Kings 9:20 f.).[62] The assimilation of this alien mass probably affected the character of the popular religion; perhaps this is reflected in the figurines common to early Israelite and Canaanite levels in city-mounds in the land. In Judah, the qādēš appeared (I Kings 14:24; 22:47)—perhaps a male functionary of the fertility cult, alien to biblical religion but known from the customs of western Semites; zealous Judean kings more than once purged the qādēš (I Kings 15:12; 22, 47; II Kings 23:7). The practice of burning children for the gods is explicitly ascribed to the Canaanites (Deut. 12:31) and the Sepharvites who were settled in the north after the exile of the northern kingdom (II Kings 17:21). In Jeremiah 7:31; 19:5; 32:35 the Judahites are censured for burning their sons and daughters on bāmōt in the valley of Hinnom. According to the latter two passages, this was the worship of Baal or Molech; yet the insistence of the prophet that YHWH "never commanded, or spoke, or imagined it" points to the God of Israel as the object of worship. The Tophet in the valley of Hinnom, where one "passed his son and daughter through the fire to Molech" was among the idolatrous appurtenances that Josiah polluted (II Kings 23:10). This practice, an imitation of the "abominations of the nations that YHWH drove out before the Israelites," is ascribed to Ahaz (II Kings 16:3). The passages about Molech in the Torah (Lev. 18:21; 20:2 ff.) may be interpreted as meaning dedication to idolatrous service; ancient opinion favored this over the notion of actually burning babies (cf. the summary given in Naḥmanides' commentary to Lev. 18:21), and latterly some support from Assyrian usage has been adduced for this interpretation. But even if with respect to Molech there is room for doubt, the expression "to burn in fire" is unambiguous evidence of child sacrifice in Judah under foreign influence.[63]

Magical beliefs common to all mankind were current in Israel. This occult realm of knowledge and power was sought directly, without divine mediation. Necromancy, sorcery, and divination were practiced (I Sam. 28; Isa. 8:19; II Kings 21:6; Ezek. 13:17 ff.), despite the prohibition in the Torah (e.g. Ex. 22:17; Deut. 18:9 ff.); pious kings enforced the ban zealously (I Sam. 28:3; II Kings 23:24), but the practices survived (cf. I Sam. 28:7; Isa. 8:19 ff.). Ezekiel denounces sorceresses who "for bits of bread and handfuls of barley" condemn to death and decree life (Ezek. 13:17 ff.). Few details are recorded, but such "abominations" are counted among the reasons for Israel's fall (II Kings 17:17; 21:6). The biblical authors, like the common folk, believed in the reality of magic, but precisely for that reason they regarded it as an encroachment on God's prerogatives. The Israelite must be "wholehearted" with God; he must submit himself wholly to him and eschew recourse to magic and all other sources of power and knowledge. God gave Israel prophets, and whatever magicians did for their clients the prophet in Israel could do for those who sought YHWH through him (Deut. 18:14 ff.).

C. Dynamic Elements in the Religion of the Monarchy: Prophecy and Reform Movements

1. Prophecy and the Monarchy

The critical and innovative element in Israelite religion was prophecy. The religion originated with a man of God: Moses, a messenger of God, who brought tidings of redemption, made the people enter into a covenant with God and fashioned the basic forms of worship. The prophet Samuel established the monarchy, and from then on tension existed between God's word and the command of the king. The monarchy became the focus of prophetic activity because the king was conceived of as the representative of the people before God (largely owing to his responsibility for maintaining the public worship); hence the king was the object of constant prophetic observation and censure.

David was served by two court prophets: "the prophet Gad, the king's seer" (II Sam. 24:11; cf. II Chron. 29:25), and Nathan, who appears as both counselor and censor (II Sam. 7:1 ff.; 12:1–15). Through Nathan the idea of a chosen eternal dynasty arose. God's promise to David—"Your house and your kingship will stand fast forever before me [reading *l^efānay*]; your throne will last forever" (7:16)—changed the conditional conception of royal election that originated with Samuel. This was a conscious, deliberate change: "I will not break my faith with him [the Davidide], as I broke it with Saul" (v. 15). This promise came to be called a "covenant," and titles "son" or "firstborn" of God that applied to Israel as God's covenant-partner (Exod. 4:22; Deut. 14:1; 32:6, 19 f.; Isa. 1:2) were attached to the Davidic king (Ps. 2:7; 89:27 f.). The Davidic dynasty was conceived as the means by which God would fulfil his covenant promises to Israel. Beside Nathan's dynastic oracle, prophecies supported the founding of the Jerusalem Temple. Tradition identified the temple site with the threshing floor of Arawna the Jebusite (II Chron. 3:1), where the prophet Gad had directed David to build an altar to commemorate the end of a plague (II Sam. 24:18, 25). An oracle on the election of Jerusalem as God's seat is found in Ps. 132:13; it accords with the divine promise to David that his son would build a house for God's name (II Sam. 7:13).[64]

While in the kingdom of Judah the election of the Davidic dynasty was conceived of as permanent, northern prophecy clung to the original conception of Samuel: kingship was conditioned upon obedience to the word of God; disobedience doomed the king and his dynasty. The prime adherent of Samuel's idea, so different from Nathan's oracle to David, was Ahijah the Shilonite, who provoked Jeroboam son of Nebat to rebel against Solomon because of his worship of foreign gods (I Kings 11:29-40). Ahijah himself later announced to Jeroboam that his house would also be cut off for his sins (14:7-15). To the end, northern prophecy maintained the notion of conditional royal election. In their passionate defense of the God of Israel, northern prophets foretold the end of dynasties and incited rebellion (II Kings 9:1-10). By so doing they contributed materially to the instability of the northern kingdom, which, in this respect differed remarkably from the stable Judahite monarchy of Davidides.[65]

According to the book of Kings, tension between prophet and king almost always arose because of an offense against God's covenant with Israel. There seems to have been a fundamental difference between the rulers and the prophets, though nothing suggests that the rulers intended to do away with the special relation of Israel to its national God. The policy of international cooperation and alliance often involved intermarriage with foreign princesses, who as a matter of course imported their familiar cults, which the Israelite kings were bound to respect and maintain. Solomon showed scruple in erecting the shrines of his wives' gods outside Jerusalem, the city of God, "on the mountain that was opposite Jerusalem, to the south of Mount *Mašhit*" (= the southern extension of the Mount of Olives; I Kings 11:7; II Kings 23:13). Yet the very patronage of these installations by an Israelite king, and the dedication of parcels of the land of Israel and funds out of the public treasury to foreign gods, enraged such zealots as Ahijah. King Asa's mother made "a 'horror' for Asherah" which, with other pagan appurtenances was purged by Asa and his son Jehoshaphat (I Kings 15:12 f; 22:47). Prophets are not mentioned in connection with these purges; to judge from the uprising against Athaliah (II Kings 11), in Judah it was the priesthood that "kept the charge of YHWH," the role played in the northern kingdom by prophets.

The Omrides, who stabilized the northern kingdom formed ties with neighboring states after the pattern set by David and Solomon. Ahab's marriage to Jezebel, the Sidonian princess, brought the Phoenician Baal into Samaria. A Baal temple was built in Samaria (I Kings 16:32), and hundreds of "prophets" of Baal and Asherah were pensioners of the queen (18:19). The vehement, protracted opposition of bands of northern prophets, among whom the figures of Elijah and Elisha stand out, indicates that they regarded this cult as dangerous to the faith of the masses (cf. I Kings 19:14, 18).

That the foreign cults in Judah never provoked such violence suggests that the danger to the national religion was greater in the north than in the south. Two reasons for this can be conjectured: the proximity of the north to such major centers of alien culture as Aram and Phoenicia with whom close trade and war relations were maintained; and the considerable Canaanite element in the population, particularly of the valleys and coast, only recently annexed to the Israelite kingdom, and as yet hardly assimilated. Queen Jezebel's zealous practice of her Canaanite-Phoenician cult, with the publicity and prominence it must have enjoyed in Samaria, not only checked the process of assimilation by officially endorsing an alien worship, but may well have attracted Israelites. Courtiers and royal merchants who had constant and close relations with the Phoenicians would have favored blurring cultural-religious boundaries, and adopting "the international style," then current, of syncretizing gods and cults.[66] We need not take literally the reproach that only "seven thousand" remained "whose knees had not bent to Baal and whose mouth had not kissed him" (I Kings 19:18), but its background was probably a considerable spread of Baal worship, especially among the aristocracy.

Since zealotry and persecution are uncharacteristic of paganism, Jezebel's war against the prophets of Israel was probably in reaction to an attack they initiated against her alien cult. If YHWH's altar on Carmel was demolished (I Kings 18:30), a Baal installation was in all likelihood demolished first. The zealotry of the prophets can be estimated from the way they incited and carried out purges when they were able to do so (I Kings 18:40; II Kings 10:1–10). A religious war broke out between the devotees of YHWH, headed by Elijah, and the worshippers of Baal, protected by the queen. King Ahab himself was hardly involved. Not he, but his wife, threatened Elijah's life; he searched for Elijah "in every nation and kingdom" not to kill him but to make him cancel the famine he decreed (I Kings 18:1–18). After his victory on Mt. Carmel, Elijah was reconciled with the king, and "ran ahead of his chariot." The king never consulted other than prophets of YHWH. What appears as religious equivocation results from differing notions of loyalty to Israel's God. The court permitted itself to enter into alliances with pagan neighbors and practiced the tactful toleration that necessarily accompanied this policy; prophecy, however, took an uncompromising position. The religious state of the mass of people may be inferred from the Elisha-Elijah stories. In them, the rural background does not appear to be pagan; no religious conflict is evident. The countryside worships YHWH loyally and as a matter of course; only in the metropolis, Samaria, and its extensions, are there Baal worshipers and followers.

This is the manifest background of the First Hosea (Hos. 1–3), who denounces Samaria's forsaking her divine husband to follow "Baals." The prophet alludes to a distinction between the people and their rulers: he calls on the "children" (the people) to rebuke their "mother" (the rulers) who played false to her "husband" (God). He foretells a forced return to the desert, where the people would be purged and made fit for a new "wedding" with its God.[67]

Joram son of Ahab removed the Baal pillar (II Kings 3:2), but no basic change was made till Jehu's rebellion which, incited by Elisha, did away with the Omrides and extirpated the Baal cult. Jehu was aided by the Rechabites, a zealot order who withdrew from city life and abstained from wine (II Kings 10:15, 23; Jer. 35). The custom of the Rechabites was one reaction to the inexorable urbanization that accompanied the advance of material civilization: the conviction that the true Israelite way of life and worship was the simple, pristine manner characteristic of the Wilderness period (cf. Hos. 2:16 ff.).[68] According to II Kings 10, Jehu did away with the Baal cult at one blow: having gathered the devotees by a ruse into the Baal temple of Samaria, he massacred them, burned down the house, destroyed its appurtenances, and then turned the site into a public toilet. The cult never again appeared in the north; the Second Hosea (4–14) speaks of it only as a phenomenon of the past (11:1; 13:1).

The marriage of Athaliah (daughter of Ahab and Jezebel) to the Judahite Joram son of Jehoshaphat brought the Baal cult into Judah. A temple to Baal was built, apparently in Jerusalem, in which one Mattan ministered as priest (II Kings 11:18). When Jehu assassinated Athaliah's son, King Ahaziah of Judah, the queen mother took over for six years. The priest Jehoiada led an insurrection against her (apparently Judah had as yet no body of active prophets), which ended with her death and the extirpation of the Baal cult. The success was crowned by a three-way covenant between YHWH, the king, and the people, to be "YHWH's people." The reign of the non-Davidide Athaliah and the

Baal worship she sponsored were evidently regarded as having broken the covenant that bound the three since the time of David. Operative here is the basic idea of the Davidides that YHWH's covenant with his people is mediated through his covenant with the royal dynasty; when the dynastic covenant is broken, so is the covenant with the people.[69] With this purge, the Baal cult disappeared in Judah till the time of Manasseh.

By the 9th century, the northern prophets had become institutionalized, and the accompanying decay began to show. On the one hand, the prophets respected the king as the mediator of God's blessing to his people, particularly in the military sphere. I Kings 20 approvingly depicts prophetic support of a beleaguered king. During an Aramean attack on Samaria, a prophet approached Ahab with a victory oracle, "that you may know that I am YHWH" (v. 28). The Aramean king was declared God's "proscribed man" ('īš ḥermī)— the relic of an ancient notion that for centuries had played no part in Israel's warfare with its enemies (v. 42). Thus prophets bestowed religious significance upon acts determined chiefly by political and utilitarian motives. They tried to raise the events of Israel's national life above the mere ambitions of kings. To them, history was the arena in which God's will was manifest—that was the message of Jehu son of Hanani (I Kings 16), of Elijah, Elisha, Micaiah, and of Jonah son of Amittai, the last of the northern prophets mentioned in the book of Kings (II Kings 14:25).

On the debit side, however, was the subservience entailed by the prophets' connection with the king, vividly portrayed in I Kings 22. Four hundred prophets were collected by the king of Israel to give him an oracle on the eve of his campaign to Ramoth-gilead (I Kings 22); their victory oracle flattered the king's vanity. Unlike the lone prophet of chap. 20, these did not come on their own, moved by a divine mission, but rather in dutiful response to a royal summons. Their message served to enhance not God's fame, but the king's, "Go up . . . and win, for YHWH will deliver into the hand of the king" (v. 12). The horns that Zedekiah son of Chenaanah produced symbolized the strength of the king, not of God, "who has the eminences of a wild ox" (Num 23:22). These prophets, in all likelihood pensioners of the king, exemplified the objects of Micah's taunt, "The prophets who mislead my people, who predict prosperity when their mouth is filled; but if one does not put something in their mouths, they declare war against him" (Micah 3:5). Their corruption is pointed up by the friendly advice the king's messenger gives to the independent Micaiah ben Imlah; "Let your message be like that of theirs; promise success!" (ibid. v. 13). Even the courtiers assumed the prophet's compliance with the royal wish.

The crisis of prophetic independence came during this period of Aramean

1.
Samaria: General view from the west

2.

Hazor: General view of Area A: a) Stratum X: Solomonic gate and casemate wall; b) Stratum VIII: House with columns from the time of Ahab; c) Stratum VI: Villa from the time of Jeroboam II   Courtesy Prof. Y. Yadin

3.
Beer-sheba: Aerial view   Courtesy Prof. Y. Aharoni

4.
Megiddo: Solomonic city-gate   Courtesy Oriental Institute, University of Chicago

5.
Tel Dan: Paved entrance of the city-gate, Israelite Period   Courtesy Prof. A. Biran

6.
Gezer: Solomonic city-gate   Courtesy Prof. W. G. Dever

7.
Ashdod: General view
of the city-gates, Israelite
Period

Courtesy Prof. M. Dothan

8.
Beer-sheba: Area of the
city-gate

Courtesy Prof. Y. Aharoni

9

Megiddo: Aerial view of palace 1723, 10th century B.C.E.

Courtesy Oriental Institute, University of Chicago

Proto-Ionic capital from Megiddo   Courtesy Oriental Institute, University of Chicago

11.
Ramat Raḥel: Wall of the
palace, the stones laid as
headers and stretchers
Courtesy Prof. Y. Aharoni

12.
Ramat Raḥel: Window
balustrade discovered in
1934
Courtesy Israel Department of
Antiquities, Jerusalem

13. Ramat Raḥel: Window balustrade   Courtesy Prof. Y. Aharoni

14.
Tell es-Sa'idiyeh: The water-system of the 11th century B.C.E.   Courtesy Prof. J. B. Pritchard

15.

Hazor: Water-system from the time of Ahab   Courtesy Prof. Y. Yadin

16.

Hazor: Water-system; the shaft and entrance to
the tunnel

Courtesy Prof. Y. Yadin

17.

Megiddo: Water-tunnel from the time of
Ahab

Courtesy Oriental Institute, University of Chicago

18.
The pool at Gibeon   Courtesy Prof. J. B. Pritchard

Gibeon: Staircase in the water-tunnel Courtesy Prof. J. B. Pritchard

20.
Tell es-Saʻidiyeh: Street flanked by houses, Israelite Period   Courtesy Prof. J. B. Pritchard

wars. The monarchy's part in international coalitions, intermarriages, and the establishment of alien cults on Israelite soil excited prophetic zealots against the kings. But Israel's struggle for survival was also regarded as a test of its God's power, and roused concern for the fame of YHWH that favored royal enterprises. Two conflicting prophetic styles arose: a prophecy of denunciation and doom directed against the king's breaches of the covenant, and a prophecy of victory over Israel's enemies, with the aim of glorifying Israel's God. The collision of these raised the problem of distinguishing false from true prophecy, first recorded in the story of Micaiah (I Kings 22). The test of Deut. 18:22 is already applied in this story: "When a prophet speaks in the name of YHWH, and his prediction does not come true—that is what YHWH has not spoken; the prophet spoke it presumptuously, you must not fear him." Accordingly, the king of Israel imprisoned Micaiah, "until my safe return," when, as a manifestly false prophet, he should be put to death.[70]

New ideas emerged from the prophecy of doom. The first martyrs came from these prophets, "servants of God," whose bloodshed God must avenge (I Kings 18:4, 13; II Kings 9:7). They originated the ideas of the "righteous remnant" who should escape the general doom, and of the foreign enemy whom God would appoint to punish the wicked of his people. In tears, Elisha foretold to the Aramean Hazael the future suffering he would inflict upon Israel (II Kings 5:12); this only fulfilled the plan of punishment for Baal worship that Elijah had already received (I Kings 19:15 ff.).

It was typical of the northern opposition prophets that they worked to fulfil their oracles. Not content with mere speech, Ahijah the Shilonite, Elijah and his contemporaries all set actions afoot, not hesitating even to incite insurrection.

Victory prophecy also produced a new idea: the king destined by God to save his people. The aged and ailing Elisha saw in Joash the man destined to deliver Israel from the ravages of the Arameans; accordingly, he ordered him to shoot "an arrow of victory" toward Damascus (II Kings 13:17). Jonah ben Amittai regarded Jeroboam son of Joash as the savior of Israel, who would restore the kingdom to its former boundaries (14:25 f.). "Messianic" hopes were thus pinned on northern kings before they were pinned on Davidides. A related conception of victory prophecy was "the day of YHWH," a time when God's judgment would fall upon Israel's enemies, with terrifying signs and portents in heaven and on earth. The description of the "day" in Obadiah may be taken as reflecting the early notion alluded to in Amos 5:18—where, contrary to the peculiar later prophetic skewing, the "day" is a joyous triumph of Israel over its enemies.[71]

2. CLASSICAL PROPHECY

The Aramean wars aggravated the social cleavage caused primarily by the urbanization of Israel. The mass of rural population grew poor and landless as the ruling class grew wealthy and powerful. Natural disasters—drought and agricultural pests (Amos 4:6 ff.)—hastened the process of dispossession. Godfearing men saw these as sure signs of God's wrath. But if misfortune chose as its victim the dynasty of Jehu, whose founder purged the land once for all of the Baal cult, its traditional explanation as punishment for worship of alien gods could no longer serve. The author of Kings has recourse to the jejune "sins of Jeroboam" to account for this time of troubles; II Kings 10:31 f.; 13:2, 6,[72] 11. Out of the crisis of faith, classical prophecy was born, with its new conception of the essence of the covenant, and a new definition of what violation of it meant.

The first of the new prophets was Amos of Judahite Tekoa. "Not a prophet nor a son of a prophet," he was called from his sheep to prophecy in Bethel during the good years of the reign of Jeroboam II. He interpreted the natural disasters that struck at that time as warnings to repent. What sins must be abandoned? Oppression of the poor, the crushing of the needy, wanton and profligate behavior. What value had an ostentatious worship that venerated temples more than of God? Morally callous, glorying in their victories, Israel had forgotten God; for that they were doomed to exile and their land to destruction.

In Amos' prophecy, the moral component of the covenant was for the first time given priority over the cultic. The worship tendered by villains was worse than worthless; it was hateful to YHWH:

> I hate, I despise your feasts
> And I take no pleasure in your solemn assemblies
> Though you offer up to me your whole offerings
> And your meal offerings, I will not accept them . . .
> Take away from me the noise of your songs;
> To the melody of your lyres I will not listen.
> But let justice well forth like water,
> And righteousness, like a perennial stream.
> Did you make sacrifices and meal offerings to me in the
> Wilderness forty years, O House of Israel? (5:21-25).

Seeking God, which Amos contrasted with resorting to (the temples of) Bethel, Gilgal, and Beersheba, meant: "Seek good and not evil . . . Hate evil and love good, and establish justice in the gate" (5:4 ff, 14 ff.). He predicted that the curses of the covenant—blasting, mildew, plague, exile and destruction (cf. Deut. 28)—would come upon Israel for violation of the moral laws. Here was a major innovation; the notions then current, deriving from the old covenant documents themselves, singled out apostasy as the sin in whose wake national doom would follow. Amos' revolutionary message, so apt for the circumstances, was not accepted. Amaziah, the priest of Bethel, expelled the prophet from the temple city under indictment for treason since he had prophesied the king's death and his kingdom's exile.[73]

After the death of Jeroboam II, Israel was wracked for years by political turmoil, civil strife, and rapid changes of kings. The kingdom became tributary to Assyria, while subject to native adventurers who battened on its misfortune. The monarchy, emptied of all spiritual content, became an institution dedicated solely to power and exploitation. Against this background, the only classical prophet of the north, the Second Hosea (Hos. 4–14), appeared.

Second Hosea berated his generation for loss of loyalty (*hesed*) and devotion (*da'at*) to God (4:1–6). Authority was gone (10:3); kingship had lost its divine sanction ("they made kings, not from me; made officers, but I knew it not;" 8:4). The people put their trust in human works—in the calf of Samaria, in the numerous altars and pillars, in the multitude of castles and fortified cities (8:14), in Assyria, and in Egypt (5:13; 7:11). Having put God out of mind, their punishment was sure: their cities would be razed, their altars torn down, Egypt and Assyria would be the lands of their exile. There was but one remedy: penitent return to God. The prophet dictated a confession: "Assyria shall not save us; we will not ride on horses, or ever again call the work of our hands 'our God'" (14:4).

Hosea was the first to denounce the power politics of the state, its reliance on weapons and alliances instead of on God. His censure of the north's worship is especially notable. Performed "on mountain tops and on hills," it was polluted with fornication (4:13 f.); Ephraim made many altars—"like heaps on the furrows of the fields" (12:12)—for sinning (8:11). Hosea repeatedly condemns the calf-images of the north—"they made a molten image of their silver . . . nothing more than a craftsman's work" (13:2), "a no-god" (8:5). No other prophet so sweepingly invalidated the people's worship, not because it was offered to other gods, but because it was Godless; a consecration of places and things instead of devotion to God.[74]

The last king of Israel, Hoshea son of Elah, is said to have done what was evil in the sight of YHWH, "only not like the kings of Israel that preceded him" (II Kings 17:2). Moreover, Hoshea is the only Israelite king exempted from the censure of having followed the evil ways of Jeroboam son of Nebat; this may hint at a removal of the golden calves, which so exercised the king's prophetic namesake. Hoshea's revolt against Assyria ended with the final exile of the north. But the literary and prophetic heritage of the northern kingdom was salvaged, transferred to Judah, and there absorbed; the exile of her elder sister bequeathed to Judah a great spiritual reinforcement. Northern influence is to be recognized in the rapid and wonderful quickening of the spiritual life of Judah at the end of the 8th century.

In the first half of the 8th century, under King Uzziah, Judah too had enjoyed prosperity and political success. As in Israel, these were accompanied by corruption and social polarization. Close upon Amos, and remarkably similar in his social message, came the first Judahite prophet, Isaiah son of Amos. His first prophecies excoriated the decay of solidarity and social responsibility, rejected the piety of the villainous Jerusalemite aristocracy, and called for repentance on pain of dire punishment.

> Hear the word of YHWH, chiefs of Sodom;
> Give ear to the teaching of our God, O people of Gomorrah.
> What do your many sacrifices mean to me, says YHWH,
> I am sated with offerings of rams and the fat of oxen;
> I have no taste for the blood of bulls and lambs and goats.
> Your newmoons and festivals I abhor; they are a burden to me;
> I cannot stand them.
> When you spread forth your hands, I will close my eyes to you;
> Even though you pray much, I will not listen;
> For your hands are full of blood.
> Wash, purge yourselves, remove your wicked deeds from my sight!
> Stop doing evil; learn to do good;
> Seek justice; defend the right of the deprived;
> Vindicate the orphan; champion the widow!
> If you are agreeable and obedient,
> You will eat the best of the land;
> But if you refuse and rebel,
> You will be eaten by the sword.
> The mouth of YHWH has spoken it (1:10–20).

The Syro-Ephraimite attack on Judah drove the prophet into the political arena. He demanded trust in God and denounced the plan of King Ahaz to call upon Assyria for help. The king did not listen to him, whereupon the prophet foretold an Assyrian attack upon Judah. Soon Damascus and Samaria bowed before the armies of Assyria, and Judah followed suit during the reigns of Ahaz and Hezekiah. Assyria's trail of ruthless and irresistable conquest opened the eyes of the prophet to a larger vision: the Assyrian world empire was merely a prelude to the final stage of God's grand design. The culmination would be the redemption forever of Israel and the world from heathen tyranny. For after YHWH had used Assyria to scourge the wicked, he would punish the pride of the haughty king who had far exceeded his commission. Assyria would fall miraculously on the mountains of Judah, and its yoke would be removed from the necks of all the nations. A righteous king would ascend Zion's throne, a shoot from the stock of Jesse, in whose time peace, blessing, and righteousness would prevail in the land. Out of fear of YHWH the nations would throw away their idols and say:

> "Come let us go up to the mountain of YHWH,
> To the temple of the God of Jacob,
> That he may instruct us in his ways,
> And that we might follow his paths.
> For out of Zion instruction goes forth,
> And the word of YHWH from Jerusalem."
> Then He will judge between nations,
> And arbitrate for many peoples;
> So they will beat their swords into plowshares,
> And their spears into pruninghooks;
> Nation will not lift up sword against nation
> Nor will they experience war any more. (2:3 f.).

The prophet's faith in the eternity of Jerusalem and the Davidic dynasty stood firm when King Hezekiah's rebellion against Sennacherib brought disaster upon Judah. Isaiah deprecated the alliance that Hezekiah made with Egypt in preparation for the rebellion; he deemed it an insult to YHWH (chaps. 30–31). When the Assyrian king crushed the rebels, devastated Judah, and laid siege to Jerusalem, the prophet was unshaken in his faith that God would not surrender his city to the blaspheming enemy. He urged Hezekiah not to comply with the Assyrian demand to open the gates, and his faith was repaid.

Three great themes thus run through Isaiah's prophecy: indignation over the moral obtuseness of the upper class of Judah; the vision of God's grand design to turn all men to him and establish his kingdom of peace and righteousness in the world; faith in the role reserved for the dynasty and city of David in the accomplishment of that vision.[75]

Partly contemporary with Isaiah was Micah the Morashtite, whose earliest prophecies precede the fall of Samaria. Micah too denounced the leaders for their cruelty, their corruption, and their refusal to be corrected. But he went beyond Isaiah in foretelling the destruction of Jerusalem for the sins of its inhabitants.

Hear this you leaders of the house of Jacob,
You chiefs of the house of Israel,
Who abhor justice and distort what is straight
Who build Zion with blood
And Jerusalem with iniquity—
Her leaders govern by bribes,
Her priests instruct for a price,
Her prophets divine for silver,
Yet they rely on YHWH, saying
"Is not YHWH in our midst?
No evil can befall us."
So then because of you Zion shall be ploughed up like a field,
Jerusalem shall become ruins,
And the temple mount a forested height (Micah 3:9–12).

A hundred years later, these outspoken words were cited in favor of the prophet Jeremiah, when he was on trial for prophesying in their tenor. At Jeremiah's trial, elders testified that not only did King Hezekiah not harm Micah, but he took his harsh words to heart and propitiated YHWH, and YHWH was pacified (Jer. 26:17 ff.). This "propitiation" may be a reference to the reforms Hezekiah made in the official worship of Judah, to be described shortly.

3. CRISES AND MOVEMENTS OF REFORM

With Judah's participation in international alliances and intrigues during the preceding reigns of kings Uzziah and Ahaz, alien usages had made their way into Jerusalem, as they had earlier into Samaria.

"For you have abandoned your Maker [reading 'ōsekā], O house of Jacob;
For they have become filled with sorcery [reading miqsām],
And with divination, like the Philistines,
And they abound in customs of the aliens" (Isa. 2:6).

Ahaz "caused his son to pass through the fire, like the abominations of the nations which YHWH drove out before Israel" (II Kings 16:3). He replaced the bronze altar of Solomon's time with a new altar modeled upon "the altar that was in Damascus" (ibid, 10–16). This tendency to imitate the surroundings was checked in Hezekiah's time.

Before Sennacherib's invasion, Hezekiah had put into effect his reforms in the realm of worship. "He removed the bāmōt and broke the pillars, and cut down the asherah and ground to pieces the bronze serpent that Moses had made, for up to that time the Israelites had been making burnt offerings to it" (II Kings 18:4). These practices probably all belonged to the worship of the God of Israel;[76] forms of worship hitherto considered legitimate were henceforth banned. The coincidence of the purged usages with objects of Hosea's denunciation suggests that Hezekiah's policy was affected by Hosea's prophecy (see below with regard to Josiah's reform). In any case, the collapse of the northern kingdom, just before Hezekiah's ascension, must have shaken Judah. The effect could only have been heightened by Micah's foretelling the destruction of Jerusalem. If in Jeremiah's time it was remembered as having caused Hezekiah to propitiate YHWH, an interrelation of the collapse, the prophecy, and the reform seems likely.[77]

Though Sennacherib failed to capture Jerusalem, for the rest of Hezekiah's reign and all through the reigns of Manasseh and Amon Judah was a vassal of Assyria. The record condemns the latter two kings for unprecedented religious adulteration—the sponsoring of pagan elements in the official worship of God throughout Judah. Manasseh is blamed for "abominations like those of the nations that YHWH drove out before Israel . . . He rebuilt the *bāmōt* that his father Hezekiah had destroyed; he erected altars to Baal, and he made an Asherah as Ahab King of Israel had done; he worshiped the whole host of heaven . . . and built altars to the whole host of heaven in the two courts of the temple of YHWH. He caused his son to pass through fire; he divined . . . practiced necromancy . . . He placed the idol of Asherah that he had made in [the temple of YHWH]" (II Kings 21:2–7). This cultic mixture reflects Canaanite-Phoenician-Aramean influence; "Horses and chariots to the sun," instituted by the "kings of Judah" (23:11), point to Assyrian influence. Now there is no evidence of an Assyrian policy to coerce vassal kingdoms to practice an Assyrian cult; where such a policy existed—as in annexed provinces—it was not such a mixture, but the cult of the imperial god Ashur that was required. Hence it is necessary to look elsewhere for the origin of the (rather typically Syro-Phoenician) melange of cults transplanted into Judah at this time.

Chapter 1 of the book of Zephaniah gives an idea of what religion in Judah was like before King Josiah's extensive reforms obliterated the work of Manasseh and Amon. Assimilation to gentile customs was rife among the Jerusalemite aristocracy. Nobles and officers dressed in alien garb; they skipped over the Temple threshold (a Philistine custom). Wealthy merchants pursued gain, doubtless in international trade. In prosperity, the worship of YHWH was halfhearted or indifferent: "YHWH can do neither good nor harm." There was a regular worship of the host of heaven and of Baal (who had priests), beside the worship of YHWH. Archaeological evidence exists for Assyrian influence in architecture and art. Among the primary channels of influence must be counted the obligatory service of units of Judah's army in the forces of Assyria during the campaigns of Ashurbanipal in Egypt, and in the construction works of his predecessor, Esarhaddon. In short, Judah was politically and militarily integrated into the Assyrian empire, a process favored by king and court. Unprecedent commercial opportunities were opened by the forceful unification of the states of the region under Assyrian hegemony, and Judahite royal merchants were not slow in exploiting them. This was the setting for the wholesale imitation of gentile customs and the decline of traditional, national religion described in the book of Kings and in Zephaniah. The impulse to assimilation came from the court—from those ruling and mercantile circles interested in integrating Judah into the lively international scene.

Was there any opposition to the religious effects of this policy? Manasseh is reported to have shed enough innocent blood "to fill Jerusalem from one end to the other" (II Kings 21:16; 24:4); to be sure, the text does not connect the bloodshed with the religious sin, but seems intent only on portraying the king as a bloody tyrant (cf. the portrayal of Jehoiakim, in Jeremiah 22:17, where no cultic wrongdoing is implied). But Jeremiah, at the very start of his career, expressly condemned that generation for doing away with an opposition: "Your sword devoured your prophets like a ravaging lion" (2:30). Considering the utter absence of prophecy during the nearly six decades of Manasseh and Amon (in an otherwise unbroken succession of prophets), these passages may be taken as indicating a bloody repression of prophetic opposition by the assimilatory kings.[78]

Just as the aftermath of Ahaz was the reform of Hezekiah, so the more extensive "apostasy" of Manasseh brought in its wake the great reform movement of Josiah's time. Josiah's political and military revival kept pace with Assyria's retreat from the west under sustained blows from its hostile neighbors. Hand in hand with political emancipation went the national-religious revival, nourished by a spirit of penitence that demanded far-flung changes in the worship of God. Josiah's purge and reformation of the cult is recorded in two versions, one in II Kings 23–24, the other in II Chronicles 34–35. A critical combination of the data of both versions yields the following reconstruction of events: In Josiah's eighth regnal year, when he was 16 years old, "he began to seek the God of his father David" (Chron.). This turning came, it may be supposed, under the tutelage of priests and prophets loyal to YHWH (such as are mentioned in II Kings 23:2). After four years a great purge of all alien cults was set afoot. It began in Jerusalem and its environs, spread through Judah, and spilled over into Bethel, the cities of Samaria, and Galilee, as the Judahites gained control of the Assyrian province of Samaria. Pagan cult installations were demolished and their priests put to death; worship of heavenly bodies and worship of

YHWH at *bāmōt*, with asherim and pillars, was stopped; the *bāmōt* were defiled and their priests gathered in Jerusalem. In the eighteenth year of Josiah's reign, a "scroll of Torah" was found in the temple, incidental to its renovation; perhaps the scroll had been stored away during the terror of Manasseh's reign. When it was brought and read to the king, he was profoundly agitated, and asked the prophetess Huldah for an oracle regarding the fate of the people and the land. She responded that Josiah's penitence assured him peace in his time. Then the king assembled the elders, priests and prophets in the temple court, read out to them the "scroll of the covenant" (= "the Torah scroll"), and pledged them to keep the covenant with their God, after having so long violated it during the reigns of Manasseh and Amon. The Passover season having arrived, it was celebrated with great pomp, in unprecedented fashion, in Jerusalem, "according to what was written in the scroll" (presumably this refers to the concentration of all ceremonies in the Temple of Jerusalem, in contrast to the former countrywide celebration of the festival). Josiah also purged away necromancy and other private cults whose impetus had come because Manasseh had adopted them.[79]

The critical opinion that the "Torah scroll" found and covenanted upon in Josiah's time was a version of Deuteronomy is based on striking similarities between the story of II Kings 22–23 and Deuteronomy. Of all the books of the Pentateuch, only Deuteronomy calls itself "this Torah scroll" as well as "the words of the covenant" (29:8, 20; 30:10; cf. II Kings 22:8; 23:2). Only Deuteronomy bans the worship of heavenly bodies, and the worship of YHWH by asherim, pillars, and at many places (contrast Ex. 20:24). The latter prohibitions aim at distinguishing the very forms—not merely the objects—of Israel's worship from those of the gentiles, in line with the Hezekian and Josianic reactions to the assimilatory trend in neo-Assyrian Judah. The old injunction, "You shall not act as they do" (Ex. 24:23) was meant to ban the worship of foreign gods; in Deut. 12:4, 30–31 it is far-reachingly reinterpreted as "You shall not act thus [as the gentiles do] toward YHWH your God." Worship at many places, a hallmark of the gentiles' cult, is thus excluded, with all its consequences. Celebration of the Passover, as well as all other festivals, is confined to one sanctuary (Deut. 16); country "Levites"—dispossessed by this new arrangement—are permitted to serve at that sanctuary "like all their fellow Levites" (= priests; 18:6–8). Finally, Deuteronomy is the only work explicitly called a "Torah scroll," with warnings and curses so terrible a king might be shaken by them (chap. 28).

This is not to say that Deuteronomy was composed at the time of Josiah's reform; indeed the narrative of I Kings 22 assumes that the secreted Torah scroll had been previously known. The disqualification of *bāmōt* priests from service at the temple altar (II Kings 23:9), a blatant violation of the magnanimous rule of Deut. 18:6–8, also suggests that the book originated independently of the reform.[80]

Signs of an ultimately northern provenience have been detected in the book of Deuteronomy: the choice of Shechem as the place where the people are to inscribe and ratify the Torah after they cross the Jordan; some remarkable affinities with the phraseology and views of the prophet Hosea (e.g. the deprecation of pillars and of many altars; a reserved attitude toward kingship). The theory that the core of Deuteronomy was composed in the north, and, after the fall of the north, brought south by fugitive scribes has much to recommend it. Having been adapted to southern conditions, its first recorded effect was Hezekiah's reform. Suppressed during the reigns of Manasseh and Amon, it emerged into the full light of history on the tide of penitence and spiritual revival that rose in the time of Josiah.[81]

By making the Torah scroll the basis of the people's covenant obligation, King Josiah in effect declared it the constitution of his realm. Heretofore no more than a religious document, the product of a creative conservation of ancient traditions, it became the binding law of the kingdom. Conduct "in accord with what was written" became the touchstone of loyalty to both God and king. The covenant made in Josiah's reign was thus the fateful step toward Israel's becoming a "people of the book"—a people defined religiously and politically by adherence to a sacred scripture.[82]

The result of Josiah's reform was to limit the public, sacrificial cult of YHWH to Jerusalem, and thus empty the countryside of all means of public worship. This situation obtained during the score of years remaining before the Exile; nor was public worship renewed among the main body of Judahite exiles in Babylonia. II Kings, Lamentations, and Jeremiah say nothing of pagan elements or even of *bāmōt* worship in the official cult after Josiah's reform. To be sure, Jeremiah and Ezekiel refer to *bāmōt* and pagan cults, but it may be supposed that these were private, without official backing.[83]

At first, Josiah enjoyed political success. During his reign the Assyrian empire crumbled before the very eyes of its victims. A cry of relief and revenge sounds in the contemporary prophecy of Nahum. He gloats over the destruction of Nineveh "the city of blood, the den of lions;" "YHWH has restored the pride of Jacob!" Josiah, full of confidence in his God, sallied to block the passage of Pharaoh Necho's army on its way through Palestine to support the remnant of the Assyrian power in Haran (609). His plan miscarried, and he was killed at Megiddo. With him died the political and religious impetus he had given to Judah. After a few years of Egyptian dominance, Judah was absorbed into the west-Asiatic domains of the neo-Babylonian empire of Nebuchadnezzar.

Habakkuk's prophecy reflects the Chaldean (= Babylonian) ascendancy, and wrestles with its challenge to faith in divine providence. The Babylonians' conquests might be taken as a divine judgment upon Assyria, but the victimization of smaller nations along the way, and the victor's ascription of his success to his "idols" demanded a response from YHWH. "Why do you look on at the treacherous, / Indifferent, as the guilty destroy the innocent." God replies that the end of the term allotted to the wicked will come; even though it should tarry, wait for it; it must come. In the meanwhile, "the righteous shall live by his faith." Evil will recoil upon the head of the evil ones; the idols will be proven worthless. Then "the land will be filled with knowledge of the majesty of YHWH as waters cover the sea." In this way the prophecy of Isaiah (Isa. 11:9) was adapted to the unexpected rise of the Chaldeans. Like Isaiah, Habakkuk also regarded the sucess of the cruel conqueror as a universal problem, to which nothing less than a universal revelation of divine power could provide an answer.[84]

Nebuchadnezzar's victory over Pharaoh Necho at Carchemish (605) decided the fate of Judah; its few remaining years were to be under Babylonian rule.

The last decades of Judah were distinguished by the long, agonized prophecy of Jeremiah son of Hilkiah, of the country priesthood at Anathoth. Even before Josiah's reform, under the pall of Manasseh's "abominations," Jeremiah had foretold the onslaught of an unnamed "nation from the north" to punish Judah's apostasy to "no-gods." Following Hosea, Jeremiah likened Israel to a wife who had broken faith with her husband. Then came Josiah's reforms and successes, and the prophet, apparently in hopes of true repentance and a change of destiny, kept watchfully silent. But Josiah met a sudden, untimely death; the new Babylonian conqueror subjugated the region, and a tyrannical king, Jehoiakim, ascended Judah's throne. The wrath of God toward Judah for Manasseh's sins seemed not to have been assuaged; Jeremiah considered the train of calamities a presage of doom for the kingdom. But the masses, believing in their virtue and in the presence of God within their cleansed temple, refused to credit Jeremiah's warnings. Early in Jehoiakim's reign, Jeremiah prophesied the destruction of the Temple and was nearly condemned to death by the irate crowd (another prophet, Uriah son of Shemaiah was actually executed by the king for a similar prophecy [Jer. 26]).[85] Jehoiakim attempted to break loose from Babylonia, but died suddenly; Nebuchadnezzar punished his successor, Jehoiachin, along with Judah's ruling class with exile. The ascension of Zedekiah opened the last phase of Judah's descent. The king was soon involved in an organization of small western states for rebellion against the Babylonian overlord. In Zedekiah's fourth year, Jeremiah announced to a conclave of the conspirators that God had decreed a universal subjection to Nebuchadnezzar, from which no city or nation could escape. But there were other prophetic voices; during that same year Jeremiah collided with Hananiah son of Azur, who prophesied the imminent triumphal return of Jehoiachin's exile. Jeremiah, on the other hand, sent a letter to the exiles which iterated the theme of a seventy-year subjection to Babylonia, but promised them a bright future afterwards. For the people of Judah and Jerusalem, however, the prospect was inexorable doom.

The rebels of Jerusalem had faith in the impregnability of the city of YHWH, which they might have grounded on Isaiah's stand and the city's successful defiance of Sennacherib a century before. Under siege, they demonstrated covenant loyalty by emancipating their slaves in exact accord with the law of the "scroll of the covenant" (symbolizing thereby their prayer for liberation from the siege). And relief came; King Apries of Egypt made a sally against the Babylonians and compelled them momentarily to lift the siege (Jer. 34; 37:5). This event indicates the state of religion in Jerusalem's last days. That economic necessity soon forced cancellation of this unprecedented measure does not lessen its significance as a manifestation of religious fervor.

Throughout the siege, Jeremiah called for surrender to the Babylonians. Suspected of intention to defect, he was thrown into prison, whence he continued to prophesy doom, until events bore him out.[86]

4. REACTIONS TO THE FALL

The fall of the kingdom of Judah did not put an end to Israelite-biblical religion. Traditions about the establishment of Israel's covenant with God included threats of misfortune for breach of it, among which defeat, destruction, and exile figured prominently. The prophets had always warned the people of such misfortunes as punishment for disobedience, so when disaster came it was perceived as the realization of prophetic warnings (which is why so many prophecies of doom have been preserved).[87] A minority of Judahite exiles in Egypt interpreted the fall as the condign vengeance of the Queen of Heaven for the cessation of her cult (apparently by Josiah), and concluded that they must propitiate the goddess by reviving it (Jer. 44). The singularity of their reaction only underlines how differently the disaster was appreciated by the bulk of its victims. The dirges in the book of Lamentations attribute the fall to God's wrath over Judah's sins. What the sins were, who committed them, and when, were matters on which different views were held. The author of the book of Kings blames the sins of Manasseh (II Kings 23:26; 24:3; cf. Jer. 15:4); the popular saying "Our fathers sinned and are gone; we suffer their punishment" (Lam. 5:7) is, at bottom, in agreement. Cynics expressed the notion differently: "Fathers have eaten unripe grapes; childrens teeth are set on edge"

(Jer. 31:28; Ezek. 18:1). The exilic prophet Ezekiel reached back to the very origins of Israel in looking for the root of the fall (Ezek. 16; 20; 23). Common to all was the conviction that Israel's evildoing was the cause. All accepted the covenant idea that Israel's destiny was not determined by such "natural" factors as its relative strength, or by some failure of its God, but by the law of retribution embedded in the terms of its covenant with God. This view opened a window to hope in the future, for if indeed sin had caused the disaster, repentance and spiritual regeneration might restore Israel to God's favor and thus to its land. Trust in the efficacy of penitence ultimately rested upon a deep faith that "the covenant with the forefathers" (Lev. 26:44 ff.) still stood, in spite of Israel's faithlessness. God remained true to his promise to the patriarchs to be the God of their descendants forever. A prayerful addition to the prophecies of Micah from the time of exile or later ends with an expression of confidence: "You will show constancy to Jacob and loyalty to Abraham, / As you swore to our fathers in olden times" (7:20). Faith in God's unilateral and unconditional covenant loyalty sustained Israel though its fall and Exile and made national revival possible when the opportunity presented itself.

CHAPTER V

THE STRUCTURE OF SOCIETY

By H. Reviv

A. Patterns of Israelite Society on the Eve of the Monarchy

BIBLICAL HISTORIOGRAPHY HAS failed to deal fully and systematically with Israelite society. Social developments, as opposed to political and religious ones, did not interest the authors of the historical sources. This is why so many aspects of the social reality in pre-monarchical Israel have not yet been closely analyzed, among them the character of tribal activity in general and its terminology.[1] A cautious approach is therefore desirable toward the pronounced all-Israelite national character of events during the period of the Monarchy.

The descriptions of the war of Ebenezer (I Sam. 4:2 ff.) and the war of Mizpah and the accompanying ceremony (*ibid.* 7:3 ff.) point to the restricted scope both of the participants and the territories involved. In a different kind of incident, such as choosing a king for Israel, described in I Sam. 8 as a national consensus, obvious local elements stand out. It is doubtful whether the election of Saul in fact extended beyond one tribe or group of tribes at the most,[2] since he ruled over a restricted area, to be compared with that ascribed to Ishbosheth (II Sam. 2:9[3]). The territorial limitations are made clear in I Sam. 11, even though the events described in this chapter are also assigned an all-national character (*ibid.* v. 8). It might therefore be argued that the action of a single tribe or group of tribes is described as inter-tribal, with repercussions, therefore, upon the nature of the all-Israelite body, discernible from the descriptions of assemblies, ceremonies, and wars. This body has left its mark upon the sources and bears a national character. Among its several names are *'ēdāh* (congregation), to all appearances the earliest and perhaps the original designation (Ex. 16:2–3; Num. 14:1–10; cf. also Josh. 18:1 ff., etc.), and *qāhāl* (community) (Prov. 5:14; cf. Num. 10:7; II Chron. 7:8). The term *qāhāl* is sometimes synonymous with *'ēdāh*. The difference between them is not sufficiently clear, perhaps of contemporary uncertainty, although some distinction can be drawn on the literary and chronological level.[4] The inclusive body of the Children of Israel is reflected also in inclusive names such as *ha-'ām* (the people), *Yisrā'ēl* (Israel), etc. The framework defined by the different names has its origin in the patriarchal, nomadic Israelite society.

Examination of the activities of the inclusive body further emphasizes the problem of analyzing material concerning the inter-tribal character. The portrayal of the war of the congregation against Benjamin—known as the "Narrative of the concubine of Gibeah" (Judg. 20–21)—as inter-tribal raises doubts about the dimensions attributed to it, especially since it is questionable whether the Israelite tribes could in fact have formed a roof organization at the period of the Settlement. Just as an inter-tribal character can be imparted to a limited event, even though its dimensions were really much more modest, so it is possible to describe a campaign, in which merely a group of tribes participated, as an action of the congregation. Nor can it be ruled out that the action of a single tribe can be turned into an action of the congregation. It must be supposed that the Israelite assemblies, within the tribe or groups of tribes, assumed the status of an activity of the whole congregation at a time when the congregation itself had become a historical memory. The legal, military, and ceremonial prerogatives which the Pentateuch and the books of Joshua and Judges assign to the congregation encourage the view that the tendency to bestow an inter-tribal character upon certain actions was a result of later internal, political, and religious considerations.

In addition to the episode of the "concubine in Gibeah," which belonged to the Joseph tribes, a similar local explanation can probably be made for the reference to the 'ēdāh in the affair of the Gibeonite cities (Josh. 9:15–19, 21). The obvious conclusion, therefore, is that during the period of the Settlement and on the eve of the establishment of the Monarchy no all-tribal or national-federal or amphictyonic structure existed in Israel. The fact that there was a tribal body with characteristics similar to those of the 'ēdāh supports this view. The very existence of the body called "men ('īš) of a certain tribe" clarifies the way a limited action came to be attributed to the organizational inter-tribal framework, whose basis in the reality of the period of the Settlement is doubtful. The "men" of the tribe comprised the members of the tribes from age groups liable for military service. Its authority and functions paralleled those of the inter-tribal assembly as described in the sources. The standing of the congregation in inter-tribal contexts compared with that of the "men" of the tribe, with similar activities within the restricted, tribal framework.

In contrast to the obscure and tendentious descriptions of the inter-tribal framework, however, the "men" of the tribe can be seen in real context, all firmly rooted in the reality of the period of the Settlement and of the United Kingdom. A number of times the "men of Ephraim" were alerted to defend their hegemony, as in the days of Gideon and of Jephthah (Judg. 7:24 ff.; 12:1 ff.). Similarly, "the men of Judah" faced the Philistines, to negotiate or to fight, and hand Samson over to his enemies (*ibid.* 15:10 ff.); the "men of Benjamin" fought to defend Gibeah (*ibid.* 20:41); the "men of Judah" are mentioned as an active military and political body at the time of Absalom's rebellion (II Sam. 19:15, 43–44; 20:4; see also p. 128). In this connection, it might be well to consider whether the appellation "men of Israel" had a basis in the reality of the period of the Settlement. It is used mainly in reference to confrontations between Judah and groups of tribes from the north, the center, and Transjordan. The first such confrontation is made clear by the events at the time of Absalom's rebellion (*ibid.* 19:12–44).[5]

As for the period preceding David, the situation in which the "men of Israel" are mentioned might well be realistic when the action is on a restricted scale, as can be seen from the verse: "And the men of Israel were gathered together out of Naphtali, and out of Asher, and out of all Manasseh" (Judg. 7:23). A national character could, of course, have been assigned to this term; the appeal of the "men of Israel" who said to Gideon: "Rule thou over us . . ." (Judg. 8:22) might be interpreted as all-Israelite, but it actually came from those who wanted the protection of a judge whose authority did not exceed a restricted area.

To sum up: The largest operative unit during the pre-monarchical period was the tribe. The activity of the *'ēdāh*, only a memory at the time of the Settlement, is an enlargement of the activity of the "men" of the tribe or group of tribes, resulting from a late ideology, or at most a tribal trend, to confer on themselves an all-Israelite image. It must be borne in mind that the tribe was not a homogeneous unit, but a loose and fragmented framework in its territorial stage, due to the conditions of permanent settlement. One might therefore wonder whence came the tribes' ability to function. The answer is to be found in the power and vitality of the sub-tribal units—the clans (*mišpāḥōt*) and families (*bātēi-'āv*).[6] Their close links and their social and economic unity gave them stability and strength under the circumstances of the Conquest of Palestine. The clans and families, in fact, determined the extent of the tribal settlement, because the division of the limited land resources in Palestine was essentially the result of the settlement of these units. Since agriculture was the basis of the Israelite economy, it necessarily led to the consolidation of limited frameworks. Hence, the ability or failure of the tribe and the "men" of the tribe to function on different levels depended on whether circumstances motivated common action and how greatly such action served the common interest of the tribal components. The willingness of the sub-tribal units to unite into a comprehensive formation therefore assumed the form of an event with a tribal character.

The clans and families, and therefore also the tribes, were headed by the elders. They led the Israelites by virtue of authority derived from early patriarchal tradition. The leadership is clearly shown in events and in decisions taken, though it is explicitly mentioned only a few times in connection with this period.[7] Biblical passages mainly emphasize the representational function of the elders, who act on behalf and with the agreement of the different social bodies. This is why the term for the tribal frameworks or components is interchangeable with the term "elders." It also accounts for the difficulty in distinguishing between the functions and authority of these frameworks and those of the elders. This overlap does, however, help to clarify the nature of the traditional Israelite leadership, because the tribe and its units acted according to the decisions of the elders. The context in which the terms for the various frameworks appear must also be interpreted as evidence for the authority and functions of the elders. Thus, for example, the "Elders of the Congregation" (*ziqnēi ha-'ēdāh*) conferred about avoiding the destruction of the tribe of Benjamin (Judg. 21:16 ff.) after the congregation proclaimed peace unto the vanquished (*ibid.* v. 13). The decision to make peace when the war of the tribes against Benjamin ended was undoubtedly made by the group of elders, who also announced it in the name of the assembly of the tribesmen.

The incident of Absalom's rebellion contains interesting alternations that shed light on the functions of the elders and their relationship to the wider bodies. Ahithophel's advice pleased Absalom "and all the elders of Israel" (II Sam. 17:4), who are thus shown to have participated with Absalom in an important political and military decision. In that same context, Absalom "and all the men of Israel" considered the advice given by Hushai the Archite better than that of Ahithophel (*ibid.* v. 14). Both pieces of advice were given before the same bodies and the term "men of Israel" comes in place of the term "the elders." These alternations are used to emphasize the fact that Hushai's advice was better and was accepted, as it were, by all Israelites, but it really shows an overlapping of functions. The elders might possibly have acted as representatives of "the men of Israel." After Absalom's death David sent his priests to the "elders of Judah" to urge them to return the king speedily to his house (*ibid.* 19:12). The answer to his message was given by the "men of Judah:" "Return thou, and all thy servants" (*ibid.* v. 15). This incident also indicates that the decision of the tribal body resulted from previous counsels and decisions that had been accepted by the "elders of Judah."[8]

Other instances, although revised in the spirit of the late inter-tribal concept, which give a realistic picture, mention the traditional leadership, where the terms and institutions are not interchanged. Military command and control of the whereabouts of the Ark of the Covenant, on the eve of the establishment of the Monarchy, were prerogatives of the elders (I Sam. 4:3). The decision to crown a king was made by elders (*ibid.* 8:4). The description of David's election by the "elders of Israel" is most realistic (II Sam. 3:17; 5:3; I Chron. 11:3). However, Saul's words to Samuel regarding the position and importance of the elders are very instructive: "I have sinned, yet honor me now, I pray thee, before the elders of my people, and before Israel" (I Sam. 15:30).

The tribal and "inter-tribal" activity described in the books of Judges and Samuel portrays the elders as the recognized and accepted leaders in Israel. The composition and character of the Israelite leadership were upset only when and where the elders did not meet the challenge of the time and had to give way to deliverers—traditionally named "Judges"—the military leaders who then acquired local government authority.[9] But the elders remained at the head of the social frameworks after the Judges had vacated the scene, thus clearly proving the unshakable authority of the traditional leadership in the pre-monarchical period and to a considerable extent in the days of the United Kingdom.

In the wake of the changes that took place in Israel after the Conquest, a new economic situation developed, based on unequal land distribution and unequal amassing of property. The sub-tribal unit went over to the barter system for supplying the necessities of life and services, since subsistence farming no longer suited the new conditions. The increasing economic gap revealed the social polarization, a characteristic of any settled, non-equalitarian society.[10] A first hint of men of property occurs in the descriptions of the personages usually referred to as the "minor judges" (Judg. 10:1–5; 12:8–15). Their property and position are emphasized by their numerous offspring, and their places of habitation and burial are recounted in detail, which points to land holdings and economic power.[11] In Saul's time Nabal the Carmelite was a "great man" a holder of considerable property (I Sam. 25:2). The term "a great man" ('īš gādōl) is also assigned to other propertied men, like Barzillai the Gileadite ("And he had provided the king with sustenance while he lay at Mahanaim; for he was a very great man" [II Sam. 19:33]); so also Shobi son of Nahash of Rabbath-ammon and Machir son of Ammiel of Lodebar (ibid. 17:27–29; cf. also Gen. 24:35; 26:13–14; Jer. 5:27; Job. 1:3).[12]

The fact that geographic details about most of the propertied men are supplied along with family affiliation is evidence of economic power and not necessarily of noble lineage. All the "great men" mentioned in the Bible were associated with land, agriculture, or animal husbandry. People in urban settlements, however, also seem to have accumulated wealth by means of trade, crafts, and the like, a possibility that must not be precluded even though no explicit evidence for it is available. They simply might not have been called by the usual term, "great men."

The men of wealth among the Israelites were at the extreme of the social polarization. The conditions which created this group gave rise also to its opposite: the freemen, who were economically and socially ostracized. Apart from slaves, they were on the lowest rung of the social ladder, and were called in the Bible "vain fellows," "empty fellows," "base fellows," an indication of the popular attitude toward them. "The vain and empty fellows" lived on the fringe of society, unsettled, propertyless and rootless. Their connections with established society were loose and frequently negative. They grouped themselves around a leader and lived by plunder and pillage or as mercenaries to any bidder, like those of Abimelech (Judg. 9:4) and Jephthah's followers (*ibid.* 11:3). Such bands also made a living by extending protection to a population in return for payment, like David's band, a group that acted as a political instrument to further David's ambitions. The members of David's band are neatly defined in I Sam. 22:2: "And every one that was in distress and every one who was in debt, and every one who was discontented, gathered themselves unto him; and he became captain over them; and there were with him about four hundred men."[13]

Jeroboam son of Nebat later utilized similar elements: "And there were gathered unto him vain men, base fellows that strengthened themselves against Rehoboam the son of Solomon" (II Chron. 13:7). In this particular case one might suspect that the author of Chronicles wanted to present Jeroboam in a negative light. It is not impossible, however, that the man who raised the banner of revolt against the house of David attracted dissatisfied elements along with the fringe group that had been affected by the economic and administrative state of affairs. So also Rezon the son of Eliada was helped by such a band to become king in Damascus (I Kings 11:24).

The traits characterizing the "vain and empty fellows" paralleled those of the men belonging to the class of the *ḥab/piru* known throughout the ancient East. The *ḥab/piru* were a side-effect of the economic structure in the Fertile Crescent and consisted of elements of inferior social standing, most of whom lacked property and a foothold in the places where they lived.[14]

An indication of the wretched position of these people is preserved in the biblical laws enacted to deal with conditions which undoubtedly also existed in pre-monarchical Israel. We should especially point to the laws whose purpose was to lessen the impoverishment of the poor settled population as a result of economic relationships. Even though the tradition of ancient eastern law, inherited by the Israelites,[15] influenced biblical law, directives and instructions in the biblical text attempt to prevent economic, social, and legal injury to those Israelites who were most vulnerable. These were obviously the substructure, the poor, the "vain and empty fellows" on the one hand, and the slaves on the other. In several passages the Israelites are warned not to covet the property of their brethren (Ex. 22:24–26) nor to expand their land holdings at the expense of others, and not only because of the sanctity of the inheritance (Deut.

19:14; 27:17, etc.). Since loans at interest and pledges to pay increased the impoverishment of the borrower and the wealth of the lender, and often led to temporary or permanent enslavement, laws were often made to alleviate such situations (Ex. 21:7; Lev. 25:10; 25:50 ff., etc.). Situations like these are well-known throughout the ancient East from other sources in different periods[16] and possibly came into existence during the Israelite period of Settlement.

Between the two extremes of the "great men" and the "vain and empty fellows" was the majority of the Israelites, who owned property of varying value and who stood on the intermediate rungs of the social ladder. The Bible only indirectly provides actual information of their activities. One such group seems to have been called "man of valor," (*gibōr ḥayil*), although it is not altogether clear whether this term was created in the pre-monarchical period or later. But in any event, the existence of this class cannot be doubted (cf. Judg. 6:12; 11:1; I Sam. 9:1; Ruth 2:1, etc.). The term "man of valor" points, on the one hand, to a connection with the army and on the other to property. The "men of valor" might in fact have been the "men" of the tribe.[17] It seems reasonable to assume that at the period of the Settlement men engaged in crafts or in other service trades were not called "men of valor" unless they owned land. This intermediate stratum seems to have been the stable element in Israelite economy and society during the pre-monarchical period.

Nevertheless, Israelite society could not at that time have been defined as a class society. The comparative balance and the absence of clear social stratification were rooted in the settlement process and particularly in the patriarchal way of life and in the economic and social purpose of the sub-tribal units, which preserved mutual responsibility and supplied the essential needs of their members. There seem to have been no definite restrictions against moving from one social group to another.

B. The City on the Eve of the Establishment of the Monarchy

Life in a permanent settlement[18] offered challenges to the Israelite families upon their settlement in the land. The nomadic elements in the Fertile Crescent were familiar with towns and urban civilization and might in the course of their wanderings have become wholly or partially integrated into it,[19] but it is not easy to estimate the Israelites' ability to manage urban life independently and with the necessary expertise. The archaeological finds from the period of the Settlement leave no doubt that ability was limited and material culture poor, lagging behind that of the Canaanites, and their towns lacked clear signs of urban organization.

The character of the Israelite township was formed along patriarchal lines which the settlers had inherited. The preservation of the patriarchal regime was a natural result of the settlement of whole sub-tribal units within the framework of a township. This also assured continuity between the nomadic period of the Israelites and their permanent settlement in the country.[20]

That affinity between the sub-tribal unit and the township developed early in the Settlement period, as is evident from several biblical passages and particularly from documentation incidentally preserved in the genealogical lists in Chronicles and the topographical lists in the Bible. This evidence—both early and late—points to the structural connection of the township with the tribal frameworks, territorially as well as organizationally.[21] Such well-known formulations as: "Ashhur the father of Tekoa" (I Chron. 2:24); "Mesha his first-born, who was the father of Ziph" (ibid. v. 42); "Shobal the father of Kiriath-jearim" (ibid. v. 50), etc. indicate that in the Israelite Settlement the clan was the main or only component of the township. Thus the dominant or only component of Tekoa was the clan of Ashhur; that of Ziph, the clan of Mesha, and so on. Of particular interest is the enumeration of a number of clans and families from one township, "And the families of Kiriath-jearim: the Ithrites and the Puthites, and the Shumathites, and the Mishraites" (ibid. 2:53); "And the sons of the wife of Hodiah, the sister of Naham, were the father of Keilah the Garmite, and Eshtemoa the Maacathite" (ibid. 4:19); "And these are the sons of Ehud—these are the heads of fathers' houses of the inhabitants of Geba, and they were carried captive to Manahath; and Naaman, and Ahijah, and Gera, were they that carried them captive" (ibid. 8:6–7); "And Beriah, and Shema, who were heads of fathers' houses of the inhabitants of Aijalon, who put to flight the inhabitants of Gath" (ibid. 8:13), and so on. Even though there is no evidence for the date of these verses, it seems reasonable to assume that complete clans or families must have settled in one township at the beginning of the Settlement.

The position of the clan and family within the framework of the township and the ancient patriarchal pattern determined the link between the township and the tribe. So long as tribal activity continued, fed by the sub-tribal units, this link was maintained, because the tribe made itself responsible for what went on in the towns within its territory. That is why biblical mention is made, not of the activity of Israelite towns in the description of events during the Settlement, but only of the activity of the tribe: no urban activity, independent of the tribe, is described in these passages. Indeed, in the only event directly involving the urban population in the period of the Judges (Judg. 19–21), the tribe of Benjamin was directly responsible for the sin of Gibeah. The shameful action of the town was punished on the tribal level and the leadership which participated in the various stages of the negotiations between the tribes was tribal (*ibid.* 20:2; 21:16, etc.). Such a passage essentially reflects early conditions which do not obtain in later periods.

It takes a long time to consolidate a township and establish an organizational apparatus that permits an urban population to act independently, directed by local interests. This process was probably not uniform and the creation of a basis for urban life in the different townships was affected by demographic, topographic, and political conditions. The economic life in the townships, which resulted in the division of labor and production, increased the interdependence of the urban population and gave local interests precedence over tribal ones. This came about with the active assistance of non-agricultural people, like the artisans.

Most of the townships never attained city status and the comparatively few that became towns did so, according to biblical descriptions, only late in the pre-monarchical period. In any case, it is hardly an accident that the independent activities of the townships and their exclusively local administration are mentioned for the first time in the book of Samuel, whereas the book of Judges describes the tribal units. The change in the Israelite Settlement is thus concretized and proves that its citizens were institutionally organized close to the time of Samuel. The change first becomes apparent when the people of Beth-shemesh and Kiriath-jearim make arrangements for the return of the Ark of the Covenant from the Philistines and determine its location (I Sam. 6:15–21). The people of those localities made decisions according to their own best interests and had the organizational means not only to make such decisions but to expedite them.

The first detailed description of an urban activity appears in I Sam. 11 when Nahash the Ammonite encamped against Jabesh-gilead and the "men of the town" requested him to "make a covenant with us, and we will serve thee" (*ibid.* v. 1). This appeal to Nahash, which points to willingness to accept a vassal alliance, is at the same time an attempt to establish an independent relationship between Jabesh-gilead and Ammon. When Nahash refused, another urban body, the "elders of Jabesh," negotiated with him, even sending a delegation to Benjamin in an attempt to summon help. It is interesting that in the region, a little earlier, a similar incident was concluded on the tribal-territorial level: According to Judg. 11:5 ff., the elders of Gilead took action and appointed Jephthah chief over them. These verses make it clear that the tribal-territorial framework was still the decision-making one and that the urban population was not yet able to deal with such problems except as part of the territory. The elders of Gilead, unlike the elders of Jabesh, were leaders who carried on negotiations and represented all the inhabitants of Gilead. A little later, Jabesh-gilead achieved sufficient organizational and social consolidation to allow its citizens to solve their problems independently of the population of Gilead as a whole.

In I Sam. 11 the men who negotiate with Nahash the Ammonite stand out: the "men of the town" (*'anšei ha-'ir*), an assembly of the free citizens, who were the permanent inhabitants, and the "elders of the town" (*ziqnei ha-'ir*), a restricted leadership body for local administration. According to the above-mentioned passage, these two groups were able to deal with the affairs of the town. The alternating references to "the men" and "the elders" in verses 3 and 5, like the change from "elders" to such general tribal terms as "congregation," etc., derive from their overlapping functions and from their status as representatives of the "men" of the town.[22]

Other passages too reflect the institution of the "men" of the town in Jabesh-gilead. In I Sam. 31:11 "the inhabitants of Jabesh-gilead" were recruited in order to take down the bodies of Saul and his sons from the wall of Beth-shean. This seems to have been decided at the assembly of "the men of Jabesh" under the leadership of the elders. In this connection, II Sam. 2:4 mentions "the men of Jabesh-gilead," whereas II Sam. 21:12 refers to "the citizens (*ba'alei*) of Jabesh-gilead." We therefore have three parallel terms, of which the two last are known to indicate urban institutions.[23] The term "citizens of the town" is not unequivocal, but in I Sam. 23:10–11 it is also parallel with "men of a town," when David considers whether he will be handed over to Saul by the citizens of Keilah. The extradition of a hostile element is a political act which might have been based on a covenant between Saul and Keilah, a common practice in the ancient East.[24] Whatever the case, David considered the extradition within the rights of the citizens of Keilah. Probably the institution of the "men of the town," like all bodies with many members, did not participate actively in all areas of urban life and the elders needed at most a formal confirmation for their decisions. The functions of leadership were concentrated in the hands of the elders.

The origin of the urban leadership is indicated by its terminology. At first, apparently, the "elders of the town" were the traditional leaders of the sub-tribal units—heads of clans and families—who had settled in the place. As separate local interests began to be recognized and to supersede tribal interests, the heads of clans became "the elders of the town," who conducted urban affairs as well as those of their own clan or household. To the traditional criteria for electing the elders were probably added those suited to specifically urban needs. In the course of time men of economic power and favored craftsmen were also counted among the elders of the town, along with the heads of traditional noble families—leaders of the sub-tribal units in the townships. Both groups had suitable positions in the representative institutions of the town, according to the specific considerations of each locality. The town became the melting pot for new elements in the population, the non-urban localities preserving more strongly the sense of familial-tribal kinship and the marked patriarchal character of their leadership.

The institutions and functions of the "elders of the town" are clearly described in those parts of the Bible that deal with the beginnings of the Monarchy. David shared his booty with the elders of the towns in the tribe of Judah to gain their sympathy and to win over the population, which usually follows its leaders: "And when David came to Ziklag, he sent of the spoil unto the elders of Judah, even to his friends, saying: 'Behold a present for you of the spoil of the enemies of the Lord;' to them that were in Beth-el, and to them that were in Ramoth of the south, and to them that were in Siphmoth, and to them that were in Eshtemoa; and to them that were in Racal, and to them that were in the cities of the Kenites; and to them that were in Hormah, and to them that were in Bor-ashan, and to them that were in Athach; and to them that were in Hebron, and to all the places where David himself and his men were wont to haunt" (I Sam. 30:26–31). The elders of the towns of Judah constituted the local bodies which decided upon the foreign relations of their settlements. I Sam. 16:4 leads to the same conclusion: The elders of Bethlehem fearfully came to welcome Samuel: " . . . and came to Beth-lehem. And the elders of the city came to meet him trembling."

The sources do not completely outline the functions and authority of the "elders of the town" in the biblical period, but it must be supposed that the urban leadership not only fulfilled the traditional leadership functions, but also those essential to the specific needs of urban life. Apart from arranging the affairs of the family and its property, the elders of the town almost certainly represented the people politically and culturally. Something of this emerges in Deuteronomy, whose background is definitely urban. The premise that this book was originally edited at the time of Josiah king of Judah in the seventh century B.C.E. is one of the basic tenets of modern Bible research, thus making possible the conclusion that the Deuteronomic reference to the elders is based on the reality of Judah at the end of the First Temple period only. Still, a connection need not necessarily exist between the crystallization of the book and the legal situations and precedents it contains, which probably reflect an earlier period. The tasks which fell upon the "elders of the town" during the period of the Monarchy, although no detailed data are preserved, constitute only a part of the affairs conducted by the municipal leadership on the eve of the establishment of the Monarchy. Deuteronomy tends to reflect established pre-monarchical situations, such as the extradition of a murderer whose act was premeditated, in accordance with the ancient custom of blood vengeance: " . . . then the elders of his city shall send and fetch him thence and deliver him to the hand of the avenger of blood, that he may die" (19:12; cf. Josh. 20:4).

The role of the municipal leadership as representative of the population is clearly delineated in the matter of breaking a heifer's neck (Deut. 21:1 ff.). The elders of the town participated in this ceremony, whose purpose was to absolve the population, within whose territory a corpse was found, from collective responsibility and guilt. This was a firmly anchored tradition in Syria-Palestine in the second half of the second millennium B.C.E. and was one of the specific tasks of urban leadership.[25] The elders as official town witnesses and executors of the accepted customs in ancient family law discharged their official duties in the matter of the man who slandered a virgin ((*ibid.* 22:13–19), and especially in the judgment of a rebellious son (*ibid.* 21:18–21). The legal function of the elders in the place designated for lawsuits is mentioned in one of the few descriptions of life in an early Israelite town: "Now Boaz went up to the gate, and sat him down there; and, behold, the near kinsman of whom Boaz spoke came by, . . . and he took ten men of the elders of the city, and said: 'Sit ye down here.' And they sat down . . . and Boaz said unto the elders, and unto all the people: 'Ye are witnesses this day, that I have bought all that was Elimelech's, and all that was Chilion's and Mahlon's of the hand of Naomi' . . . and all the people that were in the gate, and the elders, said: 'We are witnesses. The Lord make the woman that is come into thy house like Rachel and like Leah . . .'" (Ruth 4:1–11; cf. Deut. 25:5–10). Thus we see that the elders took part in legal decisions concerned with criminal acts, family matters, and economic transactions, all functions of the urban institutions in the ancient East as reflected in many documents.[26]

The Israelite township therefore crystallized into an organized and active body just before the establishment of the Monarchy. The passages quoted show that during Saul's time the Monarchy was not yet influential within the urban settlement, nor was the relationship between the Monarchy and the town established. With David, a new period began. Until then, "the elders of the town" had functioned as leaders in all spheres.

C. The Part Played by the Monarchy in the Development of Early Israelite Society

The new regime in Israel, that came into being with the establishment of the Monarchy, was extremely important in shaping Israelite society. The Monarchy left a strong imprint, assisted by economic and social processes which were already in full swing, and itself initiated many significant changes, three of which were: 1.) the break-up of the tribal framework; 2.) the consolidation of new strata among the inhabitants of the kingdom; 3.) the strengthening of the urban population.

1. The Break-Up of the Tribal Framework

It would be difficult to understand the significance of the changes which occurred when the Monarchy was established without mentioning the weakness of the tribal framework. We have already alluded to the reasons for emphasizing the economic and social functions of the sub-tribal units. Because the interests of the family and the township superseded those of the tribe, the tribe's operative strength was reduced, although it continued to act collectively as a territorial framework for clans and families. The historical link with a tribe fulfilled only a secondary function.

The rise of local interests suited the tendency for greater governmental centralization, a typical feature of the Monarchy. Since local interests weakened tribal links it became easier to establish criteria for a new territorial division according to administrative principles favored by the Monarchy. The new administration was opposed to tribal independence, to the spirit of separatism inherent in it, and, needless to say, to the traditional inherited boundaries. David and Solomon understood that their kingdom depended not a little on breaking up the territorial tribal framework. They appear to have succeeded in doing so by establishing administrative districts ruled by governors (I Kings 4:7–19). The list of the administrative districts makes it clear that not only were several tribal boundaries changed, but that even when tribal boundaries and administrative districts coincided, tribal independence was disrupted by the very existence of the districts.[27] The definition of tribal territory, with its borders and towns, as a district was a consequence of the concentration of government in the hands of the king and of royal administration and the intentional damage done to tribal sovereignty. This assumption rules out the view that a number of district boundaries constituted some kind of compromise forced by circumstance upon the Monarchy, obliging it to resign itself to a degree of tribal independence and the retention of the tribal boundaries. The districts clearly point to the growing dependence of the population on the Monarchy and its apparatus and proves the forced response to monarchical needs like taxes, conscription, corvée, etc. Centralization was speeded up by weakening the links between the population and the tribe.

Since division into districts did not begin with Saul, the evidence of the limited nature of his Monarchy is irrefutable; that it existed during the regimes of David and Solomon proves that the tribes of the time were weakening. However, the violent rebellions which occurred in David and Solomon's period reflected the tribal dissatisfaction with their policies, but the suppression of the tribal rebellions shows that the tribe was not strong enough to stand up to a contest with the Monarchy.

2. The Formation of New Strata among the Inhabitants of the Country

One of the social phenomena which marked the beginning of the monarchical period in Israel was the development of a class of people organically and economically dependent on the Monarchy. They are usually called "slaves (i.e., servants) of the king," although other designations also indicate their attachment to the army and to the administrative and household staff of the Monarchy. They are thus designated in the Bible and in Hebrew seal inscriptions and in the inscriptions from the Syrian and Mesopotamian epigraphy. [28] The term "servant of the king" refers only to attachment and not to any hierarchy (I Sam. 18:5; II Sam. 2:13; 10:2; 15:15, etc.). The class arose with the establishment of the administration and the army in the kingdom and with activity in all branches of the royal household. The methods of its establishment, no doubt, suited the requirements and the development of the institution of the Monarchy. The number of such "servants" was in direct proportion to the ability of the kingdom to maintain them by means of grants and privileges in return for their services. These methods were copied from those in the city-states throughout Syria and Palestine. [29] Even during Saul's limited rule rights and privileges were granted: "And it shall be, that the man who killeth him, the king will enrich him with great riches, and will give him his daughter, and make his father's house free in Israel" (I Sam. 17:25). We prefer the explanation according to which "free (ḥofšī) means a man freed from paying taxes and performing obligatory duties for the monarch to the one referring to the ḥupšu, known from inscriptions all over the Fertile Crescent. Since ḥupšu were an inferior class, it can hardly be supposed that belonging to this social level was considered a privilege, especially since there is no other evidence for the existence of a ḥupšu class in Israel. [30] The intricate apparatus of appointments, grants, and privileges given the "servants of the king" is clear in Saul's outcry: "Hear now, ye Benjamites; will the son of Jesse give every one of you fields and vineyards, will he make you all captains of thousands and captains of hundreds?" (ibid. 22:7–8). This exclamation shows not only the sub-structure of manpower for the "servants of the king" in Saul's time, but also the ability of the kingdom to provide them with their means of livelihood. That same apparatus is, of course, also seen in the "Manner of the King," with its links to the customs reflected in tablets of the archives of Alalakh and Ugarit, [31] "And he will take your fields, and your vineyards, and your oliveyards, even the best of them, and give them to his servants" (ibid. 8:14). A part of the grants, therefore, came from Israelite property, but another part must have come to the king as crownlands taken by conquest from non-Israelites in the country.

Saul's dependence on his tribe vouchsafed the Benjamites certain preferences, since they were the candidates for office in his court. It must be assumed that members of his father's house were the first "servants of the king," Saul's personal attendants before he was crowned, and it was his "young men" who assisted him in his wars. David, too, needed men to staff his expanding kingdom and utilized his trusted band. After Jerusalem became the capital, the "servants of the king" were augmented by foreign elements expert in areas about which the inexperienced Israelites knew little. The integration of foreigners under domination into the state organization is common practise and occurs whenever the cultural level of the conquerors is lower than that of the conquered. The reference to "Doeg the Edomite, the chiefest herdman" among his trusted servants (I Sam. 21:8, etc.) indicates that Saul, too, was assisted by aliens, although on a more limited scale. David, however, greatly expanded the use of aliens, particularly in the higher administrative echelons (II Sam. 8:16 ff.; 20:23 ff.; I Chron. 18:15 ff.; 27:25 ff.). Some of them continued in their posts under Solomon (I Kings 4:2 ff.).[32] A growing and developing kingdom required parallel growth in personnel far beyond what one single tribe was able to supply. The king used grants to achieve his aims, as did the kings of Alalakh and Ugarit, and as is illustrated by Ziba, who was given material benefits by Saul ("Now Ziba and fifteen sons and twenty servants," II Sam. 9:10; cf. 19:18), as well as by David ("Behold, thine is all that pertaineth unto Mephibosheth . . .," II Sam. 16:4; "Thou and Ziba divide the land," ibid. 19:30). An obvious analogy to this is the granting of the town of Ziklag to David by Achish (I Sam. 27:5–6).

Another group of functionaries joined the class of the "servants of the king" because of the expanding economy. New vistas opened when the kingdom entered international trade; thus, the royal establishment also absorbed seafaring merchants and others (I Kings 9:26–28; II Chron. 8:17–18; I Kings 10:15, 22, 28–29; II Chron. 9:14, 21). Construction and maintenance of real estate and movable property increased the need for experts and workers of various abilities, all of whom were employed within the establishment and maintained by the royal treasury.

Among these people were experts whose professions had been transmitted from father to son. Others had been trained by experts from Tyre who assisted the early Israelite kings according to their special needs (I Kings 7:13–14; II Chron. 2:12–13, etc.). Thus technology and professional standards advanced and economic branches previously unknown in Israel developed. At the same time the non-agricultural segment of the population became increasingly important.

The Levites were another group of unusual composition and role which became attached to the royal administration during the period of the United

Kingdom. They may not have been official members of the "king's servants," but their function made them an inseparable part of the administration.[33]

Opinion differs widely as to the meaning of the term "Levites," the origin of the Levites, and the formation of the tribe. According to some, they originated in a secular tribe which devoted itself to cultic service. According to others, they were a professional and heterogeneous group attempting to adapt to the tribal structure current in Israel. However, at the period of the Settlement, the Levites were essentially a professional group which also included families with inherited knowledge and training. They were joined by other elements who adopted their cultic occupation. The biblical data indicate that at this period and even later the Levites were not a closed framework and that the cultic functionaries hailed from all the Israelite tribes. The openness of this group is clearly brought out in the verse: "And there was a young man out of Bethlehem in Judah—in the family of Judah—who was a Levite . . ." (Judg. 17:7). The sanctification of Eleazar the son of Abinadab as guardian of the Ark of the Covenant (I Sam. 7:1) makes it clear that it was possible to officiate in the cult without belonging to the tribe of Levi. David appointed his sons and Ira the Jairite as priests (II Sam. 8:18; 20:26), and Jeroboam the son of Nebat did the same: "And made priests from all the people that were not the sons of Levi" (I Kings 12:31). Samuel is recorded in the lists of Levites although belonging to the tribe of Ephraim (cf. I Sam. 1:1; I Chron. 6:18 ff.).

The Levites lacked a land inheritance and were characterized by dispersion among the Israelite tribes; this was considered a sacred destiny (Num. 18:20 ff.; Josh. 13:14, 33; 18:7, etc.). Their dispersal came about because the holy places were located in various tribal territories and the Israelites needed religious ministrants. The Levites therefore became dependent on the population for protection. Passages dealing with biblical law and particularly the story of the Levite in the affair of the concubine in Gibeah (Judg. 19:1 f.) illustrate the dependence of the Levites. It is difficult to estimate what land holdings were at their disposal in the pre-monarchical period. Sacred service—in public or private places—does not necessarily mean that land is held in each place, and it seems more probable that their livelihood depended mainly on their occupation. It can therefore be argued that the Levites were a marginal, essentially mobile element, hiring out as priests (Judg. 17).

The inferior status of the Levites during the pre-monarchical period is the key for understanding why they were integrated into the royal administration from the end of David's reign onward, apparently on the initiative of Solomon. Decisive evidence appears in I Chron. 26:30–32: "Of the Hebronites, Hashabiah and his brethren, men of valor, a thousand and seven hundred, had the oversight of Israel beyond the Jordan westward; for all the business of the Lord, and for all the service of the King. Of the Hebronites was Jerijah the chief, even of the Hebronites, according to their generations by their fathers' houses. In the fortieth year of the reign of David they were sought for, and there were found among them mighty men of valor at Jazer of Gilead. And his brethren, men of valor, were two thousand and seven hundred, heads of fathers' houses, whom King David made overseers over the Reubenites, and the Gadites, and the half-tribe of the Manassites, for every matter pertaining to God, and for the affairs of the King." Mazar has shown that David aimed to strengthen the Israelite border districts, where the population was foreign or mixed, by settling Levites who were appointed to administer the fortified cities, i.e., the Levites' cities (Josh. chap. 21; I Chron. 6:39 ff.).[34]

The development of a social stratum dependent on the royal court had far-reaching consequences for Israelite society. This socially and economically privileged group, whose maintenance placed a heavy burden upon the state, came between the population and the king, and stimulated the centralizing tendencies of the government. It is instructive that some of the royal functionaries and officers were selected from elements without tribal and territorial links, such as the Levites and the non-Israelites. The choice was dictated both by objective conditions early in the Monarchy and by the express directions of David and Solomon. It therefore seems that the "servants of the king" helped to break up the Israelite tribal structure and to advance the royal interests just as they implemented the government's directive.

3. THE STRENGTHENING OF THE URBAN POPULATION AND ITS RELATIONSHIP TO THE KING

We have observed the inter-relationship and inter-dependence of township and tribe during the pre-monarchical period. On the eve of the establishment of the kingdom, the Israelite town was beginning to consolidate on the basis of popular self-interest and therefore severed its link with the tribal inheritance.

During David's reign the relationship between the township and the kingdom was regulated by districts. The link of township to tribe, to its territory and its leadership, weakened with urbanization, and its functions became consolidated, with increased economic and organizational dependence on the kingdom and its establishment.

In the struggle between the opposing aims the king needed allies to help him subdue those who still demanded full or limited tribal independence, and to neutralize the dissatisfied traditional leaders. The Monarchy appears to have found the allies it needed among the urban population whose tribal links were weak because of economic conditions, especially among the non-agricultural groups such as merchants, artisans, civil officers, and men of the standing army for whom the royal establishment provided work and pay. Most of the "servants of the king" benefited from the Monarchy and were interested in its ascendancy and they supported the royal interests as a means of self-advancement. The town became increasingly attached to the Monarchy as greater benefits accrued from its links with the royal administration and economy. In addition, the non-Israelite population, depending entirely upon the good-will of the king, and whose loyalty was personal rather than tribal or national, seems to have played an important part in making the town into a stronghold for the Monarchy. This was another reason for integrating them into the administrative and economic structure of the kingdom.[35]

The Monarchy's dependence on the town strengthened both the town and the king. Moreover, it is generally accepted that David's success in establishing a large kingdom can be attributed to favorable political conditions, tribal weakness, and his personal qualifications. Scholars, however, appear to have disregarded the contribution made by the internal consolidation of the towns in David's time, which helped their inhabitants to assist and strengthen the Monarchy; without this David and Solomon might not have been able to deal effectively with the problems of the kingdom.

The urban population also benefited. The town became the center of the royal administration, and the economic reservoir for investments in royal undertakings, grants, and wages. As the town adapted itself to the needs of the Monarchy it developed physically and its inhabitants progressed professionally. The Monarchy delegated to the towns well-defined and sometimes special functions, according to location, composition of population, etc. This is how store cities (I Kings 9:19; II Chron. 8:4; 11:5 ff.; 17:12, etc.) and cities for chariots and horsemen (I Kings 9:19; 10:26; II Chron. 8:6) came into being. The functions of the forty-eight priestly and levitic cities were probably assigned by David and Solomon. The towns of the royal estates were, at least in part, populated by military and professional experts (cf. I Chron. 4:23) who performed special labor services and other duties, called *mišmāʿat*.[36]

The increasingly close relationship between the town and the Monarchy necessitated a new approach in urban leadership. The attitude of the Monarchy to the "city-elders" was, in fact, ambivalent, as it was to the traditional leadership. The royal establishment affected the extent of the elders' authority by appointing official city administrators,[37] but refrained from abolishing urban leadership for fear of disorganizing the urban way of life and the foundations of the sub-tribal units in problematic areas. The Monarchy also needed the urban leadership to help with conscription, services, censuses, etc., the implementation of which was still linked to the family structure.[38] This ambivalent approach led to the integration at the municipal government level of the "elders of the

town" with the king's officials. Integration seems to have begun when the ramified royal establishment was set up, when it became clear that the municipal
leadership could be restricted. The withdrawal of authority from this leadership
was, no doubt, accompanied by a struggle similar to that which took place at
the time of the limitation of the prerogatives of the traditional leadership. In
any event, at the time of the Divided Kingdom, decisions beyond the bounds
of family responsibility were made by forums of "elders" and "governors"
(sārīm), with the urban leadership acting as official representatives.

D. Features in the Social Development of the Kingdoms of Israel and Judah

Two political entities, with a common past and a common social and cultural
background, came into being when Solomon's kingdom was divided. The division into "Israel" and "Judah," even though it had a certain basis in the period
of the Settlement and of the United Kingdom, did not obscure the cohesive
elements among the Israelites.

The scanty information at our disposal, mainly about the Southern Kingdom,
leaves no doubt that in both sister kingdoms society developed along generally
parallel lines. It is almost certain that in social structure and composition and
in the social processes of Israel and Judah no far-reaching changes occurred
which ran counter to the trends existing in the Kingdom of David and Solomon.
It therefore seems that the period following the division of the kingdom saw
the continuation of those processes which had begun in the formative period
of centralized rule in Israel.

The position held by the tribal units within society determined its character.
Unlike Judah, the Kingdom of Israel consisted of many tribes, the generally
accepted reason for the instability and political weakness of the Northern Kingdom. In contrast to this heterogeneity, the Southern Kingdom was much more
integrated internally, because of its dominant tribal position and the stability
of its ruling dynasty.[39] In Judah the distinction between "congregation," "man,"
"tribe," and "people"—in the sense of territorial and political definition—
was probably rapidly obliterated. The relative homogeneity in the Southern
Kingdom served to blur the tribal character and strengthen the Monarchy. Yet
here also the tribal division was significant, since censuses and military conscription were sometimes organized separately within the framework of Judah and
of Benjamin (II Chron. 17:14 ff.; cf. I Chron. 8:1–28, 32; cf. 4:41). At the
same time it is uncertain whether these and other biblical passages are evidence
of active tribal units or of an administrative separation. After all, not the tribes
but the sub-tribal units were the basis for the census and conscription in Judah.

Moreover, other verses indicate that the clan gradually disintegrated and the importance of family and individual gradually increased. Several biblical books appeal even for the abrogation of collective responsibility, to be understood only against the background of a weakened clan (II Kings 14:6; cf. Deut. 24:16; Ezek. 14:12 ff.). In any event, at the time of the Israelite rival Kingdoms the sub-tribal units seem to have continued to exist and function. Efforts to find allusions to or evidence for organizational forms outside family criteria for this period have not been successful. Even the supposed "guilds" are simply local family organizations (I Chron. 4:14, 21, 23, etc.).[40]

The coexistence of high officials and town elders continued in both Israel and Judah, although the increasing involvement of the Monarchy may have further reduced the authority of the urban leadership. Its participation in the legal and army systems continued, and functions that remained in its hands were given official sanction. In the judicial reform initiated by Jehoshaphat of Judah, elders became a permanent component of the appeals' court in Jerusalem by royal appointment (II Chron. 19:4–11).[41] The decisions and the forum common to the "elders of the town," "the nobles," and the "governors" in the trial of Naboth (I Kings 21:8, 11) and in the negotiations with Jehu (II Kings 10:1, 5) offer clear evidence that royal sanction was granted for the participation of the "elders" and for determining the frameworks of their authority. Thus it is clear how the terms "governors" (sārīm) and "elders" originally began to be interchanged and to appear jointly in biblical passages (Num. 22:7 ff.; Judg. 8:4 ff.; etc.).[42]

The period of the Divided Kingdom was the time of the great rise of all sections of the royal establishment, particularly in the higher administrative ranks. The functionaries in the Kingdom became strongly entrenched, and in the higher echelons offices were reserved for a few noble families who possessed much power and influence. The many privileges and benefits granted to or accumulated by high officials turned them into a strong political pressure-group, active, under certain historical circumstances, against the Monarchy. The senior officers' class was especially active (I Kings 15:9, etc.). To gain their ends, the high officials took control in many economic areas, not only to inflict their will on weak kings, but also to increase their holdings and their wealth.[43] The Bible shows that this was accomplished mainly at the expense of the poor (see below). In fact, the border between the officials and the rich became so blurred that the two were often identical because economic power was concentrated in the hands of royal functionaries and the wealthy were given offices, titles, and means.[44] This is why biblical passages often do not distinguish between the court aristocracy and the great property owners, presenting both in an equally negative light.

The serious social problems arising from unbalanced economic relations and increased social polarization were loudly voiced by those who had to fight for their economic existence. The prophets were morally concerned and frequently participated in actions to help the poor. This is one reason why the prophets took active part in deposing the house of Omri. Elisha's miraculous interference to prevent enslavement in return for a debt also strikingly illustrates the concern of Israelite prophetic circles (II Kings 4:1 f.). The harsh words used by the prophets to the high officials and the large property owners about their treatment of the people expressed the popular mood and at the same time faithfully mirrored the gravity of social conditions in both Kingdoms: "The princes (sārēi) of Judah are like them that remove the landmark; I will pour out my wrath upon them like water" (Hos. 5:10); "Therefore, because ye trample upon the poor, and take from him exactions of wheat; ye have built houses of hewn stones, but ye shall not dwell in them. . . , etc." (Amos 5:11); "Woe unto them that join house to house, that lay field to field, till there be no room . . ." (Isa. 5:8); "Hear this word, ye kine of Bashan, that are in the mountain of Samaria; that oppress the poor, that crush the needy . . ." (Amos 4:1). The merchants and landowners deserved censure: "As for the trafficker, the balances of deceit are in his hand. He loveth to oppress" (Hos. 12:8); "Hear this, O ye that would swallow the needy, and destroy the poor of the land, saying: 'When will the new moon be gone, that we may sell grain? and the Sabbath, that we may set forth corn? Making the ephah small, and the shekel great, and falsifying the balances of deceit; That we may buy the poor for silver, and the needy for a pair of shoes, and sell the refuse of the corn'" (Amos 8:4 ff.).

The deterioration of internal economic relations and the increasing social polarization necessarily led to the consolidation and organization of a "middle class"—a phenomenon typical of the period of the Divided Kingdom. The great bloc of the "men of valor" and the urban population achieved extensive economic and political power. It is not easy to know precisely the concrete form this bloc assumed in the Northern Kingdom. The picture is clearer in the Kingdom of Judah, because of the term "the people of the land" and its doublet "the people of Judah" (II Kings 14:21). As the Kingdom developed, the "people of the land" ('am ha-'āreṣ) succeeded the early "men" of the tribe and even of the "congregation." The Bible gives several reasons—doubtless not the only ones—for the appearance of the "people of the land." First, the internal structure of the Kingdom of Judah and the reduced power of the traditional leadership facilitated an organization not on a tribal but on a countrywide basis. In addition, a common denominator was achieved by the Monarchy and the "middle class" in the face of pressure from elements among the upper classes. The "people of the land" wanted to maintain the status quo to forestall disturbances and upheavals from the above-mentioned groups. This was also why the "people of the land" appeared as cooperators with the Monarchy and as guardians of the continuity of the House of David in the hope that the king might help to curb the influence of the high-placed pressure groups, just as the Monarchy recognized in the "people of the land" allies in its effort to restrain the high officials and the rich. The active and activating force in the "middle class" was probably the urban population, the long-standing ally of the Monarchy. A number of biblical passages refer to critical moments for the Monarchy, when the "people of the land" stood by the dynasty of the House of David. Even though it is nowhere explicitly stated, it must be supposed that the Monarchy repaid the "people of the land" by giving them a voice in state affairs.[45] The cooperation between the Monarchy and the "middle class" found expression in the Bible's increasing tendency to magnify the role of "Israel," the "people," the "congregation," etc., terms which signify democratization in the Kingdom of Judah.

CHAPTER VI

ADMINISTRATION

by Sh. Yeivin

A. Generalia

A NY SOCIAL ENTITY organized on the basis of a central authority, which orders affairs and executes them, necessarily needs a certain set of practical conventions on which it acts, both in executing its functions, as well as in maintaining its relations with the individuals comprised in that entity, in order to enforce their compliance with their duties, and to ensure the exercise of their rights. Moreover, any such entity, which exceeds the limits of a single settlement, even be it a central settlement with its dependent hamlets within a very limited area, requires a regional division and a hierarchical grading in organizing its functioning and carrying out its duties by latterly relations, of the population toward its ruler on the one hand, and those of the ruler toward his subjects on the other.

As a rule, where such associations grew up of themselves since prehistoric times, their growth and development were formed by local conditions and influenced by the concatenation of local events.

In Israel "kingdom" did not "descend from Heaven,"[1] but was deliberately introduced by Samuel with the express wish and consent of several tribes, and for a definite purpose: " . . . Now, set up for us a king to judge us like all the nations" (I Sam. 8:5); ". . . and that our king may judge us[2] and go forth before us, and fight our battles" (*ibid.* v. 20). Consequently, this act represented an artificial transplantation, willingly and consciously, of a "foreign" institution into the body of a society, which was based and developed, till then, on entirely different lines of tradition, namely, tribal–patriarchal customs, which to editors of later generations looked like an anarchism: " . . . every man used to do as he pleased" (Judg. 17:6; 21:25). Now, it was this clash between the actuality of a centralized rule, in spite of its being the product of a collective will, on the one hand, and the tribal traditions, on the other, that, to a large extent, moulded and formed the history of social development in Israel throughout the period of the Monarchy.

B. In the Days of Saul

When Saul became king, he actually ruled only over Mount Ephraim, i.e. the tribal allotment of Benjamin, Ephraim, and Manasseh. It may not have been accidental that a member of the smallest tribe had been made a king, but because the (tribe) elders (that represented "public opinion") did not wish to enthrone a member of a numerically strong tribe, so that he would not be able to enforce so easily his will on the whole body politic. In the course of time, Saul seems to have gained a somewhat loose control also over areas of Judah and the Valley of Jezreel (Issachar and Zebulun)—on the one hand, and the Gilead—on the other. In any case, the new king's main function lay in his military assignment, to remove the Philistine yoke from the neck of Israel. Hence, there is little wonder that the only organizational activity of which one hears during his days had been carried out first and foremost in the field of military structure: "So Saul chose for himself three thousand men of Israel; two thousand were with Saul in Michmash and in the mountains of Bethel, and a thousand were with Jonathan his son in Gibeah of Benjamin" (I Sam. 13:2). Here had been established, therefore, a military permanent nucleus, assembled in the eastern area of Benjamin's allotment;[3] probably, mainly residents of this area (as far as their origin was concerned); a third of them held at the king's place of residence (Gibeah of Benjamin), under the command of the heir apparent, Jonathan, while two-thirds were stationed at the various settlements in the vicinity ready for a call-up as need arose. There is little doubt that these settlements were burdened with their provisioning and maintenance, as far as they were not locals. It should be emphasized that actually even this nucleus had been voluntary, for those who: " . . . went with him (viz.: Saul) [were some] brave men whose hearts the Lord had touched. But there were some worthless individuals who said: 'what [can] this [man do to] save us?' thus they despised him . . . " (I Sam. 10:26–27). Saul, however, understood that he cannot enforce obedience " . . . so, he held his peace" (lit.: "He [was] like a silent [man]," meaning, he behaved as if he did not hear [them]).

As to the shaping of his internal policy, the Scriptures are silent. However, it seems plausible that he was already middle-aged when he was chosen king.[4] Consequently, one may assume that his personality had already set in the traditional patriarchal patterns of the absolute power of a head of a family (as the smallest social unit, the Hebrew *beit 'āv*). In this respect he resembled the type of a "charismatic" judge, rather than that of a king, and he reckoned on ruling his people as a whole on the same lines. The fact is, that his immediate circle of advisers comprised only members of his nearest kin: "Thus the sons of Saul were Jonathan, and Ishvi[5] and Malchishua;[6] while the names of his two daughters were, the eldest Merab, and [the name of] the youngest Michal. Then, the name of Saul's wife [was] Ahinoam the daughter of Ahimaaz; now, the name of the commander of his army [was] Abiner, the son of Ner, the uncle of Saul; [there] also [were] Kish the father of Saul and Ner the father of Abner, the son of Abiel" (I Sam. 14:49–51).[7] And if later Saul expects David to take part in a festive meal (among his nearest entourage), it should be remembered that David was by that time his son-in-law (cf. I Sam. 20:27). Again, on another official occasion, when the priests of Nob are brought before the king, one finds among those "that were standing by him (viz.: Saul)" also Doeg the Edomite (I Sam. 22:9 ff.); one should remember, however, that the latter, whether slave or free hireling, was the king's private servant, namely " . . . the chief of Saul's shepherds" (I Sam. 21:7).

We don't hear of any fiscal arrangements. It looks as if the government expenditure was financed from Saul's private income and the presents were made to the king voluntarily by individual citizens visiting him (cf. I Sam. 10:27: " . . . and they did not bring him presents . . . "). Indeed, some scholars have pointed out the proclamation announced in the camp during the campaign against the Philistines in the Valley of Elah: " . . . and (will) make his father's house free in Israel" (I Sam. 17:25); but it is highly doubtful whether this statement points to fiscal duties (whether corvée or taxes); probably it means no more than that the king promises to grant them free access to his person, without the customary "voluntary" gift on such occasions.[8]

Even in camp there are no special arrangements for a night watch, whether general or round the person of the king (I Sam. 26:7); moreover, the murderers of Ishbaal, the son of Saul, could enter his house, reach his bedroom, and leave the residence without hindrance. All this evidence points to the fact that there were no organized precautions for safeguarding the life of the ruler, whether in his residence or during campaigns.

C. How and On Which Pattern the Organization of the Kingdom Was Formed

The man who introduced and finally established the patterns of administration and the state personnel in Israel was David; it also seems that this was not achieved before the second decade of his reign,[9] when the state he ruled spread beyond its originally narrow limits, and various organizational problems began to worry him considerably. As is obvious from what has already been stated, the Israelites were inexperienced in such manner of organization and ruling. On what pattern, therefore, could David base his activity towards such an undertaking? Several scholars opined that David was guided by Egyptian practices.[10] This hypothesis seems unlikely *per se*, since in the days of David ties with Egypt were extremely loose; while traditions of Egyptian organizational patterns could hardly be current in Canaan, for the simple reason that the Egyptians never introduced there a system of governing based on their own norms, but left local administration and its ways of execution in the hands of the petty Canaanite "kinglets," who continued to rule in accordance with their traditions; the Egyptians contented themselves with the appointment of Egyptian officials responsible for levying tribute from the local rulers. Moreover, ignorance of the unknown and incomprehensible language and the difference in general outlook both prevented any socio-cultural contacts that could possibly influence such organizational "borrowing." Furthermore, it had never been proved that there existed any substantial identity between the functions of any Israelite administrative official, mentioned in the Scriptures, and those of an Egyptian official documented in Egypt (see also below).

What has been said above about Egypt applies also to Mesopotamia as a possible guiding example in matters administrative, with the additional unlikelihood resulting from geographical distance.

As against this, there existed in the Israelite area units of Canaanite rule, where traditions of centralized administrative organization were well established of old,[11] and the experience of which was readily available to David after the conquest of such. First and foremost among these, the Jebusite state in Jerusalem, which fell to David in the eighth year of his reign, and the senior officials of which he could reemploy in organizing his centralized rule, and apparently did so.[12]

While it is realized that the actual example on which David could shape his organizational activity lay near at hand, and he could utilize experienced administrators from the then recently conquered petty Canaanite city-states,[13] it should also be obvious that the problem of the manpower needed to activate the state service was far from being thus resolved. Such service comprised, especially in the immediate entourage of the king, certain main functions that could hardly be entrusted to members of the pre-Israelite populations, first and foremost among which were military and religious personnel; indeed, such posts were filled by Israelites from the very beginning (see below).

It seems that David carried out this state organization in two phases, first in the fourteenth year of his reign, and then through changes and addition in his 30th year.[14] However, from the very beginning it shows quite clearly the intention to integrate Israelite and pre-Israelite elements; moreover, though we lack definite indications on the tribal origin of the Israelites, it looks as if there had been a pronounced intention to integrate appointees from various tribes into one "national" unit, to abolish tribal separatism, and to bind individual functionaries by personal loyalty to the king, as a *nāgīd* (lit.: headman, leader) of the whole of Israel. Not only were the "mighty-men" of David (actually his personal body-guard unit) drawn from different tribes, and some of them were even non-Israelites,[15] but Ira the Jairite and the other priests of David (Abimelech and Zadok) most certainly were neither relatives of the king (like Joab, his nephew), nor even Judahites (like Benaiah the son of Jehoiada of Kabzeel; II Sam. 23:20); the same applies to Shitrai the Sharonite (I Chron. 27:29), or Zabdi the Shiphmite (*ibid.* v. 27; if he was not from Shepham [Num. 34:10], but a member of the Shuphamite [or Shephuphamite] clan of the Benjaminites [Num. 26:39]; II Chron. 8:4).

However, David's wisest and most efficient act in solving the problem of manpower for staffing his administrative service, was carried out towards the last years of his reign, when he appointed the Levites: " . . . for every affair of God and every affair of the king" (I Chron. 26:32; cf. *ibid.* v. 30), settling their various clans in appointed cities throughout the state of Israel. This arrangement solved in one stroke three rather troublesome problems: a) it stabilized the position of the Levites, who for lack of a suitably sufficient territorial allotment (at the very south of Mount Judah and the eastern part of the Benjaminite allotment) became mostly landless, tended to wander in other tribal territories (cf., e.g., Judg. 17:7; 19:11), and were apt to turn into a factor fomenting trouble and anarchy in a state but recently founded; b) created a social stratum of state employees, whose work made them by necessity loyal and devoted to the person of the king, on whom their livelihood depended; c) concentrated Israelite state elements in the recently conquered Canaanite cities, which were inhabited by a pre-Israelite population.[16]

To insure a proper flow of manpower in future organizational state service, David must have continued to support instructional institutions for the bringing-up of scribes, which must have existed in the cities recently incorporated into his state,[17] and possibly may have even opened new ones. We do not know whether such institutions were schools in the proper sense of the term; it seems rather more plausible that state-scribes, in the service of the king, each maintained a number of young apprentices whom they trained, while the latter assisted them in their official tasks. Now, if Albright's suggestion that the tablet (calendary) of Gezer is nothing but an uncouth exercise of such an apprentice-scribe,[18] this find attests to the existence of such institutions at least in the days of Solomon.[19] Obviously, such apprentices were enlisted first and foremost from the families of the scribes themselves, or their nearest kin, as well as those of their service colleagues; thus, quite naturally, the phenomenon of hereditary service élite had taken root, commonly found everywhere at all times. Already in the days of King Solomon we find among his ministers sons of those who served under

King David. The same phenomenon is attested in historical records of the kingdom of Judah during the last fifty years of its existence.

As the split in Solomon's kingdom became a definite fact, when Jeroboam had realized that he had not succeeded in overthrowing the Davidides and reigning over all Israel (see Part I, chap. VII), nothing had changed in the kingdom of Judah, as far as the problem of providing manpower for the administration of the state was concerned. The ostraca from Arad, dated to the end of the seventh century B.C.E., testify to the fact that the Levites still kept their position in the service of the state, since those ostraca mention as administrative functionaries people known (by their names) as members of Levitic families.[20] In the course of time, there are signs of the intention to integrate tribe elders in the service, as the king's appointees, especially under king Jehoshaphat (see below, p. 169).

However, circumstances in the Northern Kingdom were entirely different. Jeroboam I removed the Levites from their state posts and expelled them to Judah (II Chron. 11:13–14), undoubtedly because he considered them too loyal to the Davidic dynasty and its religious center in Jerusalem; thus he was constrained to look elsewhere for candidates to man his administration, and had no choice but to select for the purpose "from among the top[21] people who were not from the sons of Levi" (I Kings 12:31), i.e. the elders of the tribal families (*miqqᵉṣōt ha-'ām = miqqᵉṣīnei ha-'ām/ha-šᵉvāṭīm*), candidates to man the administrative services, possibly also some posts in the inner circle of the king's "ministers." At the same time one should note that the majority of the higher grades in the Northern Kingdom named in the Bible are designated by their first names only, without indication of their patronymics; thus Arza ("who [was] over the house" I Kings 16:9), Obadiah ("who [was] over the house"; *ibid.* 18:3), Bidkar "third officer"; II Kings 9:25.[22] Moreover, all kings of the Northern Kingdom who founded new dynasties are designated by their names and patronymics, or at least their places of origin or tribal gentilics, in order to stress their noble origin as notables of their tribes or cities, with the exception of two such kings of the Northern Kingdom, namely Zimri and Omri; now, only these two alone were of high military rank before ascending the throne, i.e. members of the closest circle of the king's advisers, and just these, and these alone, are "sons of no name."[23] Obviously, one has here an indication that in the Northern Kingdom, too, the rulers continued to follow David's policy, namely to choose their nearest entourage, at least partly, among people personally known to them, and not necessarily of "noble" tribal descent.

D. Center and Peripheral Areas

The first organizational act of David was the fixing of his residence at Jerusalem, which was made the capital of his kingdom, since actually it did not belong to the current allotment of any tribe till he subdued it.[24] Thus was established a national, non-tribal and over-tribal, center for the whole of Israel; then, when the Ark of the Covenant was brought into the City of David, Jerusalem also acquired the halo of a religious center (II Sam. 7).

Since the Bible does not mention any definite administrative division of Israel under Saul, it looks as if he was content to leave matters on the basis of the vague geographical areas of tribal settlement. Thus we hear that upon the death of Saul, Abner crowned his heir Eshbaal: "over [lit.: to] the Gilead and over [to] the Ashuri[25] and over [to] Jezreel, and over [on] Ephraim and over [on] Benjamin and over [on] Israel in its entirety" (II Sam. 2:9). Thus the territory over which Eshbaal ruled is here described with reference to tribal allotments and geographic regions, some of which are ethnic (Gilead = the allotment of the Israelite tribe of Manasseh, at least partly; Geshuri = the area of the Aramean state of Geshur).

It has already been said (above, p. 151) that David's organizational activity shows his clear understanding that a centralized and enduring state of Israel could not be established, unless the various elements of its population be interlaced into a web of one national-territorial unit which would gradually at least eradicate the particularism of its variegated tribal and ethnic elements. This same realization guided David also in his administrative division, which he apparently introduced in the course of the second decade of his reign.[26] It should be pointed out that in this case he could not have been guided by the example of the small Canaanite city-states, but blazed his own trail.

True enough, the first record of administrative territorial division is found in the Bible narrative of Solomon's days, which apparently is to be attributed to the latter part of his reign; but there is little doubt that it mirrors the circumstances obtaining under David.[27] That division, like the general organization of the state services, was carried out in two phases (see above, p. 150), and it, too, reflects David's general tendency to abolish tribal particularism. Thus, e.g., the Plain of Sharon was divided into two separate provinces (the third: Arubboth, Socoh, and all the Valley of Hepher; the fourth: all the region of Dor), instead of adding it to the territory of the Josephites, to which they belonged in theory (cf. Josh. 16:4, 8; 17:9, 10); the allotment of Ephraim, part of the allotment of Manasseh, and during the first phase probably also that of Benjamin, were incorporated into one province (the first one: Mount Ephraim); parts of the allotments of Manasseh, Zebulun and Asher were incorporated into one province (the fifth one: the Valleys of Jezreel[28] and Beth-shean). On the other hand, there seem to be indications of an effort not to make this purpose too obvious, thus the frame of Dan's tribal allotment was kept (the second province: Aijalon, Makaz, and Sha'albim with Beth-shemesh and Elon-beth-hanan), probably partly because it ceased, long before that, to be an actual tribal allotment, after the migration of the Danites northwards;[29] tribal boundaries were kept also in the case of Issachar (the tenth province);[30] and in the second phase also of Benjamin (the eleventh province). It seems that also the area of settlement of the various Manassite clans in the Gilead was divided into two (the sixth province comprising the southwestern Bashan plus the northeastern Gilead; and the seventh: encompassing the central and southwestern Gilead); while the delimitation of the twelfth province is not quite clear, it seems to have included the southern Gilead (the land of Sihon), and possibly a narrow strip of the eastern Gilead which joined it to the southern Bashan (the land of "Og king of Bashan," who resided at Edrei;[31] the eighth and ninth provinces seem to have kept their old tribal attribution, perhaps just because they comprised several Canaanite enclaves,[32] and also because of their rather vague northern delimitations. Under Solomon the area of the ninth province alone seems to have been enlarged, probably only after the twentieth year of his reign: "in Asher and Bealoth" (I Kings 4:16); now, as the district of Bealoth (=$M^{e'}iliyye$) belonged, according to the description of the boundaries of tribal allotments, to the allotment of Naphtali, there is little doubt that it was annexed to the province of Asher (the eighth), in order to compensate it for the loss of the twenty towns (the land of Cabul), transferred to Hiram (of Tyre, I Kings 9:10–14). Consequently, it follows that the list of administrative divisions and their governors, as presented in the Bible, is to be attributed to the second half of Solomon's reign; such a dating is further strengthened by the fact that two of the governors were married to the king's daughters: Ben-abinadab (of the fourth province) to Taphath (*ibid.* 4:14); and Ahimaaz (of the ninth province) to Basemath (*ibid.* v. 15).

When the kingdom of Solomon split, both Judah and the Northern Kingdom were constrained to introduce new administrative divisions for fiscal and economic reasons. As to the Northern Kingdom, it kept within its area ten complete provinces out of the original thirteen of united Israel,[33] for it did not include the whole province of Judah and large parts of two more provinces: the eleventh (Benjamin, the major part of which remained attached to Judah), and second (the old territory of Dan, see Part I, chap. VII), the northwestern part of which was attached to Mount Ephraim (by the Northern Kingdom), the eastern part— absorbed by Judah, while a large area in the southwest came into the hands of the Philistines.[34] Consequently, Jeroboam I divided the eastern part of his largest province (eighth: Naphtali) into two: a) Ijon, Dan, and Abel-beth-maachah; b) all Chinneroth (from the surroundings of Hazor southwards unto the southern border of the province on *Naḥal Yavniel* (Wādȳ Fejjaz). Thus, he completed the number of twelve provinces (cf. I Kings 15:20); as to the thirteenth province (the privileged one, for purposes of leap years), he may have carved it out round his capital Shechem (the fertile valleys of Socher and Hammichmethath).

As far as Rehoboam was concerned, whose areas were reduced with the lessening of the territory under his rule, we have no direct indications of his deeds; but there may be a hint of such activity in the list of "cities for defence," (lit.: for [class of] beleaguerment)[35] which he fortified. Accordingly, one may assume that Judah was then divided into six provinces: 1) Bethlehem, Etam, and Tekoa (1st province, northeastern Judah); 2) Beth-Zur, Socoh, and Adullam (2nd province, north-central Judah); 3) Gath (= Moresheth-gath, Mareshah, Ziph (3rd province, a strip of central Judah, stretching from the north-west to the south-east); 4) Adoraim, Lachish, Azekah (4th province, western Judah and its Shephelah); 5) Zorah and Aijalon (5th province, remainders of the 2nd province of united Israel, at the northwestern end of Judah); 6) Hebron (the southern part of central Judah, with the Negeb, which have been connected, owing to their relative aridity).[36] The 7th district (the privileged one, taxable only in leap years) comprised Jerusalem and its surroundings (see below), together with that part of Benjamin's allotment that was contiguous with it, either since its final boundary on the north had not yet been fixed owing to the changing fortunes of war between the two rival states (see Part I, chap. VII), or because that part of the Benjaminite allotment had been included in the privileged district to attract the Benjaminites.

With the stabilization of the northern frontier under Jehoshaphat, when he initiated several administrative reforms in his kingdom, it seems that one of his first acts in this connection was a new administrative division of the country based on the return to the system of thirteen provinces: eleven in the Judahite allotment and two in the Benjaminite one, a system reflected, according to many scholars, in the lists of Judahite and Benjaminite towns in the book of Joshua (15; 18).[37] This list is based on a geographical-regional division: "on the frontier of Edom with Negeb" (one province, Josh. 15:22–32); "in the lowland" (three provinces, *ibid.* vv. 33–44); and "in the mountains" (five provinces, *ibid.* vv. 48–60); "in the wilderness" (one province, *ibid.* vv. 61–72);[38] the total comes to ten provinces; however, in the Septuagint the list contains an additional verse (between vv. 59 and 60), which describes a narrow strip of land near Jerusalem, from Tekoa to Shoresh, which would add another province.[39] When the provinces of Benjamin are added, and these two based also on a geographic-regional basis: east of the watershed (one province, Josh.

18:21–24), and west of it (one province, *ibid.* vv. 25–28), one arrives at a total of thirteen provinces, based on the same principle that governed the division of united Israel.

Any one who accepts Mazar's view, that the ostraca uncovered by the excavators of Samaria in 1910 reflect the extent of the Northern Kingdom in the early years, and in the late years, of the reign of Jehoahaz, the son of Jehu, must find in these documents clues to the administrative division in those days.[41] It may possibly be significant that the number of places (including clan-units [of Manasseh: Abida and Shemida]) from which came the natural produce specified in the ostraca, comes to thirteen in those ostraca that date to the years 9 and 10 (of Jehoahaz's reign), while in such that date to the years 15 and 17 (only one) the number of places is reduced to ten. However, some ostraca bear only fragmentary inscriptions, lacking indications of date and place (four ostraca), only place (three), or only date (one from *Ḥaṣērīm*, three from Shemida).[42]

The areas controlled by Judah and the Northern Kingdom expanded and contracted several times in the vicissitudes of their existence as recorded in our sources; but we lack any clue, whether in the Bible or in external documents, if and how administrative divisions were changed as a result.

This paragraph, however, cannot be concluded without mentioning one more hypothesis concerning the subject under discussion, namely the well-known impressions (on jar-handles); "*lammelek*" [= "(belonging) to (or: of) the king"] followed by one of the four names: Hebron, *Mmšt*, Socoh, Ziph. Yadin suggested that these impressions are connected with a reorganization of the administrative division of the state, both for fiscal and enlistment (either military or corvée) purposes. He identifies the four *n. pr. l.* as centers of administrative divisions: Hebron (Mount Judah), Socoh (the *Shephelah* [= lowland] of Judah), *Mmšt* (= the Nabatean Mampsis; the Negeb), Ziph (eastern Judah).[43] Yeivin, who considers the suggestion, as a whole, quite plausible, disagrees with the identification *Mmšt*, and assigns the Negeb region to the province of Hebron (on account of their common relative aridity); he suggests, though hesitatingly, the possible identification of *Mmšt* with Tel 'Erāny (Tell es-Sheykh 'Aḥmed-el-'Areynȳ).[44] Without concerning himself with the problem under discussion, Ginsberg had suggested, already a long time ago, that the word *Mmšt* should be considered not as a *n. pr. l.*, but a dialectical pronounciation form of *mmš[l]t* (=*memšel(e)t* = government, ruling; in which the silent *l* is assimilated to the following *th*) referring to the seat of the government, namely Jerusalem.[45]

As to the administration of the subjugated countries, the Bible hints at two simultaneous systems. In some countries the king of Israel is said to have appointed governors; thus in Aram-Damascus and Aram-Zobah (II Sam. 8:6), as well as in Edom (*ibid.* v. 14), where this system continued to function till, at least, the late reign of Jehoshaphat (I Kings 21:48; cf. II Kings 3:9; see Part I, chap. VII); while in others the subjected kings continued to rule as vassals, as in the case of Talmai, the king of Geshur (cf. II Sam. 13:37); it seems that the same system applied in the land of the Ammonites, though its defeated king (Hanun son of Nahash, who fell in battle, or was dethroned) was replaced by his brother Shobi, the son of Nahash (cf. II Sam. 17:27); as to Moab, no information is available, but judging from what the Mesha Stele tells us of the situation under the Omrids of the Northern Kingdom, a vassal king was apparently suffered to rule there. On the whole, circumstances do not seem to have changed in the split states, with the exception of Edom after the reign of Jehoshaphat. The areas conquered by Uzziah in Philistia were apparently annexed to Judah, as the king's private domain. While we do not know how Josiah administered the regions of the Northern Kingdom which he annexed ("from Geba [probably 'Geba of the Cavalry' in Josephus = Tel el-'Amr[46]] to Beer-sheba," II Kings 23:8); on the Philistine coast he probably followed Uzziah's policy.[47]

E. Administration of the Country: The King's Suite

On the ambivalence of the king's status at the head of his companions, both theoretically and in practice, and on his role as (superior) judicial authority as well as military leader (see chap. I).

This ambivalence guided David and his successors both in their attempts to balance the power evenly between the elders (the heads of tribal families) and the appointees of the king, chosen both from among the Israelites and the notables of the pre-Israelite population, who were more at home in administrative matters. The same tendency is reflected in their efforts to smooth the inherent contradiction between the tribal-patriarchal traditions on the one hand, and the centralized royal rule on the other, while trying to channel the energies and activity of all the servants of the king into a common runnel of territorio-political attitudes to their function, and loyalty to the king's person (see Part I, chap. V).

This inner struggle moulded to a large extent the concatenation of events in united Israel, as well as in the units into which it split later; and at least in Judah it seems that these efforts were crowned with a certain modicum of success and firmly established the loyalty to the reigning dynasty.

The Bible preserved three "concentrated" lists of "the king's servants" at the time of united Israel, which should be viewed as official records of the companions nearest to the ruler, "cabinets," so to speak, of David and Solomon.

Two of these concern the reign of David. One (II Sam. 8:15–18) is most probably to be dated to about 992 B.C.E.[48] This list records six high functionaries (= *sārīm*), and makes mention of "the sons of David." Highest in status here, listed immediately after the king, is "[he who is] over the army," who undoubtedly won this high standing not only since he was David's nephew, but mainly owing to the importance of his job in a state created during and because of the incessant struggle, first with a foreign potential conqueror (the Philistines), then in prolonged efforts to stabilize its position and its frontiers against actual and potential threats on the part of its nearest and farther neighbors. The "general" is followed by a civil appointee "the recorder" (see below, p. 161); after him are listed the two priests; followed again by a "civil" appointee, namely "the scribe" (see below, pp. 161 f.); then the commander of the unit of "mighty men" (cf. I Chron. 27:7) and foreign mercenaries ("the Cherethites and Pelethites," II Sam. 8:18). The record ends with the phrase: "and the sons of David (were) priests" (*ibid.* v. 18).

It seems that the second list (II Sam. 20:23–26), is to be dated to about 977 B.C.E. It shows some changes (in comparison with the first) due to changed circumstances.[49] The commander-in-chief still maintained his position at the head of the list, but second to him is listed here the commander of mercenaries, for during the rebellion of Absalom the latter not only proved his personal loyalty to the aging king, but because the necessity for relying in emergencies on the "permanent" army, so to speak, "the mighty men" (= the king's bodyguard and the mercenaries, as against a general levy, became quite obvious on that occasion; in the third place is listed a new functionary "he who is over the *mas*" (= corvée, levy), whose appointment and importance become fully plausible as a result of the growing building activity of David (both civil, cf. II Sam. 5:11; I Chron. 14:1; and military, cf. I Chron. 11:7, but mainly the evidence of excavations) in the later years of his reign (more especially his preparations for the construction of the Temple, I Chron. 28:11 ff.); after him are mentioned "the recorder" and "the scribe"; finally, the two priests, to whom is added here a third (not of priestly descent!: Jair the Gileadite).

The third list dates to the days of Solomon (I Kings 4:4–6: "and these are the high officers [= *ha-sārīm*], which he had"). This list should probably be dated to the second half of his reign, since several allusions seem to point in this direction. The (high)-priest mentioned here is apparently the grandson[50] of Zadok, the priest who anointed Solomon; moreover, some of the other high functionaries are sons of members of king David's suite; also, it is impossible to separate this list from that of the "twelve officers over all Israel" (*ibid.* vv. 7–20) in which are included two who married daughters of king Solomon (*ibid.* vv. 11, 19); while one province in that list of governors is cited as including an additional area, the annexation of which is only plausible during the second half of Solomon's reign.

Solomon's suite comprises nine high functionaries; now their respective order in the list is entirely different from that of his father. First comes the (high)-priest, then two "scribes" (sons of David's scribe), "the recorder," "he who is over the army,"[51] "he who is in charge of the officers" (= governors of the provinces), a priest, who is "the king's friend," "he who is over the house," and lastly "he who is over the forced labour."

The two lists of David show that only two categories of functions were filled by Israelites, the priesthood and military command, for naturally, they could not have been entrusted to non-Israelites; while organizing-administrative functions were delegated to members of the pre-Israelite population, undoubtedly as a result of their previous experience in Canaanite city-states. It is reasonable to assume that David's "scribe," whose name seems to have been Hurrite, came from Jebusite Jerusalem; but the name of the father of "the recorder" and that of the officer in charge of the corvée-levy seem to be essentially Phoenician, so that these officers possibly came from newly conquered city-states in the northern part of the country.[52] At any rate, the lists prove David's efforts to integrate the pre-Israelite population with the Israelites into one state-body.

On the other hand, Solomon's list of his suite reflects the changed circumstances. First and foremost, the importance of the commander-in-chief declined, so that he is relegated to the fourth place (after the two most important "civil" officers). This is quite comprehensible in the light of the external conditions in Solomon's days, and his lessened necessity to wage wars. Instead, the list is headed by Azariah, the son of Zadok, the (chief)-priest (see above, note 50); this position, too, seems plausible in the light of the importance of the Temple in Solomon's days, both as a symbol of the close relation of the dynasty of David to the God of Israel, as well as its being a factor uniting all the tribes of Israel and strengthening their adherence to .the ruling dynasty (see Part I, chap. V). Then, "the recorder" and "the scribe" changed places, for the former is listed after the two scribes. One also notes the decline in importance of the functionary "who is over the forced labour," who was named first among the "civil" officers in the days of David, while in Solomon's list he is cited in the ultimate place. Solomon's list also contains four new appointments: a second scribe, an official in charge of the governors (of provinces), a "king's friend," and an officer "in charge of the house." As against these, there is no mention of an officer in charge of the unit of "mighty men" and the mercenaries, perhaps because the man who filled that post under David now became commander-in-chief, and concentrated in one hand the leadership of the whole military establishment, including the Israelites conscribed from the various tribes. Furthermore, there are no new appointees from the pre-Israelite population; but the most notable feature of the list is the nascence of the hereditary bureaucracy, in which a number of families concentrate in their hands the "ministerial" functions from one generation to another, a phenomenon reflected in the Bible till the days of the Babylonian abolition of the Judahite kingdom.[53]

The Bible does not contain lists of the kings' suites after the split of united Israel. Only some hints appear in different Scriptures. When Jehu had rebelled against the Omrides and Joram was assassinated, the former sent letters to Samaria: "to the rulers of Jezreel, to the elders and to those who brought up Ahab's children . . . " (II Kings 10:1);[54] but those who answer him actually are: " . . . he who is over the house, and he who is over the city, and the elders and those who bring-up . . . " (*ibid.* v. 5). It is quite likely that the listing of 'him who is over the house" at the head of the answerers (see Part I, chap. VII) shows that the record deals with the king's suite. Then, again, in Judah we hear during the reign of Jehoiakim, that in the office of "the scribe," in the king's palace: "all the officers sit, Elishama the scribe, and Delaiah son of Shemaiah, and Elnathan son of Achbor, and Gemariah son of Shaphan, and Zedakiah son of Hananiah, and all the officers (= *ha-sārīm*; Jer. 36:12). This, too, is possibly a list of the king's suite, for two of the enumerated officers were scribes (Elishama and Gemariah, *cf. ibid.*, v. 10), and Elnathan may have been the commander-in-chief under Jehoiakim.[55]

F. The Administration of the Country: The Functions of the King's Suite

The primacy of the commander-in-chief, which is so obvious under the circumstances in the days of David, seems to have been kept by the holder of this office in the Northern Kingdom. The fact is reflected not only in the decisive influence of these officers on the history of kingship there, but actually sounds in the words of Elisha, who asks the Shunamite woman as a matter of fact: " . . . do you (wish me) to speak (on) your behalf to the king or to the commander-in-chief? . . . " (II Kings 4:13). Not so in Judah, where the grading already introduced by Solomon, who placed the (high)-priest and the most important "civil" functionaries before the commander-in-chief, seems to have continued.

The commander-in-chief's duty was not only to lead the people's army in war, which was really first and foremost the king's obligation, but also to to take care of proper mobilization whenever needed (cf. II Sam. 20:4–5; and see above). That is why Joab was put in charge of the census (II Sam. 24:2), which was aimed at properly organizing conscription on numerical data, as well as fixing taxation on a just distribution of this burden, be it mobilization for corvée-work or imposition of taxes in kind.

The "recorder" is mentioned in the Scriptures relatively frequently and yet one does not learn from these references anything concerning his functions. Those scholars who contend that David had shaped the organization of his state on Egyptian patterns, have suggested that he was a sort of official "herald" (*whm.w ni.sw.t*), an opinion which they try to bolster philologically with the rather unusual meaning of *hazkārāh* as appeal, say call out (cf., e.g., Ex. 20: 24).[56] This suggestion is not supported by any evidence from the Scriptures, and it seems hazardous to define the nature of a function by an unusual meaning of a word. Only by analogy, which is itself not quite certain,[57] may one perhaps learn something about the function of the "recorder." Since in David's days he is listed first in the hierarchy, but in the course of time the primacy passed to him "who is over the house" (see below, pp. 163–164), it is possible that the former was, like the latter, in charge of economic matters of the state, what one should call today "chancellor of the Exchequer," and as such held state documents (concerning economic and policy matters), and was responsible for keeping them. With the passing years, when the charge of fiscal and economic matters has been transferred to other officials, he only remained in charge of the upkeep of archives, and as such his function is translated in most of the ancient translations.[58]

The title of "the scribe" testifies to his functions, as de Vaux so fittingly put it: "this official was both the king's private secretary and the secretary of state."[59]

In the course of time, the work entrusted to the scribe grew, so that Solomon was obliged to appoint two secretaries, the sons of David's secretary;[60] and and two secretaries are listed in Jehoiakim's suite ("Elishama the scribe . . . and Gemariah the son of Shaphan," Jer. 36: 12; cf. *ibid.* v. 10). Apart from the scribe, frequently mentioned in the scriptures (in the days of David, Solomon, Joash of Judah [II Kings 12: 11; II Chron. 24: 11], Hezekiah, Josiah, Jehoiakim), we possess a seal: "[belonging] to Amos the scribe," which—by its paleography and ornamentation—should be assigned to the mid-8th century B.C.E.; now, quite possibly this was the father of the prophet Isaiah, who may have served as the scribe of king Uzziah, which fact would explain the special status of Isaiah in the court of Hezekiah.[61]

This official was THE scribe. But it is quite obvious that there were also scribes in other government offices, and—as is quite probable—there existed private scribes; such were: "Jonathan, the uncle of David, adviser, a man of understanding, and he [was a] scribe" (I Chron. 27: 32). Of other official scribes there is mention of: " . . . scribe (of) the commander-in-chief" (Jer. 52: 25).[62] Baruch son of Neriah, Jeremiah's private "scribe" (= secretary; voluntarily?), apparently had some official standing, for to him was entrusted, in the presence of witnesses, the contract of acquisition (= *sēfer ha-miqneh*) by Jeremiah (Jer. 32:12).

The function of the official (= *sār*) "over the corvée (work)" was to organize and supervise the mobilization of forced labour and its smooth functioning. A sufficiently detailed account of the way this levy worked is given in the account of the early reign of Solomon, "so king Solomon levied forced labourers from all Israel . . . thirty thousand men . . . ten thousand a month in relays; a month they were in Lebanon and two months at home" (I Kings 5:27–28). In addition were enlisted: " . . . seventy thousand burden bearers and eighty thousand hewers [of stone] in the mountain" (*ibid.* v. 29); it is to be presumed that these corvée-men, too, worked on the same rotation principle as the former. The actual execution of the mobilization and the work done by the levies, were supervised by: " . . . the officers superposed over the work three thousand and three hundred who handled the people with a strong hand (*ibid.* v. 30). These supervisors were chosen from the various tribes, each having a supervisor from its own tribe, like: " . . . Jeroboam the son of Nebat," who was in charge: "of all the corvée work[63] of the House of Joseph" (I Kings 11:26–28). It is evident that such a heavy burden of forced labour roused disaffection and finally led to open revolt (*ibid.*). The revolt was suppressed, and Jeroboam took refuge in Egypt (*ibid.* v. 40).[64] But Solomon was astute enough to learn his lesson. Consequently, a reorganization of corvée levies was effected in the latter part of his reign (*ibid.* 9:18 ff.): "all the people that were left of the Amorites, the Hittites . . . them did Solomon levy as forced labourers. But the Israelites he did not make into slaves, for they were his fighting men, and his attendants, and his officers [= *sārāw*] . . . his supervisors, five hundred and fifty who handled the [corvée] people who did the work with a strong hand" (*ibid.* vv. 20–23). In these circumstances the lessened status of him "who is over the corvée" (see Part I, chap. V) is quite comprehensible; and with the reduction of building activity the number of "superposed officers" who "handled the people . . . with a strong hand" also declined.

The split states continued to execute public works, which necessitated levies of forced labour. Not only various scriptures testify to this fact in the days of Rehoboam–Jeroboam; Asa, under whom is mentioned a levy without exemptions: " . . . none exempt" (I Kings 15:22); Jehoshaphat; Omri, and Ahab; Joash of Judah; Uzziah and Jotham; Hezekiah; Manasseh; Josiah; and Jehoiakim; more specific evidence comes from numerous excavations in Jerusalem, Samaria, Megiddo, Taanach, Hazor, Lachish, Tel-Ḥāsī, Tel ʿErāny, and other places. In spite of this, there is no longer mention (in the Bible) of an officer "over the corvée [work]." It is quite possible that no such special official was appointed in the split kingdom, since this function was transferred to another officer;

perhaps the commander-in-chief, as the functionary in charge of census and recruiting.

Solomon's list includes three additional officers in the king's suite. One "over the governors" (lit.: the superposed [officers]) whose function is clear: in charge of the governors of provinces and responsible for the official discharge of their duties. After the split of united Israel no such officer is mentioned. It is to be assumed that in Judah his function was no longer relevant, owing both to the restricted area of the country, and—at various times—the reduction in the number of provinces (see Part I, chap. VII); it seems that in the Northern Kingdom, too, such an officer was no longer appointed. One may possibly surmise that his function was transferred to the officer in charge of fiscal and economic matters, namely "he who is over the house" (see below, p. 164).

Another new member of the king's suite was "the friend of the king." Indeed, such a title is mentioned in connection with David's officials (see below, p. 166), but it seems that at that time he was not included in the king's immediate suite. This function was traditionally Canaanite, for not only is it mentioned in the el-Amarna letters: [lu]ruḫi šarri, 228, line 11), but also in the suite of Abimelech the king of Gerar (in the Patriarchal age): "Ahuzzath, his friend, and Phicol, his commander-in-chief" (Gen. 26:26). After the split of united Israel such an officer is no longer recorded in the Scriptures; it is possible that such officers (friend and counsellor) became known in the course of time as: "those who behold the face of the king"[65] (cf. Jer. 52:25).

Finally, an officer "over the house." Although in Solomon's list he is placed one before the last, as time went on he acquired a status of primacy. In how short a time this had been achieved we learn from the first mention of this officer in the Northern Kingdom; for the fourth king of this state was killed (approximately 885 B.C.E.), as: "he was . . . drinking himself drunk in the house of Arza who was over the house . . ." (I Kings 16:9); some years later, when Ahab goes on a tour of his kingdom during a famine, he calls upon: " . . . Obadiah who is over the house" to accompany him (ibid. 18:3). It is quite possible that the kings of the Northern Kingdom made a special effort to advance the status of this officer, so as to counterbalance the important position of the commander-in-chief (see above), in order to play off the "civil" service, so to speak, against the military chiefs; all the more so if the former were king's appointees chosen from "nameless people" (= b^enei b^elī šēm; see above, p. 152).

To some extent, the steady rise in the standing of this officer may be explained by his close proximity to the king's person in everyday matters, seeing that he was in charge of his household affairs;[66] on the other hand, a contributory cause may have been the fact that with the abolition of the post "over the preposited" (= governors of the provinces; see Part I, chap. V), who as such concentrated in his hands fiscal and economic powers, for he supervised the officials: "... who approvisioned the king and his household, each man his month in a year ..." (I Kings 4:7), the officer "over the house," taking over the functions of the former, gained preponderant standing in the king's suite. This status is fully reflected in its enthusiastic description by the prophet Isaiah: "... will I call for my servant, Eliakim, the son of Hilkiah; and will invest him with your [viz.: Shebna, who is over the house] robe, and will gird him with your sash; and I will hand over your [viz.: as above] authority to him, and he shall become a father to the inhabitants of Jerusalem and to the house of Judah. And I will place the key of the House of David upon his shoulder, and he shall open and no man shut, and shall shut and no man open." (Isa. 22:20–22).

The high standing of him "who is over the house," as second to the king, is also attested by the fact that after the destruction of Jerusalem and the First Temple, when Judah became a Babylonian province, the man appointed as governor was Gedaliah, the son of Ahikam (II Kings 25:22), while all scholars agree that he is none other than "... (belonging) to Gedaliah who is over the house," of the impression found at Lachish.[67] There is little doubt that his pro-Babylonian attitude, which must have been known to the Babylonian authorities, helped; but other pro-Babylonian high officials were known at the time,[68] so that one may assume that the fact of Gedaliah's having been "over the house" was a decisive factor in his appointment as governor of the new province.

G. THE ADMINISTRATION OF THE COUNTRY: OFFICERS NOT INCLUDED IN THE KING'S IMMEDIATE SUITE

In addition to the two lists of David's suite, there exists in the Scriptures a mixed list of his officials, arranged in three groups: "the officers of the tribes of Israel" (I Chron. 27:15–22), each one of whom is given the title of "leader" (=nāgīd); "the officers of the substance (lit.: property) of king David" (ibid. vv. 25–31); various officers (ibid. vv. 32–34). The mention of an officer, who "was with the king's sons" (= tutor), and the inclusion of Ahithophel, attest that this list must belong to the earlier part of David's reign (between the conquest of Jerusalem and the rebellion of Absalom; on the other hand, the mixture of officers later included in the immediate suite of the king with such that were not, may possibly point out that it should be ascribed to a time prior to the initiation of the first suite (993 B.C.E.). One may therefore assume that at first David sought to temper the centralization of power by recognizing a sort of a "council" of tribe leaders, which would put a stamp of a seemingly voluntary agreement with the king's decision formed by him on the basis of state considerations. Even the title of these "leaders" (= *nāgīd*) was symbolic of the "democracy" of kingship: just as each one of the officers named was a leader of his tribe, so was David the leader (= *nāgīd*) of all Israel (II Sam. 5:2), a leader among leaders, a sort of *primus inter pares*;[69] only in the course of time, as David considered his grasp of authority firmer, after his first military successes, and perhaps since his effort to rule through persuading the "council of leaders" proved not quite easy, that he established his first suite of companions.

The list of "leaders" also exhibits another interesting aspect. It enumerates thirteen "leaders," one of priests (= of Aaronids; I Chron. 27:17, in addition to the "leader" of Levites), and twelve of the twelve tribes of Israel. However, two tribes, Gad and Asher,[70] are not included in this list; in compensation, the Josephites (in the narrower sense[71]) are divided into three tribes: Ephraim, half the tribe of Manasseh, and half (of) Manasseh in the Gilead. In this connection, one should compare the situation reflected in the Song of Deborah: ten tribes are mentioned there;[72] Manasseh is not mentioned, instead of whom appear Machir (with Ephraim and Benjamin in Cisjordania) and Gilead (with Reuben in Transjordania, while no record is made of Gad, who also is not named at all. Need one conclude, then, that the number of twelve tribes of Israel was well known and approved in Israelite tradition, but what actually was included in this number was not yet definitely fixed during the early reign of David? Furthermore, Asher and Gad had crystallized into definite tribal units only in the course of David's reign?[73]

The second group of officers mentioned above is rather interesting, inasmuch as it proves that the economy of the state in David's days, at least during the early part of his reign, is still exclusively agricultural, including breeding of animals, and home-industries based on agricultural produce (wine and oil), with the addition of resources acquired as booty and tribute from conquered lands (king's treasury). Interesting, too, is the ethnic composition of the list. Naturally, the officer in charge of the king's treasury (lit.: [warehouses of] treasures) is an Israelite notable. So are those in charge of central stores of grain (I Chron. 27:25), of: "them who did the work of the field . . . " (*ibid.* v. 26), of those "over the herds [that were] in valleys" (= home herds of agriculturers; *ibid.*, v. 29); officers in charge of " . . . the vineyards . . . and the increase of the vineyards for the wine cellars . . . " (*ibid.* v. 27), of " . . . the olive [tree]s and the sycamore [tree]s that were in the lowland . . . " (*ibid.* v. 28), of: " . . . the herds that fed in the Sharon . . . "[74] (*ibid.* v. 29), and of: " . . . the she-asses . . . " (*ibid.* v. 30), were described by association with their places (of origin?), i.e., whether Israelites of no "noble" descent, or non-Israelites; the officer in charge of: "the cellars of oil" (*ibid.* v. 28) bears an Arab (?) name without any accompanying gentilicon or associative nickname; while those in charge of: "... the camels ..." (*ibid.* v. 30), and of: "... the small-cattle ..." (*ibid.* v. 31) were definitely non-Israelite, an Ishmaelite and a Hagrite respectively. It follows that the Israelites were considered expert in cereal agriculture and handling of domestic cattle; those expert in growing fruit-trees and handling domestic industries based on their produce, as well as animal husbandry on a large scale, were doubtfully Israelite; while raisers of beasts of burden and small cattle were definitely non-Israelite.

The third group seems to enumerate all the king's officers at the time, including: two "counsellors" one Israelite, who is also a scribe; and a member of the pre-Israelite population[75]), an officer: "... with the king's sons," i.e. a "bringer-up" in charge of their education (cf. II Kings 10:1, 5), a king's friend, two[76] military chiefs, and one priest (Ebiathar);[77] see Part I, chap. V.

This early list already reflects the tendency of David to integrate Israelites (mainly in posts which could not be entrusted to non-Israelites) and elements of the pre-Israelite population into one unit of service loyal to the dynasty.

The Bible also gives a list of Solomon's governors of provinces (I Kings 4:7–20); here, again, is reflected the tendency to enlist the services of both tribal notables (nine governors) and king's appointees, be they Israelites (one governor), or individuals chosen among the pre-Israelite population (two governors); again kneaded together into one administrative whole. Moreover, there seem to be indications of an intention not to appoint local notables as governors, for Ben-Hur (a member of an obviously Judahite clan) is serving as a governor at Mount Ephraim (*ibid.* v. 5), while a member of an apparently Gileadite clan (Ben-Deker) serves in the 2nd province (the eastern part of the former allotment of Dan).

Apart from the officers discussed above, the Bible and contemporary external documents allude to the following officials:

1. *Governor* (*niṣāv* or *n*ᵉ*siv*). In charge of an administrative division (see Part I, chap. V) under Solomon. After the split of united Israel, Jehoshaphat continued (or renewed?) this office in Judah (II Chron. 17:2); but in the Northern Kingdom these officials were called "officers of the counties" (= *sārēi ha-m*ᵉ*dīnōt*; I Kings 20:14). The *n*ᵉ*sīv* title was applied also to governors of conquered countries appointed by the king, wherever the former rulers, or their replacers, were not left on their thrones as vassals (II Sam. 8:6, 14; I Kings 22:48).[78] Preposited officers' (= *sārēi niṣāvīm*) were officials supervising the execution of public works or various assignments undertaken by the state. These were "they who ruled with a strong hand the people doing the work" (I Kings 5:30; cf. 9:23); apart from the above there was an officer appointed from every tribe over the corvée levies.

2. "(He who is) *over the burden*" (= *'al sēvel*). It is not quite clear whether this officers functions included only the actual enlistment of the levy and arrangement for its employment, or he was also supervising their work, as responsible for the proper doings of the "preposited officers" (above, p. 166). Such an officer was Jeroboam son of Nebat, in his early career, whom Solomon appointed: " . . . over all the burden of the house of Joseph" (I Kings 11:28).

3. *Governor of the City* (= *sar ha-'īr*). A government appointee in charge of the affairs of a certain settlement. The existence of such an officer is proved also by results of excavations (city planning—at Megiddo, Tell Beit-Mirsim, Tel 'Erāny, Tell en-Naṣbeh; paving of streets—at Megiddo, Tel 'Erāny, Lachish; city drainage—at Megiddo, Tell Beit-Mirsim, Lachish). The Bible mentions by name city-governors in Samaria (I Kings 22:26) and in Jerusalem (II Kings 23:8; II Chron. 34:8) and in country towns (the "officer of Menuhah," Jer. 51:59).

The city-governor was responsible for order and security (I Kings 22:26), with the help of night guards that patrolled the streets (Cant. 5:7). Possibly several city-governors functioned at the same time, at least in Jerusalem (cf. II Chron. 29:20).[79]

4. (*The*) *Son of the King.* The real meaning of this title is still in dispute. References in the Bible seem to suggest that he was not a high-grade officer, for he is listed after the city-governor (I Kings 22:26; II Chron. 18:25), and is responsible for arrests (*ibid.*; Jer. 36:26; 38:6). Moreover, the great majority of the persons bearing this title never came to the throne. Consequently, Clermont Ganeau's suggestion, that the title should not be taken literally, but as a title of a minor official, seems plausible.[80] Perhaps one may explain it as a case parallel to what actually took place in Egypt; at the beginning some one of the sons of David or Solomon used to be appointed to this minor post, and in the course of time the title had been kept, even when sons of kings were no longer the sole appointees to this function. Thus, during the days of the Middle Kingdom in Egypt, a son of the reigning pharaoh (usually the crown-prince) used to be appointed governor of Kush, and was titled "the King's son of Cush"); the title had been kept by the pharaohs of the New Kingdom, though the governors were no longer of royal blood.[81] As against this, Rainey sought to prove (basing himself on Ugaritic parallels)[82] that officials so entitled were really princes of royal descent, but his proofs are irrelevant, for nobody has ever doubted that royal princes were frequently appointed as high or even lesser-grade officers; yet there does not exist a shred of evidence that they ever had been assigned to such minor functions. Apart from references in the Bible there exist also four seals of officials so entitled: "(belonging) to Elishama (the) Son (of) the

King,"[83] "(belonging) to Ge'alia (the) Son (of) the King,"[84] "(belonging) to Manasseh (the) Son (of) the King,"[85] "(belonging) to Jehoahaz (the) Son (of) the King."[86]

5. *Sārīs*. Two such officials are named in the Bible: "Nathan-melech the *sārīs*" (II Kings 23:11), and: "Ebed-melech the Cushite a man (who is a) *sārīs*" (Jer. 38:7 ff.); but the actual office is mentioned in several Scriptures, in which it is obvious that this was a minor official, who served as a messenger on various occasions. The title is derived from an abbreviated Assyrian title: *ša rēš [šarri]* (= he who is by the side of the king), and the way it is transcribed (and pronounced with a sibilant *s*) proves that it could not have been borrowed before the days of Middle Assyrian, but it should be assumed that it was not borrowed by the Israelites before the appearance of Assyrian influence in the second half of the ninth century B.C.E. There is no trace of evidence of the emasculation of such officers. The first biblical reference to such maltreatment is in Isa. 56:3 (post-exilic); however, even assuming that the above-mentioned Ebed-melech described as "a man (who is a) *sārīs*" (i.e. eunuch) was castrated, the reference is to a non-Jew in the Neo-Babylonian period, when this disfigurement is current in Mesopotamia.

6. *Na'ar* (= boy). Occurs several times in the Bible, apparently referring to a butler (fiscal servant; e.g. Ziba, II Sam. 9:2, etc., who had been the personal slave of Saul and his heirs) or a personal valet, whether a slave or a hireling (Gehazi, the *na'ar* of Elisha [II Kings 4:12, and elsewhere], who seems to have been a hireling). A butler seems also to have been the owner of the seal: "(belonging) to Eliakim the boy of Yokhan," who had apparently been in charge of the private domain of King Jehoiachin of Judah, after the latter's exile. Impressions of this seal were uncovered in the excavations at Tell Beit-Mirsim, Beth-shemesh, and the mound of Ramat Rahel.[87]

7. "*They Who See the Face of the King*."[88] This title occurs only in the reign of Zedekiah as a designation of several persons in the closest entourage of the king (II Kings 25:19; Jer. 52:25). We do not know when this title was introduced into Judah, but it seems to have been borrowed from Assur, where a similar title was in use, and there, too, the function of its bearers is not clear;[89] it probably continued in use in the neo-Babylonian empire, whence it was borrowed by the Achaemenids, under whom these were the seven members of the council of state: "who sat the first in the kingdom" (Esther 1:14). In Judah perhaps they succeeded the "friends of the king" (above, p. 163), for after the days of Solomon the latter are not mentioned, while the title "counsellor" (= adviser) is last mentioned in the prophecies of Micah (4:9) about the middle of the eighth century B.C.E.

The administration of justice included:

8. *Judge*. It looks as if in united Israel the administration of justice was in the hands of the local tribal elders (cf. II Sam. 14:7), only the appeal against their verdicts having become a royal prerogative (cf. *ibid.* 15:2 ff.). Apparently, only Jehoshaphat has given in Judah a semblance of royal approval (II Chron. 19:5) to their appointment in accordance with the statutes of Deuteronomy (6:18).[90]

Associated with the judge in the latter codex is:

9. *Sōṭēr* (= officer). Only once is such an officer personally named in the Bible, "Maaseiah the ruler"; (Chicago translation: the notary; II Chron. 26:11), who is associated in this case with a military scribe; but this function is frequently mentioned in the books of Chronicles in association with Judges (e.g., I Chron. 26:29; or Levitic officers, II Chron. 19:11), as well as other functions (e.g. I Chron. 27:1). It seems that the biblical references to these officers indicate that their task was to find the people (sued by law, called up for enlistment, or corvée-work), and to see that they are properly dealt with.

Fiscal officers included:

10. (Tax)-Collector. In 1966 Avigad published a seal, acquired in Jerusalem: "(belonging) to 'zry/w hgbh." He interpreted the last group of letters as derived from *gōv*, *gōvai* (= locust), in accordance with the ornamentation under the inscription.[91] This author considers such an interpretation linguistically impossible; consequently, he reads it as *ha-gōveh* = collector, i.e. an official in charge of collection of taxes in kind;[92] with this function should be connected those impressions of individual seals on jar handles (sometimes even accompanying the *lammelekh* [royal] stamps [see above, p. 156], uncovered in Israelite layers from the end of the eighth century B.C.E. onwards, for their owners seem also to have been such collectors. The fact that all such impressions contain but a few names, sons and fathers (mainly Azariah/Ezer, Zaphan, Shebna/Shebanyo, Menahem), seems to point also to the hereditary nature of this bureaucracy.

11–12. "*The Men Who Toured*" and the "*Pedlars*." The two functions are mentioned under Solomon in connection with his income in gold (I Kings 10:15). It therefore seems likely that imports and exports and possibly also the distribution of commercial commodities inside the country were then a state monopoly, and those occupied in such professions were government appointees: "the men who toured" were agents dealing with imports and exports, for which purpose they were "touring" foreign lands, while the "pedlars" were in charge of distribution inside the state.

13. Agent (= *sōkēn*). This designation occurs in the Bible only in a derogatory use (Isa. 22:15), and there is no evidence that there ever was such a function in Israel, though the title is found in a Phoenician inscription towards the end of the eleventh century B.C.E.[93]

In 1962 Naveh published a fragmentary ostracon, inscribed in black ink, the major part of the inscription on which had faded;[94] he read what remains: "... *tṣb'l* (a personal name in his opinion) ... / ... *šāqal kesef ṣᵉqālīm 'arbaʿah* ... *šay*." Even before publication this author thought that the letters in the upper line should be divided otherwise " ... *taṣiv ʿal* ... " (= you should put over, put in charge). If this reading is correct, it may possibly indicate that certain government posts were sold to the highest bidder; and perhaps may hint at farming out of the collection of taxes in kind, as was the case in the Ottoman empire[95] even some 60 years ago.

14. *Sār* (= official of high rank). This title applies to every senior government official, whether in civil or military service. Thus, in eulogizing Abner (after his murder) David says: " ... for a *sār* and a great man fell this day in Israel" (II Sam. 3:38), and he called Abner first *sār*, a government appointee, before saying "a great man"—a notable among his people.

15. *Servant of the King.* Theoretically, all government officers were "servants of the king" (cf. I Kings 1:47). As a particular title of a certain individual this appellation occurs twice in the Bible: "Asaiah a servant of the king" (II Kings 22:12; II Chron. 34:20), but these Scriptures do not give us any hint of the officer's functions, except the evidence that he belonged to the *élite* of officialdom, for he is associated there with the (high)-priest, senior officials, and THE scribe. Then, again, there exist three seals: "(belonging) to servant of the king": Shemaʿ Obadiah, and Jaazaniah (apparently a military officer).[96] They date from the end of the eighth century (Shemaʿ) to the end of the seventh century B.C.E. (Obadiah and Jaazaniah).

In this connection should be mentioned an additional category of seals bearing the words: "(belonging) to X, servant of Y," and Y is always a name of a king. Of the four known seals of this category one was unearthed at Megiddo; it belongs to the Northern Kingdom: "(belonging) to Shemaʿ (the) servant (of) Jeroboam."[97] Most scholars ascribe it to the reign of Jeroboam II, but this author attributes it to the days of Jeroboam I;[98] the other three were acquired from dealers and are of Judahite provenance: "(belonging) to *'byw* servant (of) *'zyw*"[99] "(belonging) to *šbnyu* servant (of) *'zyw*,"[100] "(belonging) to *'šn'* servant (of) *'ḥz*."[101] These seals date from the tenth (if the first mentioned belongs indeed to the days of Jeroboam I) to the eighth century B.C.E. We also possess four similar seals from the kingdoms of Ammon,[102] Ashkelon,[103] and Byblos,[104] dating from the eighth (Byblos) to the seventh (Ammon; Ascalon); century B.C.E. It seems likely that this title applied to high officials especially close to the person of the king owing to their position (if *šbnyu* is the known Shebna, then because he became later "who is over the house"), or to their intimacy with the king. Since, however, such an official was likely to serve several successive rulers, at least in Judah, the title was probably changed in the course of time to the more general "servant (of) the king" (cf. the time span indicated above).

16. *Nāgīd* (= leader). This title designated the oldest among the elders of the smallest units, who was recognized as the chief of a tribe (cf. I Chron. 27: 16 ff.), and also the king (see chap. I). Figuratively, it is applied once in the Scriptures to the most prominent among the king's sons (II Chron. 11:22). The tribe of Levi, too, and the priestly clans had such leaders; however, the LEADER of the priests was not necessarily the high-priest, but it was probably he who was known as the "leader of the House of God" (I Chron. 9:11); it is further probable that this title was shortened to: "the leader of the House" (Azrikam, under Ahaz, II Chron. 28:7), contrary to the opinion of other scholars, who consider the bearer of this title to have been the leader of the royal palace,[105] for the senior official in charge of the palace was "he who is over the house," while under Ahaz it was most probably Shebna (Isa. 22:15); it also seems that there were several "leaders" (of the House of God) simultaneously (II Chron. 35:8).

17. *Appointee* (= *pāqīd*). It seems that this was merely a general term applying to anyone appointed to a government post. A parallel term was the phrase "possessor of appointments," by which term a certain Irijah son of Shelemiah son of Hananiah (Jer. 37:13) is called in the Bible. A similar conclusion may also be drawn from another verse: "and Jehoiada installed appointees (in) the House of the Lord" (II Chron. 23:18, and in the parallel text in II Kings 11:14 it says: "and the priest installed, etc. . . . "). The term also occurs in the plural (masc.): " . . . the officers of hundreds, appointees [of] the host . . . " (II Kings 11:15; II Chron. 23:14): similarly: " . . . them that did the work of the appointees [in] the House of the Lord" (MT, II Kings 12:12).

18–19. *Governors and Deputies* (= *paḥōt u-sᵉgānim*). These titles have been borrowed from Assyrian terminology. During the period of the monarchy they were applied only to the neo-Babylonian administration (Jer. 51:23). Other occurrences in the Bible also apply only to foreign nations (Isa. 41:25—neo-Babylonian empire?; Ezek. 23:6—Assyrian; Mal. 1:8—Persian). Only the title *peḥāh* applies once in the Bible to Solomon's reign: "the kings of 'Erev and the *peḥāh*s of the land" (I Kings 10:15), but the whole phrase is problematical[106] and may possibly be the work of a post-exilic editor.

CHAPTER VII

TRADE AND COMMERCE

by M. Elat

A. Internal Trade

1. Products For Trade

THERE ARE FEW passages in the Bible which mention either the purchase and sale of merchandise or the accompanying commercial activities.[1] Existing references deal largely with trade in agricultural produce, upon which the economy of Palestine was based and which was the major source of livelihood. The sellers of agricultural produce were apparently the producers themselves or the owners of the land on which the produce was grown.[2] In the category of transactions involving agricultural surplus, we should also include the sale of clothes, when the seller himself was the manufacturer. Weaving and the sale of the work of her hands was one of the activities of the "virtuous woman," who devoted herself to caring for home and family (Prov. 31:1–31; esp. 19, 24). The discovery of large quantities of spinning and weaving implements in excavations of private residences, rather than in special workshops, confirms the fact that Israelites generally wore homewoven garments.[3]

2. Manufacture

The picture was different as regards crafts requiring specialization. These included weaving expensive fabrics, forging copper and iron, gold- and silver-smithing, wood- and metal-work, pottery, the preparation of spices and medicines, etc.; archaeological finds indicate that these crafts were practiced in special workshops. Metal workshops have been found in many places,[4] and in En-gedi a special workshop was discovered where resin was prepared from medicinal and aromatic plants which grew in the area.[5] Pottery workshops have been found in other places.[6] Crafts such as these were occasionally concentrated in certain regions and among specific families whose skills were passed from generation to generation, and whose living derived from them. Chemical tests on shards bearing the inscription *la-melek* ("to the king:") and the place-name Hebron, or Socoh, confirm that the clay for the pottery came from the Hebron area.[7]

This concentration of crafts is also corroborated by the biblical tradition about the descent of certain craftsmen from specific families and forefathers. Thus, for example, the workers of copper and iron were linked to "Tubalcain, he was the forger of all instruments of bronze and iron" (Gen. 4:22).[8] In these families the craft was passed down from father to son: in the genealogical record of the tribe of Judah (I. Chron. 4:1–23) we find "the sons of Shelah the son of Judah: Er the father of Lecah, Laadah the father of Mareshah, and the families of the house of linen [byssos] workers at Beth-ashbea; and Jokim, and the men of Cozeba, and Joash, and Saraph. . . . These were the potters and inhabitants of Netaim and Gederah; they dwelt there with the king for his work" (vv. 21–23). This genealogical list also mentions the sons of Joab, a descendant of Kenaz; Joab was "the father of Ge-harashim [valley of craftsmen], so called because they were craftsmen" (v. 14). We have no information as to what metal was worked by these smiths, or by those who lived in "the valley of craftsmen" near Lod and Ono, in the period of the Return (Neh. 11:35). Families and individuals among the returning exiles were occasionally identified by their family craft tradition. Among the builders of the wall around Jerusalem in the days of Nehemiah, we find "Uzziel the son of Harhaiah, goldsmith [sōrfim]," "Hananiah, of the perfumers' clan," and "Malchijah, of the goldsmiths' clan" (Neh. 3:8, 31). During the First Temple period potters lived near the "Potters' Gate" (ša'ar ha-ḥarsīt), one of the several gates of Jerusalem (Jer. 19:2; cf. Jer. 18:2–4), and there was also a "bakers' market" (ḥūs ha-'ofim, Jer. 37:21; cf. below, p. 175), which was apparently a street in which were concentrated bakers and their shops.[9]

3. MEANS OF PAYMENT

Whenever the Bible mentions purchase or sale, the reference is to payment in measured silver, not to barter. Food was paid for in silver (II Kings 6:25; 7:1; Isa. 55:1–2), the price of a field was set in silver (II Sam. 24:24; I Kings 17:24; 21:2; Jer. 32:9–11; cf. Gen. 23:17), various services were paid for in silver (I Sam. 9:8; II Sam. 18:12; Zech. 11:12), and ransom or damage compensation payment were also made in silver (I Kings 20:39; cf. Ex. 21:32–35).

4. AREAS OF CONCENTRATION OF TRADE

Commerce in Israel took place in the cities, but the Bible has no special word for the part of the city where commercial activity was centered.[10] The modern word for market (šūq) appears only three times in the Bible in the sense of "street," since it had not yet developed its secondary meaning in connection with commerce.[11] A similar transfer of meaning took place with the words ḥūṣ, ḥūṣōt; although they later refer to markets, but in the Bible they simply mean passages or roads between houses.[12] That commercial activity did not take place in the ḥūṣ is indicated by Jer. 37:21: the prophet was imprisoned within the walls of the palace and on the orders of the king was provided with "a daily loaf of bread from the ḥūṣ of the bakers, until all the bread of the city was gone." This "ḥūṣ of the bakers" was undoubtedly a street with bakeries that supplied bread and baked goods to the palace, and possibly also to the general population. Shops and places of commercial activity apparently gravitated to certain streets in Jerusalem, as is indicated by Zephaniah's prophecies about Jerusalem (1:1–11): "A cry will be heard from the Fish Gate, a wail from the Mishneh . . . Wail, O inhabitants of the [Maktēš]. For all the traders ['am kᵉnaʿan] are no more, all who weigh out silver are cut off." "'Am kᵉnaʿan" (Canaanites) in these verses (and in others, as we shall demonstrate below) apparently refer to merchants.

Shops and workshops were dispersed among the various ḥūṣōt of Jerusalem can also be inferred from the excavations at Hazor, where buildings serving such purposes were found in the residential quarter of the eighth-century B.C.E. city.[13] This may explain why the Aramaic Targum sometimes renders ḥūṣōt as "māḥōzīn" (Num. 22:39; Lam. 2:19; 4:14), which also means "markets," a place where stores and stalls are found.[14]

As in other ancient eastern civilizations, trade in Israel was carried on near the gates of the city.[15] Because the people had to enter and leave by the gates, which also served as centers of social life, they became gathering points. Farmers therefore brought their surplus for sale there, and merchants their wares. Some gates specialized in and were named for certain types of merchandise in Jerusalem were the "Fish Gate,"[16] the "Sheep Gate,"[17] and the "Pottery Gate."[18]

We cannot determine the distribution of shops in the streets of Jerusalem, Samaria, or other cities, nor the extent of commerce at the city-gates. Commerce, however, seems not to have strongly influenced the patterns of life and thought of our period: the prophetic literature and other literary works of the time, which reflect the various aspects of contemporary life, make little mention of commercial life or of those involved in it.

5. THE LAW, THE MONARCHY, AND TRADE

Biblical literature in general, and the biblical legal codes in particular, seldom refer to trade. Only in two legal passages denouncing the use of false weights and measures is there an echo of commercial activity (Lev. 19:35–36; Deut.

25:15–16). The prophecies of Amos and Micah also refer to the deceptive use of weights and measures by the rich of Judah and Samaria (Amos.8:5; Micah 6:10–11). Both from the Bible and from archaeological evidence we know that measures of volume and weight were determined by the king: the story of Absalom mentions "the king's weight" (II Sam. 14:26). and in fact "shekel" weights distributed by the authorities have been found at many archaeological sites of the seventh and sixth centuries B.C.E.[19] These measures were apparently not standard throughout the kingdom, but only in the royal administration: they were used in the collection of taxes, on the royal estates, in the distribution of rations to royal servants, etc.[20] Weights of non-uniform size without markings have also been found; it is impossible to identify them, but they were probably used outside of the royal administration. It appears, then, that even in the enforcement of uniform and obligatory weights and measures, the foundation of regular commerce and trade, the range of royal intervention was very limited, restricted to matters in which the crown itself was directly involved.

The absence in Israel of governmental and societal interest in trade becomes even more apparent when comparison is made with Hittite and Mesopotamian law in various epochs, which devoted a great deal of attention to trade and merchants.[21] Assyrian kings of various periods claimed to have established fixed prices for basic commodities, to prove concern for their subjects and desire for just rule.[22]

The intervention of Israel's Monarchy in economic life in general, and in particular, is more evident in relation to religion and ritual. The Pentateuch commands observance of the Sabbath, forbidding work (Ex. 23:12; 34:21; etc.), a prohibition that was in fact observed in the monarchic period (Amos 8:5; cf. II Kings 4:23).[23] Perhaps the prohibition on work and trade on the Sabbath was enforced by governmental authorities; in the early days of the Second Commonwealth, before a central legal authority had crystallized in Judah, this law was not observed, and only the authority and power of Nehemiah forced the inhabitants and traders of Jerusalem to abstain from trade within the city on the Sabbath (Neh. 13:19–22).[23] This seems to be the reason why the *coup d'état* against Queen Athaliah broke out on the Sabbath (II Kings 11:6–9), the day when the People of the Land, who cooperated with the High Priest Jehoiada in the *coup d'état*, customarily assembled in the Temple (II Kings 11:16–20). Tradition directed that the people come to the Temple on the Sabbath for convocation and assembly and to bring offerings of incense (Isa. 1:13).[24]

6. The Nomenclature of Trade

In the description of Solomon's commercial activity we find for the first time terms for trade and traders in Israel: "Traders (*'anšei ha-tārīm*) and merchants (*mishar ha-roklīm*)" (I Kings 10:15), and the "king's merchants" (*sohărei ha-melek*) who were occupied in horse-trading (I Kings 10:28; II Chron. 1:16). The efforts of Gordon and Albright to ascribe trading activity to the patriarchs as well, on the basis of Hamor's statement to Jacob, "You shall dwell among us and the land shall be before you; dwell in it and move about [*seharuha*—see below, p. 178] and acquire holdings in it" (Gen. 34:10; cf. v. 21), and on the basis of Joseph's words to his brothers, "and you can move about [*sahăru 'et*] the country" (Gen. 42:34),[25] are not sufficiently substantiated. Speiser, Saggs, and others have convincingly refuted their arguments by showing that the root *shr* in these verses refers to travel and wandering, not to trade. Nor is there any apparent connection between the patriarchs' activities and livelihood, described in Genesis, and any type of trading.[26] The words derived from the root *shr* have a double meaning: either involvement in trade or movement, wandering, vagabondage, etc. Thus, in the passage in Jeremiah (14:18). "If I go forth into the field, then behold the slain with the sword! And if I enter the city, then behold, them that are sick with famine! For both the prophet and the priest move around [*sahăru*] through the land, and know it not," the root is to be understood in the latter sense. Landsberger has also joined in the argument about the activities of the patriarchs in Shechem and Egypt, claiming that the above verses from Genesis refer to commercial activity. He bases his claim on the syntax of the phrase in question, *sahăru 'et hā-'āres* (*sahăru* "the land," not *bā-'āres*, "in the land"), which in his opinion means trading, not moving about and wandering.[27] This claim, however, cannot withstand criticism, as Hebrew is not consistent in the use of prepositions with certain verbs. Thus the Bible gives us both "your going through this great wilderness [*'et ha-midbār*] these forty years" (Deut. 2:7) and "I have led you forty years in the wilderness [*ba-midbār*]" (Deut. 29:4 [5]).[28] The same inconsistency occurs with the root *sbb*, whose meaning is almost identical with that of the root *shr*. This verb appears in the description of similar situations and in conjunction with the same nouns, but with varying prepositions: we find both "the men of the city surrounded the house ['*al ha-bayit*]" (Gen. 19:4) and "The men of the city surrounded the house ['*et ha-bayit*]" (Judg. 19:22), meaning in both cases that the men (of Sodom and Gibeah respectively) besieged their neighbors' houses.

Not only is there no evidence or tradition that the patriarchs were involved in trade, but in Israel trading was regarded as a Canaanite activity. The most common biblical term for trader is "Canaanite," applied to traders both in

Israel and abroad. Isaiah prophesied about Tyre, "whose merchants were princes, her merchants [Canaanites] were the honored of the earth" (23:8), and Ezekiel termed Babylonia "a land of trade ['ereṣ kᵉnaʿan].... a city of merchants" (17:4).²⁹ The term was specifically used of merchants in Israelite society: Hosea condemns "a trader [Canaanite] in whose hands are false balances, he loves to oppress" (12:7), and the proverbial virtuous woman sold her woven products to "the Canaanite" (Prov. 31:24). Job mentions the activities of "Canaanites" in parallel with those of the ḥabārim, a term synonymous with "traders" (40:30; 41:6).³⁰ Zephaniah prophesied that a loud crash would rise out of Jerusalem on the day of the Lord: "For all the traders ['am-kᵉnaʿan, people of Canaan] are no more; all who weigh out silver are cut off" (Zeph. 1:11). Canaanites also continued to take part in the trade of Jerusalem during the period of the Return; it is reported that Tyrians "dwelt also therein, who brought fish and all manner of ware" (Neh. 13:16), and it is apparently no coincidence that Jerusalem's merchants lived near the Nethinim (Neh. 3:31), a group of foreign origin.³¹

In addition to "Canaanite," other terms were used to describe the people who took part in Solomon's international commerce: tārim and roklīm (I Kings 10:15), and soḥărēi ha-melek ("the kings merchants" who were occupied in horse-trading; I Kings 10:28). Some scholars claim that the word tārim is a corruption of the Aramaic taggārim which is formed from the Akkadian tamkāru.³² There is, however, no need to assume this corruption; tārim may be formed from the root twr, which means to spy, to explore, to act as an emissary, to travel from place to place.³³ Thus 'anšei ha-tārim means emissaries, making the two expressions, "'anšei ha-tārim and "mishmar ha-roklīm" parallel. This same parallelism occurs in a letter of the king of Alashia (Cyprus), which is found in the el-Amarna archives. In this letter the king refers to the same person once as his lu mār šipri-ia (my emissary) and once as tamkāri-ia (my merchant),³⁴ for in the ancient Near East royal emissaries fulfilled both diplomatic and economic functions. The roklīm, as well as the tārim, were, according to our passage, traders on an international scale, similar to the roklīm who served the king of Assyria (Nahum 3:16), and to the foreign importers of Tyre, whom the prophet also calls roklīm.³⁵

In the period of the Second Temple, however, the meaning of rokēl came to be limited to "retail merchant" (Neh. 13:20 and, perhaps, Cant. 3:6). Thus, the author of II Chron. 9:14 changed the words "trade of roklīm," used in I Kings 10:15, to the simple "traders" (soḥărim), as it was clear to people of his generation that those involved in King Solomon's trade were not retail merchants.

B. Foreign Trade

Most of our knowledge of the foreign trade of the Israelite kingdom is extracted from the account of Solomon's reign, particularly in I Kings 10 and the parallel II Chron. 9. The author emphasizes these trading activities in order to impress the reader with the glory and splendor of Solomon in the international community of rulers far and near.[36] In the view of the author, Solomon merited his status because of the wisdom promised by God at the outset of his reign: "And I will give you both riches and honor, so that no other king shall compare with you, all your days" (I Kings 3:13). The account also emphasizes fulfillment of the promise: "So King Solomon exceeded all the kings of the earth in riches and in wisdom. And all the earth sought the presence of Solomon to hear his wisdom, which God had put into his heart" (I Kings 10:23–24). Because of his motivation the narrator did not trouble to label these activities commercial, and we can learn their nature only from his description of them.

1. The Account of the Visit of the Queen of Sheba

The story of the Queen of Sheba's visit to Solomon's court accords with the historiographic tendencies of the narrator. She came to Jerusalem because she had heard "of the fame of Solomon because of the name of the Lord, [so] she came to test him with riddles" (I Kings 10:1). She brought gifts with her, of the type which Arabians traded in: "a hundred and twenty talents of gold, and a very great quantity of spices, and precious stones: there were no spices such as those which the Queen of Sheba gave to King Solomon" (I Kings 10:10; II Chron. 9:9). The emphasis on the large amount and high quality of the spices and other gifts is not without good reason: the text apparently refers to myrrh and frankincense, extracted from shrubs that grow only in the southern part of the Arabian peninsula and in certain areas of East Africa; such spices were marketed by Arabian traders during the period of the Israelite Monarchy and later.[37] In accordance with contemporary diplomatic etiquette, Solomon reciprocated with gifts, some selected by him, others requested by the Queen herself: "And Solomon gave to the Queen of Sheba all that she desired, whatsoever she asked beside that which Solomon gave her of his royal bounty" (I Kings 10:13).

Despite the legendary quality of the story, it reflects the commercial aspect of the meeting: the phrase *liš'ōl ḥēfeṣ* ("to ask for something desired"), describing the exchange of gifts between the two monarchs, is also often found in the report of the negotiations between Solomon and Hiram, whose commercial nature is clear. Hiram wrote to Solomon, "I am ready to do all your desire ['et kol ḥefṣᵉkā] in the matter of cedar and cypress timber. . . and you shall meet my desire ['et ḥefṣī] by providing food for my household" (I Kings 5:22–24, English version 8–10). A similar formula for negotiating the exchange of "gifts" between kings is common in the el-Amarna Letters; these are understood to be commercial negotiations, although their explicit definition as such is lacking. [38] In their correspondence with Pharaoh, the various kings repeatedly use the formula: "That which you wish of my land, write and I will see to it that they shall bring it to you, and I shall write of that which I wish of your land, and you shall send it to me. [39] In the light of these parallels, it seems that the Queen of Sheba came to Solomon not only "to test him with riddles," but also for trade negotiations. Solomon controlled the trade routes and the countries over which the Arab camel caravans then traveled on their way to the lands of the Fertile Crescent; without Solomon's cooperation, the Arabians could not be assured of the regular conduct of their trade. [40]

2. THE VOYAGES TO OPHIR

Another element of Solomon's greatness is contained in the short descriptions of the voyage to Ophir. "King Solomon built a fleet of ships at Ezion-geber, which is near Elath on the shore of the Red Sea, in the land of Edom. And Hiram sent with the fleet his servants, seamen who were familiar with the sea, together with the servants of Solomon, and they went to Ophir and brought from there gold, to the amount of four hundred and twenty talents, and they brought it to King Solomon." [41] Tyrians were included in these voyages primarily because of their shipbuilding and sailing skills, [42] but they were also particularly valuable because of the commercial nature of the voyages to Ophir: the Sidonians were experts in sea trade and even had special organizations of sea traders, called ḥbr, as we learn from the report of Wenamun. [43]

Gold, precious stones, 'almugīm wood, ivory, monkeys, and parrots were brought from Ophir. Opinions vary as to the identification and location of Ophir: some place it in India, others in southern Arabia, and still others in East Africa or on either coast of the Red Sea. [44] H. von Wissmann has recently adduced an additional point in favor of the view that Ophir was in southern Arabia. He claims that the almug wood in the list of goods from Ophir (I Kings 10:11–12; II Chron. 9:10–11) and from Lebanon (II Chron. 2:7) [45] is identical with a certain type of juniper growing on the Libanese mountains and on the Asir mountains east of Aden in southern Arabia, which are covered down to the coast with large forests. [46]

Other scholars have correctly noted that many of the goods from Ophir were also brought from the land of Punt, where the pharaohs sent expeditions via the Red Sea as early as the time of the Ancient Kingdom.[47] On the basis of written reports of these expeditions, depictions of flora and fauna on reliefs, and lists of the merchandise from Punt, scholars have identified it with various spots on the African coast of the Red Sea, or even with parts of the opposite Arabian coast.[48] The fact is that some articles from both Punt and Ophir were to be found on both sides of the Red Sea.

If the identification made by most scholars of Ophir with Punt is correct, we can learn more about Solomon's expeditions to Ophir from the description, found in the temple of Deir el-Bahri, of an expedition sent by Queen Hatshepsut (1490–1468 B.C.E.): "[The arrival] of the king's messenger in God's Land, together with the army which is behind, him, before the chiefs of Punt; dispatched with every good things from the court [of Egypt]."[49] It can therefore be concluded that emissaries from the king of Egypt on diplomatic assignments were also supplied with goods and authorized to carry on trade in the name of their king; this combination of commerce and diplomacy appears in other New Kingdom documents as well.[50] The goods which the Egyptians exchanged with the princes of Punt are not specified, nor does the Bible mention what Ophir received in return for its goods; Glueck surmised that Solomon's and Hiram's sailors exchanged copper from Timna for the products of Ophir, but Rothenberg's discoveries make it doubtful whether these mines were still being exploited in the days of Solomon.[51]

Ophir was particularly famous for its gold, which was known as "Ophir gold" or as "fine gold of Ophir" (*ketem 'Ophīr*); the phrase "gold of Ophir" has been discovered on an eighth-century B.C.E. ostracon from Tell Qasileh.[52] The biblical stories about Solomon stress the fact that he had much gold because of his ties with Ophir and the Arabians.[53] Gold existed in large quantities in southern Arabia and especially in Nubia (east Africa);[54] during the time of the New Kingdom period, the Egyptians ruled the latter area and made voyages to the former and was therefore the most important source of gold for all of eastern Asia. Letters to pharaoh found at el-Amarna repeatedly request him to send gold to Asian kings, which is like "dust" in his land.[55] With the decline of Egypt in the twelfth and eleventh centuries the ties with gold-producing lands were cut, and in the tenth century the Israelite kingdom, which controlled part of the Red Sea coast, was able to assume Egypt's former commercial role with these countries. The Israelite kingdom, furthermore, commanded the routes to the Fertile Crescent used by the Arabians, among whose wares, according to the Bible and to Assyrian documents, gold was important. It is therefore not coincidental that our sources for Solomon's prosperity particularly emphasize the great quantities of gold that he possessed.

3. Economic Ties with the Kingdom of Tyre

The cooperation between Israel and Tyre in sea voyages to Ophir was only part of the wider economic cooperation between the two kingdoms in the tenth century.[56] In addition to their geopolitical situation, the two countries also complemented each other's needs, thanks to the physical characteristics and the particular economic structure of both; it is perhaps for this reason that of all the countries we are told only of the goods which Israel exchanged with Tyre.

Hiram undertook to supply Solomon with timber from Lebanon for use in his many and elaborate building projects. In return, Solomon agreed to provide Hiram's professional woodcutters with Israelite laborers, as well as "twenty thousand cors of wheat as food for his household, and twenty thousand cors of beaten oil" (I Kings 5:20–25; English versions 6–11). According to Ezekiel's lament about the city, Israel was in fact Tyre's main source of agricultural produce. In the period of the Return, just as in Solomon's time, cedars for the construction of the Temple were bought from Tyrians and Sidonians in return for "food and drink and oil" (Ezr. 3:7).

Israel's rich agricultural yields account for the tradition that it was a land of "wheat and barley, of vines and fig trees and pomegranates, a land of olive trees and honey, a land in which you will eat bread without scarceness, you shall not lack anything in it" (Deut. 8:8–9).[57] Where the Assyrians ruled, they also exploited the land's agricultural surpluses a conclusion to be drawn from various documents: an administrative document from the Nineveh archives (*ABL* 1201) testifies that in the province of Samaria the Assyrians collected corn taxes (*ŠE nu-sa-ḫe*) and, according to a contemporary legal document, three *ḥomer* (*imēr*) of wheat were sold "according to the *sūtu* measure of the land of Judah (*mat Ya-u-di*)."[58] It is impossible to determine from this latter document why two men in Nineveh conducted their transaction on the basis of a Judean measure, but the fact that such a measure was employed in the grain trade implies that Palestinian produce reached the markets of distant Mesopotamia. We do not know whether goods from the province of Samaria and from the Judean kingdom reached Mesopotamia only by means of taxes or also through normal business channels, but these documents certainly attest to agricultural surpluses in Palestine, even during periods of political weakness.

Solomon's control over the lands east of the Jordan, long renowned for the bounty of their agriculture, was certainly a contributory factor in trade agreements with Hiram of Tyre, based as they were upon the export of Israelite agricultural produce. Ezekiel, in a verse cited above (27:17), refers to the "wheat of minnith," apparently named after Minnith in Ammon or nearby (Judg. 11:33).[59]

King Jotham received a yearly tribute from the Ammonites, "a hundred talents of silver and ten thousand cors of wheat and ten thousand of barley" (II Chron. 27:5), and we can assume that other areas of Solomon's empire with high agricultural yields were exploited to further his commercial interests.

However, the terms of the commercial agreement with Tyre put Israel at a disadvantage from the start. Israel's trade, derived, as we have seen, from agricultural production, which depends heavily on the weather. Besides, since Israel was not Tyre's only neighbor with agricultural surpluses, Israelite economy and trade were therefore extremely sensitive to natural disasters and political reverses. Tyre, on the other hand, not only possessed valuable and desirable timber easily transported by sea, but also marketed other goods which were specialized and consequently of great value.[60] Thus, in the latter half of Solomon's reign with the deterioration of the geopolitical situation of the kingdom of Israel and the fortunes of the Davidic dynasty, including its great empire, the balance of trade shifted in favor of Tyre. Agricultural surpluses no longer sufficed to pay for the construction timber, gold, and technical knowledge supplied by the Tyrian kingdom; Solomon was therefore obliged to cede to Tyre the fertile agricultural land on the border between the two countries, the region of Cabul in western Galilee,[61] thus fixing the border between Tyre and Israel for generations to come.[62]

4. SOLOMON'S HORSE TRADE

The Bible reports: "And Solomon had horses brought out of *Miṣrayim* and Que, and the king's merchants received them from Que at a price. A chariot came up and went out of *Miṣrayim* for six hundred shekels of silver, and a horse for a hundred and fifty, and all the kings of the Hittites and the kings of Aram brought them by export through them" (*b^{e}yādām yōṣi'ū*; I Kings 10:28–29; similarly, II Chron. 11:16–17). Despite the obscure nature of these verses, they attest the profitable exploitation of transit trade by the kingdom of Israel, as a result of its control over the routes between Africa and Asia Minor.

The kingdom of Que extended along the Cilician coastal plain on the southeastern part of the Anatolian peninsula. Northeast of it lay the land of Muṣri, known to us from various epigraphic sources and from II Kings 7:6 by the name of *Miṣrayim*.[63] North of this land, in the mountains of Cappadocia, there were, according to documents and inscriptions from the second and first millennia, important horse-breeding centers, from which horses were exported to various parts of Mesopotamia, in particular the neo-Assyrian empire.[64] Routes led directly from Asia Minor into Mesopotamia, but Palestine made contact with Cappadocia via the Cilician coast, at that time controlled by the kingdom of Que. Solomon's merchants may possibly have sent their consignment of horses by ship from the Cilician coast to the ports of Palestine, since the Septuagint says, "They brought them out by sea" (κατα᾽ θάλαϲϲαν), in place of the words of the Masoretic Text, "They brought them by export through them." Canaanite tradesmen did indeed transport cattle by ship to Egyptian ports, as Egyptian wallpaintings depict.[65] A clay seal discovered at Knossos indicates, furthermore, that boats carrying horses were plying the seas as long ago as the Late Bronze Age.[66]

Naturally, transit trade was conducted only in transferable silver currency, in contrast to Solomon's other foreign commercial dealings, which as we have seen were usually based on barter.

Solomon's political control of Syria and Palestine, whose peoples neither raised nor used horses, apparently gave him a monopol in the sale of horses and war chariots to all the vassal kingdoms—"to all the kings of the Hittites and the kings of Aram." In addition to income, this monopoly gave Solomon control over the chariot forces of his subject kingdoms. The royal merchants active in this trade were experts. A similar situation obtained in the Assyrian empire, where vassal kingdoms bought their horses through the Assyrian kings.[67] The Bible emphasizes the profits of Solomon's monopoly by noting the high prices paid for horses and chariots supplied by the royal merchants. The Masoretic text appears to have exaggerated the price; the Septuagint quotes fifty shekels of silver for a horse and one hundred for a chariot, prices identical with those paid in Babylonia a hundred years before.[68]

5. Ḥūṣōt

The biblical account of the war between Ahab of Israel and the king of Aram offers additional information about the international trade practises of Israel, Judah, and their neighbors. After Ahab defeated Ben-Hadad of Aram-Damascus at the battle of Aphek, Ben-Hadad suggested: "The cities which my father took from your father I will restore, and you may establish [tāsīm lᵉka] ḥūṣōt for yourself in Damascus, as my father did in Samaria." Ahab agreed to this suggestion, saying "I will send you away with this covenant;" the account ends: "So he made a covenant with him and sent him away" (I Kings 20:34).[69] The meaning of the term ḥūṣōt, used here in a political context, is not clear. If, however, we assume that ḥūṣōt refers to places of concentrated economic activity,[70] we can infer that the defeated Ben-Hadad agreed to grant trade concessions to Ahab's merchants in Damascus, similar to those in Samaria once granted to the king of Aram-Damascus.

The root swm ("and you may establish [tāsīm] ḥūṣōt for yourself in Damascus, as my father did in Samaria"), when used by the Bible in a political context, refers to the activity of the stronger party *vis-à-vis* the weaker, and means to appoint to a position, to establish something within the territory of the weaker party, or to impose some legal obligation.[71] The *ḥūṣōt*, therefore, should not be likened to the *kārum* institution of the early Assyrian and Babylonian periods in Anatolia and the cities of Babylonia; the merchants of the *kārum* traded in the foreign land on the basis of political and economic equality between their homelands and the states in which they operated.[72] The *ḥūṣōt* of Aram and Israel had a status similar to that of the colony of merchants from Ura extant in Ugarit in the fourteenth century B.C.E. These merchants acted on behalf of the Hittite king, whose vassal, the king of Ugarit, was responsible for their safety.[73] The *ḥūṣōt* offered Ahab in Damascus were similar to the *kāru* maintained by eighth- and seventh-century Assyrian kings in Arvad: from a letter apparently sent to Esarhaddon (ABL 992), we learn that the king of Assyria had special rights in the port of the kingdom of Arvad, which was under Assyrian hegemony—a special *kārum* (quay)[74] was held by the Assyrian king for the exclusive use of his men. The writer of the letter complains that Jakinlu, king of Arvad, was preventing ships from docking at the "*kārum* of the king of Assyria" (lines 16–17) and trying to attract vessels to his own dock, apparently in order to profit from docking the ships and from trade in their goods. The letter, which is partially damaged and difficult to read, further mentions individuals close to the Assyrian king and to merchants acting on his authority (rev. 6–10).

We know nothing of the nature of the commercial activity of the residents of *ḥūṣōt* in Samaria or Damascus; our sources are silent on the subject. The mere existence of such *ḥūṣōt*, however, is enough to confirm the fact that the Omride kings actively participated in international trade, as a result of their geopolitical situation. Further evidence for their activity in this field is the attempt by Jehoshaphat of Judah to reactivate the voyages to Ophir, and the role of his ally Ahaziah, king of Israel, in this attempt (I Kings 22:49–50; II Chron. 20:36–37). The stories about Solomon's monarchy clarify the commercial purpose of these voyages as does the phrase describing the cooperation of the two kings in the Ophir voyages: "He joined him [*vayeḥabrēhū*] in building ships to go to Tarshish."[75]

We have no further direct information about foreign trade during the monarchic period. It is reasonable to assume that when the geopolitical situation was similar to that of the Solomonic or Omride periods as it was in the days of Jeroboam son of Jehoash, king of Israel, and Uzziah and Jotham of Judah, the two kingdoms took part in international trade. But because of the nature of biblical historiography and the complete lack of epigraphical evidence about the economic activities of the kingdoms of Judah and Israel, this assumption remains without direct support. From archaeological finds and from information about the types of merchandise in the storehouses of the kings of Judah and Israel, however, we can conclude that commercial ties were maintained with countries far and near. We need mention only two examples. The remains of Egyptian alabaster jugs were found in the Omride palace in Samaria, one of them engraved with the name Osorkon II (861–829 B.C.E.).[76] The prophet also tells us that the caravans which passed through Sinai on their way from Judah to Egypt were loaded, "carrying their riches on the backs of asses and their treasures on the humps of camels" (Isa. 30:6). These snippets of information add to our knowledge of the international transactions of the kings of Judah and Israel, but they are not substantial enough to tell us as much about its nature as we know about Solomon's commercial activity.

Our information indicates that foreign trade was initiated by the crown and conducted on its behalf. It rested on two factors: 1) the existence of agricultural surpluses in Palestine, the product of favorable climatic conditions and the diligence of the people in developing and preserving the land. Trade in these surpluses was mainly with the kingdom of Tyre, a natural customer because of its unique economy and its proximity to Israel. 2) Particular geopolitical conditions which allowed Judah and Israel to participate in international trade by virtue of their control over international routes or parts of them. This, however, was largely transit trade; while it produced profits for the royal court and raised the standard of living of those close to it, it had only a limited influence on the local economy or on the occupational distribution of the country's inhabitants.

Agriculture was the primary source of livelihood for the people of Israel as long as they remained in their homeland. Even in the generation which saw the Destruction of the Second Temple, Josephus could still write of his nation:

Ours is not a maritime country; neither commerce nor the intercourse which it promotes with the outside world has any attraction for us. Our cities are built inland, remote from the sea; and we devote ourselves to the cultivation of the productive country with which we are pleased.[77]

CHAPTER VIII

THE ARCHAEOLOGICAL SOURCES FOR THE PERIOD OF THE MONARCHY

by Y. Yadin

A. STRATIGRAPHY AND CHRONOLOGY

THE UTILIZATION OF archaeological findings as evidence for under-standing the history of Palestine during the time of the Monarchy often encounters difficulties because it involves two different disciplines: archaeology and history. This is because, while excavating the mounds of cities mentioned in the Bible or extra-biblical sources, the excavators are inclined to make use of knowledge derived from these sources in order to arrive at a more precise date of the layers uncovered. This is natural and in many cases appropriate. However, in making use of the results of excavations the excavator must take care to distinguish adequately between conclusions based on pure archaeological finds and those influenced by historical documentation. For this reason and in order to present to the reader, who is not a professional archaeologist, the finds transmitting the material culture of the period of the Monarchy, we must first clarify the chronological and stratigraphical facts in some of the key Palestinian mounds. In our selection of mounds, we decided to limit ourselves to those cities of the period which are of historical importance and which have been the sites of large-scale excavations from which we can draw definite or nearly definite chronological conclusions. The order in which these mounds are to be considered is based on their geographical position, from north to south.

1. DAN

The excavations of this important site[1] brought to light two main buildings related to the period in question: the cult site in the north of the *tell*, and the fortifications and the city-gate in the south.

The Bāmāh ("high place"). The latest excavations show that the Israelite cult site was built on the remains of an earlier place of worship. From the time of the Monarchy, three main stages can be distinguished. (1) The earlier building (stage A), whose remains were found covered by a layer of ashes with pottery of the tenth century B.C.E., was rectangular and measured approximately

6 × 18.4 m. The excavator, A. Biran, is apparently justified in linking this building, whose character has not yet been sufficiently clarified, with the activities of Jeroboam I, the son of Nebat (I Kings 12:31). (2) The main part of the building uncovered in the excavations belongs to the second stage (B) which, according to the potsherds of the first half of the ninth century B.C.E. found there, can be approximately attributed to Ahab's reign. This building is almost square (18.7 × 18.2 m.); its exterior walls are built of ashlar stones in the typical manner of the Israelite period: the stones in the two lowest courses are placed as headers, and in the upper courses are laid as headers and stretchers. The style of the dressing of the stones is also typical of this period (see also below). The monumental staircase built on the southern edge of the *bāmāh* should be attributed to the third stage (C) in the eighth century. The cultic character of this site was preserved throughout the Hellenistic and Roman periods, when the building was enlarged. Biran assumes that the building served as an open *bāmāh*. The state in which the remains were uncovered does not permit this assumption to be proved or disproved. Thus we have here the earliest Israelite cult building of the *bāmāh* type that can be dated with reasonable certainty. The latest excavations there brought to light a small horned altar, as well as a possible *propylaeum* leading to the *temenos*.

The Gate and Fortifications

The fortifications of Dan at the time of the Monarchy consisted of a massive wall,[2] 4 m. wide,[3] a monumental gate, and a paved road leading from the gate into the city, apparently ending at a further, interior, gate. The importance of the gate and the fortifications has several aspects. The foremost problem is dating their construction; it is natural that Biran initially attributed these fortifications to the reign of Jeroboam I, i.e., the end of the tenth century. This conclusion was, in his opinion, strengthened by the pottery finds there,[4] and no doubt this is the earliest date to which the construction of the fortifications can be attributed. On the other hand, on the basis of the fill discovered on the site in the excavations of 1972, a later date for the construction of the fortifications, viz., the reign of Omri, might be considered. The conclusion that these fortifications do not precede the period of the divided kingdom is of great importance for the study of the methods of fortification, and bears upon the dating of other fortifications built similarly (see below, Beersheba).

The gate itself consists of two elements: the outer city-gate which leads to a large piazza, and the gate-building proper, with four rooms, two on each side. The plan is similar to that of Megiddo from Ahab's reign and to that of the earliest gate discovered at Beersheba, as well as to the gate at Tell el-Kheleife (Eziongeber?). On the piazza, to the right of the gate when entering, a structure was

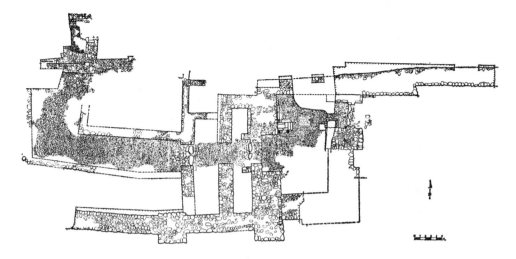

Fig. 1. Tel Dan: City-Gate, Area A.
A. Biran, *IEJ*, 26 (1976), 203.

uncovered, built of ashlar, with columns in its four corners. Three of the bases of the columns were found *in situ*, decorated in a style common in the towns of the neo-Hittite kingdoms of that period. The excavator presumes that the columns supported a kind of canopy which covered the structure, in which may have stood the throne of the king or a statue of cultic significance.

2. HAZOR

The excavation of this town, whose ruins were identified with certainty with Tell el-Qedah,[5] forms one of the foundations of the stratigraphy of an Israelite town dating from the United Monarchy until its destruction in 732 by Tiglath-pileser III. The reason for this lies in the wealth of knowledge derived both from written sources and from the identification of the strata with known historical events, as well as from the large areas excavated in uncovering the various strata. The two clear strata which limit the dates of the other strata uncovered are stratum X from the reign of Solomon and stratum VA from the reign of Pekah and the destruction of the town by Tiglath-pileser III. The other strata—at least four, not counting the intermediate phases—can be dated between 930 and 730, a period of 200 years. Thus it is possible to date the strata within a margin of 30–50 years. An additional find from stratum VI, indicating that this town was destroyed by an earthquake, enables us to date this stratum to the days of Uzziah king of Judah and Jeroboam II king of Israel (cf. Amos 1:1; Zech. 14:5) and thus to limit still further the dates of the other strata.

Stratum X

The buildings here were identified with the construction activities of Solomon, corresponding both to the stratigraphical and pottery finds and to the literary account that Hazor was built by Solomon together with Gezer and Megiddo (I Kings 9:15). The discovery of identical fortifications at Megiddo and Gezer finally confirmed this dating.

The fortifications comprise two clear elements: a gate with six rooms (three on each side) and two towers (one on the right and one on the left) and a casemate wall. The excavations proved conclusively that Solomon's town covered only the western half of the mound and that its area did not exceed approximately 26 dunams. This overall system of fortifications, identical to that discovered at Gezer and Megiddo, but not at other sites, shows that it was planned on behalf of a central authority. According to the archaeological data thus far known it can be stated that the existence of a casemate wall, a six-room gate, and two towers alone allow us—without additional data—to attribute this system of fortifications to the reign of Solomon.

Between the lowest layer of stratum X (XB), from the time of Solomon, and the foundations of stratum VIII from the time of Ahab, three intermediate building phases were uncovered: XA and IXA-B, which should be attributed to a period of approximately 60 years. In the final phase of stratum IX a thick layer caused by burning was discovered, which might be attributed to the activities of Ben-Hadad in c. 885.

Stratum VIII

This stratum—from the time of the greatest prosperity and expansion of Hazor—entirely changed the appearance and character of the town. It extended over the whole area of the mound; public buildings, including a strong citadel, a storehouse, and underground water installations in case of a siege were constructed. Historical reasoning, the pottery finds (ninth century B.C.E.), and the chronological limits of the early and late strata enable us to attribute the building of this city to the reign of Ahab.

In addition to the expansion of the town area in this stratum, the fortifications are now characterized by a new massive wall instead of the previous casemate one. Traces of this wall were discovered in the eastern area, which was now part of the town limits, on every side. On the other hand, in the western area, the new wall was built on the foundations of the previous casemate wall wherever its remains could be distinguished and in many places it was clear that the case-

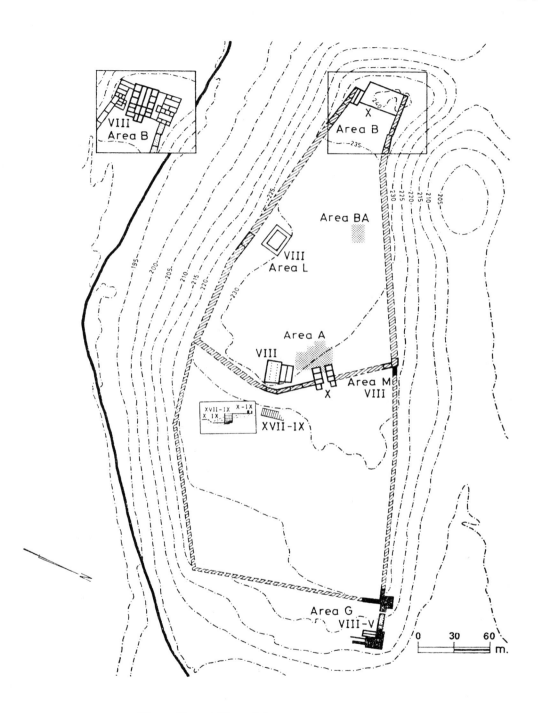

Fig. 2. Hazor: Plan of the Iron Age fortifications.

mates had been filled in with earth and stones, thus achieving a massive wall here also. The gate from Solomon's time and the adjacent casement wall, which now stood in the middle of the new town, were completely destroyed and new buildings erected on their ruins, or the casemates used for storage purposes and the like. For the first time it became clear from these excavations that between the periods of Solomon and Ahab there had been a significant turning-point in the fortification system of Israelite cities: the change-over from casemate walls to massive walls. This phenomenon can be explained by the appearance of the battering ram in the Assyrian armies at the beginning of the ninth century. Against these mighty breaching machines it was necessary to strengthen the walls of the principal towns which had been built as fortified cities (see also below).

The recently discovered water-supply system for times of siege has been attributed, on the basis of stratigraphical considerations, to stratum VIII; it undoubtedly forms part of the fortification works of that period, similar to Megiddo and possibly also to other sites. The structure of this installation is particularly interesting, and helps us to understand and classify the other waterworks. First a perpendicular shaft was dug, intruding into the earlier settlement layers until it reached bedrock. This shaft was padded with giant supporting walls to prevent the intrusion of loose earth. When the rock was reached, the shaft was hewn into it. About 15 m. above what is assumed to have been the water-level, a tunnel was dug which slanted down to the required depth. Into the sides of the shaft, four-meter-wide steps were hewn, allowing for two-way traffic up and down. In contrast to the waterworks at Megiddo (see below), the tunnel was not directed to the springs outside the town, but continued within the limits of the mound until it reached water-level. In this way, the water-supply was entirely guarded against any possible action by a besieging enemy.

The Storehouse

One of the monumental buildings erected in this stratum is in the center of the mound and consists of three halls: one is broad (measuring 13.5 × 20.7 m.) with two rows of columns, and is flanked by two narrow halls. Architecturally, it resembles somewhat the stables at Megiddo (see below), but has, in contrast to these, no stone-made troughs and no holes in the columns for tying up animals. It can therefore be assumed that this was a public building, apparently for storage. This assumption is also supported by the character of the two narrow halls; their floor is paved and one narrow entrance serves both. It is possible that in the main hall the goods were kept in storage vessels (e. g., jars and *pithoi*), and in the side halls scattered on the floor or stored in sacks. This type of room of great width, with a ceiling supported by columns, is common in Israelite construction of storehouses and stables as well as of buildings serving other purposes.

The Citadel

In the western and best protected edge of the mound, a large citadel was discovered, its ground floor planned according to the four-room principle of one broad hall and three long rooms, also one of the distinctive marks of the buildings of the monarchical period. This citadel, built on the remains of a fortress of stratum X, was erected on the very edge of the mound, its walls doubling as the city-wall. This principle also seems to mark the city fortifications at the time of the Monarchy.

The outstanding architectural elements of the citadel included a couple of proto-aeolic capitals, one of which is decorated on both sides; it probably crowned a free-standing column. These capitals are very similar to those found at Samaria and Megiddo.

The general style of building of stratum VIII—including the use of ashlar at the corners of the building—is similar to that at Megiddo and Samaria of the same period, although of inferior quality.

In stratum VII, signs of deterioration in the maintenance of the city's public buildings are recognizable. There is also a change in the town's general image, expressed in its growing civilian rather than military character. This city was destroyed by a huge conflagration, possibly attributable to attacks by the Arameans at the end of the ninth century, which may also have caused the destruction discernible in many buildings at Dan.

Stratum VI

In this stratum, signs of reorganization are recognizable in the city, chiefly in the residences of the well-to-do. From this period are preserved the most impressive private buildings of the Israelite period. The fact that the destruction of the city at this time occurred because of an earthquake allows us to date its end by the earthquake mentioned in Amos 1:1 at the time of Jeroboam II. If this is correct, it gives us an additional means of determining the absolute date of the strata of Hazor, in addition to the period of Solomon.

Stratum V

The destruction caused by the earthquake was quickly repaired and we can see that the builders of the next city—stratum V—made use of many of the earlier buildings. In some areas there are clear signs that during the existence of this city the fortifications were strengthened (VA), presumably in an effort to forestall the danger of an Assyrian attack at the time of Tiglath-pileser III. Stratum V was destroyed by a huge conflagration, undoubtedly attributable to the conquest by Tiglath-pileser III.

Stratum IV

This stratum represents a poor settlement—still Israelite in character—constructed on the ruins of the town and its fortifications. It can be assumed that after the town was destroyed some of the previous inhabitants resettled there under the protection of the Assyrians.

Using all this information, we can date the strata of Hazor in the period of the kings of Israel as follows:

Stratum	Date	Historical source (or period)	Remarks
XB	C. 950 B.C.E.	Solomon's city I Kings 9, 15	Fortified town in the western half of the mound
XA	End of tenth century		
IXA, B	Early ninth century		This town may have been destroyed by Ben-Hadad in c. 885 B.C.E.
VIII	Ninth century—Ahab		The town is re-fortified and expands over the whole mound
VII	Second half of ninth century		Signs of deterioration
VI	First half of eighth century	Destruction by earthquake Zech. 14:5; Amos 1:4	
VB	Second half of eighth century	Menahem	
VA	Destruction in 732 B.C.E.	II Kings 15:29 (Pekah)	
IV	End of eighth century		Open city

Thus the Hazor excavations are the most important source in the north of the country for dated finds from the period of the Monarchy.

3. MEGIDDO

The excavations at Megiddo, although not conducted in an orderly manner, threw much light on the material culture—particularly the architecture—from the time of the kings of Israel. Changes in the leadership of the expeditions led to a lack of continuity in the interpretation and publication of the material, so that it is difficult to accept some of the basic conclusions of the excavators. In particular, the attribution of the well-known stables to the time of Solomon caused differences of opinion among scholars. This conclusion of the excavators had already been shaken by Crowfoot and Kenyon, mainly on the basis of an analysis of the building style and the pottery finds. Following the discovery of Solomonic strata at Hazor and Gezer (see below), the author undertook five short seasons of excavations on the site, in order to ascertain what layers belonged to the period of the Monarchy.[6] An analysis of the relevant strata at Megiddo, although complex, is necessary here, even though this volume is not basically archaeological, because this is the only possible way to reach a number of fundamental conclusions in connection with the history of the Monarchy. We shall limit ourselves to the statement of the main facts and to some remarks concerning a number of conclusions arrived at which contradict the conclusions of the previous excavations.[7]

The starting point for the description is Stratum IVA, in which were discovered two complexes of the well-known stables, the massive wall 325, and a gate with six rooms and two towers, also attributed to this stratum.

Because of the association with the chariot towns of Solomon, the excavators of Megiddo attributed it to Solomon's period (although Megiddo is not defined specifically as a chariot city). More precisely stated, in the first stage the excavators did not attribute to this town the six-room gate, but a later gate with four rooms, which was discovered integrated in the massive wall 325. The excavators themselves noticed the stratigraphical difficulty deriving from this attribution. On the south side of the mound, the foundations of a splendid palace (1723), built in the Israelite style, were uncovered *below* the above-mentioned wall. Furthermore, in a similar stratigraphical position an additional monumental building (1482) was discovered, which had been partly covered by the foundations of the complex of the southern stables (1576). The stratum of these buildings was designated stratum IVB by the excavators, because the number VA had been given to another stratum discovered in the other areas of the mound below the stable complexes. The building of stratum IVB, and in particular the palace 1723, were of ashlar, dressed and laid in an identical manner to that of the six-room gate, which is also characteristic of the building method of the kings of Israel at Samaria (see below).

With these discoveries, the Megiddo excavators faced a difficult problem. Because the stables, the gate, and the wall were attributed to the time of Solomon, and because the architectural style of the structures in stratum IVB was identical with that of the structures above them, there were only two ways to attribute them: either the palace had been built by David as an isolated fortress destroyed when the town was rebuilt by Solomon, or they had been built by Solomon in an earlier building phase, and later, when the town was built according to a uniform plan, they were destroyed by Solomon himself. Both alternatives raised many logical as well as historical difficulties. It is difficult to assume that the most splendid building discovered at Megiddo would have been destroyed at the hands of the man who built it—Solomon; if, indeed, it "was in the way" of the line of fortifications, a means could easily have been found to include it in the city-wall. From the historical viewpoint, those buildings were difficult to attribute to the time of David, not only because the Bible states specifically that Megiddo was built by Solomon (I Kings 9:15), but because David—by reason of his many wars, particularly across the borders—had no time to build cities; he did not even construct the Jerusalem Temple. The stratigraphical confusion was partly solved by Albright and Wright,[8] when they proved that strata IVB and VA are one and the same; but this was not sufficient, since it assumes that a whole town with all its components, not simply an isolated citadel, had been built by David.

Checking the conclusions reached by the excavators of Megiddo proved necessary for another reason. At Hazor and Gezer (see below), it was found that Solomon's fortifications, connected with the six-room gate, belonged to the type of case-mate walls, while at Megiddo, according to the excavators, Solomon built a massive wall. It is an accepted axiom that the fortification system planned by a central ruler is uniform and adjusts to the problems of warfare at a specific time. It was difficult to accept the assumption[9] that the fortification system of Megiddo was different because it served as a chariot city and was therefore specially fortified.[10]

Five seasons of excavations were therefore carried out at Megiddo in the years 1960, 1961, 1966, 1967, and 1971, in order to clarify the relationship between the buildings of stratum IVB and those above them, and in particular to clarify the fortification system of the stratum IVB city, which, according to the excavators' conclusions, was—as mentioned above—without fortifications.

The excavations were concentrated near the northern complex of the stables, at the spot where the massive wall 325 and the stable complex itself had been well preserved, and proved without doubt that palace 1723 and building 1482 were not isolated structures. Another palace—6000—and alongside it the remains of another large building were discovered here. These structures, uncovered below wall 325 and the stable complex, were built of the ashlar characteristic of the Israelite building methods. Furthermore, the repertory of pottery vessels found *in situ* is identical to that found at Hazor in the stratum of Solomon. On the other hand, a considerable number of potsherds clearly belonging to the ninth century was found among those extracted from the

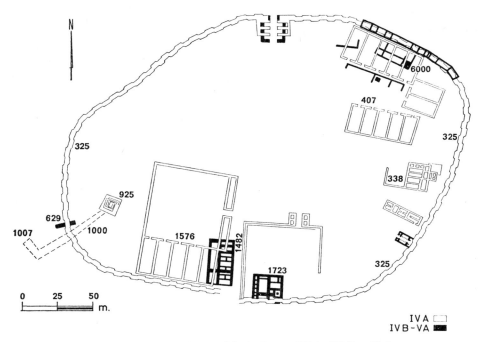

Fig. 3. Key plan of Megiddo in Strata IV A, IV B—V A.

fill of wall 325. Thus it becomes evident from both the stratigraphy and the pottery that the city of stratum VA–IVB has to be attributed to the reign of Solomon, and the city of stratum IVA with its stables and walls to the ninth century, apparently built by Ahab (see below). Several of the walls of the buildings of stratum VA–IVB had been robbed, with clear evidence of the robbers' trenches. It can be assumed that the builders of stratum IVA, who changed the entire character of Megiddo, extracted many fine ashlar stones from Solomon's city and re-used them in their own buildings. Thus it becomes understandable why earlier excavators of Megiddo came upon almost none of its remains.

The excavations in the vicinity of the "new" palace—6000—also proved that adjacent to it existed a casemate wall and that the massive wall 325 had been built on its ruins. The casemate wall was discovered on both sides of the palace, whose exterior wall also forms the city-wall. The section of the fortifications east of the palace—where the slopes of the mound are steepest and most easily defensible—is of field stones and the casemate system is similar to that discovered on other sites, particularly at Tel Beit-Mirsim: sometimes the casemates form part of the buildings, which continue into the interior of the town, and sometimes they are an independent unit whose divisions do not extend beyond the wall.[11] On the other hand, the casemates to the west of the palace, which continue in the direction of the gate, are built solidly of ashlar. Here too, however, the wall facing outward toward the slope is of field stones. This system of casemates undoubtedly formed the city-wall and was not part of the palace courtyard, as can be verified from the location of the large building discovered south of palace 6000. The plan of palace 6000 is also interesting: a broadhouse whose parts remind us of the type of the *bīt-ḫilāni* at Zinjirli of approximately the same period,[12] an example of the influence of Phoenician architecture on the buildings of Solomon's times.

These discoveries proved clearly that the new-found complex—the palace and the casemate fortifications—should be attributed to stratum VA–IVB, counting the strata from top to bottom, but stratigraphically confirmed by counting from bottom to top. The Megiddo excavators discovered between strata VA and VIA an additional stratum of a modest unfortified city which they called VB. B. Mazar established it as belonging to the reign of David, having attributed the destruction of stratum VIA to David's activities.[13] Indeed, both in the area of the eastern casemates and that of palace 6000 and the western casemates, structures clearly belonging to this stratum were discovered underneath the buildings of VA–IVB and above stratum VIA. Thus the stratigraphical "circle" is clearly closed.[14]

These new discoveries also necessitated a re-check of the huge structure discovered at Megiddo: the underground installations for supplying water in times of siege. In fact, two of these were uncovered which permitted access from inside the city to the spring at the foot of the mound on its southern side: (1) A perpendicular shaft (925) and a tunnel (1000) which led from the town to the spring, which was blocked from the outside by a strong wall built for this purpose; (2) A "passage" on the southern side, built of ashlar, which also led to the spring through the slope of the mound. This passage (or "gallery" 629, as it was called by the Megiddo excavators) was found blocked underneath the massive wall 325, attributed by the excavators, as mentioned, to the time of Solomon. The considerations of the excavators in connection with the relative dates of the two water installations were logical: the "gallery" which led to the open cave precedes the shaft and tunnel. Since the excavators attributed wall 325 to the reign of Solomon, they dated the water installations to the twelfth century. The new facts necessitated additional excavation near the "gallery," which proved conclusively that from the stratigraphical viewpoint the "gallery"— built of ashlar laid as headers and stretchers—was constructed in the period of the palaces and fortifications of Solomon's reign. On one of the stones of the "gallery" a mason's mark was observed, identical with those on the stones of the palaces and stables (where they were found in secondary use).

It could therefore be concluded that the shaft and tunnel, as well as the stables, had been built at the time of Ahab. As we have seen above, similar waterworks of the same period were discovered at Hazor, allowing us to draw conclusions about the difference in character in the town at the time of Solomon and that of Ahab. During the reign of Solomon, a fortified administrative center existed here, commanding not only the principal artery of the Megiddo pass, but serving also as the center for Solomon's commissioners in all matters of administration and ceremony. This situation fits Solomon's period, which in general was relatively peaceful, permitting commercial and administrative-economic activities to develop. On the other hand, Megiddo of the Divided Monarchy (which reached its zenith during the reign of Ahab) became a "fortified city" with all the accoutrements: strong city-walls, an easily defensible basis for chariots, and, most important, sophisticated installations for the supply of water in times of siege. As at Hazor, the city developed this character as a result of the decisive change in the political and strategic situation at the beginning of the ninth century, with the increase of strength of the Arameans and Assyrians, and the permanent threat against the northern kingdom.

The new stratigraphical facts discovered in the latest excavations also enable us to understand correctly the development of the city-gates at Megiddo. On top of Solomon's six-room gate were first discovered two more gates. Since the earlier of these two gates was found by the excavator, Guy, bonded into the massive wall (325), he attributed it to the reign of Solomon. When Solomon's real gate was discovered, the later excavators (Loud and Lamon) attributed it to stratum III, the last city at Megiddo to have been fortified. The excavators now faced an additional difficulty when it became evident that the gate in question (500) consisted, in fact, of two different stratigraphical phases. Since they could attribute both to stratum III only, they called the earlier IIIB and the later III.

But as it seemed unlikely that two gates had been constructed in one stratum, they arrived at the strange conclusion that in fact only "gate III" had existed, explaining IIIB as a mistake made by the builders who, when they realized this, interrupted its construction. With the discovery of the true stratum of Solomon, it is now possible to attribute the gates as follows:

The six-room gate—stratum VA–IVB, casemate wall (Solomon).

The four-room gate—gate IIIB, stratum IV (the house of Ahab).

The two-room gate—gate III—stratum III (the time of the Assyrian conquest).

These conclusions compel us also to assume that the construction of the six-room gate, which is of ashlar, is not, as the excavators thought, a foundation built underground, but the stone foundation for the brick gate. Indeed, the road made of well-beaten earth should be attributed to this phase and not to the city of stratum VB, which was, as we have realized, an open city.

To our great regret, the excavators did not leave any unexcavated areas near the gates and therefore it is difficult to find out the exact development of the area near Solomon's gate in the period immediately following the destruction of the town at the time of Shishak.[15]

We can conclude with the following table of strata of the Iron Age (for the convenience of the reader, the periods preceding the Monarchy are included):

Stratum	Date	Remarks
VII A	Twelfth century—the period of Ramses III and VI	The first Iron Age city. "Philistine" elements
VI B	End of twelfth century and first half of eleventh century	Poor stratum built on the destruction of stratum VIIA. Open city. "Philistine" elements
VI A	Second half of eleventh century	Large developed city with considerable "Philistine" elements. Destruction by a great conflagration, apparently by David
V B	The time of David	Small open city
V A–IV B	The time of Solomon	Large city—administrative center—with several palaces, a six-room gate, casemate wall, "water gallery"
IV A		Several phases: mainly a city of chariots, fortified by a massive wall and underground water installations
III	The time of the Assyrian conquest 732 B.C.E.★	
II	The time of Josiah	Open settlement with fortress
I	Strata later than the period of the Monarchy	In fact, several phases

★ According to the original proposal of Albright, which he later abandoned (see *AASOR*, 21–22 (1943), p. 2, n. 1, and Y. Yadin, in: A. Malamat, ed., *The Kingdoms of Israel and Judah*, Jerusalem, 1961, p. 104, n.86 [Hebrew]).

4. SAMARIA

The Samaria excavations, like those of Hazor and Megiddo, are to be recognized as most important sources for the understanding of the material culture of the Israelite Monarchy; they are important, furthermore, for the chronological dating of the Israelite pottery. This is because Samaria served the kings of Israel as a capital city, and splendid buildings, representing the best of Israelite architectural tradition, were constructed there. Much knowledge can also be derived from historical sources concerning its rise and fall. However, scholars are divided about the exact interpretation of the archaeological finds, but since this has recently been dealt with exhaustively and lucidly[16] we shall here restrict ourselves to clarifying a few fundamental problems connected with the stratigraphy and dating of the finds. The main discussion derives from two basic assumptions made by one of the excavators, Kathleen Kenyon, on which she based the dating of the buildings and the pottery of the various strata. One of these assumptions is historical, i.e., that Omri built the city on top of a hill on which no earlier settlement had existed in the Israelite period; the second assumption is a clear-cut archaeological-methodological one: the statement made by Kenyon that the ceramic material in the make-up of the floors of the buildings belongs to the same period as the buildings. Following these assumptions, Kenyon fixed the date of the pottery in the fill of the floors of the first building stratum to the time of Omri. The scholars opposed (Albright, Aharoni, Ruth Amiran, Wright) pointed out that this pottery precedes the time of Omri and can be compared with that discovered on other sites (Megiddo, Hazor) and dated from the tenth century and the beginning of the ninth. They concluded, therefore, that before Omri built his palace, there existed on the site a poor settlement whose ruins served—among other purposes—as building material and fill for the floors of Omri's buildings. And indeed, Avigad showed[17] that, according to the excavation report itself, it is possible to distinguish several rude walls stratigraphically preceding the period of the monumental buildings. As a result of these differences in conception, those who oppose the conclusions of the excavator distinguish between the period of the building and of the pottery. In fact, as is shown in the following table, this difference is of great importance methodologically and in terms of the pottery, but the conclusions of the "opposition" do not differ basically from those of the excavators insofar as the date of the beginning of the monumental building at Samaria is concerned. For the convenience of the reader, we provide a table prepared by Avigad[18] (see next page).

Without clear data, it is difficult to determine the merits of the points under discussion. For our purpose it is sufficient to say that the opinion of Kenyon and Avigad—namely that the two main phases distinguishable at the beginning of the building activities are to be attributed to Omri (phase I) and Ahab (phase II)—seems to us preferable to that of Wright, who attributes phase I to Omri-Ahab, and phase II (the phase of the "casemates") to Jehu. It should be pointed out that the bulk of the finds in question were discovered only on the Acropolis.

And now let us define and describe briefly the nature of the two main early building phases: To the first building phase (I) we can attribute, basically, a wall or partition (called by the first scholars who dealt with it "the inner wall") which

Period	Kenyon Buildings	Kenyon Pottery	Wright Buildings	Wright Pottery	Avigad Buildings	Avigad Pottery
Early Bronze Age	—	+	—	+	—	+
Rural settlement (Shemer's estate?). Tenth-early ninth centuries	—	—	—	1–2	Wall remains	1–2
Omri (882–871)	I	1	I	3	I	3
Ahab	II	2			II	
Jehu (842–814)	III	3	II		III	
Jeroboam II (789–748)	IV	4	III	4	IV	4
End of Israelite settlement	V–VI	5–6	IV–VI	5–6	V–VI	5–6

surrounded a kind of rectangular precinct, measuring from east to west approximately 180 m. in length and about 90 m. in breadth, i.e., a rectangle exactly twice as long as broad. The wall is about 1.60 m. thick and is built of ashlar finely-dressed in the typically Israelite style, with the oblique marks of the chisel recognizable. The stones are laid systematically and precisely as headers and stretchers. This wall was built exactly as was the one discovered at Ramat Raḥel (see below). In the southwestern corner of this area were discovered the remains of a monumental building, probably containing a central courtyard surrounded by rooms. This seems to have been the main part of the palace in its narrow meaning of the king's house.

The second building phase (II) consists principally of a large extension of the summit of the hill, achieved by constructing huge retaining walls on the steep slopes and filling in the hollow space between them and the natural rock (technically this can be compared to the work of Herod on the Temple Mount). From the technical point of view, these retaining walls were built as casemates to prevent the collapse of the thick retaining walls (in the steep north, the overall thickness of the wall reaches 10 m.) because of the pressure of the fill. These walls were constructed of two parallel walls connected by partition walls. The hollows created between the walls were filled intentionally with earth and crushed stones. The area of the summit was thus enlarged by about 17 m. towards the north and by about 30 m. towards the west. Later, storage and administrative buildings were constructed in the enlarged area, where—among other finds—the famous ostraca were discovered. In the southwestern corner, outside the enlarged area, the remains of further monumental buildings were discovered, attributable to the expansion of the town at the time of Jehu or Jeroboam II. In addition, another splendidly constructed building was discovered about 150 m. east of the corner of the summit walls; it may have been the outer gate of the summit citadel.

The generally accepted scholarly opinion is that the house of Baal built by Ahab (I Kings 16:32) was erected within the precincts of the Acropolis, although in the excavations no remains identifiable with a building of this kind were discovered. It seems now to the present writer[19] that this house of Baal was possibly erected outside the area of the citadel of Samaria, on the site called "the city of the house of Baal" (II Kings 10:25–26), similar to the buildings which, in the opinion of the author, were erected by Athaliah in the vicinity of Jerusalem (see below, Ramat Raḥel).

To conclude this short survey, we can say that, in spite of scholarly differences of opinion concerning the details of construction, the buildings discovered at Samaria—together with those at Hazor and Megiddo—permit us to reconstruct with certainty the architectural system common during the Israelite Monarchy in the tenth-ninth centuries B.C.E. (We shall deal with this problem in detail, see below, pp. 225 ff.)

5. TIRZAH TELL EL-FARʿAH (NORTH)

An interesting conjunction between the biblical narratives and the archaeological finds was revealed in the excavations at Tell el-Farʿah (North), identified by excavator Père R. de Vaux, following Albright, with Tirzah. These findings are also related directly to the excavations at Samaria. The mound lies about 15 km. east of Samaria, near the opening of Wadi Farʿah, and it controls the important pass between the Jordan Valley and the mountains.[20]

The period we are concerned with is represented by the four (or rather five) latest strata, I–III.

Stratum III: The earliest of these, stratum III, was built on the ruins of the Late Bronze Age town. It existed for quite a long time, and the excavator distinguished a considerable number of phases of repair, as for instance the rise of the street level by about half a meter during its existence. The potsherds found in its top level date from the tenth and early ninth centuries. On the basis of these finds and the biblical data (I Kings 16:15–18), the excavator attributes the stratum's complete destruction to the conquest by Omri. Characteristic of this stratum are the houses of the "four-room" type.

The two intermediate strata between III and II (hereafter the "intermediate strata A–B"):

Intermediate stratum A: Above the ruins of the town of stratum III, several well-constructed buildings were discovered, in which simple ashlar stones were used. In the opinion of the excavator, the construction work on these buildings was not completed because Omri moved his residence from Tirzah to Samaria.

Intermediate stratum B: A number of rude buildings found in the area with foundations higher than the "unfinished" buildings of the intermediate stratum A were attributed by the excavator to a short-lived phase, dated by the pottery finds to the ninth century.

Stratum II: In the opinion of the excavator, this stratum is clearly distinguishable from the preceding strata by its well-constructed buildings—some of them the "four-room" type—which prove economic prosperity. The bulk of the pottery of this stratum is from the eighth century B.C.E., the time of Jeroboam II until the destruction of the town by the Assyrians. The excavator distinguishes between the "residential houses of the rich" and the poor ones.

Stratum I: In this stratum only a few buildings were discovered since much of it has eroded and was destroyed by natural forces and agricultural cultivation. The finds of Assyrian potsherds of the "palace-ware" type prove conclusively that it has to be attributed to the period after the Assyrian conquest.

The dates of the strata at Tell el-Far'ah are given in the following table:

Stratum	Date	Remarks
Stratum II	Tenth and early ninth centuries. Destruction by Omri	I Kings 16:15 ff.
Intermediate str. A.	Beginning of Omri's reign	Several unfinished buildings
Intermediate str. B.	Poor settlement of the ninth century	
Stratum II	Eighth century. Destruction by the Assyrians in c. 723	Fine buildings proving economic prosperity
Stratum I	Period of the Assyrian conquest in the (eighth) seventh century	Assyrian pottery of the palace ware type

6. TELL QASILEH

The most important period of the excavations at Tell Qasileh, which were conducted by B. Mazar and later by A. Mazar, is that of the settlement of the Philistines and the Sea-Peoples, preceding the Monarchy. The wealth of pottery finds and their stratigraphical attribution enable us to follow the development of the material culture of this period, although much is still unknown. Particularly worth mentioning is the latest discovery of a unique Philistine temple. The excavators attribute to the period of the Monarchy a number of strata which show the expansion of the Israelite settlement in this district. The following table of strata, based on that published by the excavators, shows the main stratigraphy of the site in the period in question.

Stratum	Period
IX 2 IX 1	The period of the United Monarchy in the tenth century B.C.E.
VIII	Ninth century B.C.E.
VII	Eighth century B.C.E. Destruction by the Assyrians

7. TELL EN-NAṢBEH (MIZPAH?)

The stratigraphy of the buildings within this town is not quite clear; however, the mighty fortifications discovered in their entirety, together with others found in a lesser state of preservation or insufficiently uncovered, have made this site one of the most interesting sources for understanding the development of town planning and fortification.

We shall start our analysis of the finds with the latest and also the most complete architectural remains, i.e., the massive wall with the offsets and insets, the towers, and the two-room city-gate. The foundations of this mighty wall (whose average width is more than 4 m.) were undoubtedly laid at the time of the Divided Monarchy, apparently, in the opinion of the excavators, at the time of Asa, in the early ninth century. This conclusion fits its type and also the biblical source (I Kings 15:22), if this mound indeed contains the remains of the city of Mizpah. All phases of the wall, however, as uncovered by the excavations, appear not to date from the same period; in fact, the excavators noticed several recognizable building phases, in particular in the various towers.

The city-gate—one of the finest preserved from the time of the Judean kings—

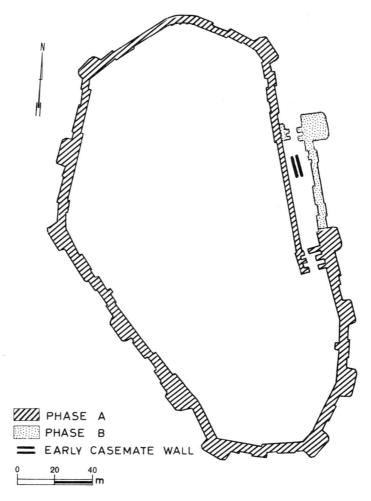

Fig. 4. Tell en-Naṣbeh: Plan of the Iron Age fortifications.
According to Y. Yadin.

consists in the main of two rooms (see plan) enclosed by four pilasters, two on each side. In front of the gate is a square with benches similar to those found in the rooms, thus offering us a fine example of a gate fulfilling a communal function. In one of the outer pilasters (the right one from inside the town), a long, horizontal depression was found that fitted the horizontal bolt when the gate was open; in the opposite pilaster, a depression for the bolt when the gate was locked. This is an authentic example of the biblical expression "gates and bars" (Deut. 3:5). About 60 m. south of this gate, a massive building was discovered, with walls 2.2 m. thick, adjacent to and built into the massive wall. Its plan is similar to that of a four-room gate, but its northern pilaster juts out farther to the west than do the two southern pilasters. Wampler, one of the authors of the excavation report, has suggested, with some reservations, that this is an earlier gate which for some reason went out of use when the northern gate was built. Two points strengthen this theory: (1) The tower belonging to this building is particularly big and strong and the section of the wall which leads from it to the northern gate is not fitted to it. (2) In the section south of the northern gate, part of a thick wall was uncovered, which continued in the direction of the wall of the western tower of the northern gate. From all this it seems to the present writer that the southern, four-room gate existed in the first building phase. In this phase, the wall continued and reached its western side (see the suggested plan). This phase can be dated with certainty to the ninth century, since all agreed that the "southern gate antedates the northern one."

Later, apparently in the eighth century, the fortifications were altered and strengthened; the northern two-room gate characteristic of this period was built by lengthening the eastern wall northward from the earlier gate-tower, while section A of the wall, which closed the gate on the west, went out of use and was shortened, thus closing the new gate on the west.

In addition to these two fortification systems, there were uncovered, within the area enclosed by the walls, the remains of fortifications in which an element of casemates could be recognized.[21] This, the earliest of the Israelite phases, can be dated to the period of the United Monarchy. If the preceding analysis is correct, this is a fine example of the development of the walls and gates in the Judean cities, corresponding to the Israelite kingdom (see also below).

8. BETH-SHEMESH

Here we will mention only the results of the excavations at Beth-shemesh (Tell Rumeileh) connected with the fortifications of the town, since the rest of the material—although of some importance with relation to isolated finds—cannot be exhaustively and exactly dealt with stratigraphically and chronologically. The stratum which interests us here was called IIA by G. E. Wright,[22] since this is the first stratum which can be attributed to the United Monarchy. Judging from the stratigraphy, the history, and the pottery, Wright fixed its date at the time of David. He suggests its end in the final days of David and the beginning of Solomon's, an exact dating that needs confirmation by additional excavations. But in any case, scholars agree that this stratum should be attributed to the tenth century.

This was apparently the last fortified town to have existed on the site, a fact which fits, in Wright's opinion, the biblical statement that Rehoboam fortified the neighboring Zorah (II Chron. 11:10). The fortifications of that town are in fact composed of a casemate wall which closed a breach in the wall of the earlier town.[23] The fortifications of Beth-shemesh thus fit the general idea that in the days of the United Monarchy the casemate wall was the generally accepted system of city fortifications in Israel and Judah.

9. GEZER

The excavations at Gezer have served, since the publication of their results by the first excavator, Macalister, as a source of information and despair alike. The failure of the excavation report to solve the complexity of the stratigraphical finds and their connection with the pottery even led to erroneous fundamental conclusions concerning the development of the city at the time of the Monarchy. After the excavations at Hazor and Megiddo on the one hand, and the new Gezer excavations conducted by the Hebrew Union College under the direction of W. Dever and J. Seger[24] on the other, it is now possible to solve part of the complex problem, and in particular to select the relevant facts. When the gate and casemate wall from Solomon's time had been discovered at Hazor, the present writer suggested that similar fortifications could also be observed at Gezer in the place called by Macalister the "Maccabean Castle."[25] This assumption, based on the similarity in plan as well as on the biblical verse (I Kings 9:15) stating that Hazor, Gezer, and Megiddo were built by Solomon, has now been definitely confirmed by the new excavations, which not only uncovered the

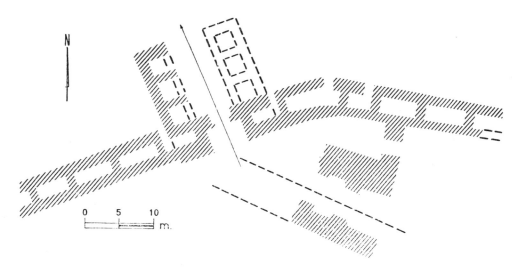

Fig. 5. Gezer: Reconstruction of the Solomonic fortifications.

whole of the gate building, but also fixed its date in the tenth century on the basis of the pottery found in its floors. This discovery offers most impressive evidence for the centralized planning of the fortifications of the key towns at the time of Solomon, built in accordance with one identical plan.

The new excavations brought to light another important fact for our subject. In contrast to the earlier assumptions based on Macalister's report, it now became clear that Gezer continued to exist uninterruptedly even in the ninth and seventh centuries. Thus, *inter alia*, it is possible to identify without hesitation the relief of Sargon II, which shows the conquest of the town of Gazru, with Gezer in Palestine. Together with the reliefs of Sennacherib depicting the conquest of Lachish, these form the only two detailed reliefs which represent towns in Palestine at the time of the Monarchy.

10. JERUSALEM

Within our limited framework we cannot examine in detail all the archaeological finds in Jerusalem that bear on the period of the Monarchy. But we must consider here some of the new discoveries which strongly illuminate a number of key problems as well as previous discoveries connected with the history of the town at the time of the Monarchy.[26]

The Eastern Hill—the Ophel: Two principal discoveries here by K. Kenyon are worth mentioning. Although not completely solving a number of problems, they open certain new possibilities for the study of the history of the city by explaining some of the difficulties heretofore impeding our research. Kenyon's excavations proved that the "Jebusite bastion" and the walls connected with it—discovered in previous excavations on top of the hill—date not from the time of the First Temple but from the Hasmonean period. It also became clear that these constructions were built on the destruction debris of Jerusalem from the end of the First Temple period. In spite of the importance of this discovery in itself, it would not have been complete without the discovery of the fortifications of the town on the slopes of the hill. These showed not only that the area of Jerusalem at the time of the early Monarchy reached fifty dunams—an area comparable to that of other royal cities during that period—but also provided a solution to one of the riddles connected with the problem of supplying water to the town during a siege.

It is well known that two principal systems of water-supply for use during a siege were discovered on the eastern hill. One is the famous Siloam tunnel, apparently hewn at the time of Hezekiah, the other is called "Warren's shaft." The latter in fact consists of two systems combined to make one: a sloping tunnel and a vertical shaft. Until the latest excavations it was accepted that in the period of the Monarchy the entry from the town into the shaft system lay outside the assumed city-walls, a fact which, if true, would have nullified the value of this system. It now becomes clear that the entry to this system lay within the fortified area, and thus is congruent with the kind of water-supply systems known from other sites (see below). At the same time, the continuing difficulty of understanding some of the principal problems connected with the fortifications should be pointed out, including when their construction started and how long they existed. An assessment of the excavator's assumption that this system of fortifications existed from Middle Bronze Age II until the seventh century will have to be reserved until the publication of the full excavation report. Among the few architectural finds discovered here, mention should be made of a proto-Aeolian capital found near a wall built of ashlar in the common Israelite style, absolutely identical in appearance and details with those found at Ramat Raḥel. This capital is attributed by the excavator to the time of Solomon (see below).

The Temple Mount and its Vicinity: Among the relevant discoveries of B. Mazar, who is excavating in this area, the date of a system of rock-cut tombs hewn in the Phoenician style has not yet been finally fixed, but the excavator's opinion that they should be attributed to the ninth-eighth centuries B.C.E. seems reasonable. In any case, the existence here of these tombs can be explained only by assuming either that during the period in question the city had not yet extended to the western hill, or that this hill was enclosed by a separate wall and the burial area lay in fact outside the walls.

Western Hill: Two new facts discovered in the latest excavations (Kenyon—Tushingham, Amiran–Eitan, Broshi–Bahat, Avigad) oblige us to re-check some of the accepted ideas about the development of Jerusalem across the western hill at the time of the Monarchy.

First, in the whole area of the western hill, remains, clearly from the time of the First Temple, were discovered, some of them dwellings. Their exact date still needs checking, but it is reasonable to attribute them to the eighth or seventh centuries. The most important discovery was made by Avigad in the Jewish quarter of the Old City, where a massive wall, 6.4–7.2 m. thick, was uncovered.[27] It runs in a general north-south direction and has been dated by the excavator to the days of Hezekiah or Manasseh, probably the former. The excavator believes that the wall surrounded the *mishneh* ("second quarter" or "second city"), which in his opinion existed on the eastern spur of the western hill. The continuation of the wall to the south has not yet been discovered and the excavator assumes that it also surrounded the Siloam pool in such a way that the latter was included within the fortifications. This important subject, i.e. the exact line and date of the wall, will certainly occupy the excavators for some time to come, but it is already obvious that the discovery of this wall has opened a new chapter in the study of the extension of the town on the western hill.

11. RAMAT RAḤEL

A direct link exists between the excavations in Jerusalem and the discoveries made at Ramat Raḥel.[28] The importance of the latter derives from two different interrelated aspects, the first purely archaeological, the second the interpretation of the archaeological finds in relation to the historical sources. The main discovery at Ramat Raḥel was a monumental building constructed of ashlar, hewn and laid in a manner identical to that of the Samaria buildings of the ninth century. Discovered also were a considerable number of proto-Aeolian capitals, identical to the one discovered in the Ophel and similar to those from Samaria, Hazor, Megiddo, and other tenth-ninth century sites. In addition, a unique find should be mentioned—a stone balustrade, made of little pillars, with drooping palmettes and capitals in the style of the proto-Aeolian capitals. The excavator, Y. Aharoni, is undoubtedly right to compare this balustrade with those carved in a number of ivory reliefs from Samaria, Arslan-Tash, and Nimrud, depicting the well-known figure called "the woman at the window." At the end of the excavations, the excavator distinguished two distinct periods belonging to the Judean Monarchy, which he called strata VB (the earlier) and VA. In fixing the dates of the strata, he frequently hesitated and changed his mind. His last position is that the earlier stratum began to exist in the eighth century or possibly the second half of the ninth. Aharoni now attributes the second building phase to the reign of Jehoiakim (earlier he identified the building with the *beit ha-ḥofšīt*, "a separate house" of Uzziah [II Chron. 26:21], on the basis of the pottery finds and the biblical sources [Jer. 22:14], where the building of a "wide house" is attributed to this king).

The excavator has recently also attributed to the early stratum the monumental building (the royal citadel) architecturally identical in all its details with the later building. The main objections to his views are: The architecture under discussion is identical in all its features to that of the buildings at Samaria and other sites in the ninth-century Israelite Monarchy, thus making it impossible to dissociate the buildings at Ramat Raḥel from their parallels. One should therefore look for a period during the reign of the kings of Judah, when not only did the Israelite Monarchy strongly influence Judah, but when such monumental building activities could be carried out. These conditions seem to be most adequately met by the reign over Judah[29] of Athaliah, who also built here a "house of Baal,"

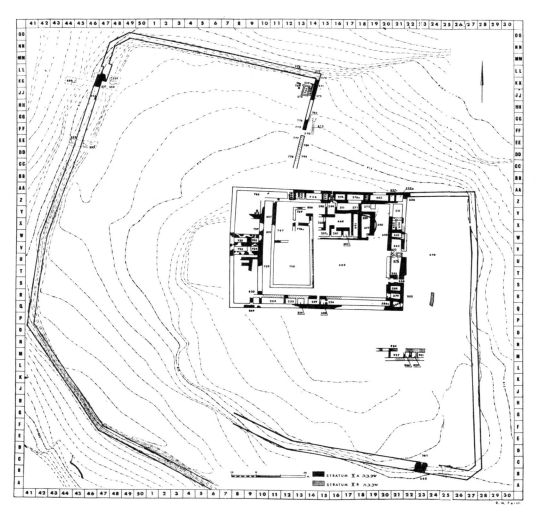

Fig. 6. Ramat Raḥel: General plan of the Iron Age Citadel, Strata V A—V B.
Y. Aharoni, *Excavations at Ramat Raḥel: Seasons 1961 and 1962*, Rome, 1964, fig. 6.

whose remains can be seen in the original building phase at Ramat Raḥel.[30] Stratigraphically, the early citadel (stratum VB) cannot be distinguished from the original phase of the monumental building which was attributed *entirely* to stratum VA. This building, destroyed or possibly never completed, was restored and reconstructed in the seventh century. To this restoration period should be attributed the late pottery finds in the fill of the floor. If the excavator were right in his suppositions, then the architecture at Ramat Raḥel would be a complete exception and would represent a renaissance in Judah of the building style of the ninth century, after an interval of 250 years. On the other hand, if our above-mentioned suppositions are correct, then the buildings at Ramat Raḥel fit well into what we know of the building methods of the ninth century, which were no doubt influenced by Phoenician architecture.

12. TELL BEIT MIRSIM

This mound can be called a key site not because the towns built on it had ever been of particular importance, but because of the systematic excavations conducted there by Albright, as well as his detailed publications. In these, the excavator also deals with the complex of archaeological problems in Palestine having a direct or indirect relationship to the finds from this site. Although the basic evidence concerning the development of town planning during the period of the Monarchy is quite clear, there is a dearth of stratigraphical finds connected with the details of the sub-periods.

Albright divided the strata of the Iron Age into two main groups: B, the early, and A, the late. From the early group, only the last phase, B 3, is relevant to our subject; this is the phase attributed to the tenth century, the time of the United Monarchy. Period A, which is also subdivided into several phases, ended, in the opinion of the excavator, with the Babylonian conquest. It is worth mentioning that a seal impression was found from the end of the period, *l'lyqm n'r ywkn* (similar to those at Beth-shemesh and Ramat Raḥel), which Albright attributed to the time of Jehoiachin.

From the point of view of town planning, the fortifications and the adjacent buildings are of particular interest. Tell Beit Mirsim is an instructive example, showing that the system of fortifications in tenth-century Palestine was one of casemates, as this is in fact the only wall existing on the site which was established during that century (phase B 3)—if we attribute it, with Albright, to the time of David, or else to that of Solomon. In any case, this town was probably destroyed at the time of Shishak's campaign. Mainly the northwestern region of the town was destroyed and the casemate wall repaired later—at the beginning of the Divided Monarchy—by broadening the outer wall to a width of two meters. In spite of this, the use of the fortification system of the casemates continued until the town ceased to exist. From this it can be concluded that the town that existed here (in Albright's opinion: Debir—Kiriath-sepher) at the time of the Judean Monarchy was *not* a key city specially fortified against assault by battering rams during a siege, as were other sites from the end of the tenth or the beginning of the ninth century. In Albright's opinion, the town reached its zenith in the eighth century, and although it was restored after Sennacherib's conquest, it never completely recovered.

13. LACHISH[31]

Excavation was discontinued here in 1938 after the murder of the director of the expedition, J. L. Starkey. It is particularly famous because of the important finds from the Bronze and Iron Ages. From the latter, the best-known are the "Lachish Letters," discovered in the city-gate, within a destruction layer caused by fire. Because the work was interrupted at an early stage, however, the excavators did not succeed in uncovering enough from the period of the Monarchy to permit thorough understanding of the process of settlement on the site right from the beginning of this period. In fact, we know little of the strata of the town in the early centuries of the first millennium.

In addition, although the divergent lines of the city fortifications can be followed clearly, it is difficult for the time being to fix with certainty the date of construction, in their entirety or in various phases. For these reasons and also because what is known up to now has already been summarized several times, we shall concentrate on several of the problems connected with the excavations and not describe the finds themselves.

We can say that the key problem in the archaeology of the period of the Divided Monarchy in Judah hinges on the dating of the destruction of strata III and II, the only two strata from the period of the Monarchy that were relatively extensively uncovered. Strata V–IV, which represent the beginning of the town fortified during the Monarchy (the reign of David and Solomon, in the opinion of several scholars, or the reign of Rehoboam, as evidenced by the Bible and in the opinion of the excavators), have hardly been excavated, and everything said about them at present is hypothetical. On the other hand, the discussion of the destruction date of stratum III is of great importance, not only in terms of the excavations at Lachish, but also in terms of dating the different strata in the Judean key cities in general. The reason is that of all these towns (Arad, Beersheba, Tell Beit Mirsim, and others), Lachish is the only one that offers external historical evidence for assigning one of its destruction dates to Sennacherib. The excavators of the site as well as other scholars naturally took great trouble to identify the stratum considered to have ended with this destruction. Thus a clear and almost unique criterion would exist for determining the characteristics of the pottery from the end of the eighth century, which could also be used for other sites. An additional element in this problem is that the well-known seal impressions (la-melek) were also found in stratum III. Therefore its exact dating is also of great importance for the dating of this find, which is among the most important from the period of the Monarchy because it throws light on the system of military and civilian administration in the Judean kingdom. Archaeologists differ widely on this subject, and until it is finally settled we must realize that some of the conclusions of excavators at other sites are not absolutely certain. Olga Tufnell's final report on the excavations attributes the destruction of stratum III to Sennacherib, and the end of stratum II—which, according to this opinion, lasted more than a hundred years—to the final destruction by Nebuchadnezzar in 587 or 586. This view is supported by several scholars, among them Aharoni, who based the dating of the strata at Arad and Beersheba (see below) on this assumption. Starkey, the director of the excavations, Albright, Wright, Yeivin, and particularly Kenyon differed, maintaining that the town of stratum III was destroyed at the time of the first campaign of Nebuchadnezzar (c. 597), while stratum II was destroyed during his second campaign, about ten years later. Their reasoning is based on the fact that stratum II is a very poor one and it is inconceivable that it existed for a hundred years; additionally, in their opinion, the pottery of stratum III, including the seal impressions *la-melek*, particularly of the two-winged type, is characteristic specifically of the seventh century. Basing himself on a detailed analysis of the loci where *la-melek* stamps of the two-winged type were found, which—as is generally agreed—belong to the seventh century, Lance recently reached the conclusion that some of these impressions were found in stratum III.[32] In his opinion, this offers additional proof that this stratum was destroyed not in 701 but during the seventh century.

In conclusion, it should be pointed out that at the present stage of research it is difficult without further excavations to decide one way or the other about this central problem; it is therefore to be hoped that the excavations Ussishkin is conducting on the site will concentrate first of all on solving this problem.[33]

A number of additional problems connected with this site should also be mentioned. Until now, no casemate wall has been discovered in the system of fortifications surrounding the town. This apparently would strengthen Tufnell's view that the massive fortifications of the city, consisting of a wall with insets and offsets, were first erected by Rehoboam, as stated in the Bible (II Chron. 11:11–12). On the other hand, the gate of the first system of fortifications seems not yet to have been discovered in its entirety; part of it is apparently still hidden in the non-excavated area. Indeed here, as the excavators pointed out, at least six pilasters of the earlier gate have been discovered. This problem too can be solved only by an additional excavation, which should verify whether the gate has four rooms, similar to the gates of the early ninth century, or six, like those of the end of the tenth century (see below, Ashdod), or—which seems less reasonable—that it is the same type as Solomon's gates.[34]

Another problem, not less interesting, relates to the character and periods of the Israelite citadel, or palace, discovered in the center of the western half of the mound. So far, only the substructure (as the excavators call it) or the platform of the palace has been uncovered; in it several structural phases can be

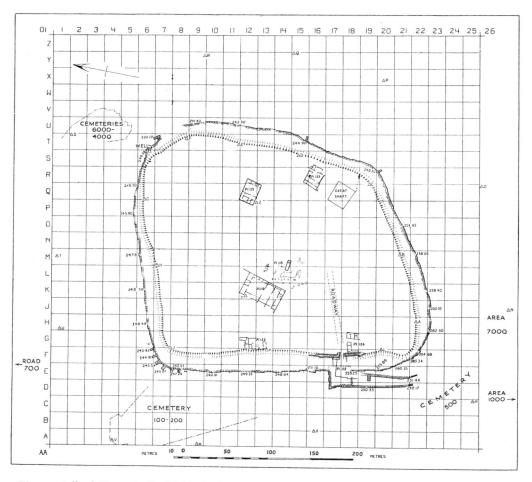

Fig. 7. Tell ed-Duweir (Lachish): Reference grid, triangulations, buildings, and cemeteries.
Olga Tufnell, *Lachish* III, London, 1953, pl. 108.

distinguished. Their attribution to specific kings is, according to our present knowledge, only speculative.

This analysis of the central problems of Lachish at the time of the Monarchy can be concluded with a short survey of the buildings of stratum I, which the excavators attributed to the time of the Persian conquest and the Hellenistic period (there is a difference of opinion about the date of some of these buildings). First, the temple, called by the excavators "the solar temple," should be mentioned. The site has recently been re-excavated by Aharoni because he assumes that the building is similar to the one he discovered at Arad (see below) and therefore belongs to the Israelite period. In fact, however, the excavation confirmed the opinion of the earlier excavators that the building was constructed in the Hellenistic period.[35]

The second important building attributed by the excavators to the later periods was discovered on the destroyed foundations of the Judean palace-citadel. This building is of a monumental character and of a high architectural standard, possessed of vaults and columns with round drums on stepped and comb-dressed bases. The scholars have sought parallels to it; lately the opinion has been expressed that it is an Assyrian palace and should be attributed to the early seventh century.[36] However, a comparison of the method of dressing (see below), and in particular the shape of the column bases, compel us, it seems, at the present stage, to accept the opinion of the excavators that the building was constructed in the Persian or possibly even in the Hellenistic period.[37]

It should be pointed out that in spite of the importance of the excavations at Lachish, the stratigraphical data thus far found there, and especially their dates, are still under discussion, so that much caution is required at the present stage when considering historical conclusions or archaeological datings of other sites based exclusively on these finds.

14. ASHDOD

The importance of the excavations at Ashdod derives from the fact that these are the first systematic excavations to be conducted in a Philistine town.[38] We shall have to follow up the finds of stratum 10B, dating from the second half of the eleventh century, since they will help us to date and understand the later strata, which belong chronologically to the period of the early Monarchy in Israel.

In this phase, the town area expanded and for the first time what may be called the "lower city" was found. The remains so far discovered prove that this town was unfortified; in the quarter excavated, mainly potters' installations were discovered. In the next phase (stratum XA), the area of the lower city was fortified, and Ashdod became one of the largest cities in Palestine at that time. The city-gate—a tower with rooms on both sides—recalls the gate of Philistine-Canaanite Megiddo of stratum VI. In Dothan's opinion, this gate was destroyed in the first half of the tenth century by David at the end of his reign or, even more likely in the excavator's opinion, by Pharaoh Siamon in c. 960 B.C.E. The destruction of the town, or of its fortifications, was so complete that for several decades at least the gate remained in ruins, proved by some kilns directly opposite the gate, which blocked the passage through it. This phase is, in fact, an intermediate one between the preceding stratum 10 and the following stratum 9, which interests us particularly. In this stratum, the beginning of which should be attributed to the late tenth century or the early ninth, the town was impressively re-fortified. Of particular interest are the city-gate and its wall, which were excavated. The gate, thus far unique (perhaps similar to the one discovered at Lachish which originated in strata V–IV, see above), is of a type between 'Solomon's gates' and 'Ahab's gates;' it has three rooms on each side, but lacks the fourth pair of rooms that made a kind of tower in Solomon's gates. The corners of the brick-built gate were of ashlar stones similar to those then common in Israel. The adjacent wall is massive (about 5 m. broad) and also characteristic of the period.

This gate and its wall existed until—in Dothan's opinion—they were destroyed by Uzziah who, as evidenced by the Bible (II Chron. 26:6), broke down the walls of Ashdod. Particular mention should be made of the destruction wrought in the next stratum (8), in which was discovered a great number of burials where there had been thousands of skeletons. This destruction should probably be attributed to Sargon II in 712, not only because of the biblical evidence (Isa. 20:1), but mainly because of the fragments of a monumental inscription of Sargon himself discovered in the excavations. And finally it should be mentioned that in the strata of the last phase of Ashdod from the period of the Monarchy (strata 7–6), some Hebrew weights were found (pīm, neṣef), as well as a two-winged la-melek stamp (class III). The excavator ascribes these finds to the reign of Josiah, who also ruled over the neighboring Meṣad Ḥashavyahu. The total destruction of stratum 6 should be attributed to Nebuchadnezzar. The possibility of dating some of the strata by linking them with clear historical events will contribute much towards further clarification of the dates of the pottery in the ninth-seventh centuries B.C.E.

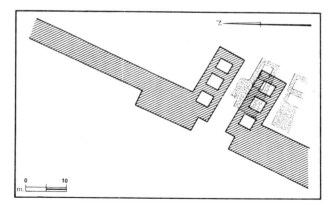

Fig. 8. Ashdod: Gates in Area M. ▦ Gate from the end of the 11th and beginning of the 10th centuries B.C.E. ▨ Gate from the last third of the 10th century B.C.E.

M. Dothan, Qadmoniot 5 (1972), 9.

15. ARAD

Arad in the period of the Monarchy was confined to a small citadel measuring only about 50 × 50 m. Seven strata are attributed by the excavator, Y. Aharoni,[39] to this period.[40] The first citadel was erected in stratum XI and had a casemate wall, a system of fortifications characteristic of Solomon's time.[41] In stratum X, attributed to the reign of Jehoshaphat, the citadel was fortified with a massive wall, about 3–4 m. thick, which, in the opinion of the excavator, continued to exist until and including stratum VII, and in the opinion of the present writer, until and including stratum VI. According to the excavator, "in the course of time, thinner walls were built paralled to the first wall, inside the citadel, so that a kind of casemate wall was achieved." An additional casemate wall was built in the last stratum, i.e., stratum VI.[42] Among the most important finds from Arad are many Hebrew ostraca, their bulk addressed to Elyashiv son of Eshyahu, and a sanctuary (or, in any case, a site with obvious cultic significance).

The plan of the cult building was compared by Aharoni to the plan of Solomon's Temple in Jerusalem, and described by means of terms borrowed from those of the Temple, such as 'ūlām (porch), hēḵāl (main room), dᵉvīr (inner sanctuary or holy of holies), and also "Jachin and Boaz." There is in fact, however, no similarity at all between the plans of this building (a courtyard with an altar, surrounded on two sides by long rooms and on its short side by a broad room containing a cult niche) and Solomon's Temple, as will be shown below.

The various dates suggested in the excavation reports for the periods when the sanctuary or parts of it went out of use as a result of religious reforms instigated by Josiah or Hezekiah, kings of Judah, should be taken with caution.[43]

It is difficult to accept these conclusions, not only because they do not conform to the logical process of the building of towns and their destruction, but chiefly because they are based on the dates suggested by Aharoni for the "casemate walls" of the late strata, which he attributes to the period of various kings of Judah. These casemate walls are in fact partly built of stones dressed with the combed pick[44] characteristic of the Hellenistic and Roman periods and for which no parallel has yet been found in the buildings of the period of the Monarchy.[45] Thus it can be assumed that these casemate walls belong to the Hellenistic citadel (stratum IV), whose very deep foundations reached down to bedrock.[46] The as yet unpublished fact, supporting the view of the present writer, was discovered during the fourth season of excavations in 1965.[47] It emerged that the casemate wall had not only not been destroyed by the foundation trench of the Hellenistic tower of stratum IV, but had been built at the same time as this tower and leans on its wall.

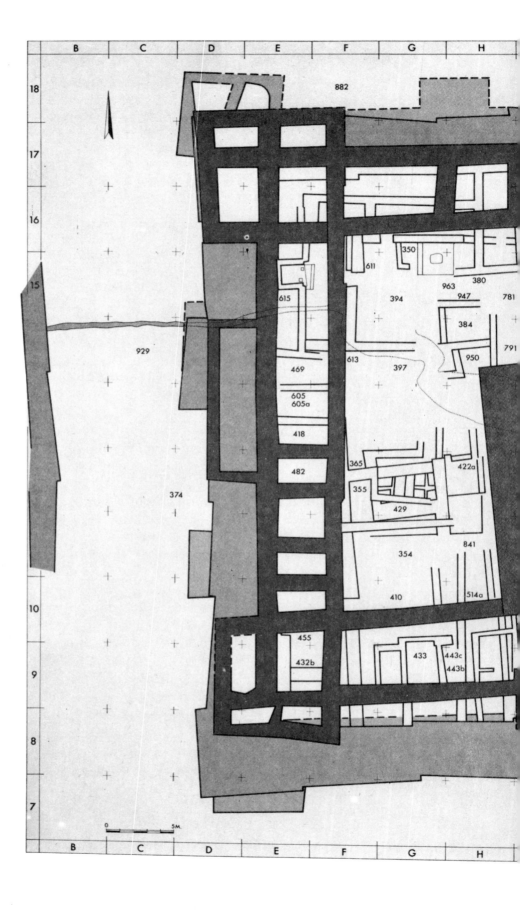

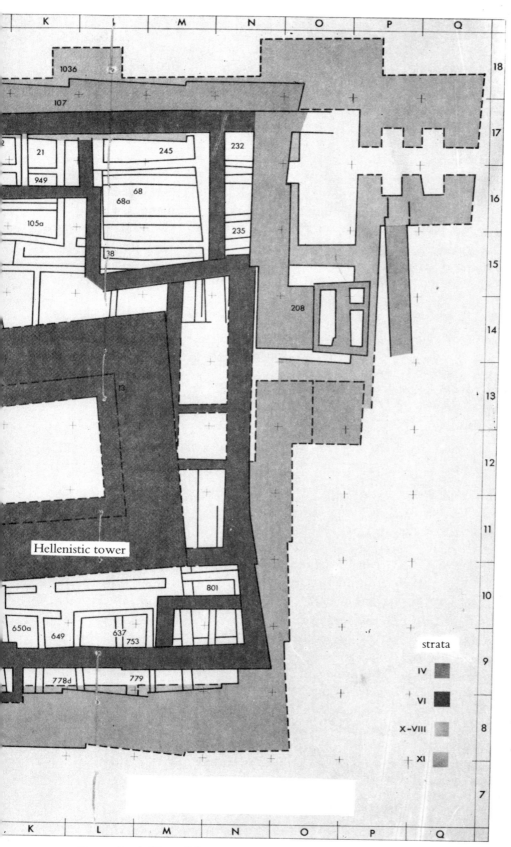

Fig. 9. Arad: Plan of the Israelite citadels, Strata VI–XI.
Y. Aharoni, *Arad Inscriptions*, Jerusalem, 1975, 6.

The fact that the wall is not Israelite, but late and intruded through the Israelite strata may also explain another important phenomenon, which the excavation report does not do satisfactorily. In the fourth season, an interesting group of four seals was discovered, three of them "Elyashib son of Eshyahu," the main addressee of the ostraca. Now, according to the stratigraphical interpretation of the excavator, based on the dating of the above wall, these seals were found "below the layer of destruction by fire of stratum VII,"[48] while the ostraca were found in a room nearby, but in stratum VI.[49] It is clear, however, that all the material was found in the same room[50] and the same stratum, the difference between the two loci having been caused by the very late wall which cut through the earlier buildings in the process of excavating for its deep foundations.[51] The excavator defines the stratigraphy and the dates of the strata at Arad thus: "In a relatively short period between the middle of the tenth and the early sixth centuries, there are many strata and it is, therefore, possible to attribute each stratum to a limited time span and to *well-defined historical events*. Arad is now the mound with the most detailed stratigraphy in Judah from the Israelite period II and it will be possible to base a more exact chronology for the various mounds in Judah on the many types of pottery vessels found in the various strata."[52] It is desirable, for the reasons given, at the present stage and before the final published report on the excavations, to consider the above historical and chronological conclusions with much caution.

16. BEERSHEBA

An important recent excavation, directly related to the period of the kings, is that of Tell es-Saba', identified with biblical Beersheba. The excavator, Y. Aharoni, declared that the aim of the excavation was to find the temple which, according to Amos 5:5; 8:14, existed there.[53] After the third season of digging,[54] the excavators arrived at the following conclusions about the stratigraphy of the site at the time of the Monarchy: Stratum V—tenth century— the reign of Solomon,[55] a city fortified with a massive wall, 4 m. thick. According to the report on the first three seasons,[56] this solid wall was built into the debris of Iron Age I. According to the schematic sections thus far published[57] and dated,[58] this solid wall was erected on an artificial glacis 6–7 m. high, made of river pebbles and layers of grey soil, ashes, and brick material. At present it is difficult to understand the relation between this glacis, which the excavator believes was built to give the mound an impressive observation post, and the earliest strata of settlement, into whose destruction layer the wall was built. The excavators thought initially that after its destruction a weak casemate wall,[59] had been built on the summit of the mound in stratum IV, but after the fourth season,[60] they decided that these were merely retaining walls, built in stratum II, for the new glacis constructed during this period. They have now concluded, therefore, that the solid wall continued to exist in stratum IV. A casemate wall, constructed in stratum III, continued to exist in stratum II. Stratum II, the last fortified settlement at Beersheba, was destroyed, the excavators believe, at the end of the eighth century by Sennacherib,[61] an opinion based on the alleged similarity between the pottery found in this stratum and that of Lachish, stratum III.[62] Two gates have been found so far: the upper, from strata III–II, with four rooms, two on each side, and the lower, originally attributed to Solomon and now to David, also with four rooms, two on each side, and a massive tower.[63] In the opinion of the excavator, the plan of the gate is very similar to the one at Dan, and the fact that they differ in plan from Solomonic gates makes it probable that the gates of Dan and Beersheba were constructed in the days of David.[64] Among the public buildings discovered in the excavations, special mention should be made of a construction complex in the style of the stables at Megiddo, the storehouse at Hazor, and other places (see below). The excavator also points out that a shaft of the kind found at Megiddo and Hazor was discovered,[65] but until its excavation is complete its purpose remains uncertain, since there is no spring in the vicinity, as at Megiddo, and the level of the ground-water and the floods in the wadi is very low.

By the end of the 1975 season, no temple had been discovered. On top of the mound some cult and votive objects had been found, but their non-Israelite character is absolutely clear.[66] They include a cylinder seal (the figures and inscription carved in the positive and not in the negative, proper in a seal) in a provincial Babylonian style, whose inscription mentions the name of one Rimūt-ilāni son of Adad-idri.[67]

The discovery of a jug with the inscription qdš[68] cannot yet be considered proof of the existence of a temple, but the large horned altar found in the 1973 season suggests some kind of cult site or high-place.[69]

17. TELL EL-KHELEIFE (EZION-GEBER)

Since the excavations of this site in the Gulf of Elath, conducted in 1938–1940, have not yet been fully published, there are still many problems that cannot be solved or even exactly defined. The excavator, N. Glueck, thought at first that he had found here a smelting site from Solomonic times, but B. Rothenberg[70] showed that the central building did not serve this purpose. An additional study by Z. Meshel[71] clarified the character of the early buildings; Glueck's last reports of the excavations, published before his death,[72] accepted the above corrections, and the following description of the principal buildings, their character, and stratum, is based on these studies.

To the first stratum (I) should be attributed a massive square structure, most of which is the "four-room" type, each side about 13 m. long. This building, a kind of administrative fort, was surrounded by a square courtyard (with sides 45 m. long), its walls built as casemates. This stratum should be ascribed to the reign of Solomon, which fits the biblical sources, the building style, and the pottery finds.

In the next stratum (II), the character of the site was changed, its square area enlarged (each side about 60 m. long) and fortified by a solid wall with offsets and insets; this wall was strengthened by a glacis, a moat, and a further wall. On the south of the precinct was discovered a large gate with four rooms, two on each side, and a fortified tower on its east. Its similarity to the Megiddo gate in its plan of stratum IV and the gates at Dan and Beersheba leaves no doubt that it should be attributed to the ninth century.[73] The town of stratum III was built long after the previous town had been abandoned. In this stratum was found a signet-ring with the inscription *lytm* ("belonging to *ytm*"), which has been attributed by some to Jotham king of Judah.

The excavator attributes the town of stratum IV to the Edomite settlement on the site, which began at the end of the eighth century. In this stratum were found several handles with the impression *lqws'nl 'bd hmlk* ("belonging to *qws'nl*, servant of the king"), clear evidence of its Edomite character. The next stratum (V) belongs to the period after the Babylonian conquest.

Whether or not we accept the identification with Ezion-geber,[74] the results of the excavations of this important site can throw much light on the material culture at the time of the Monarchy. It is especially noteworthy that the types of fortification in the various periods fit those discovered on other sites in the country.[75]

18. En-gedi

We conclude the analysis of the main architectural and stratigraphical features from the time of the Monarchy with En-gedi because the excavations here[76] showed clearly that the settlement on Tel Goren existed only at the end of the period of the Monarchy and after the Babylonian conquest. The Israelite settlement (stratum V) is outstanding in that it consisted mainly of workshops and installations dedicated to the production of perfumes and fine oils. The excavation is important from the biblical-historical viewpoint because its finds prove that the settlement was not founded before the second half of the seventh century. This is directly related to the town-list of Judah in Joshua 15:62 and to the date of compilation. On the other hand, it should be stressed that other finds from En-gedi[77] testify to the possible existence there of another settlement (not necessarily on Tel Goren) during the eighth century, whose exact site and character have not yet, however, been determined.

B. Architecture in the Period of the Monarchy

1. Building Methods and the Architectural Elements

One most impressive feature from the period of the Monarchy, proving both the high standard reached by the masons at that time and the contacts with and influences of the neighboring countries, was the treatment of building stones: the method of dressing and laying them, and the use of them in building construction. An analysis of this style is essential not only for comprehension of the building method itself, but also for the chronological implications and for the understanding of the plans and functions of the buildings.[78] As in the preceding periods, bricks and unworked or little-worked stones were the usual building material, the stones used mainly for foundations and bases, the bricks for the upper parts of the walls. It can be assumed that the walls were generally plastered. But the monumental architecture in the period of the Monarchy really excels where splendid ashlar stones are used; the remains of these are usually found in royal buildings, particularly from the tenth and ninth centuries. Although the earliest examples of this kind of construction were found at Megiddo from Solomon's time, the principal ones date from the ninth century from the area of the northern Israelite kingdom. The similarity between this architectural style and those in the neighboring countries, particularly Phoenicia, suits the chronological and geographical frameworks described above. Solomon's reign is outstanding, also according to the biblical evidence, in its relation to and dependence on the building art of Tyre. The same is true of the kings of Israel after the division of the kingdom, as is also indirectly shown by the building style in Judah at the time of the Divided Monarchy which—except for Ramat Raḥel, to which we shall return below—is different from the style of the ashlar buildings previously mentioned. This is evident, for instance, in the central royal building, the "palace," in Lachish, already begun during the reign of Rehoboam. It is built of partly-dressed stones, but not of ashlar of the style under discussion, as are the buildings at Tell en-Naṣbeh (including the gates), Tell Beit Mirsim, Beth-shemesh, Beersheba, etc.

Most of the buildings using ashlar are constructed according to two—or sometime three—methods, which can all be reduced to a common denominator. The aim of the builder in the better examples was ultimately to build the part of the wall visible above ground level of smoothly dressed ashlar. During the period under consideration, this was achieved by using a broad chisel, which dressed the stone with diagonal strokes, an arduous task. The stones were then laid in the system of headers and stretchers, i.e., one stone laid so that its long side was turned to the front (stretcher), the next one (or the next two or three) with the short side to the front (header). In general, the wall was built with two faces and on the same pattern of headers and stretchers, and the hollow space between the two faces was filled with rubble and little stones. The system of headers and stretchers itself was enough to effect the joining required to strengthen the wall and to make it one structural unit. The foundations of the wall, those parts that from the beginning were intended to be below floor level, were also built in the header and stretcher technique, but the dressing of the stones was different. The masons tried to save on the dressing where it was not needed for the actual building; the central part of the face of the stone was therefore left undressed or only partly dressed, and the margin was dressed, sometimes just one or both of the sides, and only in rare cases all four edges. These margins were smoothed to make possible the use of a plumb-line and a horizontal string. This economy, as we have said, was used mainly on the hidden parts of the walls or in those sections where a smooth dressing was not aesthetically necessary. It follows—as the first excavators of Samaria had already noted—that the margins were by no means an ornamental element and that the walls with smoothly dressed stones were always intended to appear above the floor. This building method in itself necessitates at least final dressing when the stones are laid in their courses, a logical assumption supported by evidence from the excavations: in excavations of foundations and in the fill between the ashlar stones, many splinters and flakes which had been chipped off during the dressing of the stones were found.

A third system was used for the building of the very base of the wall. After the foundation trenches had been hewn into the rock, there sometimes were laid what can be called the bases: half-dressed stones placed in headers only. The reason for this was to obtain a horizontal layer onto which the upper courses could be laid between the foundations and the upper parts. These distinctions are very important also for stratigraphical reasons; thus, for instance, if a number of smoothly dressed courses are found *below* the level of a certain floor, it can be assumed either that this is not the original floor or that the builders initially intended these parts to be visible above the surface. Perhaps we can assume that the face of the walls—and certainly the interior of the building—even if it was smoothly dressed, had been covered either with plaster or wood (see Solomon's Temple). This was essential for the top parts made of bricks, but perhaps also for those built of stone, to keep out the rain. In Megiddo, Hazor, and Samaria, it is often possible to see that between several stone courses a narrow course of wood had been laid.[79] This was structurally necessary to prevent the collapse of the building as a result of earthquakes or other tremors caused by the elements.

The use of ashlar stones dressed with a broad chisel and the typical margins was, as stated, found at Megiddo (beginning in Solomon's reign), Samaria (ninth century), and Hazor (ninth century). In the light of these facts, it is difficult to accept the statement that the building discovered at Ramat Raḥel was originally constructed at the end of the seventh century. Such a phenomenon would be entirely exceptional, and for this and other reasons[80] we can assume that the building was originally erected in the ninth century, at a time when Israelite influence on Judah was strong.[81] It should be stressed that the other buildings uncovered in Judah from the eighth-seventh centuries were never built of ashlar of this type.

To conclude this discussion of the methods of stone dressing and building, we must return to the problem of the "comb dressing" at Arad. In the light of what has been said, it is obvious that these considerations, which seem merely technical, are in fact of prime importance in relation to the chronological problems of the results of the excavations of this site and thus also for the historical conclusions drawn from them. This kind of dressing has never before been found on any building stones from the time of the Monarchy, either in Palestine or the neighboring countries.[82]

One of the outstanding elements in the Israelite monumental buildings are the columns and the capitals commenly called proto-Ionian (or Aeolian). These capitals, whose Canaanite-Phoenician origin is proved by similar designs on various objects in those countries, have thus far been discovered at Megiddo (possibly by Solomon's time), Hazor, Samaria, Jerusalem, Ramat Raḥel, and Medeibi in Transjordan.[83] In most cases, the relief is carved on one broad side of the rectangular capital only. Exceptional capitals with two carved faces have been explained by the excavators of Megiddo as a failure of the stone mason in carving the one side, making it necessary for him to carve the other. However, capitals of this kind have subsequently been discovered at Hazor and Samaria, and today we can assume that they were set on top of quadrangular columns with their faces turned not to the front but toward the jambs. The capitals with only one carved face were used for the pilaster near the door-jambs, while those with both faces carved were used on proper columns (Illustration 10).[84]

Additional elements, also originating in Phoenician building, are the decorated windows and low balustrades made of small columns with proto-Ionian capitals. This type has generally been found in the decorated ivories from Nimrud, Arslan-Tash, and Samaria. In these ivories a woman's head is always shown looking out of the window, the motif called "the woman at the window." One of the important discoveries made at Ramat Raḥel was such a balustrade, thus offering additional evidence for the influence from the north in the ninth century on the architecture at Ramat Raḥel. These windows are constructed of a series of window posts and recessed lintels, as a result of which the window becomes narrower towards the interior (*hallōnēi šᵉqufim 'ăṭumīm*, "windows of narrow lights"—A.V.; "windows with recessed frames"—R.S.V.; I Kings 6:4).

2. THE FORTIFICATIONS

No other subject in the field of architecture, planned by a central authority, bears the stamp of royalty to a greater degree than the system of fortifications, particularly those of key towns or towns intended from the outset to withstand a long siege or, in the language of the Bible, *'ārīm lᵉmāṣōr*, "cities of defense" (II Chron. 11:5), or *'ārei ha-mᵉṣurōt*, "fortified cities" (*ibid.* 11:23; 12:4). Furthermore, one finds here a certain adherence to rules, since the fortifications were planned in response to the changing methods of enemy warfare. It should also be remembered that, since large-scale fortifications of towns demanded extreme effort, planners tried to restrict the major elements or methods of fortifications to the most vital cities, where it was certain that the enemy would use all machines and implements at his disposal. In certain instances, the fortifications were designed to strengthen resistance against revolt or tribal raids or the attacks of smaller peoples without elaborate siege machines. In such cases the building program could be somewhat reduced and simpler methods used.

Thus certain guide lines of planning common to or typical of each period can be distinguished from the above analysis of the major excavations in "cities for defense" against a strong exterior enemy or in cities of less importance from this point of view. We have seen, for instance, that during Solomon's reign the system of casemate walls was common in most key towns. The system saves much building effort and the wall itself and its vicinity can at the same time be exploited for dwellings and storage, but it does not provide maximum defense against battering rams. From this we deduce either that in this period sophisticated battering rams did not exist or that there was little danger of invasion by an enemy thus equipped. Such conditions were well suited to the tenth century, since not only was this a generally quiet period in Palestine, but the immediately threatening armies had not yet acquired this perfect siege machine. For this reason it is difficult to accept without decisive proof the assumption of the excavators that the building of the fortifications of massive walls at Beersheba should be attributed to Solomon's reign (or to David's; see above). There was no military or other justifications for this. The stratigraphy and pottery published thus far do not, as mentioned above, necessitate drawing this conclusion, and at the present stage it is reasonable to assume that the wall post-dates Solomon's reign[85]—was built either during Rehoboam's reign or even later—in particular after Shishak's campaign, which occasioned (or rather brought in its wake) a fundamental reorganization of the fortifications of the cities in Israel and Judah.

The above analysis shows clearly that, with the late tenth century and especially in the early ninth, a decisive change occurred in the fortifications of the "cities for defense." From that point on mainly solid walls are found, as at Dan, Hazor, Megiddo, Tell en-Naṣbeh, Lachish, Arad, Tell-el-Kheleife, Ashdod, and also Beersheba. On the other hand, wee see that in several places, as for instance at Tell Beit Mirsim, the casemate wall continues in use (although here too with additional thickness and strength), even in the later period. We can conclude from this that in the ninth-seventh centuries the kings of Judah did not see in the town existing on this site a key city, "a city for defense," for which it was worth making the maximum fortification effort. An additional interesting phenomenon is that the system of the casemates continues in the fortifications of the Acropolis (as in Samaria), for structural reasons as well as because it was superfluous to fortify the Acropolis against battering rams: once the armies had overcome the main city fortifications, the fall of the Acropolis to the battering rams was only a question of time.

The renewed use of casemates in some isolated forts or small mounds should be similarly interpreted. At these places (e.g., Beersheba, with an area of only 12 dunams), where there was no intention of resisting strong armies equipped with battering rams, the problem of saving space within the town area was more important. The casemate walls provided both sufficient defense against attacks from the enemies in the south (Egypt, which did not use battering rams, Edom, and others) and dwelling space and storage room for the standing army.

The factual state of the city walls according to periods is summarized in the table on page 230.

Regularity in planning is equally discernible in the fortifications of the city-gates; here it is even easier to follow the different types according to their periods. We see again that in the tenth century, during Solomon's reign, the large gate with six rooms and two towers is the most common. In the late tenth century, a transitory type is common (Ashdod and possibly also Lachish), i.e., a gate with six chambers with different types of towers or without any at all. With the beginning of the ninth century (or the end of the tenth), a four-room gate clearly takes over. Only from the early eighth century does the two-room gate appear, used together with the four-chamber type. This phenomenon can also be summarized in a table on page 231.

Type of fortification	Dan	Hazor	Samaria	Megiddo	Tell en-Naṣbeh	Gezer	Beth-shemesh	Tell B. Mirsim	Ashdod	Arad	Beersheba	Lachish	Kheleife
Casemate wall in the 10th century	[?]	+	No fortified settlement	+	+(?)	+	+	+		+	+	[?]	+
Casemates in acropolis, in small settlements in 9th–7th cent.			+					+			+		
Solid walls, end of 10th and following centuries	+	+	[?]	+	+				+	+	+	+	+

3. THE WATER SUPPLY SYSTEMS FOR TIMES OF SIEGE

There is a direct connection between the fortification efforts of the kings of Israel and Judah in the 'cities for defense' and the great installations for water supply in times of siege. Without the latter, cities could have been subdued by a comparatively short siege and the whole massive power of the fortifications might have been useless. In fact, just because the strategy of the kings of Israel and Judah was based during various periods on the assumption that the prospect of a long-drawn-out siege would deter attacks by the great empires in their campaigns against each other, they expended more effort on these projects than did their great neighbors. Indeed, there is no more impressive feature in the fortification system of several of the cities in Israel and Judah at the time of the kings than these installations. Water systems for times of siege have thus far been discovered at Hazor, Megiddo, Ibleam, Gibeon, Jerusalem, Lachish,[86] Gezer,[87] and perhaps also Beersheba.[88] The excavation results show that most of these waterworks were not made before the ninth century, when the city fortifications were re-strengthened for the reasons mentioned.

Type of gate	Dan	Hazor	Samaria	Megiddo	Tell en-Naṣbeh	Gezer	Beth-shemesh	Tell B. Mirsim	Ashdod	Arad	Beer-sheba	Lachish	Kheleife
10th cent. Solomon's reign 🕮		+	Was not yet built	+		+							
Transitory type, late 10th cent. 🕮									+			+	
Four-room gate, with or without towers— 9th century and sometimes subsequent centuries 🕮	+			+	+(?)	+					+		+
Two-room gate, 8th– 7th cent. 🕮		(?)		+	+	+		+				+	

We can divide the water installations into two main groups:

(a) A conduit which draws water from a spring lying at the foot of the mound, outside the fortifications, into the city area, by means of a shaft and tunnel or a tunnel only (Megiddo, the second installation at Gibeon, Ibleam (?), the Siloam tunnel in Jerusalem);

(b) Reaching the groundwater or spring within the area of the city itself (Hazor, the first installation at Gibeon, Warren's shaft in Jerusalem, Gezer).

The second type was, of course, more secure, but the hydrogeological conditions were not always suited to its exploitation. According to the inscription of Mesha, it can be assumed that these installations in their entirety were called 'šwḥ, kl'y 'šwḥ,[89] although their different parts were called tunnel (Jerusalem) or pool (Gibeon).

4. PUBLIC AND PRIVATE BUILDINGS

The four-room building: The four-room building is characteristic of the period of the Monarchy (in fact, beginning with the late period of the Judges).[90] In these buildings we can distinguish three long rooms and a broad one equal in length to the sum of the narrow sides of the three long rooms. It can almost certainly be assumed that the central long "room" was an open courtyard. This type of building, without parallel in the neighboring countries, is an original Israelian creation and adequately suits the needs of a well-to-do family. We can also assume that the broad room of the building had a second story, on the evidence of a fine building of this type discovered at Hazor.[91] This type of dwelling also forms the basis for the plan of the citadels—palaces of the higher functionaries in the Israelite period—a fine example of which has been found at Hazor (the citadel, strata VIII–V). Y. Shiloh[92] distinguished an additional type of the four-room building with an annex of a further long room on the side, whose length equals the sum of the length of the long rooms and the width of the broad room. Such buildings (Tell el-Far'ah, North, strata III, II; Tell Beit Mirsim, "West Gate" building) apparently also served as dwellings for high officials or town rulers.

There are two more noteworthy types of buildings for the rich, common in the cities of the period of the Monarchy, both of which have a courtyard. In one the courtyard lies in the center, with rooms on both its sides,[93] in the other the courtyard lies in a corner, with the two rows of rooms along two adjacent sides. A very fine example has been found at Hazor, stratum VI, from the eighth century.[94]

There are, of course, other dwellings with different plans, adapted to the standard of their owners and the local topography.

The three-room building: Among the public buildings common during the period of the kings (with the exception of the Acropolis palaces, as in Samaria), special mention should be made of a type of large building with a uniform plan: three long units, divided from each other by two rows of pillars or by walls, or by the two elements in combination.

From the several fine examples of this type[95] discovered on many mounds, a magnificent one is the "pillared building" at Hazor, stratum VIII. Undoubtedly these buildings often served for storage ($misk^en\bar{o}t$, in the biblical terminology).

In some cases there probably also existed a second story, at least over part of the building. At Hazor, two additional long and narrow halls with cobbled floors were discovered. Presumably grain was stored, either in bulk or in sacks, in these halls, while the principal rooms were used mainly for jars holding oil and wine.

The motivating reason for this type of building is structural: lack of ability to build a ceiling over a large rectangular building without intermediate walls or other support. In fact it can be said that the plan of these buildings is basically similar to that of the later basilica which were built thus for similar reasons. Therefore, not every large building with three long rooms should necessarily be considered a storehouse. On the contrary, one might say that every structure that needed a large hall and that could not be covered by a wall-to-wall ceiling was built by this method.

Having arrived at this conclusion, we approach the problem of the stables at Megiddo. The two stable complexes discovered in stratum IVA (about Ahab's time) are in fact composed of a number of long adjacent halls, each of which is divided by pillars into three long units. The fundamental difference between these buildings and the storehouses is that in Megiddo fine troughs were hewn out of ashlar stones set between the pillars. Furthermore, in the pillars (which supported the ceiling) were holes to tether the horses. Doubts have recently been expressed as to whether the Megiddo buildings indeed served as stables, a hitherto commonly accepted assumption.[96] Pritchard bases his opinion on several assumptions: (a) the similarity of the plan to that of the storehouses; (b) the depth of the troughs, which in his opinion does not suffice to hold an appropriate quantity of grain; (c) the absence of built stables in the ancient world in general. Whether Pritchard is right or wrong, his reasoning does not stand up to criticism.[97] The Assyrian reliefs (from the reign of Ashurnaṣir-pal II) clearly show not only that built stables did exist, but also that the hollow in the troughs was not particularly deep. This is in fact extremely advantageous, since it permits the correct grading of the quantity of fodder, and at the same time keeps the horses from lowering their heads too much and scratching their necks. The "storehouse" theory does not explain either the existence of those fine troughs, which were executed with great craftsmanship, or the tether-holes in the pillars. And lastly, in contrast to the storehouses adjacent to the stables at Megiddo is the important additional element of a large courtyard with a water pool in its center. From the foregoing it can be concluded that large buildings with three long units did not necessarily all serve the same purpose: they may have been storehouses, stables, or other public buildings requiring a large rectangular space.[98]

Temples and cult buildings: The archaeological discoveries supply evidence for the fact, confirmed by the biblical sources, that there existed in several towns during the period of the Monarchy cult structures, which should not always be called temples but in most cases can be described as "high-places" *(bamot)*. A typical complex of this kind was discovered at Megiddo from the time of Solomon,[99] in the southwestern corner of a broad-house, in a spacious building adjacent to the city-wall, about 30 m. to the west of "Solomon's gate." Fundamentally, this building, which lies in the general direction of south to north,[100] consists of a broad unit in the south, from which one enters into a long hall, at whose entrance stood two stone columns and at whose back was a square room. To the west of this hall lies a unit the length of the building, to its east a row of rooms. In other words, we have here a four-room building, which, as we have seen, was common to the magnificent buildings of the period. The complex of cult structures discovered to the west of the entrance to the broad unit (a courtyard?) contained three small stone incense altars, several "incense stands," of clay and of stone, and also a considerable number of imported Cypriot and "Cypro-Phoenician" vessels, including perfume bottles and similar ware.

It is difficult in this whole complex to see a temple proper. The impression is rather that the vessels served for a house cult which included burning incense, but not offering animal sacrifices. The existence of similar incense altars in other places at Megiddo also proves that this is not a sacred building, but that these are cult objects found in various buildings.

Of an entirely different character is, of course, the high-place found at Dan, dealt with at the beginning of this chapter. Both the architectural features and the Bible attest that here we have a monumental cult building. If we accept the excavator's (Biran's) suggestion, we have to assume that the "high-place" consisted of a raised square platform, reached by monumental steps. It is to be regretted that the remains discovered are not sufficient for an understanding of the plan of the high-place.

The only building thus far discovered in strata belonging to the period of the Monarchy which might be called *miqdāš*, a "temple" or "sanctuary," or which might at least have been erected wholly for cult purposes, is the temple at Arad, since here, in addition to the other cult structures, an altar for burnt offerings was found in the courtyard. In principle, the plan of this temple, which lies in a general east-west direction,[101] consists of a square courtyard surrounded on three sides by built units. In fact, we have here essentially the plan of a four-room building (thus there is some similarity to the "cult building" at Megiddo): a central inner space (a courtyard), a long hall along the entire length of the building (in the south), a long room in the north of the same length as the courtyard, and a broad room in the west. The outstanding difference between this and the usual four-room building is the rectangular niche (1.5 × 9.5 m) in the western wall of the broad room. Three steps led to this niche; on them were found two stone incense altars of the type discovered at Megiddo, which had gone out of use. In the niche, a stone *maṣēvāh* with a rounded top was discovered, and in the middle of the northern side of the courtyard an altar measuring about 2.5 × 2.5 m. The altar is built of field stones, but on its top lies a large slab of flint.

As already stated, we undoubtedly have here a building with all the characteristics of a sanctuary. It is difficult, however, to accept the excavator's version that the building plan is similar to that of Solomon's Temple in Jerusalem. Thus there is a certain inaccuracy in calling the unit between the altar and the broad-room by the term *'ulām*, hall, porch; furthermore, it is impossible to speak here of the sequence *'ulām, hēkāl, devīr*, "porch," "main hall," and "holy of holies" as similar to that of Solomon's Temple, because in the last case the whole building was a long house divided into three sub-units of equal width.[102] The discovery of ostraca bearing the names Meremoth (*mrmwt*) and Pashur (*pšḥr*), in the vicinity of the temple in its latest phase, seems to strengthen the opinion of the excavator that we have here a sanctuary connected with the cult of YHWH. However, we have to await the publication of the study of the bones of the sacrificial animals before we can arrive at a final opinion. It is worthwhile in this connection to mention S. Yeivin's suggestion[103] that the sanctuary belonged to the *kittiyim*, those mercenaries often referred to in the ostraca. Only the final and full publication of all the finds will make possible a critical examination of several important problems connected with this important cult building.

CONCLUSION

We should stress in conclusion that our intention is not to present all the stratigraphical data from the period of the Monarchy. Not only would this be impossible in the present framework, but in a book of mainly historical interest it would not even be profitable. We have dealt, therefore, in particular and at some length, with certain problematic aspects of the finds—finds of which the historian often makes use without being in a position to check the archaeological facts. Since the opinions expressed here are obviously those of the author, the reader is therefore advised to make use in every instance of the detailed bibliography attached to this chapter.

CHAPTER IX

CRAFT AND INDUSTRY

by E. Stern

A. CRAFTSMEN

EXPERT ARTISANS who possessed specialized knowledge and experience in a particular craft are generally referred to in the Bible by the name of their professions, such as bakers, cooks, perfumers, weavers, laundresses, potters, scribes, etc. Some of these occupations, like cooking, baking, and laundering, were common household tasks, but archaeological evidence clearly attests that even those crafts which presumably required expert knowledge, such as spinning and weaving, dyeing, and even pottery-making and metal-working were often carried out on a small scale within the household for domestic needs, or as small industries to supplement the family's income (cf. the description of the "woman of valor," Prov. 31:10 ff.).

Because of its many requirements, the royal household probably employed specialists to perform the normal household tasks of cooking, baking, etc., as did the Temple household in Jerusalem.

Craftsmen often acquired their specialized skills within the framework of the tribe. The Kenites, for example, were known as metal workers.[1] In Palestine, however, these were family occupations and the members of such families were all concentrated either in the same village or in several adjoining ones, so that the area in any case became the center for a particular kind of production. Archaeological finds, furthermore, confirm that specialization was generally connected with proximity to the necessary raw material: dyeing of woolen cloth at Tell Beit Mirsim, wine and oil at Beth-shemesh, spices at En-gedi, etc.

Several decades ago, Mendelsohn suggested that the term "family" (*mišpāḥāh*) appearing in certain passages in the Bible refers to guilds of craftsmen. Thus he interprets the "families of the house of the linen workers" (I Chron. 4:21) as a family (or guild) of specialists.[2] The Bible also mentions "families" of potters (I Chron. 4:23), scribes (*ibid.* 2:55), goldsmiths, and merchants (Neh. 3:32). Since the Bible does not provide details of the method of organization of the families of artisans, other relevant documents must be examined—in Babylonian, Ugaritic, and Phoenician.

Artisan guilds, or "families," worked in "houses." The full name occurs only once in the Bible as "the house of work" (*bēit 'avōdāh*) (I Chron. 4:21) and usually appears in the shortened form of "house," such as "potter's house," "house of the wine," "house of the winepress," etc. Several houses of this type are mentioned in the Bible, together with their products. In the village of the "house of Ashbea" was located the "house of the linen workers." In Netaim and Gederah there were apparently potteries. Some scholars even interpret the "ivory houses" built by Ahab in Samaria as workshops for ivory carvers. But when the Bible refers only to "houses" it cannot be known what was produced there. In the roster of "families" in I Chronicles, "Jokim, and the men of Cozeba" (4:22) are mentioned, and it is possible that the members of these families worked in the "houses of Achzib" mentioned in Micah 1:14.[3] Possible confirmation of this suggestion is offered by an ostracon discovered at Lachish in a room which served as the archive of a court official, which contains the names of nine men of the "house of A[chzib]" connected with the royal workshop there.[4]

Some of the so-called families were organized solely for the purpose of supplying the needs of the elaborate and advanced households of the king and the Temple, and some were under their direct authority (cf. "occupied in the king's work," I Chron. 4:23). It is also probable that certain of the ordinary industries, especially those connected with supervising weights and measures, were under royal supervision, as is attested by numerous stamps on handles of store jars bearing names of royal officials. Seals and stamps bearing the names of artisans have been found: "Belonging to Naṣarel the goldsmith" (*lnṣṭ'l hṣrp*), "Belonging to Amoṣ the scribe" (*l'mṣ hspr*), "Belonging to Jehu son of the artisan" (*lyhw' bn h'mn*), etc.[5]

B. HOUSEHOLD WORK
Grinding, Kneading and Baking, Cooking, Washing

Typical household tasks performed by women included the preparation of bread and the related occupations of grinding, kneading and baking, as well as cooking, drawing water, and washing clothes. In the houses of the rich and in the royal household these duties were carried out by slaves and handmaidens, specialists in particular tasks (I Sam. 8:13). Cloth was prepared in the home—spinning, weaving, dyeing, etc.—on a small scale and for family needs.

Grinding. The two types of vessels used for grinding were mortars and grindstones. They were made of basalt or other hard stones and have been found in great numbers in excavations in strata from the Iron Age. The mortars had the form of a bowl standing on a tripod and the pestles were cylindrical with a wide working surface and a narrow top.[6] The grindstone was more efficient,

DANIEL S. WRIGHT

21.
Reconstruction of a
"four-room house"
from Shechem

Courtesy Joint American
Expedition to Tell Balaṭah
(Shechem) and Prof. G. E.
Wright

22.
Remains of "four-room house" from Shechem, Israelite Period

Courtesy Joint American Expedition to Tell Balaṭah (Shechem) and Prof. G. E. Wright.

23.

Megiddo: Remains of a house, Israelite Period. Note two rows of
columns, used to support the roof   Courtesy Oriental Institute, University of Chicago

24.

Beer-Sheba: Living quarters, western section of the city

Courtesy Prof. Y. Aharoni

25.
Hazor: Store-house with
pavement in front; Stratum
VIII

Courtesy Prof. Y. Yadin

26.
Beer-sheba: Store-houses in
the eastern section of the
city; Stratum II

Courtesy Prof. Y. Aharoni

27.
Megiddo: Granary in Stratum III

Courtesy Oriental Institute, University of Chicago

28–29.
Megiddo, Stratum IVA: Section of the stables (above) after excavation; (below) reconstruction
Courtesy Oriental Institute, University of Chicago

30–31.
Arad: (above) Holy of Holies in
the temple; (below) altar in the
temple courtyard
Courtesy Prof. Y. Aharoni

32–33.
Lachish: 10th century B.C.E. sanctuary (above) cult objects *in situ*; (below) sanctuary after
clearing   Courtesy Prof. Y. Aharoni

34.
Beer-sheba: Four-horned
altar of hewn stones
(reconstruction)
Courtesy Prof. Y. Aharoni

35.
Dan: South wall of *bamah* from the period of Ahab   Courtesy Prof. A. Biran

36.
Tell 'Aitun: Israelite tomb. Note incised lines flanking the entrance and animal heads carved in the wall   Courtesy Prof. D. Ussishkin

37.

Village of Siloam: Inscription from the tomb of the "Royal Steward"   Courtesy British Museum

38.

Khirbet el-Kom: 8th–century B.C.E. funerary inscription

Courtesy Prof. W. G. Dever

39–40.
Village of Siloam:
(above) Double-burial
niches. Note head-rests;
(below) interior of the
large tomb

Courtesy Prof. D. Ussishkin

41–42.
Khirbet el-Kom: Entrance and
interior of tomb no. 2
Courtesy Prof. W. G. Dever

43.
Jerusalem: Entrance to a tomb (Israelite Period) on the eastern slope of the western hill
Courtesy Prof. B. Mazar

however, and the rubbing and friction combined to produce a larger amount of flour. In her study of the development of the grindstone in Palestine, Ruth Amiran concluded that over a period of thousands of years the form of the grindstone underwent no changes.[7] It had, moreover, the same form in different cultures at great distances from each other. It consisted of two stones, the upper one rubbing and crushing the grain which had been poured onto the lower, larger stone, which apparently stood on a mat or a piece of cloth where the ground flour was collected. These two stones are common to all historical periods starting with the Neolithic.[8] A new type, developed in the Iron Age and known as "grindstones with a frame," had a perforated upper stone so that the grains could be passed through the hole without interrupting the grinding process. Another innovation was a bar fitted through a groove in the upper stone to turn it. This type of grindstone increased both efficiency and convenience[9] and was in use throughout the period of the Monarchy.

The ground flour was divided into categories according to quality; the most finely ground was considered the choicest. The Bible differentiates between fine flour and simple coarse meal (I Kings 5:2). Another category is added in an ostracon found at Arad: "the first flour," which is also interpreted as fine flour.[10]

Kneading. The technique of kneading dough can be learned from a pottery model from the time of the Monarchy which was uncovered in excavations at Achzib. A woman is shown kneading loaves of bread on a trough-shaped four-legged table.[11] The table seems to have been built especially for kneading, but simpler vessels, such as large stone or clay basins, were probably more commonly used.

Baking. Baking ovens were built in the courts of houses. The remains of numerous ovens have been uncovered in excavations, usually with only the bases preserved. Most were built of a thick layer of unfired clay coated on the outside with potsherds to increase insulation. When damaged, the ovens were recoated. Judging from the round bases that have been preserved, the complete oven was about half a meter high and was shaped like a pointed or rounded dome with an opening pierced in one of the sides. At Tell es-Sa'idiyeh in Transjordania, a common kitchen containing many ovens, probably to serve a number of families, was uncovered from the period of the Monarchy.[12]

Baking vessels found in excavations from the First Temple period consist mainly of round trays with perforations in the base, which archaeologists call baking trays. A round flat loaf could have been baked on this tray.[13] The Bible mentions, among others, the "griddle" and "stewing pan" (Lev. 2:5, 7) which were used for baking with oil, but these vessels cannot be distinguished today.[14] The baking was apparently done in a very hot oven after the removal of the coals.

Cooking. The pot set on the fire is the cooking vessel most common in the Bible (II Kings 4:38; Ezek. 24:3–4; II Chron. 35:13). Most pots were of clay and a few of copper (Lev. 6:21).

Many potsherds, undoubtedly belonging to cooking vessels, have been found in excavations, foremost among them the so-called cooking pot because of its shape, its coarse clay and the fact that in excavations it was frequently found standing on an oven, its sides blackened with soot. The cooking pot of the Bronze and Iron Ages was open, but a lid was added in the Persian period.[15] Other cooking vessels mentioned in the Bible cannot be unequivocally identified.

In the courtyards of the king and of the Temple were large kitchens in which expert cooks were employed (I Sam. 8:13; 9:24). The remains of a set of dishes apparently used by the Aramean royal household in the ninth century B.C.E. were discovered in northern Palestine. At Tel Dan a bowl was found with the inscription, *ltb(h)y'* ("belonging to the cooks"), and at 'En Gev a store jar inscribed, *lšqy'* ("belonging to the cupbearer").[16]

Laundry. The clothes were usually washed by the women of the household. How they did it can be inferred from the Hebrew verb *kbš*, treading, which suggests that the clothes were cleaned primarily by treading with the feet. Egyptian reliefs indicate that this method was universally practiced by ancient peoples. The clothes were washed at the settlement's main water source, whether spring or pool. Thus, for example, the "fullers' field" in Jerusalem was near the upper pool (II Kings 18:17; Isa. 7:3). The Bible mentions two kinds of washing substance: *bōrīt*, which was produced from the ashes of plants, and *neter*, one of the natron salts. Potash was used for whitening.[17]

C. MAKING CLOTHES
Spinning, Weaving, Dyeing, Dress

Spinning. In the First Temple period fabric was made into cloth by the threefold process of spinning the thread, weaving it into cloth, and cleaning and dyeing the wool.

The thread was generally spun by drawing and twisting the fiber at the same time, and then winding the finished thread into a ball. Animal fibers—the wool of sheep and the hair of goats and camels—were usual, but vegetable flax was also used.[18]

The Bible shows that spinning was one of the typical household tasks performed by women in their leisure time (Ex. 35:25; Prov. 31:19). The wealthy employed handmaidens and slaves, since spinning in itself was not considered a respected occupation (II Sam. 3:29).

Fig. 10. Tomb of Ṭhuti-nefer: Wall-painting showing spinning and weaving establishment.
Eretz–Israel VI (1961), p. 45.

The exact method of spinning used in Palestine in First Temple times cannot be known, because several different ones appear on Egyptian reliefs, wall paintings, and wood models. Scholars, furthermore are divided as to the meaning of the two terms connected with spinning in the book of Psalms, although it is generally accepted that the *kīšōr* is the spindle, a narrow rod with pointed ends, one of which is attached to a whorl (*pele̱k*), a weight that gave momentum to the

Fig. 11. Tomb of Kheti at Beni Hasan: Wall-painting showing various spinning techniques.
Eretz–Israel VI (1961), p. 43.

spindle. Since most of the spindles were wooden, very few have been uncovered in excavations, and those few have been bone. Whorls, however, have been found in large numbers, most of them, from the Iron Age, of stone, but some of bone, as well as numerous clay whorls made of broken pottery fragments reshaped and perforated in the center. Some have geometric decorations and are concave, conical, biconical, and even flat disc.[19]

The depictions of spinning in Egyptian sources have been studied by Trude Dothan, who concluded that at least three spinning methods were used:[20] 1) the suspended spindle, by which the spinner draws the thread with upright hand from a coil in front of him and twists the spindle on his thigh with his other hand; 2) the supported spindle, by which the spinner draws the thread with upright hand from a bowl in front of him and rolls the spindle on his thigh; 3) the grasped spindle, by which the thread is drawn from a bowl in front of the spinner through a forked stick down to a spindle turned with both hands. In this method several threads are usually twisted into one. In a similar technique, also depicted on Egyptian reliefs, the thread is drawn through rings above the bowl instead of the forked stick, and the spindle is turned with both hands. Proving that these or similar methods were used in Palestine are the many spinning bowls which have been discovered, identical in shape to those on the Egyptian reliefs. Although both stone and pottery bowls of this type were found in Egypt only the latter were found in Palestine. They are made of well-fired clay and are shaped like ordinary bowls, but have handles inside on the base. Although handles usually appear in pairs, either connected or separate, some bowls have only one handle and others two pairs. These bowls have been found at many sites from the Late Bronze and Iron Ages in Palestine.[21] The Egyptian bowls are earlier, from the Twelfth Dynasty, indicating that they were of local origin.

The uses of the spinning bowls can be determined from the Egyptian sources. They served as receptacles for the ball of fibers being spun and may also have been filled with water for wetting the threads, especially those that were twisted. The handles inside the bowls held the balls of thread securely in place, making it possible to spin several threads from different balls at the same time without tangling. The friction of the threads wore grooves into the handles.[22]

Weaving. Like spinning, weaving also began as a domestic task performed chiefly by housewives in biblical times in Palestine.[23] Fine weaving of special fabrics like linen, however, was done by expert craftsmen (I Chron. 4:21).

The Bible makes little mention of how weaving is done. The warp and woof of linen and woolen garments are referred to in Lev. 13:47 ff. Types of specially woven cloth occur in the description of the tabernacle, as, for example, in the

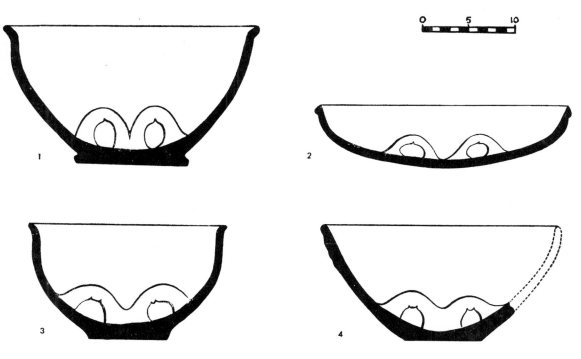

Fig. 12. Spinning-bowls from Palestine.
Trude Dothan, *IEJ*, 13 (1963), 98.

description of the high priest's robe of ephod: " . . . it shall have a binding *ma'ăseh 'ōrēg* round about the hole of it, *k^efî tahărāh* that it be not rent" (Ex. 28:32). The term *kefî tahărāh* is obscure, but *ma'ăseh 'ōrēg* apparently refers to a type of fabric. The term *ma'ăseh ḥōšēv* also appears several times (Ex. 28:6; 36:35; etc.) and seems to refer to cloth woven in special designs. Fabric woven in colored patterns of different hues is apparently called *ma'ăseh rōqēm* (*ibid.* 26:36). Other types are *tašbēṣ*, perhaps a checked weave (Ex. 28:4), and *ša'aṭnēz*, a cloth described in the Bible as a combination of wool and linen. It is forbidden to wear such cloth because it is a "mixed species" (Deut. 22:11).

Several types of textiles are listed in the Bible, such as woolen or linen garments (Lev. 13:47). Fine woolen cloth was called by the color it was dyed: *'argāmān*, *t^ekelet*, and *šānî* (and see below). Linen fabrics also had several names, the plain called simply cloth. *Shēsh* (Ezek. 27:7) is the Egyptian name for fine-quality linen. In Ex. 39:28 "linen breeches of fine twined linen" refers to a fine double-ply thread. Fine linen in Mesopotamia and Syria was called *būṣ*, the name appearing in the biblical phrase for "the house of the linen workers" in Judah (I Chron. 4:21).[24] *'Eṭūn* was another fine Egyptian fabric (Prov. 7:16). The linen cloth ḥūr is mentioned in Esther 1:6 together with *karpās*. *Mešī* (usually translated ("silk") is referred to Ezek. 16:10, 13 but it cannot be identified.

The art of weaving consists of passing the crosswise weft threads through the lengthwise warp threads, which are stretched (cf. Lev. 13:48 ff.) on a loom or frame. Egyptian reliefs, wall paintings, and wooden models show several different techniques of weaving, some of which were still practised by Arab *fellahīn* a generation ago.[25]

In the story of Samson and Delilah are terms connected with weaving (Judg. 16:13–14), apparently describing in a fragmentary way the horizontal loom whose use was widespread in that period. Among the features of the Philistine armor a component of the loom appears, the "weaver's beam" (I Sam. 17:7; II Sam. 21:19), probably the bar which separated the odd warp threads from the even ones. According to Yadin, the shaft of the javelin and the weaver's beam are similar in their general appearance; both are long and narrow; the loops of the javelin served for throwing it and those of the weaver's beam for tying the threads.[26]

Neither the Bible nor archaeological finds furnish sufficient data to determine which of the Near Eastern weaving techniques current in biblical times were employed in Palestine. While the horizontal loom is mentioned in the story of Samson and Delilah, more definite evidence is available only for the weighted-loom type. Loom weights have been found in Palestine from the Middle Bronze Age to the Persian period and later.

Fewer weaving than spinning tools have been uncovered in excavations in Palestine. Of the loom itself only the weights were made of clay and thus only these have survived. Wherever the looms were burnt or destroyed several weights were found on the spot. At Lachish a weaver's workshop from the end of the period of the Monarchy was excavated. A weighted loom, of which only one charred post had been preserved, had stood on a raised and paved platform with a group of clay weights at its foot. A vat for dyeing was found, as was a seal inscribed *lḥlqyh bn m's*, which had probably belonged to the artisan.[27] Several more workshops have also been found recently at Tel Amal, near Beth-shean. One workshop in stratum IV, from the tenth century B.C.E., was built on the plan of the four-room house. Its middle room contained some kind of heating apparatus or oven. The equipment in the shop included a great many cooking pots, jugs, juglets, storage jars, and stone tools, such as mortars, and other tools whose function is unknown. There were several groups of stone weights, each group containing scores of weights, arranged in rows. The largest group had 60 weights. The way in which the weights were arranged indicates that they had belonged to a vertical loom. The charred remains of looms were found near each group of weights. In each group the number of weights and their sizes varied, the number depending on the width of the fabric, the size on the quality and thickness of the yarns.

Above this settlement stood the remains of a later settlement (stratum III, also from the tenth century B.C.E.), built according to the same plan and construction methods, and demonstrating that the Beth-shean Valley was a major center of weaving in the time of the First Temple. The especially large quantity of spinning bowls found there have already been noted.[28]

The majority of the loom weights found in excavation in Palestine were of pottery and only a small number of stone.

Weights from the Bronze Age were elliptical in shape, from the Iron Age spherical, with a central hole,[29] and at the end of the Persian period, generally pyramidal, as in the Hellenistic period. Some of the weights were made by the weaver himself and crumbled easily because they were only lightly fired. Those produced by a professional potter were well fired.

Bone tools which had probably been used in weaving have also been found. They are thin and flat with a point at one end and a hole in the other and may have served as shuttles for carrying the weft through the shed or for beating in the weft. Bone spatulas, rectangular shaped on one side and on the other pointed and glossy from use, were probably used to raise groups of threads from the web in weaving intricate designs.[30] The threads could be more easily separated, by using either the pointed ends or animal horns. The numerous needles (of bone and bronze) found in excavations were probably also employed in weaving or plain sewing.[31]

Although no actual remnants of clothing were found in excavations from the First Temple period,[32] a large and varied collection of clothes and textiles from the time of Bar-Kokhba were uncovered in the "Cave of the Letters" in Naḥal Hever in the Judean Desert. These are woven fabrics of flax and wool and furnish valuable information about weaving techniques, which had persisted in part from the time of the First Temple.[33]

Dyeing. Judging from the clothes shown on wall paintings and reliefs, it is evident that most garments were colored. The Bible provides no details of the dyeing process but it mentions colored clothes (Judg. 5:30) and cloth, as already noted, is listed by its *šānī t*e*kelet* color.[34] In the opinion of most scholars, the colors *būṣ*, *t*e*kelet*, and *'argāmān* were obtained on the Palestinian coast from the murex, a snail whose blood is purplish-black, apparently the color of *t*e*kelet*. With the addition of other substances, the color could be changed to purple (*'argāmān* and *šānī*).[35]

The extraction of purple dye on the Palestinian coast is attested at Tel Mor near Ashdod, where a third-century B.C.E. installation for obtaining dye from murex shells was uncovered. It was composed of two superimposed plastered pools interconnected by a pipe. A channel led from the pools to a small pit which held the dye. The clothes were probably immersed for dyeing in the pools. The surplus dye flowed into the lower pool from which it could be removed by means of jugs (several were found in the pool) and re-used. A deep cistern near the pools supplied the necessary water; at its base were found hundreds of murex shells.[36]

The art of purple-dyeing was mainly in the hands of Tyrians, specialists in this craft. In the time of Solomon this work was performed by an artisan from Tyre (II Chron. 2:6, 13). Aram is also listed in Ezek. 27:13 as an exporter of purple and linen clothes.

While simple dyeing of woolen yarns and flax may have been done at home, more complicated work, especially of luxury fabrics, was an art practised by experts whose lore was transmitted from father to son. Several dye plants from the eighth-seventh centuries B.C.E. have been excavated in Palestine, the best known at Tell Beit Mirsim, and others at Beth-shemesh, Tell en-Nasbeh, Bethel, and Gezer.[37]

The dye plants at Tell Beit Mirsim were found scattered throughout the area of the city. Although only six or seven were unearthed in the excavations, Albright believed that the site contained as many as forty plants run by a number of families specializing in this profession. Each installation consisted of two round stone vats, almost all about 80 cm. in height and diameter. In the hollow of the vat was a small container, 30 to 45 cm. in diameter, with a small mouth.

The vat had a deep groove around the rim and a hole through which the liquid returned. Near the vats were plastered cisterns and a bench on which large store jars were set. In several of the plants there were pottery jars containing lime and at least one storage jar held potash, both undoubtedly essential ingredients in dyeing. Large perforated stones, perhaps to press the surplus dye out of the cloth, were also found. The many cisterns in the area provided the abundant water necessary. First the dye was poured into the vats with the fixing material and after the wool had been immersed several times it was wrung out and laid to dry. Albright determined the method of dyeing in Tell Beit Mirsim by observing dyeing workshops in Hebron in 1930. The type of dye was the essential difference. The Hebron dyers used indigo imported from the east, apparently cheaper than the excellent dyes of antiquity; they also put potash and lime into the vats and added the dye two days later. A small amount of indigo went into the first vat and double the amount in the second. The cloth was immersed on the third day, ordinary cloth receiving two baths in the two vats, fine fabrics as many as ten. The size of the vats at Hebron makes it evident that those at Tell Beit Mirsim were too small to hold a whole garment, which probably had to be dyed in sections.

In the opinion of Albright, the dye plants at Tell Beit Mirsim used the cold bath method, which means that the dyes were not heated before absorption. The tenth-century-B.C.E. dye plants at Tel Amal seem to have employed various techniques. Stone mortars were found there for pounding the substances from which the dyes were produced, as well as resin, which the excavator considered one of the dyeing ingredients. The large number of cooking pots unearthed were used for heating or cooking the dye. The type of stone vat common in Judah and Benjamin did not appear here.[38] In two dye plants from later periods found at En-gedi and Tel Mor the vats were also built-up and plastered installations.

A large variety of colored fabrics were among the textiles in the "Cave of the Letters" in the Judean Desert from the time of Bar Kokhba. These provided material for the first comprehensive study of the composition of clothing dyes, which presumably carry on the tradition of the First Temple period.[39]

Dress. The Bible refers to types of cloth in the First Temple period mainly in terms of their composition, woolen or linen (see above), and by their means. Most of our information about dress of that time is therefore drawn from external sources, particularly reliefs and archaeological finds.

These sources indicate that the majority of the people usually wore a single garment, a custom reflected in the prohibition against taking away a poor man's garment (Ex. 22:25–26) and in an ostracon from the seventh century B.C.E. found at Meṣad Ḥashavyahu. The ostracon is a peasant's plea to the governor of the citadel to return his coat, confiscated as punishment for idling at work: "Hosha'yahu son of Shobai came and took thy servant's garment . . . I am absolved of guilt. Please return my garment . . . be merciful to him and restore the garment of thy servant."[40]

The basic dress of the Israelite farmer and soldier seems to have been the short 'ēzōr ("kilt"), which was wrapped around the waist and reached the middle of the thigh. The maḥălāṣōt (Isa. 3:22; Zech. 3:4) is also often interpreted as a short garment covering the loins. The Bible mentions an 'ēzōr of leather (II Kings 1:8), although they were usually of flax, fastened by a belt of cloth or leather from which hung such objects as a dagger and personal belongings like a seal, stone weights, and valuables. Several belts have been uncovered in tombs of different periods in Palestine, but usually only the bronze coating and buckles are preserved. Ornamented bronze belts of soldiers from the Middle Bronze Age have been found at Jericho and Tell el-Far'ah (north). Weapons—daggers and war axes—were attached to them. Leather and bronze belts have also been found in Iron Age tombs at Tell 'Aitun. Ordinary citizens wore simple cloth belts or expensive colored ones of the kind offered by Joab as a prize for killing Absalom (II Sam. 18:11).[41]

The upper part of the body was either left bare or covered with a short-sleeved tunic, apparently the k^e*tonet* (II Sam. 13:18–19; Cant. 5:3), worn above the kilt. Over this in cold weather a dress-like garment (*simlāh*) (Ex. 22:26; Deut. 24:13) or cloak (*m^e'īl*) were worn. Both of these were outer clothes; the distinction between them is not very clear. Reliefs and wall paintings from the time of the First Temple and earlier show that the upper garments, the k^e*tonet*, *simlāh*, and *m^e'īl*, were usually multi-colered (cf. Joseph's "coat of many colors," Gen. 37:3). The seams were embroidered and trimmed with colored tassels along the edges of the garment and the hem.

The main sources for the details of dress in the First Temple period are Assyrian reliefs portraying Israelites. One relief, the Black Obelisk from the time of Shalmaneser III (858–824 B.C.E.), shows messengers of the Israelite king Jehu bearing tribute to the Assyrian king. Another major source is the well-known series of reliefs from Sennacherib's time depicting the storming of Lachish and its defense by the inhabitants of the town (701 B.C.E.).[42]

On the Black Obelisk the Israelites are dressed in long, tightly fitting garments, open in front and ornamented at the edges, with a similar long garment over it. Neither had collars. The Israelite warrior in the relief of the siege of Lachish wears a short kilt, a short-sleeved tunic, and a turban-like headdress, made of a length of cloth wrapped around the head and forehead. Important citizens were dressed in long close-fitting garments reaching the ankles. These clothes were of a solid color and unornamented.

In excavations at Ramat-Raḥel a sherd from the seventh century B.C.E. was found bearing the figure of a man, whose dress and figure are distinct copies of the style on Assyrian wall paintings. A contemporary sherd from En-gedi shows a man's figure in the same style.[43] Several additional details can be gleaned from some of the ivories from the Iron Age in Palestine[44] and from contemporary statues and ivories from sites in Transjordania, Syria, and Phoenicia, but it is doubtful that these depict the typical dress of the men of Israel and Judah.

With the exception of the kilt, men and women seem to have dressed similarly. Women apparently also had a variety of head coverings. The relief of the siege of Lachish shows the women wearing the same kind of clothes as the men, with the addition of a long narrow mantle with a head covering. The Bible (Isa. 3:18–24) lists a variety of women's clothes, unidentifiable today, and unable to be compared with the dress of women shown on contemporary monuments. Some of the biblical terms, however, seem to designate foreign dress.[45]

Very little of our knowledge of dress in the period of the Monarchy is drawn from archaeological finds, which consist mainly of buttons and toggle pins made of some solid material. Numerous stone and clay buttons with two holes for attaching them to the garment, have been found in excavations.[46] Bronze toggle pins, which are very common, were in Bronze Age times usually shaped like a long needle with a hole in the center. The needle was inserted in the cloth and secured with ties concealed in the hole and laced around the two ends. From the tenth century on, the needle-pin was replaced by a more efficient toggle pin resembling the modern safety pin but larger. Toggle pins underwent minor changes in detail from time to time; they continued to be used in Palestine during the Hellenistic and Roman periods.[47]

D. POTTERY

In the First Temple period, as in earlier periods, pottery vessels were the most common in domestic use. The mass of ceramic evidence in excavations reveals that most pottery was intended for the household—for cooking, baking, and storage. Pottery vessels were used to store wine, oil, perfumes, wheat, etc. for payment of taxes as well as to transport goods between countries, both overland and by sea. Figurines, stands, goblets, and chalices for cultic use were also fashioned of clay.

It is no wonder therefore that large numbers of pottery vessels were required and that pottery workshops probably existed in every village to fill the needs of the local population and even of a single family.[48] A study of the various Iron Age ceramic types in Palestine shows that the pottery differed from place to place within the country. It is possible today to determine whether vessels were manufactured in Judah, Samaria, Galilee, the coastal plain, the Negeb, or Transjordan, since each area had a characteristic ceramic tradition. Where the products of a particular workshop were distributed can also be established.

The biblical references to pottery and its manufacture supplement the archaeological finds. Since workshops were located in almost every village the potter's craft was well-known and the parables and rhetoric of the prophets made frequent use of ceramic terms (Isa. 45:9; Jer. 18:6; etc.). Several of these descrip-

Fig. 13. Egypt, Middle Kingdom: Pottery-making.

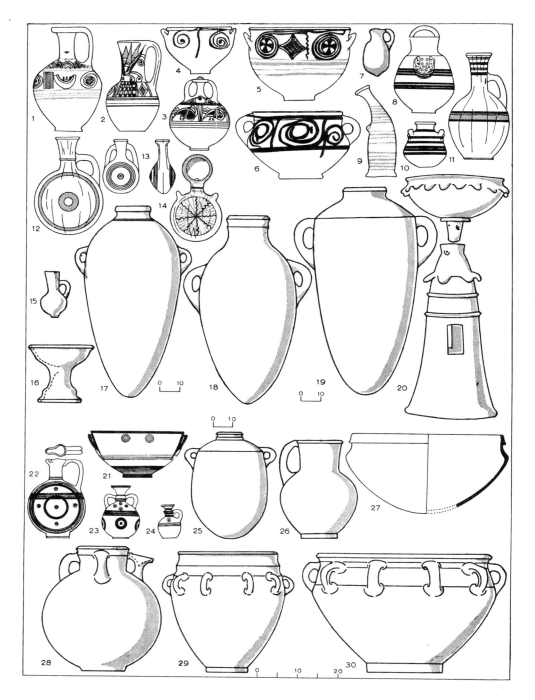

Fig. 14. Typical Iron Age pottery from Palestine.
N. Avigad, *Encyclopedia Miqra'it* IV, 1962, cols. 173–174.

tions are sufficiently detailed to enable us to determine the ancient techniques of pottery manufacture (cf. especially Jer. 18:2–4), while others tell us how the vessels were used (Lev. 6:21; 14:5; Num. 5:17; Jer. 32:14, etc.).

Pottery production methods are fully revealed by the many archaeological finds[49] and since most of them have still not changed, they can be compared with methods used in Arab villages.[50] Potters' workshops, complete with equipment, have been found in several excavations, most notably the "potter's cave" at Lachish from the end of the Late Bronze Age—beginning of the Iron Age.[51] Here were found several pits and depressions, in one of which were the potter's tools, two sets of potter's wheels, a small mortar for crushing ocher for painting, shells, smooth pebbles and worn potsherds for burnishing, and a mold for figurines. It also contained raw material. Another depression, containing many unfired pots, seems to have served for drying and storing the pots. A third pit, according to the excavators, contained the potter's wheel which he worked while sitting at the edge of the pit.

Kilns have been uncovered at such sites as Tell el-Far'ah in Samaria and Mt. Yeruham in the Negeb.[52] They were two-storied, the lower story for the fuel and the upper story for the pots that were to be fired. Although these kilns predate the Israelite period, it is not likely that methods of production changed radically from the Bronze to the Iron Ages.

Potter's tools have also been found at many sites. Wheels of basalt from the Bronze and Iron Ages were discovered at Megiddo and Tell el-'Ajjul.[53] They indicate not only that potter's equipment in Palestine underwent no alteration for thousands of years, but they also help us reconstruct ancient production methods.[54]

In addition to the potters who provided for domestic needs and private commerce, there were apparently families of potters in Judah who specialized in pottery for government use, i.e., the jars for storing taxes in kind which were concentrated in special warehouses. These (especially the storage jars) bore seals stamped *la-melek*, with symbols of the Judean kingdom and the names of four Judaean cities: Hebron, Ziph, Socoh, and *Mmšt* (unidentified). Other vessels bore stamps of rosettes, concentric circles, etc. Some scholars believe that the Judean families of potters mentioned in I Chron. 4:23 were members of a potters' guild in the exclusive employ of the king. Others suggest that they were regular potteries licensed to produce royal and ordinary vessels of a guaranteed standard measure.[55]

E. METAL WORKING

The metals known from the Bible are copper, iron, gold, silver, and lead, but there is no comprehensive biblical term for all metals. Judging from the archeological finds, the Hebrew word for copper ($n^e\underline{h}o\check{s}et$) actually denoted both pure copper and bronze, an alloy of copper and tin, widespread in Palestine in this period.

Ores, copper deposits, and a small amount of iron occur in Palestine, mainly in the Arabah and Sinai areas, which were distinguished as "a land whose stones are iron, and out of whose hills thou mayest dig $n^e\underline{h}o\check{s}et$" (Deut. 8:9). Gold, silver, and lead, on the other hand, were not mined in Palestine and had to be imported.[56]   The biblical references to working gold and silver (Prov. 17:3; 27:21; Zech. 13:9, etc.) mean secondary metallurgy, like fashioning vessels, jewelry, or useful objects from imported ingots.

Copper-working usually consists of two main stages: 1) extracting the raw material from deposits as native copper ores and melting it into ingots, and 2) making the ingots into finished products, such as tools, weapons, cult objects, household goods, and jewelry.[57] In the major metallurgical centers of the ancient East, such as the Caucasus, Anatolia and Cyprus, these stages were simultaneous while Palestinian archaeological finds indicate a clear distinction between the two. The first stage occurred in the vicinity of the mines in the Arabah and the finished products were manufactured by expert craftsmen in settlements in the interior of the country.

The copper mines and iron deposits in the Arabah were explored by N. Glueck and B. Rothenberg.[58] In Glueck's opinion, the copper extracted from the mines scattered along Wadi Arabah and especially Naḥal Timna' was smelted at a central plant at Tell el-Kheleifeh, which he identified with Ezion-geber. He attributed this activity to Solomon, who needed vessels for the Temple and articles for export, which were shipped from Ezion-geber. Rothenberg has shown, on the other hand, that Naḥal Timna' and not Tell el-Kheleifeh was the manufacturing center of the area. Mining and smelting camps were located at Naḥal Timna' and there was no need for a regional industrial center. Other finds, such as cartouches of pharaohs of the Nineteenth Dynasty, indicate that the mines in Naḥal Timna' were worked mainly at the end of the Late Bronze Age and not during the Iron Age. They were operated by the Egyptians, probably within the framework of royal expeditions to Sinai.

Excavations at Timna also revealed numerous details of its mining and smelting processes. The copper was collected in the form of concentrates (up to 80 per cent) extracted from the bedrock in southern Naḥal Timna' and Naḥal 'Amram. The concentrates were crushed and scattered by the wind near rock-cut cavities near the mining site. The wind blew away the lime of the crushed rock, leaving in the bottom of the cavity only the heavy metal nuggets, which were collected and transported to the nearby smelting camps, where they were crushed once again, mixed with charcoal, and smelted in furnaces. The smelted copper collected at the bottom of the furnace in the form of a round bar, like the complete copper bar found at a site in Wadi Arabah. Near the furnaces and in the smelting camps were many tools, including stone-crushing tools and mouths of clay bellows, as well as numerous slag heaps.

The identity of the artisans working in this camp has not been definitely established but some of them may have been Kenites, whom the Bible calls the first metallurgists (cf. Gen. 4:22),[59] and some may have been Midianites. These mines and others in Naḥal Arabah had apparently also been operated in the Iron Age, although not so intensively. At all events, the methods of mining were well known—and a poetic account is preserved in Job 28:1–11.

Palestinian metallurgy mainly consisted, as stated above, of re-smelting the copper ingots and shaping them into finished products. Metal-working of this type was common in many Palestinian towns. According to the Bible, the vessels for the Temple were cast in the Jordan Valley between Succoth and Zarethan (I Kings 7:45–46). The wide distribution of metal-working is also clearly attested by archaeological finds. Crucibles and furnaces for casting copper and iron have been found not only in places far apart from each other but also in places which lack raw material, such as Tell Deir 'Alla in the Succoth Valley, Tel Ḥarashim in Upper Galilee, Tel Zeror, and Tell Qasile in the Sharon, Gezer, Beth-shemesh, Tell el-Ḥesi, Tell el-Far'ah (south), and Tell Jemmeh in the Shephelah.[60] Numerous molds for casting tools and weapons, ornaments and figurines have been discovered at other sites, like Hazor, Megiddo, Shechem, and Tell Beit Mirsim.[61] The high level of local metal-working is clearly demonstrated by the numerous metal objects of Palestinian origin.[62]

In the twelfth-eleventh centuries B.C.E. bronze continued to be the primary useful metal employed in Palestine and only rarely were objects manufactured of iron. From the tenth century, however, the number of iron objects increased and subsequently replaced bronze.[63]

Metal was also used for agricultural tools.[64] Excavations at various sites have uncovered many plow-blades, scythes and sickles, saws, spades, etc., as well as the three prongs of the pitchfork and the cultic trident (I Sam. 2:13).[65] Many tools were found for metal-, wood-, and leather-working, including blades of axes, saws, knives, pliers, nails, fishhooks, and various other pointed objects.[66] A great number of bronze and iron weapons have been excavated, notably swords, blades of spears and javelins, arrowheads, war axes, coats of armor, etc.[67] Ritual objects mainly included figurines—of bronze and the more costly silver and gold—and also tripods, used as stands for libation and incense bowls. Of ordinary household utensils mostly bowls, jugs, and juglets have been found.[68] The numerous ornaments include bracelets, earrings, rings, and beads made of every metal known—iron, bronze, copper, silver, and gold.[69]

The great majority of these objects were produced in Palestine as is attested both by the biblical evidence (see above) and the large number of crucibles and molds for casting found in excavations. In Ashkelon a metallurgist's workshop from the Persian period was excavated, where metal figurines and weights had been cast.[70] Lead objects, only rarely recovered, are usually figurines and weights (including fishing weights). Gold and silver by weight was the main form of currency.

F. AGRICULTURAL PRODUCTS
Wine, Oil and Perfume

In years of abundant harvests an agricultural surplus allowed the farmers to prepare food for future consumption like raisins and wine made of grapes, dried figs, honey made of figs, dates, and perhaps carobs, oil, and spices. These products were meant both for local needs and for export to neighboring countries. Some may even have been grown wholly for export, as is indicated in the Bible: "Judah, and the land of Israel, they were thy traffickers; they traded for thy merchandize wheat of Minnith, and *pannag* and honey, and oil, and balm." (Ezek. 27:17). Of these products *pannag* cannot be identified. Wine, the most important product, as the excavations attest, strangely enough is not mentioned here. Wheat was probably exported in the form of kernels. While the archaeological evidence gives us no information about the production of fruits and fruit-honey, many installations have been found which shed light on the production methods of wine, oil, and perfumes.

Wine Production. That this was the principal industry based on agricultural produce is attested in almost every excavated site in Palestine in the form of wine cellars, wine presses, jars for storing wine, and other vessels.[71]

The biblical descriptions of techniques of preparing wine are meager and do not detail its various stages.[72] Our information is therefore derived mainly from Egyptian monuments and from the wine presses and cellars of the First Temple period uncovered in different parts of the country,[73] especially at Gibeon. The discoveries there enabled the excavator to trace the entire process of wine production.[74] According to his reconstruction of the various stages of work, the grapes were first trod upon in rock-cut presses large enough for two or more treaders to stand on. The grape juice, skins, stems, and seeds flowed through the press (shaped like a pool with a slanting bottom) into settling basins where the foreign matter was separated from the liquid. The juice was then transferred into containers for the first fermentation. Here the half-fermented juice was again purified of the heavier sediments and poured into large storage jars, which

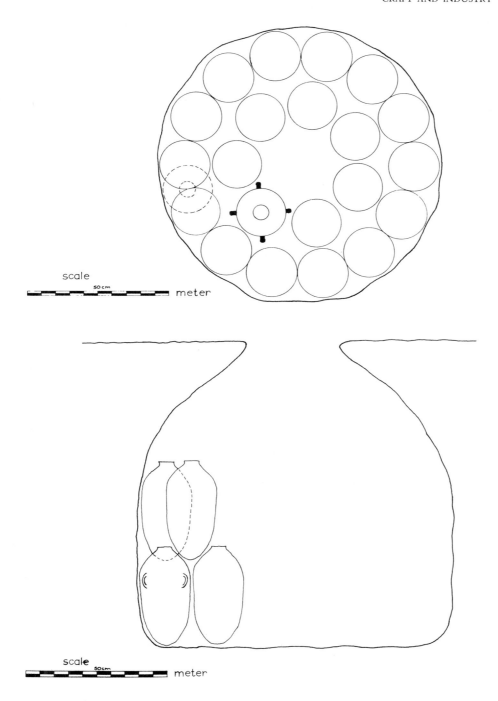

scale   meter

scale   meter

Fig. 15. Gibeon: Plan of wine cellar with jars (above). Section of wine cellar with jars (below).

J. B. Pritchard, *Winery, Defenses and Soundings at Gibeon*, Philadelphia, 1961, figs. 52–53.

were lowered into round rock-cut cellars and placed in rows along the walls. The height of the chamber allowed the jars to be set in two tiers. Since the cellars were not deeply dug, they could be easily filled and emptied. An average-size man could stand on the floor of the cellar, lift a heavy storage jar, and pass it to another man outside without using a ladder. The diameter of the cellars was about 2 meters and the width of the entrance about 65 cm., wide enough for a man to pass through and narrow enough to be blocked easily by a stone slab. When the entrance was sealed, a constant cool temperature, excellent for fermentation, could be maintained. The storage jars were left in the cellar until fermentation was complete, after which they were removed and marketed.

Aside from the various kinds of grape wine, wines were prepared from other fruits, especially dates, a wine popular mainly in Egypt and Mesopotamia. The "juice of pomegranate" (Cant. 8:2) may perhaps indicate wine prepared from this fruit.

Evidence was found at Gibeon that, before marketing, the contents of the large storage jars were funneled into smaller, two-handled jars. In Pritchard's opinion, the wine was sealed in these jars by pouring a few drops of olive oil over the wine to keep it from contact with the air, and then plugging the jar with a clay stopper (several of which have been found in the excavations) held tight by a leather strip. The stopper was also sealed with mud or bitumen. Clay stoppers or wine jars have been found in many other sites in Palestine. One from Beersheba is stamped with the seal either of the official responsible for shipping the wine or of the owner of the jar.[75]

In addition to storage jars and pottery decanters, wine was also marketed in skins (*nevel*). In the ostraca from the storehouses at Samaria dealing with the dispatch of wine appears the formula: "a *nevel* of old wine," which may refer to a standard unit of volume, since it was customary to designate quantities by types of receptacles. Another ostracon from the Persian period from Ashdod reads: "the vineyard of Zabadiah *pg*" (*krm zbdyh pg*); the last word has been interpreted as the initials of *plg grb'*, i.e., a vessel with a capacity of half a *grb*. A storage jar from the excavations at Achzib is inscribed with the measure *grbn*. Ostraca from Tell el-Kheleifeh and Elephantine record that deliveries of wine were measured by decanters (*lagīn*).[76] Nevertheless, wine was generally measured by the units of volume common in the period and not by the receptacles (see below). Thus for example an ostracon from Arad reads: " . . . give to the *Kittiyim* 3 *bath* of wine,"[77] the way quantities were designated on most other ostraca of the First Temple and Persian periods found at Shiqmona, Samaria, Beersheba, Tell el-Kheleifeh, and other sites in Palestine.

Wine is also designated by types, several of which appear in the Bible, such as *tīrōš*, "new wine" (apparently unfermented), *rekah*, which appears to be wine made from perfume (cf. Cant. 8:2), and perhaps also s*e*mādar. The last variety is attested on a sherd of a storage jar inscribed "*lpqḥ smdr*" which Yadin interprets as a type of wine sent to king Pekah son of Remaliah.[78] Other varieties of wine not mentioned in the Bible occur on ostraca from the First Temple period, among them "old wine" on an ostracon from Samaria, and "wine of basins (*ha-'aggānōt*)" and "sour wine" on ostraca from Arad.[79] On a stone seal from the Second Temple period found near Mozah is the word *temed*, a kind of drink mentioned in the Mishnah.[80]

Wine was also frequently given the name of its provenance and at times also the name of the owner of the vineyard, recalling the biblical "wine of Lebanon," "wine of Helbon," and in the Elephantine documents, "wine of Sidon" and "wine of Egypt."[81] This was the practice for wines produced both in government vineyards and private cellars. Among the keepers of the royal property were special officials responsible for "the increase of the vineyards for the wine-cellars."[82] A variety of wines was sold in the markets, judging from the contents of many ostraca, inscriptions, and seal impressions. A seventh-century B.C.E. decanter from the Hebron area is inscribed with the words: "wine of *kḥl*," i.e., wine from the locality of *Kḥl*. Another handle of a wine jar bears the inscription "*hmṣh š'l*" i.e., from the village of Mozah and the name of the wine grower Shu'al.[83] At Gibeon the local wine produce was incised on the jar handles, the usual formula being: "*gb'n/gdd/r*" followed by personal names. This is generally understood to represent the provenance of the wine, i.e., Gibeon, and the names of the owners of the vineyards. Opinion is divided, however, as to the meaning of *gdr/d*. Pritchard interprets it as "wall enclosure" referring to a part of the vineyard, whereas Avigad considers that here too it is a personal name.[84] Support for the first theory can perhaps be found in the standard formula of the Samaria ostraca and also in a sherd from Ashdod which refers to "Zabadiah's vineyard."

The custom of denoting wine by its provenance is best illustrated in the seal impressions. In the opinion of many scholars, the storage jars from Judah bearing the *la-melek* stamp and name of one of the cities of Hebron, Ziph, Socoh, and *Mmšt* refer to wine-producing localities. F. M. Cross is probably correct in assuming that only wine jars bore these stamps: "Wines are known by their district. It is the key to their taste and quality. But it matters little where grains are grown or oil is pressed."

Stamps with place names again appear in the Persian period, the best known of which are the *Yehud* stamps, which also mention Jerusalem and Mozah. Inscriptions on stone jars from Shiqmona refer to "wine (*ḥmr*) of *gat carmel*(?)," and in another stamp (from the Second Temple period), the city of Gezer is mentioned.[86]

The *la-melek* stamps often bear other symbols, one the rosette, and another, concentric circles, apparently a schematic version of the rosette. The rosette is none other than an imitation of an impression of wine cellars from the islands of Rhodes and Thasos,[87] and the same interpretation should probably be given to other symbols appearing on handles of wine jars, such as "David's shield" stamped on several vessels from Gibeon and "Solomon's shield" on the Jerusalem stamps.[88] Further confirmation may be an ostracon of the Persian period from Tell el-Kheleifeh referring to the dispatch of wine in jars to an official called *qrplgš*, an exact transliteration of the contemporary Greek term for tax collector in the islands of Thasos and Kos.[89] This was the period where the first Greek wine jars with Greek letters stamped on their handles reached the coast of Palestine.[90] It can thus be assumed that at the end of the Israelite period and in the Persian period the inhabitants of Palestine copied the methods of marketing from their Phoenician and Greek neighbors.

Oil. Second in importance to the production of wine was oil and, as stated above, most of the olives in Palestine were destined to become oil. Next to wine, oil was the most important article of trade in Palestine. In the First Temple period it had a variety of uses and served, aside from food, for lighting, washing, and lubrication, for preparing cosmetics, and for medicinal and cultic purposes.[91]

The Bible mentions various categories of oil, mostly by their uses: "pure oil beaten for the light," or simply "anointing oil," "holy oil," "beaten oil," "rich oil," and "fresh oil." Oil was also mixed with perfumes: "perfumer's ointment (*shemen roqeah*), "oil of myrrh." The Samaria ostraca refer to "fine oil" (*šmn rhṣ*).[92]

Ostraca from the First Temple period found at Tell Qasile, Arad, and Beersheba deal with deliveries of oil by quantity, using the formulas: "For the king one thousand and one hundred (log of) oil;" "on the 24th of the month Nahum sent oil by means of the Kittyim—one." A storage jar from the Persian period found at Kadesh-barnea is inscribed with the letter *shin* and the numeral 5, which M. Dothan interprets as "oil 5," or, five measures of oil.[93]

The oil referred to in these ostraca was probably olive oil, but the liquid measure employed by the senders cannot be known. Shipments of oil also designated quantity by receptacles which apparently were ancient measures, such as the *nevel* (see above). Other storage vessels referred to in the Bible were the *pāk* (jug), *qeren* (horn), and *ṣapahat* (decanter) (I Sam. 10:1; 16:13; I Kings 17:14). Oil in larger quantities was kept in storage jars, as evidenced by olive presses found throughout Palestine. These storage jars are of the usual type and cannot be distinguished from wine jars.

Little information can be derived from the Bible about methods of producing

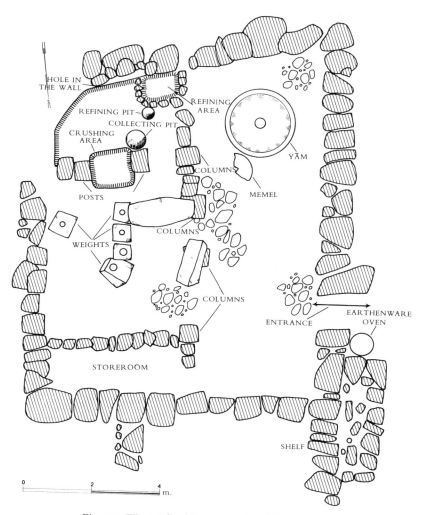

Fig. 16. Tirat Jehudah: Plan of an oil press.
Ruth Hestrin and Z. Yeivin, *Qadmoniot*, 4 (1971), 93.

oil, nor from Egyptian or Mesopotamian sources, since olives were not grown there. A single description appears in Micah 6:15: "Thou shalt tread the olives, but shalt not anoint thee with oil." The verb *drk* here is telescoped into an inclusive description of a complex operation, for the hard olive could surely not be trod upon as easily as the soft grape. The wealth of archaeological finds fully bears out this assumption and enables us to trace the process of oil pressing. Remains of olive presses from the First Temple period have been found in many sites in Palestine, the most important being at Shiqmona, Gezer, Beth-shemesh, and Tell Beit Mirsim. They date from the tenth to the seventh centuries B.C.E.[94]

A comparison with Roman presses at Chorazin and Tirat Yehudah[95] reveals that the oil-producing methods had undergone only slight modifications, which was insignificant and confined only to the form. Detailed descriptions are also contained in talmudic literature. Moreover, the operation of the ancient olive presses can be reconstructed by comparing them with the installations and techniques used today in villages in Judea and Samaria. An olive press found in a walled farm in Tirat Yehudah from the second century B.C.E. was recently reconstructed outside the Israel Museum in Jerusalem. The following account is given of its method of operation:[96]

"The production of oil consisted of two main stages: crushing or grinding the olives into a soft paste and then pressing them, two separate operations. The olive press stood in a room 12 by 10 meters, divided by a row of columns. Near the entrance on the right side was placed the crushing apparatus and beyond the columns the pressing apparatus. The former consisted of two main parts, both of stone: the *yām* and the *memel* (*B. Batra* 4:5). The *yām* is the conical stone on which the olives were set and the *memel* the wheel which turned on the *yām* to crush the olives. The diameter of the *memel* (usually of harder stone than the *yām*) was half that of the *yām*. The olives were ready for squeezing after about two or three turns of the wheel and were then transferred to special baskets (called *'ăqālīm* in the Mishnah), similar to those used today in Judea and Samaria. They are made of tightly woven ropes and are about 60 cm. in diameter. After having been filled with crushed olives to a height of 7–12 cm. they were piled on top of each other on a plastered surface between the two presses. A small pit nearby received the oil that dripped from the crushed olives even before the pressing. This was apparently the 'first oil,' described in the Mishnah (*M^enaḥot* 8, 4–5) as fuel for lighting lamps.

The press was composed of the press itself, the collecting pit, *b^etulōt* ("posts"), the beam, and the weights (*Bava Batra* 4:5). The press was a sloping surface cut in the rock to a depth of 70 cm., with a corner hole which led to the collecting pit, also cut 60 cm. into the rock. Twelve to eighteen baskets of olives were piled up in the press to a height of at least 1.2–1.5 m. On the top basket was set a stone slab which was pressed down by a large wooden beam in the process of extracting the oil. One end of the beam was inserted into the wall and a stone weight hung on its free end to increase the pressure. Since the distance between the beam's free end and the point of pressure on the baskets was double that of the distance between this point and the wall end, the weight hanging on the free end pressed on the baskets with a force double its weight. A row of five pyramidal weights with lopped-off ends was discovered in the olive press from Tirat Yehudah. The upper ends had horizontal perforations about 10 cm. in diameter and another vertical perforation descended from the top to reach the horizontal hole. The five were of different weights, averaging about 300 kg. each.

On either side of the press, standing 1.5 m. high, were two square stone posts, the b^{e}tulōt, in the language of the Mishnah (B. Batra 4, 5). Above the posts was a heavy horizontal rod to which the beam was secured while the baskets were set in place. The squeezing began with the hanging of the weights at the end of the beam, an operation requiring the labor of five men, four to raise the rod—two on either side—and the fifth to tie the rope to the beam. After having been secured, the weights remained suspended from the beam. The whole pressing operation, including setting up the weights, took some ten hours. The oil flowed into the pit in the corner of the press, where it stood for several hours, during which time the oil rose to the surface and the sediment settled at the bottom. At the end the oil was drawn into separate vessels.''

Although this description fits the operation of the olive presses of the First Temple period there were nevertheless minor differences, such as the shape of the weights, which at the end of the First Temple period, were generally round or oval, in the Second Temple period mainly pyramidal. In the First Temple period store jars or small stone basins sunk in the ground were often used instead of the more efficient rock-cut collecting pits.

Olive presses varied in capacity from the smallest, which provided for the needs of one family, to the largest, which was of almost industrial proportions. The larger the press, the greater the number of its components. The seventh-century B.C.E. olive press at Tell Beit Mirsim had three beams and 18 stone weights, whereas the small press from Tirat Yehudah had only one beam and five weights.

Perfumes. Perfumes were widely used in the First Temple period, as the numerous varieties and names of perfumes in the Bible indicate. The aromatic plants include 'ăhālōt (aloes), bāsām (apparently the 'āfarsāmōn of the Second Temple period), ḥelb^{e}nāh (gelbanum), loṭ (laudanum), mor (myrrh), nāṭāf, n^{e}kōt (tragacanth gum), nard, ṣorī (balsam), qiddāh (cassia), qānēh (calamus), cinnamon, q^{e}ṣi'āh (cassia), and sh^{e}ḥēlet. [97]

Perfume was usually mixed with oil to produce cosmetics, anointing oil, medicine, and libation oil. In a pure state it was used as fragrant incense powder, which was burnt on special libation altars. On a limestone, box-shaped altar found at Lachish was an inscription beginning with the word l^{e}vōntā', i.e., an altar for offering frankincense. [98] Many similar altars from the end of the First Temple period and the Persian period have been found at other sites. Larger stone altars in the form of a table with four horns, also libation altars, are known from the Israelite period. Incense was also offered on stone spoons in the shape

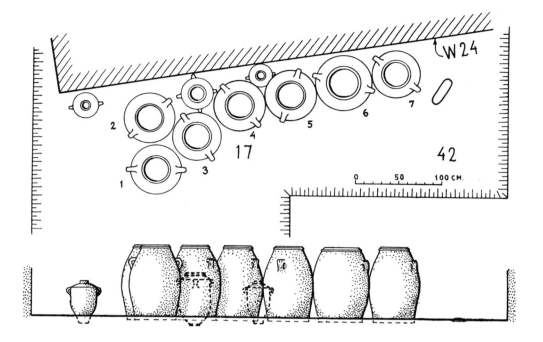

Fig. 17. En-gedi: Plan of a perfume workshop.
B. Mazar and I. Dunayevski, *Atiqot* V (English series) (1966), 26.

of palms of hands.[99] Pottery vessels generally considered incense burners include stands, chalices, and censers.[100] All of these indicate the extensive use of perfume for libations in the First Temple period in Palestine in addition to the sacrifices required for the central cult in Jerusalem. Aromatic powdered spices for everyday use were kept in bags or special boxes.[101] Their main use, as stated above, was for cosmetic oils: "And the fragrance of your oils than any spice" (Cant. 4:10); for use by men: "It is like the precious oil upon the head, running down upon the beard (Ps. 133:2); and especially for women who apparently had special tables and utensils for cosmetics. Small stone bowls, juglets, and bottles found in excavations in strata from the Israelite and Persian periods are believed by excavators to have held cosmetics. Perfumes also served as medicinal plants (Jer. 8:22) and in the popular death cult (cf., for example, John 19:39–40).

Perfumery was a craft in which women were occupied, blending the perfumes for secular purposes (I Sam. 8:13). This profession apparently included cooking the aromatic plants and mixing them with oil. The Temple ritual required large amounts of perfumes which were mixed by priestly families, whose main occupation this was: "Others of the sons of the priests prepared the mixing of the spices.[102]

Most of the perfumes mentioned were brought to Palestine from other countries, primarily Sheba in South Arabia. The kings of Judah kept them in treasure houses with their silver and gold (Isa. 39:2). The Bible states that tragacanth, balsam, and laudanum were grown in Gilead and exported to Egypt and Tyre. Balsam continued to be cultivated in Gilead at least up to the end of the Monarchy.[103] There is archaeological evidence that other varieties of perfume, henna and balsam (apparently *'ăfarsamōn*), were cultivated and processed at En-gedi, where the mild climate was particularly suitable. Vineyards of henna at En-gedi are referred to in the Bible (Cant. 1:14). Recent excavations at En-gedi have revealed in the courtyards of the Israelite houses a large number of installations and vessels, among them a unique type of clay barrel. A row of these barrels was found in one spot and near it another row of seven barrels set very close together. Around the barrels were scattered various pots, clumps of henna, perforated clay balls of different sizes, small bowls, plates, and juglets. Courtyards of other buildings in the north and south parts of the mound contained similar concentrations of barrels and finds. Beneath a burnt layer in the

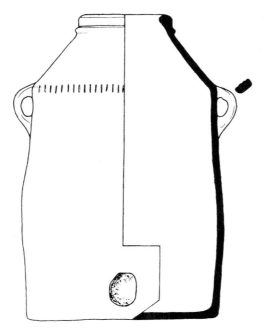

Fig. 18. En-gedi: Clay barrel.
Courtesy Prof. B. Mazar

court of one building (No. 207), which contained a spacious court with small rooms on one side, numerous finds were revealed including clay barrels, pottery, scales, "shekel" weights, a hoard of silver ingots, and a large stone seal inscribed with the name Tobshalom. Judging from parallel finds in the Near East, these had been workshops which produced various kinds of perfumes, particularly balsam, for which En-gedi was famed in antiquity.

The art of perfumery, according to Egyptian and Greek sources, as well as the Talmud, was mainly practised by women. The apothecary's diverse vessels resembled ordinary kitchenware, like barrels, pots, basins, bowls and cups, and grindstones for crushing the aromatic plants. The large quantities of water necessary were stored in large receptacles. The water, mixed with a certain amount of oil, was heated or boiled in pots, and while it was cooking spices were added. Some perfumes were cooked with interruptions, for many days, until the ingredients were thoroughly blended and dissolved in the boiling oil, and were then transferred to flasks and bottles or other suitable containers.

All this needed expert knowledge, art, and experience, which the apothecaries acquired over a long period of time. The secrets of the trade were guarded within the guild of perfume growers and apothecaries who were organized, as stated above, on a family basis. It can be assumed that at the end of the Iron Age (the time of Josiah and his successors), En-gedi was a royal estate and that both the perfume growers and the apothecaries were in the service of the king. [104]

CHAPTER X

DWELLINGS AND GRAVES

by E. Stern

A. HOUSES

BECAUSE OF THE paucity of description in the Bible, the houses uncovered in archaeological excavations at various Iron Age sites provides us with most of our knowledge of the typical dwellings in the time of the First Temple. These remains have made it possible to reach clear conclusions concerning the principal external and internal features of the typical Israelite dwelling and even to trace certain changes in the plans of the houses. [1]

Numerous houses, built on the plan known as the "four-room house," [2] have been found at many sites far removed from each other, as, for example: Hazor, Megiddo. Shiqmona and Tel Mevorakh in the north; Shechem, Tell el-Far'ah, Tell en-Naṣbeh, and Ai in the Samaria region and Benjamin; Tell Qasileh in the Sharon; Jerusalem, Beth-shemesh, Lachish, and Tell Beit Mirsim in Judah; Tell el-Ḥesi, Tell esh-Shari'ah, and Tell Jemmeh in the Shephelah; and recently Beer-sheba, Tel Masos, Ramat Matred, and Tell el-Kheleifeh in the Negev; and Tell es-Sa'idiyeh in Transjordan. [3] In its primary form, the four-room house originally consisted of four separate units: a broad rear room, which was the main living area, and three long parallel rooms extending from it. Partition walls or rows of monolithic stone pillars separated the middle room from the other two. This middle area was apparently an inner court open to the sky as well as the entrance to the house. Doorways in the court opened into the other three rooms, which were generally roofed and used for living and storage. In the court there were usually cisterns, silos, ovens, grinding stones, etc., indicating that it was the scene of most of the domestic work. Many sites disclosed the remains of remains of stairways leading to a second story generally built above the rear room. [4]

The houses in Palestine did not always follow the same basic pattern. Although the broad back room was common to all of them, some had only three or even two rooms, others more than four. The major advantage of the four-room house seems, therefore, to have been its flexibility, the ease with which additional side rooms, as well as a second story, could be attached. Conversely, the number

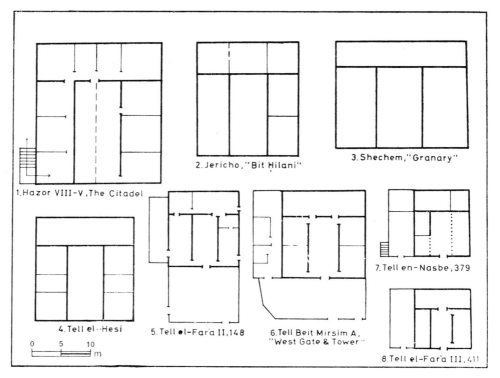

Fig. 19. Plans of typical four-room buildings.
Y. Shiloh, *IEJ*, 20 (1970), 184.

of rooms could also, if desired, be reduced. A second advantage of this plan was that not only could all the ordinary household tasks, such as milling, cooking, and baking, go on inside the building, but so could the more complicated ones of pottery-making, spinning, weaving, etc. A few domestic animals were probably also kept inside.[5]

Entire blocks of houses of this type have been excavated during the last few years, with excellent examples from Beersheba and Tell es-Sa‘idiyeh in Transjordania.[6] At the latter site a residential quarter was uncovered, consisting of a block of twelve houses of uniform plan and dimensions. Six had entrances on the street on the west side and the other six had entrances on the east side. A partition wall separated the two groups. The streets, which were 1.5 meters wide, also served as drainage channels for rainwater from the roofs. The houses, 8 by 5 meters, each had a large room whose roof was supported by a row of four pillars. An adjacent court paved with small stones contained grinding stones and an oven for baking bread. The room was used for sleeping and for such household tasks as spinning and weaving. Every house had a small storeroom

Fig. 20. Tell en-Naṣbeh, Stratum I A: Section of dwelling quarter, including four-room houses.

at the back. Despite its limited area, this small house was capable of fulfilling all the functions of the four-room house, albeit under more crowded conditions.

An entire Israelite city was uncovered in excavations at Beersheba. The city was well-planned, with several blocks of houses of the four-room type placed alongside an area of storerooms built in the same design.[7]

From the excavations at Ai and Tel Masos, it can be concluded that the four-room house first appeared in Palestine in the eleventh century B.C.E. (and perhaps as early as the twelfth century), at the time of the Israelite settlement, and continued to exist in Israel until the Assyrian conquest and in Judah until the Destruction of the First Temple when it went completely out of use. Since no examples of this type of house have been found outside of Palestine, Y. Shiloh seems justified in calling its plan an "original Israelite concept." The plan seems to have particularly suited the tastes and requirements of the ancient Israelite, whether urban dweller, craftsman, or farmer. Moreover, public buildings—palaces, citadels, stables, storehouses, etc.—found at Hazor, Megiddo, Tell en-Naṣbeh, Tell Beit Mirsim, Beersheba, etc.,[8] were built on the same plan, on a much larger scale.

Apart from the buildings based on the four-room plan, palaces and monumental structures have also been uncovered at Tel Dan, Hazor, Megiddo,

Samaria, Jerusalem, and Ramat Raḥel, some of them utilizing a different plan, e.g., the Syrian *bīt ḥilāni*), and a different style.[9] These buildings were constructed of ashlar stones, with rough marginal dressing, laid in headers and stretchers. Their ornamentation—proto-Aeolic capitals, window balustrades and stepped crenelation, apparently Phoenician in origin—mainly distinguish them from the four-room house.[10] The history of this type of building parallels that of the four-room house, having originated in Palestine in the eleventh century B.C.E. and continuing until the Assyrian conquest of the kingdom of Israel and the final destruction in Judah.[11]

A third type of building, known as the "open-court house," made its appearance toward the end of the Iron Age.[12] Although differing from its predecessors in that the rooms were arranged irregularly around a square court, it was essen-

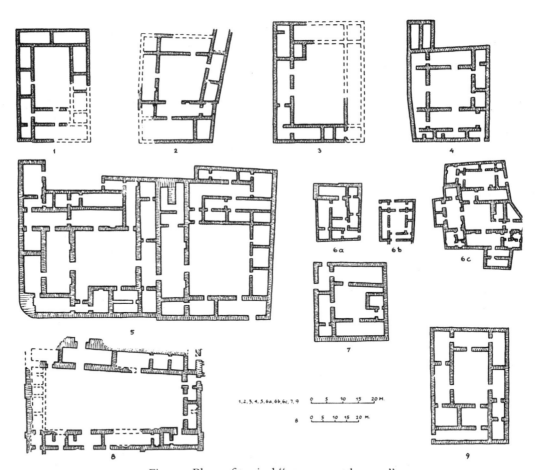

Fig. 21. Plans of typical "open-court houses."
Ruth Amiran and I. Dunajevski, *BASOR*, 149 (1958), 27.

tially similar to the four-room house because it too was closed to the outside and afforded privacy for the activities within the house. This plan is generally believed to have had its origin in Mesopotamia, arriving in Palestine in the wake of the Assyrian conquest. The assumption is confirmed by the fact that this house plan had been adopted in the northern Assyrian provinces established on the ruins of the Israelite Kingdom and occurs on every site where complete buildings were unearthed: the fortresses in stratum III at Hazor and stratum II at Megiddo, public buildings (1369, 1052) in stratum III at Megiddo, and the contemporary residential quarters at Megiddo and Dothan.[13] Isolated buildings of this type were also erected in Judah in the seventh century B.C.E. In the Babylonian and Persian periods the courtyard plan predominated in all parts of Palestine and completely replaced the earlier four-room house.[14]

The great majority of Israelite buildings, irrespective of their plan, were built on stone foundations topped with mud brick. The more imposing structures were wholly of stone. As was revealed at Hazor, Megiddo, Samaria, and Ramat Raḥel, the Israelites employed the header and stretcher method of ashlar construction, i.e., the ashlars were laid alternately on the narrow and long sides. Some of the stone walls consisted of piers of ashlar blocks at intervals with a rubble fill. Brick walls sometimes had a thin protective layer of stones (usually only on outer walls facing the street).

An almost constant feature of Israelite houses, particularly those with four rooms, was monolithic stone pillars supporting the roof. The pillars, of square or rectangular section and fashioned from a single stone from 1 to 2 meters long, are characteristic of Israelite building in general.

The floors of the houses were of stone and packed clay, often with a layer of well-beaten ḥawwār chalk. Buildings at Beersheba were found to have been constructed above layers of ashes.[15] Remains of roofs have been preserved at Shechem and Tell es-Saʿidiyeh.[16] The finds at Shechem indicate that ceilings were made of large tree trunks sawn in half and laid in pairs with the rounded side up. Fragments of roof beams have also survived at Beersheba and En-gedi, those at the former site of cedar wood, and at the latter of palm trees.[17]

A mixture of chopped straw and reeds, up to some 5 cm thick, was laid on the rafters and repaired and thickened before the approach of the rainy season. Many heavy stone rollers, used for packing clay on the roof to prevent leaking, have been uncovered in excavations.[18]

Rainwater was caught on the roofs in clay or stone pipes and ran through gutters into the cisterns that have been found in most of the courts of Israelite buildings.[19] These cisterns, which were coated with lime plaster and sealed with stone slabs, provided the household with its own water supply for the greater part of the year. Albright attributed the invention of waterproof cisterns to

Fig. 22. Megiddo, Stratum III (period of the Assyrian occupation): Section of a dwelling quarter.

the Iron Age, considering it the factor which made settlement possible in sites lacking a permanent water supply. Recent discoveries, however, indicate that this type of cistern existed in earlier periods as well.[20]

B. TOMBS

Burial was of great importance for the ancient Israelite as for other peoples. Man's final resting place was considered the continuation of this mortal abode, a theme reflected even in the terminology. Burial inscriptions from the time of the First Temple refer to the burial cave as a "room." Just as man during his lifetime chose to live with his family in his own home and native city, so he chose to be buried. Israelites were therefore generally buried in a burial plot purchased by the head of the family for use for generations. Some prepared their own graves during their lifetime (Isa. 22:15–16; this may explain Absalom's monument (II Sam. 18:18). Barzillai the Gileadite was voicing the general desire when he asked David "Pray let thy servant return that I may die in my own city, near the grave of my father and my mother" (II Sam. 19:37) and also Nehemiah who beseeches the Persian king for permission to return "to the city of my fathers' sepulchres" (Neh. 2:3, 5). Jacob, in his final testament, stipulates: " . . . bury me with my fathers in the cave that is in the field of Ephron the Hittite, in the cave that is in the field of Machpelah, to the east of Mamre, in the land of Canaan, which Abraham bought with the field from Ephron the Hittite to possess as a burying-place. There they buried Abraham and Sarah his wife; there they buried Isaac and Rebekah his wife; and there I buried Leah" (Gen. 49:29–31). Gideon was buried in this manner (Judg. 8:32), as was Samuel (I Sam. 25:1) and many others. This also explains the building of David's family tomb in Jerusalem and the tomb of the Israelite kings in Samaria (II Kings 13:13; and see below). If someone died far from his home, his family brought his body for burial in the family tomb; thus, for example, Jacob (Gen. 49:29), Samson (Judg. 16:31), and several Judean kings who died outside of Jerusalem (II Kings 23:30; II Chron. 25:28). To be deprived of proper burial in the family tomb was considered a terrible misfortune (cf. "your body shall not come into the tomb of your fathers," I Kings 13:22). Casting a body out of a grave showed contempt for a person (Isa. 14:19; Jer. 8:1–2). Not to be buried in the right place was also considered a punishment, conversely, to be interred with close relatives was an honor. The prophet from Bethel requested to be buried with the man of God from Judah: "When I die, bury me in the grave in which the man of God is buried; lay my bones beside his bones" (I Kings 13:31). It is interesting to note that the priest Jehoiada was buried " . . . among the kings, because he had done good in Israel, and toward God and His house" (II Chron. 24:16).

Burial entailed numerous rites of mourning. Some of the rites mentioned in the Bible are fasting for seven days, rending the garments, wearing special mourning clothes, abstention from anointing, women wailing, mourning feasts, burning incense and spices.[21] These customs have left their traces in archaeological finds from Israel and the neighboring countries. The sarcophagus of Ahiram king of Byblos in the tenth century B.C.E., contains a relief depicting a procession of mourning women with torn clothes, some clapping their hands and tearing their hair in an access of grief. Some scholars think that the other side of the sarcophagus portrays a mourning feast. Clay figurines of mourning and lamenting women have been found in Israel.[22] Numerous wall paintings in Egypt depict in detail the very complex burial customs of that country,[23] confirming the fact that certain Egyptian and Palestinian burial rites had features in common. The Near-Eastern practice of sacrificing to the dead may also have been prevalent in Palestine, as is evidenced by several biblical passages and by archaeological finds (see below).

The Bible offers only a few details about the forms of the tombs. The frequent verb ḥṣb suggests a grave hewn in rock. Some graves like Rachel's (Gen. 35:20 and perhaps also Absalom's (II Sam. 18:18) apparently had a kind of building or monument built over them. Compare also Josiah's question concerning the

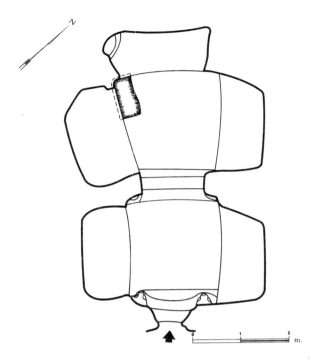

Fig. 23. Tell 'Aitun: Plan of a typical Israelite tomb.
D. Ussishkin, *Qadmoniot* 4 (1972), 88.

common grave of the prophets from Samaria and Judah: "What is yonder
monument (*ṣiyyūn*) that I see?" (II Kings 23:17).

A great number of Iron Age tombs have been unearthed in Israel and serve to
supplement the biblical descriptions. Characteristic of this period was the sub-
terranean family tomb generally hewn into the rock. Natural caves were also
adapted for burial purposes. Most tombs consisted of a stepped slanting shaft
(*dromos*) leading down to the entrance, which was sealed by a rolling stone
(usually a dressed stone slab). A few steps led from the entrance to the chambers,
whose numbers increased with the number of burials. The dead were laid,
with the offerings made to them, on raised shelves cut into the rock along the
walls. Niches were cut into the walls of some tombs to hold oil lamps. Because
these were family tombs and the dead were buried there for successive generations,
the skeletons and offerings were periodically pushed into a heap in one of the
corners. More frequently, however, a deep pit was dug in the floor of the tomb,
where the earlier remains were thrown. Most pits were sealed with a stone slab,
but some were so full that a wall had to be built to prevent overflowing. In a
number of tombs an additional opening in the roof led to an above-ground
monument (*nefesh*). A round stone projection in one of the corners of an

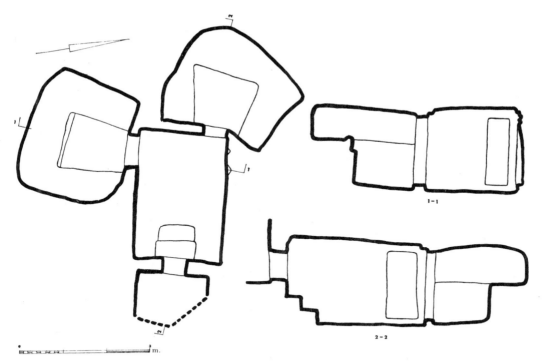

Fig. 24. Khirbet Beit Lei: Plan of tomb cave.
J. Naveh, *IEJ*, 13 (1963), 75.

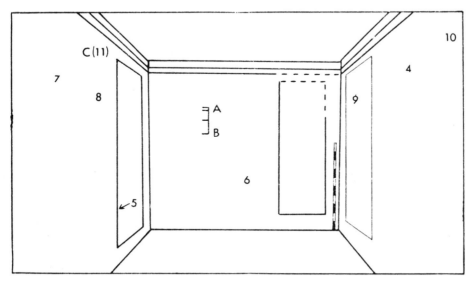

Fig. 25. Khirbet Beit Lei: Ante-chamber of the tomb.
J. Naveh, *IEJ*, 13 (1963), 76.

"Ammonite" tomb in 'Amman (see below) was interpreted by the excavators as such an above-ground monument.

Not all the tombs uncovered in Palestine were of the ordinary rock-hewn type with shelves. This type of tomb, however, is found in all parts of Palestine[24] and was used throughout the Iron Age, from the twelfth century B.C.E. to the fall of the First Temple, and also, as recent excavations show, during the Persian period.[25]

Several generations of the same family buried their dead in one tomb and ceased only when the tomb was completely full. Often, after a gap of several centuries, the tombs were re-opened and re-used apparently by different families.

The tombs, as mentioned, contained many funerary offerings, particularly household objects and personal effects of the deceased, such as pottery, cosmetic articles, jewelry, weapons, seals, etc. Unusual decorations have been found, like those in the tomb excavated at Tell 'Aitun, which was decorated with carvings of lions' heads along the stairway to the burial chamber. At Amaziah (Khirbet Beit Lei) a tomb was found with graffiti of human figures and ships, and at nearby Khirbet el-Qom wall paintings in a geometric design and the relief of an out-stretched hand. Incised and painted burial inscriptions were also found at these two sites. An inscription at the Khirbet Beit Lei tomb recorded several names and two unusual prayers, which Cross has read: "I am YHWH thy God; I will accept the cities of Judah, and will redeem Jerusalem," and "The (mount of) Moriah thou hast favored, the dwelling of YHWH."[26]

Three inscriptions were found in the tomb at Khirbet el-Qom, the longest of which includes the name of the deceased and a curse against anyone who defaces the inscription. The other two refer to two brothers buried in the tomb: Uzzah and 'Ophai sons of Nethanyahu (additional proof that these burial caves served as family burial plots). Besides the usual grave accompaniments, the dead were also provided with figurines of gods and various animals, probably employed in the then popular cult of the dead. According to Sukenik, several Israelite tombs in Samaria contain evidence of sacrifices to the dead.[27]

Of singular interest are the monumental tombs in Jerusalem from the First Temple period, situated in the City of David (Ophel) and Siloam Village. At the former site, Weill excavated in 1913/14 a group of tombs which include three very large ones that he called the "Tombs of the Kings of the Davidic Dynasty" and attributed to the kings of Judah succeeding David. These kings had been buried "in the burial field which belonged to the kings" (II Chron. 26:23) and were later transferred to "the garden of Uzza" (II Kings 21:18; 26). The tombs had the form of a vaulted tunnel, a kind of giant sepulchral chamber, about 17 meters long. A recess at the back was apparently intended to hold a sarcophagus. A fourth structure, also considered a "royal tomb," was built on

Fig. 26. Khirbet Beit Lei: Figure with 'lyre' on tomb wall.

J. Naveh, *IEJ*, 13 (1963), 77.

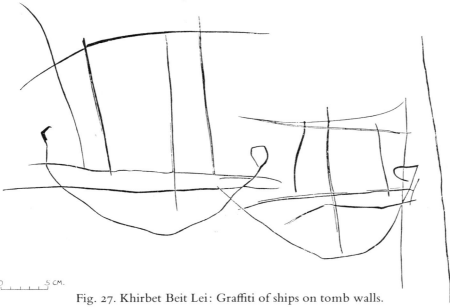

Fig. 27. Khirbet Beit Lei: Graffiti of ships on tomb walls.

J. Naveh, *IEJ*, 13 (1963), 80.

the plan of the shaft tombs, with a vertical entrance shaft and a side room.[28] Another series of tombs, uncovered in Mazar's excavations, were cut into the rock of the eastern slope of the western hill, opposite Robinson's Arch. Most of them consist of a rock-cut shaft, from which an entrance leads to a spacious burial chamber. As was mentioned above, there was a square opening in the ceilings, interpreted by Mazar as a *nefesh* (monument), covered on the outside with stone slabs or a gable-shaped structure.[29]

Jerusalem's main necropolis in the First Temple period was on the slopes of Siloam Village. Most of the surviving tombs had been cut along two parallel stone terraces. Tombs of several types were found, some with a narrow *dromos* and a narrow rectangular chamber with a gabled ceiling and a trough-shaped niche cut along the length of one wall. Others had a small dromos, a rectangular room with a gabled ceiling, and a wide shelf cut into one wall. Still others were identical to the tombs common in Palestine, with a small dromos and a square room containing shelves on three sides. Tombs with double (adjoining) chambers were also found.

Of the scores of tombs found in Jerusalem, three monumental structures cut into the upper terrace are the most impressive. Two of these are unique in their plans and in the Hebrew inscriptions which have survived on their lintels. The better known, called the "Tomb of Pharaoh's Daughter," was hewn out of a monolithic block and apparently terminated at the top in a pyramid. Only a single letter of its inscription has been preserved. A similar sepulchral monument has been found recently on the stone terrace continuing inside the village. A fragmentary inscription in Hebrew on its lintel reads: "burial of . . . the one who op[ens] . . . ," and was probably a memorial and a warning against opening it.

The third tomb consists of two regular burial chambers connected by a corridor. Both chambers have trough-shaped niches. In the first room, which has the only exit, there is space for two burials, the other for only one. A burial inscription appears above the single entrance and mentions a person called " . . . yahu who is over the house." Avigad has suggested identifying him with Shebna (cf. Isa. 22:15–16). A shorter inscription was cut into the solid rock façade of the second room: "(Tomb) chamber in the side (or slope) of the rock (or mountain)."[30] Whether the tomb belonged to Shebna or another official whose title was "who is over the house," these cave tombs are an imposing and unique remnant of the necropolis in the Siloam Village, where high officials of the Judean Kingdom were interred.[31]

It should be noted that there is a close resemblance between the tombs of all types in Jerusalem and the Phoenician shaft tombs and sepulcher monuments found in Palestine (Achzib) and Cyprus. The influence of Phoenician architecture

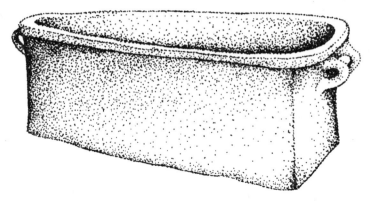

Fig. 28. A typical Assyrian pottery coffin, discovered in an 8th-century-B.C.E. tomb near Amman.

E. Stern, *Qadmoniot* 6 (1973), 8.

was evidently as pronounced here as it was in building ornamentation (see above).[32]

Apart from the ordinary Judean and Israelite ones, tombs have been found from the Iron Age and Persian period which can be attributed to other peoples. Thus a group of eight tombs found near 'Amman has been ascribed to the Ammonites on the basis of pottery and seals,[33] but their form resembles the typical Palestinian tomb.

Some scholars have recently suggested that the family bench tombs originated in the Mycenean culture and reached Palestine with the settlement of the Philistines.[34] In confirmation they cite the group of tombs of similar plan from Tell el-Far'ah (south) from the beginning of the Iron Age, which contain anthropoid clay coffins ascribed to the Philistines. Similar coffins have been found at Beth-shean and Lachish[35] and 'Amman, Sahab, and Dibon in Transjordan.[36] All the tombs at these sites, however, had been destroyed and their forms can not be known. At Tell 'Aitun, on the other hand, a typical bench tomb was uncovered, which contained Philistine pottery but not anthropoid coffins.[37]

Other foreign burial customs include re-interment in pottery coffins in typical Assyrian style, a mainly seventh-century B.C.E.[38] practice in Samaria and 'Amman.

Cremation was another foreign custom and can be definitely attributed to the Phoenicians. Evidence of it has been uncovered at several sites on the coastal plain. At Athlit, Johns excavated a cremation cemetery from the end of the Iron Age which contained burials on open hearths. Remains of carbonized wood, human bones, and funerary offerings were preserved. Only one tomb at the site contained a typical Phoenician jar with ashes. Other cemeteries have been found by Petrie at Tell el-'Ajjul and Tell el-Far'ah (south) and recently at Achzib and Tell er-Ruqeish. [39]

Fields of burials in urns of very similar types are now well known from Phoenician settlements in the western Mediterranean (Carthage, Motya, etc.). It should be noted that the cemeteries at Athlit provide evidence that the Phoenicians in Palestine stopped cremating their dead at the end of the seventh or beginning of the sixth century B.C.E., when they adopted the practice of burial in various kinds of rock-cut tombs. Several types of tombs were used, among them simple pit graves, but the majority were typical shaft tombs. There were also more complex constructions of two rooms, an anteroom and the burial chamber. The ceiling of the chamber was sometimes of stone slabs, over which a tombstone was erected. Several tombstones found at Achzib were inscribed with the name of the deceased. [40]

NOTES

CHAPTER I

KINGSHIP AND THE IDEOLOGY OF THE STATE

[1] I have used here the traditional term *miṣvat ha-melek* even though it would be more appropriate to call the chapter *mišpaṭ ha-melek*, since it is linked with *mišpaṭ ha-kohănīm* (Deut. 18:3) in the framework of the law code which pertains to conditions in the land of Canaan.

[2] Topically this matter is related to Solomon's dream (I Kings 3:5–14; II Chron. 1:7–12) and Solomon's prayer (I Kings 8:12–26; II Chron. 10:3–17).

[3] Cf. Jacobsen's treatment of what is known about the political-ideological development of Mesopotamian society, "Early Political Development in Mesopotamia." *ZA*, 52 (1957), 91–140 (= *Toward the Image of Tammuz and other Essays*, ed. by W. L. Moran [Cambridge, Mass., 1970], pp. 132 ff.).

[4] H. Frankfort, *Kingship and the Gods*, Chicago, 1948, p. 339.

[5] As is done, e.g., by the "Myth and Ritual" school, upon the conjecture that the peoples of the ancient Near East, including Israel, had a common ideological-religious substratum. A survey and criticism of this approach can be found in M. Noth, "Gott, König, Volk im Alten Testament," *ZThK*, 47 (1950), 157 ff. = *Gesammelte Studien zum Alten Testament*, München (1966), pp. 188 ff.; F. I. Rosenthal, "Some Aspects of the Hebrew Monarchy," *JSS*, 9 (1958), 17.

[6] Apart from II Kings 20:14–19, the term *medīnāh* appears only in the later biblical books—Ezek., Eccl., Lam., Esther, Dan., Neh. By and large it is used for secondary administrative units within the kingdom—provinces of a sort—either inside or outside Israel. Sometimes it is parallel to *mamlākāh*, e.g. Ezek. 19:8; Eccl. 2:8; Lam. 1:1.

[7] The political organization of the Gibeonites, who apparently were not indigenous to Canaan, was a confederacy of cities, ruled over by elders (gerontocracy). Even though the Bible likened Gibeon to a metropolis, a seat of royalty (Josh. 10:2, cf. II Sam. 12:26), a king of Gibeon is never mentioned (cf. Josh. 9–11; I Sam. 21). Among the Philistines, who originated in the Aegean, monarchical government apparently developed after contact with the inhabitants of Canaan. Perhaps one of the five Philistine governors (*serānīm*) who ruled the cities of the Pentapolis at times took over command of the joint army and while he held office would be called "king" (I Sam. 21:27–29; I Kings 2:39–40). Cf. B. Mazar, "The Philistines", *Proceedings of the Israel Academy of Sciences and Humanities* I, no. 7, Jerusalem (1964).

[8] Cf. Ex. 15:18; Isa. 24:23; 52:7; Jer. 10:10 Micah 4:7; Zech. 14:9, 16; Ps. 47:9; 96:10; 99:1; 146:10, etc.

[9] See, e.g.: Ex. 15:2 ff.; Isa. 34:1 ff.; Hab. 3:8, 13; Ps. 68, etc.

[10] See especially Isa. 33:22.

[11] A survey of the scholarly discussion of this subject with extensive bibliography is

given by W. Moran, "A Kingdom of Priests," *Gruenthaner Memorial Volume, The Bible in Current Catholic Thought*, ed by J. L. McKenzie, New York (1962), pp. 7–20; G. Fohrer, "Priestliches Königtum (Ex. 19:6)," *ThZ*, 19 (1963), 359–362 = *Studien zur Alttestamentlichen Theologie und Geschichte* (1949–1966), *BZAW*, 115, Berlin (1969), 149–153.

12 The etymology of the noun *s^{e}gullāh* is uncertain. In Ugaritic (*UT* 2060:16, 7, 12) and in Akkadian documents from Boghazköi (*KUB* III, 57:4, 5, 6) it appears to have the connotation of "pledge," "covenant." It has a similar meaning in biblical Hebrew, as can be learned from its recurring formulaic employment (Deut. 7:6; 14:2; 26:18; Mal. 3:17; Ps. 135:4; Eccl. 2:8; I Chron. 19:3).

13 In this connection, *goy* is synonymous with '*ām* (cf. Deut. 7:6; 14:2; 26:18). The qualitative differentiation made by E.A. Speiser does not apply here. See his: "'People' and 'Nation' of Israel," *Oriental and Biblical Studies*, ed. by J. J. Finkelstein and M. Greenberg, Philadelphia, 1967, pp. 160–170.

14 Biblical and extra-biblical parallels show that the word *mamlākāh* in this and some other passages has the same meaning as *melek*— "king," e.g. Deut. 3:21; I Kings 10:20; Ps. 68:33; Amos 7:13—where *beit mamlākāh* is parallel to *miqdaš melek;* I Kings 5:1: *mamlākōt* = II Chron. 9:26: *m^{e}lākīm;* I Sam. 10:18 MT: *mamlākōt*, V: *regum*. Similarly in Phoenician inscriptions, *mmlkt* = *mlk*. Cf. H. L. Ginsberg, *Studies in the Book of Daniel*, New York (1948), index s.v. *mmlkt; idem*, *BASOR*, 111 (1948), 25. Additional examples are adduced by Moran, *op. cit.*, pp. 11–13. *Gōy-mamlākāh* should be considered a hendiadys, a composite designation of Israel's national essence (cf. I Kings 18:10; Isa. 60:12; Jer. 18:7–9; II Chron. 32:15, etc. See Moran, *ibid*). In like manner, *kohănīm* should be understood as complementing *qdš*, being synonymous in meaning. For the purpose of parallelism the two bilateral expressions were broken up and the two halves rejoined cross-wise. On this matter,

cf. E. Z. Melamed, "Break-up Pattern of Stereotype Phrases, etc.," *Scripta Hierosolymitana*, 8, Jerusalem (1961), 115–153; S. Talmon, "Synonymous Readings in the Textual Traditions of the Old Testament," *ibid.*, p. 335 ff.; Y. Avishur, "Pairs of Synonymous Words in the Construct State (and in Appositional Hendiadys) in Biblical Hebrew," *Semitics*, 2 (1971–72) 17–80. In the adjectival construct *mamleket kohānīm*, the *nomen rectum kohānīm* defines the *nomen regens mamleket* = *melek*, just as in the parallel phrase *qdš* defines *gōy*. The statement purports to define Israel's peculiarity as a treasured people: priestly sanctity will distinguish the kingdom, i.e., the people and its ruler.

15 This idea is reflected in the words of the Psalmist (114:1–2), who states that when Israel went out of Egypt, the people was God's holy dominion: *hāitāh Y^{e}hūdāh l^{e}qod^{e}šō, Yisrā'ēl mamš^{e}lōtāw.* Cf. further II Chron. 29:21, where the triad, *Y^{e}hūdāh, miqdaš, mamlākāh*, serves to define the national entity of the Judean kingdom. On the interchange of *mamlākāh-memšālāh* in Ps. 114:2, see below, note 21.

16 *V^{e}hāyītī lāhem le'lohim-vihyitem lī s^{e}gullāh* (Ex. 19:5) are mutually complementary. Cf. further Ezek. 37:23; Hos. 2:25, and contrast *ibid*. 1:9 and perhaps also 3:3–4.

17 Cf. further Deut. 34:5–7; Josh. 24:29–30 = Judg. 2:8–9; *ibid.* 12:7, 10, 12, 15.

18 This is emphasized in the traditions about Moses, the prototypical divine emissary (see, e.g., Ex. 4:1–17; 19:9), and is echoed in God's words to Samuel: "for they have not rejected you, but they have rejected me from being king over them" (I Sam. 8:7).

19 The tradition of Saul's coronation after defeating the Ammonites puts the agreement *post factum* (I Sam. 11; 12:12).

20 The term was introduced by Th. Jacobsen to define the ancient Mesopotamian form of government. (See: Th. Jacobsen, "Primitive Democracy in Ancient Mesopotamia," *The Image of Tammuz, etc.*, pp. 157–162.) It was subsequently applied to the Israelite society

in the biblical period. See, for instance: C. V. Wolf, "Traces of Primitive Democracy in Israel," *JNES*, 6 (1947), 98–108; R. Gordis, "Primitive Democracy in Ancient Israel—The Biblical Edah," *Alexander Marx Jubilee Volume* (New York, 1950), pp. 369–388. Cf. S. Talmon, "The Judean 'Am-Ha-aretz in Historical Perspective," *Papers of the Fourth World Congress of Jewish Studies* I, Jerusalem, 1967, pp. 71–76. P. A. H. de Boer totally rejected the claim that there was any democratic element in the Israelite form of government in the biblical period: "Israel n'a jamais été une démocratie" ("Vive le Roi," *VT*, 5 [1955], 227).

21   The verb *mšl*, used there, and *mlk* which is widely employed in biblical Hebrew, are synonymous. Cf., e.g., Zech. 6:13: " . . . and he (Zerubbabel) shall bear royal honor, and shall sit and rule (*umāšal*) upon his throne," with I Kings 1:35: " . . . and he (Solomon) shall come and sit upon my throne; for he shall rule (*yimlok*) in my stead . . . " (similarly, vv. 17, 24, 30). See also H. T. Boecker, "Die Beurteilung der Anfänge des Königtums in den deuteronomistischen Abschnitten des I Samuelbuches," *Wissenschaftliche Monographien zum Alten und Neuen Testament*, 31 (Neukirchen, 1969), 20. The synonymity of the terms undermines M. Buber's contention that מָשַׁל here implies a formal government which is conceived as essentially different from monarchy (*Königtum Gottes*, Berlin, 1932, pp. 3 ff.).

22   M. Buber discerned two strata in the book of Judges, one anti-monarchical and the other pro-monarchical (*op. cit.*, pp. 57 ff.). However, this conjecture is open to criticism and must be re-examined. See Talmon, "In those Days there was no King (*melek*) in Israel," *Proceedings of the Fifth World Congress of Jewish Studies* I, Jerusalem, 1969, pp. 135–144 (Hebrew), and A. Malamat, *Judges*, pp. 147–151, 318 ff.

23   The issue was discussed by E. H. Maly, "The Jotham Fable—Anti-Monarchical?" *CBQ*, 22 (1960), 299–305. See also U. Simon,

"Jotham's Fable—The Fable and its Interpretation and Literary Framework," *Tarbiz*, 34 (1964), 1–34 (Hebrew).

24   Y. Kaufmann correctly demonstrated that Gideon's declaration has absolutely nothing to do with a theocratic priestly government but is advocating a prophetic-emissary form of government. (See *Tol^edot*, I–III, pp. 694 ff.).

25   It is often held that Gideon only refused in theory, but in actual fact accepted the monarchy. See G. Henton Davies, "Judges VIII," *VT*, 13 (1963), 151–157.

26   Reading with J. Kennedy, *An Aid to the Textual Amendment of the Old Testament*, Edinburgh, 1928, pp. 28, 104, *mikol ṣārēikā* instead of MT: *b^ekol 'āreikā*, which is mostly emended to *v^ekol sārēikā uš^efāṭūkā*. See, among others, J. Wellhausen, *Die Kleinen Propheten*, 3, Berlin (1898), p. 19; W. R. Harper, *Hosea*, Edinburg, ICC, 1910, p. 400; M. J. Buss, The Prophetic Words of Hosea, Berlin, *BZAW*, 111 (1969), p. 74; BH, etc. NEB presupposes: *v^ešofteikā b^ekol 'āreikā*.

27   See Y. Kaufmann, *ibid.* pp. 697 ff. Hosea's criticism of government and of rulers in his day is found in such other passages as 7:3–7; 8:4, 10, etc., most of which show opposition to an independent Ephraimite monarchy (*ibid.* 1:4–5).

28   These traditions are not of one cloth, and all or part of them are probably not contemporaneous with the events. However, the basic realistic non-mythical quality of the Israelite monarchy is discernible in the matter-of-fact presentation of Samuel's negotiations with the elders of Israel.

29   The expression usually has negative connotations. See, e.g., II Kings 17:15; Ezek. 5:6–14; etc.

30   The distinct affinity with Edom is reflected in the patriarchal and the Conquest traditions (Num. 20:14 ff.; Deut. 2:3 ff.), and also in prophetic literature (Amos 1:11; Obad. 10–12; Mal. 1:2).

31   Nöldeke's suggestion to identify the first name in the roster—*Bela' ben B^e'ōr*—with

Bilᵉʿām ben Bᵉʿōr who was Moses's contemporary (Num. 22–24), is reasonable. He may be the unnamed king of Edom, referred to in Num. 20:14. *Hădād ben Bᵉdād*, who smote Midian in the plains of Moab (Gen. 36:35), could have been Gideon's contemporary, who also vanquished the Midianites in that area. It is therefore possible that the last one mentioned in the list—Hadar (in I Chron. 1:51, Hadad)—ruled in Edom in the days of Saul (I Sam. 14:47). See: Th. Nöldeke, *Untersuchungen zur Kritik des Alten Testaments*, Halle, 1869, p. 87; Ed. Meyer, *Die Israeliten und ihre Nachbarstämme*, Halle, 1906, pp. 376–377; J. R. Bartlett, "The Edomite King-List of Gen. XXXVI, 31–39 and I Chron. 1, 43–50," *JThS N.S.*, 16 (1965), 301–314; *idem*, "The Land of Seir and the Brotherhood of Edom," *ibid.* 20 (1969), 1–20; Y. Kaufmann, *op. cit.*, p. 781.

³² It cannot be determined whether Shobi son of Nahash from Rabbat Bᵉne Ammon who helped David in his flight before Absalom (II Sam. 17:27) was of the royal line, though this is probable.

³³ The formula *melek lᵉMōʾāv* (Num. 22:4) resembles that found in Gen. 36:31 with reference to Israel—"*lifnēi mᵉlok melek livnēi Yisrāʾēl.*" In other passages, Balak is called *melek Mōʾāv* (Num. 22:10; 23:7; Josh. 24:9; Judg. 11:17, 25; Micah 6:5).

³⁴ S. Morag identified the Moabite name מישע with the Hebrew noun *mōšīaʿ*, and put forward the hypothesis that the name was given to that king on account of his military victories (*Eretz-Israel*, 5 [1958], 138–144 (Hebrew).

³⁵ An explicit allusion to primogeniture in Moab or Edom is found in II Kings 3:27, depending on whether one interprets the verse as a reference to Mesha's son or, as seems preferable, to the son of the Edomite king (thus David Kimḥi, quoting his father, and also some modern commentators).

³⁶ A. Alt, "Die Staatenbildung der Israeliten in Palästina," *Kleine Schriften*, II, pp. 1–65.

³⁷ The proposed identification of *mišpaṭ*
ha-melek (I Sam. 8:9–17) with *mišpaṭ ha-mᵉlūkāh* (*ibid.* 10:25) is debated in scholarly circles. See: M. Segal, *The Books of Samuel*², Jerusalem, 1956, p. 81 (Hebrew); S. Talmon, *mišpaṭ ha-melek*, A. Biram Jubilee Volume, Jerusalem, 1948, pp. 45–56 (Hebrew); E. E. Halevy, "*mišpaṭ ha-melek*" *Tarbiz*, 38 (1969), 225–230; J. Pedersen, *Israel, its Life and Culture*, London 1946, III–IV, p. 99; M. Noth, *Überlieferungsgeschichtliche Studien*, Königsberg, 1943, p. 58; J. de Fraine, *L'aspect religieux de la royauté israélite*, Rome, 1954; E. Mendenhall, *BA*, 27 (1954), 71; G. Fohrer, "Der Vertrag zwischen König und Volk in Israel," *Studien zur Alttestamentlichen Theologie und Geschichte*, pp. 330–351; H. Wildberger, "Samuel und die Entstehung des Israelitischen Königtums," *Baumgartner Festgabe, ThZ*, 13, (1957), 442–469.

³⁸ F. Horst distinguished two layers here: the basic law and its legal exegesis. See: F. Horst, *Das Privilegrecht Jahwes*, Göttingen, 1930, pp. 87, 99; L. Köhler, *Die hebräische Rechtsgemeinde* (1931), p. 17 ff.; J. Pedersen, *Israel*, III–IV, p. 101; K. Galling, "Die israelitische Staatsverfassung in ihrer vorderorientalischen Umwelt", *AO*, 28, 3/4 (1929), 32; A. Alt, "Die Heimat des Deuteronomiums," *Kleine Schriften*, II, pp. 250–275; G. von Rad, *Studies in Deuteronomy*, London, 1953, pp. 50, 62; Hempel, *Die althebräische Literatur*, Wildpark-Potsdam, 1934, pp. 140 ff.; K. Rabast, *Das apodiktische Recht im Deuteronomium und im Heiligkeitsgesetz*, Berlin, 1948, pp. 10 ff.

³⁹ See: S. Talmon, *loc. cit*; E. A. Speiser, *Judges*, 280–287; I. Mendelsohn, Samuel's Denunciation of Kingship in the Light of the Akkadian Documents from Ugarit, *BASOR*, 143 (1956), 17–22.

⁴⁰ However, such statutes were not recorded in the Bible because all legislation was concentrated in the Pentateuch and attributed to Moses. The Law of the King in Deuteronomy seeks to anchor the laws pertaining to the king in that formative period.

⁴¹ Similar traditions about reading a document and committing it to writing are

recorded about Moses (Deut. 31:14–30) and Joshua (Josh. 8:32–35; 24:19–26). Compare further the acts of Josiah (II Kings 23:1–3 = II Chron. 34:29 ff.) and Nehemiah (Neh. 10).

42   See Mendelsohn, *op. cit.*

43   See Num. 20:14–21; 21:21–35; 31:1–54; Deut. 2–3, etc.

44   Cf. Y. Yadin, *The Art of Warfare in Biblical Lands in the Light of Archaeological Discovery*, Ramat Gan, 1963, 243 ff.

45   Even David did away with most of the chariot horses which he captured, leaving only a hundred (II Sam. 8:4, cf. Josh. 11:6, 9). A cavalry and chariotry force was actually introduced in Israel only by Solomon (I Kings 10:26; 5:6–8).

46   καὶ τα βουκόλια Septuagint: "and your cattle." The combination "your cattle and your donkeys" reflects a standard element in the agricultural economy of that period (I Sam. 9:1–51; 11:5; cf. Job 1:3, 14; 42:12, and Gen. 12:16).

47   It seems that originally the reference was to *ʾăvādîm* in the sense of the king's officers (cf. I Kings 9:22), a title familiar from ancient seals. However, in Samuel's polemic wording of the Statute of the King the honorific term was given a negative slant by placing it next to *ʾăvādîm ušᵉfāḥōt*.

48   Perhaps it should be "your olives" *zēitēikem* as in v. 15.

49   It is probable that *vᵉnātān lᵉsārīsāv vaʾăvādāv* is a synonymous reading of *vᵉnātān la ʾăvādāv* in v. 14. The term *sārīs* is used mainly in the late books of the Bible (Jer., Isa. 40 ff., Esther, and Daniel), and is not found at all in Joshua, Judges, and Samuel. In the Pentateuch it is used only with reference to Pharaoh's court. The term is first applied to an Israelite royal officer in I Kings 22:9.

50   Taxation may have indirectly spurred the national economy because it forced the farmer to increase production so as not to have to lower his standard of living as a result of the king's levy on his produce.

51   See: A. F. Rainey, "Compulsory Labour Gangs in Israel," *IEJ*, 20 (1970), 191–202;

S. Talmon, "The New Hebrew Letter from the Seventh Century B.C. in Historical Perspective," *BASOR*, 176 (1964), 29–38, and bibliography there.

52   H. Frankfort, *Kingship and the Gods*, Chicago, 1948, p. 339: "The Hebrews knew that they had introduced it [i.e., the kingship] on their own initiative, in imitation of others and under the strain of emergency."

53   For an analysis and a definition of the term used here, see C. Pateman, *Participation and Democratic Theory*, Cambridge, 1970.

54   See: J. A. Soggin, "Zur Entstehung des alttestamentlichen Königtums," *ThZ*, 15 (1959), 401–418; *idem*, "Charisma und Institution im Königtum Sauls," *ZAW*, 75 (1963), 54–65. M. Buber, "Die Erzählung von Sauls Königswahl," *VT*, 6 (1956), 113–173.

55   For the synonymity of *šōfēṭ* and *meleḵ* see, e.g., Hos. 13:10; 7:7; Ps. 2:10, etc. Further, Micah 4:14, where *šōfēṭ Yisrāʾēl* refers to the king of Judah. Cf. S. Feldman, "Biblical Motives and Sources," *JNES*, 22 (1963), 102; W. Richter, *Die Bearbeitungen des Richterbuches in der deuteronomischen Epoche*, Bonn (1964), p. 130.

56   Although etymologically different, the terms *nāsīʾ* and *meleḵ* are often used as synonyms in biblical literature. This fact should be the starting point for any attempt to explain Exekiel's preference for *nāsīʾ* in his vision of the future Israelite kingdom, without discarding altogether the traditional title *meleḵ*. Cf. Ezek. 37:24: *vᵉʿavdî Dāvîd meleḵ ʿălêihem* with v. 25: *vᵉʿavdî Dāvîd nāsīʾ lāhem*.

57   Cf. e.g., I Sam. 9:16 with Isa. 19:20 in reference to Ex. 3:7, 9; 6:2–8, and with the formula of salvation repeatedly employed in the book of Judges, and see Boecker, *op. cit.*, pp. 20–22.

58   I Sam. 9:16–17; 10;1; 13:14; 25:30; II Sam. 6:21; 7:8, etc. and also Ezek. 28:2.

59   See Y. Kaufmann's treatment of the subject "Nathan the Prophet at the King's Court," *Collected Essays*, Tel Aviv, 1966, pp. 180–184 (Hebrew); M. Noth, *Gesam-*

melte Studien zum Alten Testament, München, 1960, pp. 334–35; G. W. Ahlström, "Der Prophet Nathan und der Tempelbau," *VT*, 11 (1961), 113–127.

⁶⁰ The phrase is redundant and is employed here for the sole purpose of evoking an association with Nathan's prophecy: II Sam. 6:8. There it is material, since it harks back to I Sam. 16:11.

⁶¹ A. Alt, "Das Königtum in den Reichen Israels und Judas," *VT*, 1 (1951), 2–22 = *Kleine Schriften*, II, pp. 116–134.

⁶² The Assyrian kings Esarhaddon and Ashurbanipal were not first-born and were appointed rulers already in their fathers' lifetimes.

⁶³ Cf. A. L. Oppenheim, *Ancient Mesopotamia*, Chicago, 1964, pp. 124–126.

⁶⁴ For biblical references to priest-kings, see Gen. 14:18 and Ps. 110:4; II Sam. 8:18 (cf. I Chron. 18:17). The combination is also found in Phoenician inscriptions, e.g., *tbnt khn 'štrt mlk ṣdnm.* Cf. H. Donner–W. Röllig, *KAI* I, 2–3 (Text 11, 1; 13, 1; 14, 5); M. Noth, *op. cit.*, n. 5, p. 194.

⁶⁵ See E. A. Speiser, "The Idea of History in Ancient Mesopotamia," *Oriental and Biblical Studies*, Chicago, pp. 270–312; *idem*, "Authority and Law in Ancient Mesopotamia," *ibid.*, pp. 313–324.

⁶⁶ See B. Mazar, "The Aramean Empire and its Relations with Israel," *BAr*, 25 (1962), 98–120 = *BAr Reader*, II, New York, 1964, pp. 127–151; *idem*, "The Philistines and the Founding of the Kingdoms of Israel and Tyre," *Proceedings of the Israel Academy of Sciences*, I, 7, Jerusalem, 1966, 356–377; A. Malamat, "The Kingdom of David and Solomon in its Contact with Egypt and Aram Naharaim," *BAr*, 21 (1958), 96–102 = *BAR* II (1964), 84–98.

⁶⁷ Most of these terms are derived from Nathan's prophecy (II Sam. 7:12–14), which is the most concentrated expression of biblical Israel's monarchistic ideology. Cf. further the metaphorical reference to the king in court-etiquette fashion as "angel of God" (I Sam.

29:9; II Sam. 14:17; 19:28; Zech. 12:8).

⁶⁸ G. Widengren, *Sakrales Königtum im Alten Testament und im Judentum*, Münster, 1955, pp. 62 ff.; A. R. Johnson, *Sacral Kingship in Ancient Israel*, Cardiff, 1955; M. Noth, *op. cit.*, (n. 5), 157–191.

⁶⁹ See K. H. Bernhardt, "Das Problem der altorientalischen Königsideologie im Alten Testament," *VTS*, 8 (1961) pp. 67–90.

⁷⁰ See *Enc. Miqr.*, IV (1962), s.v. *melek, melūkāh*, esp. cols. 1085, 1088; G. H. Fohrer, *Israels Staatsordnung in Rahmen des Alten Orients, op. cit.*, pp. 309–329; Soggin, *op. cit.*, p. 5.

⁷¹ The Sumerian King List opens with the words, "When kingship came down from heaven." See: S. N. Kramer, *The Sumerians*, Chicago, 1963, pp. 328–331; Th. Jacobsen, *The Sumerian King List*, Chicago, 1939; A. J. Sachs–D. J. Wiseman, "A Babylonian King List of the Hellenistic Period," *Iraq*, 16 (1954), 202–211; A. L. Oppenheim, *op. cit.*, p. 145.

⁷² Individuals of foreign extraction were completely assimilated into the Israelite society and could even be found in the king's entourage; cf. Doeg the Edomite (I Sam. 22:18).

⁷³ See: J. A. Soggin, "Der offiziell geförderte Synkretismus in Israel während des 10. Jahrhunderts," *ZAW*, 78 (1966), 179–204.

⁷⁴ See: S. Talmon, "The Biblical Concept of Jerusalem," *Journal of Ecumenical Studies*, 8 (1971), 300–316.

⁷⁵ Similarly, Assyrian kings credited themselves with military ventures which never took place or in which they did not take part.

⁷⁶ A. Malamat compared these groups with similar bodies in Sumer, emphasizing their institutional character: "Organs of Statecraft in the Israelite Monarchy," *BAr*, 28 (1965), 34–65. This view is opposed by G. Evans, "Rehoboam's Advisers at Shechem," and "Political Institutions in Israel and Sumer," *JNES*, 25 (1966), 273–279, but note Malamat's reaction answer in *BAr Reader*, III (1970), n. 9. See also H. Tadmor, "'The People' and the Kingship in Ancient Israel: The Role of Political Institutions in the Biblical Period,"

Journal of World History, XI, 1–2 (1968), 1–23. For a different interpretation of such phenomena, see S. Talmon, "The Judean 'Am Ha'aretz," *Papers of the Fourth World Congress of Jewish Studies*, I, Jerusalem, 1967, pp. 71–76.

77 In the chronistic summaries of assassinated kings there is not one occurrence of the term *ug^evūrātō* which is commonly found concerning kings who died while still in power: *v^eyeter divrĕi . . . ug^evūrātō* is found in connection with David (I Chron. 29:30), Asa (I Kings 15:23), Jehoshaphat (*ibid.* 22:46), Hezekiah (II Kings 20:20) in Judah, and with Baasha (I Kings 16:5), Omri (*ibid.* 16:27), Jehu (II Kings 10:34), Jehoahaz (*ibid.* 13:8), Joash (*ibid.* 14:15), and Jeroboam (*ibid.* 14:28) in Ephraim.

78 This is emphasized in the book of Samuel before and after Saul's election (I Sam. 15:1, 17–19; 13:13–14; 15).

79 The reference is missing in the parallel account in I Kings 1:38–48, where only an anointing by Zadok and Nathan is recorded (v. 45).

80 The parallel in II Chron. 23:11 reads: "Jehoiada [the priest] and his sons anointed him."

81 Cf. II Sam. 19:11: "And Absalom whom we anointed over us died in war," as a parallel to the term *melek* used in *ibid.* 15:10.

82 See: E. Kutsch, "Salbung als Rechtsakt im A. T. und im Alten Orient," *BZAW*, 87 (1963).

83 This distinction is based on the terminology introduced by M. Weber in *Gesammelte Aufsätze zur Religionssoziologie*, III, Das *antike Judentum*, Tübingen, 1921 = *Ancient Judaism*, transl. H. H. Gerth and D. Martindale, Glencoe, Illinois (1952); J. A. Soggin, "Charisma und Institution im Königtum Sauls," *ZAW*, 75 (1963), 54–65.

84 Or possibly: by this name the Lord will call him: "our righteous [one]."

85 To distinguish from M. Buber's attempt in his *Königtum Gottes*, Berlin, 1932 (= *Kingship of God*³, transl. R. Scheimann, London, 1967), to discern in the book of Judges the religio-political credo of biblical Israel.

CHAPTER II

LITERARY CREATIVITY

1 Cf. M. Lichtenstein, "Dream Theophany and the E Document," *Journal of the Ancient Near Eastern Society of Columbia University*, I, No. 2 (1969), 45–54.

2 Cf. the list of Priestly expressions in S. R. Driver, *An Introduction to the Literature of the Old Testament*, Meridian Books, 1956, 131–135.

3 We have listed Priestly passages which are more or less complete but have not mentioned brief sections or isolated verses from P, since they are numerous but not essential for our discussion. The asterisks designate chapters of composite nature: P and JE interwoven.

4 Seven pairs of clean animals (7:2) are needed, according to J, for use in sacrifices to be offered after the Flood (8:20), which is something that P does not acknowledge.

5 See M. Weinfeld, *Tarbiz*, 37 (1968), 110.

6 On the orientation of P, see M. Weinfeld, *Proceedings of the American Academy for Jewish Research*, 1969, 117–139.

7 M. Weinfeld, *Deuteronomy and the Deuteronomic School*, Oxford, 1972.

8 W. M. L. de Wette, *Dissertatio critico-exegetica, qua Deuteronomium a prioribus Pentateuchi libris diversum, alius cuiusdam recentioris auctoris opus esse monstratur*, 1805.

9 The foundations for Source criticism were laid by Jean Astruc in *Conjectures sur les mémoires dint il paroît que Moyse s'est servi, pour composer le livre de la Genèse*, 1753.

10 See M. Weinfeld, "Deuteronomy," *Enc. Judaica*, V, cols. 1577–1578.

11 Such as the laws of the first-born (15:19–23), the Passover (16:1–8), and the tithe (14:22–29).

12 See M. Weinfeld, *Deuteronomy and the Deut. School*, pp. 59–129.

13 J. Wellhausen, *Prolegomena to the History of Ancient Israel*, the Meridan Library, N. Y., 1957.

14 Y. Kaufman, *Tol^edot*, I, pp. 113 ff.

15 See below in connection with cultic instruction. For parallels to the Day of Atonement and its rites and to the institutions of the year of Release (*š^emiṭṭāh*) and the Jubilee Year, see Weinfeld, *Beth Mikra*, 49 (1971), 11, 15–16 (Hebrew).

16 See the arguments of S. R. Driver, *Journal of Philology*, 11 (1882) 201–236, versus F. Giesebrecht, *ZAW*, 1 (1881), 177–276, who maintained that the Priestly language was late. For most decisive proofs against the lateness of the style of P, cf. A. Hurvitz, *RB*, 81 (1974), 24–56.

17 The book of Deuteronomy is the first to be entitled "the book of the Torah." The older sources still speak about *tōrōt* (instructions) of various types. See *Sefer ha-tōrāh*, *Enc. Miqr.*, V, cols. 1099–1100 (Hebrew).

18 See M. Weinfeld, *'am qadoš v^egōi gādōl*, *Molad*, 185–186 (Dec., 1963), 662–665 (Hebrew); idem, "Pentat." *Enc. Judaica* XIII, cols. 236–239.

19 For the historical background of the book of Genesis, see B. Mazar, *JNES*, 28 (1969), 73–83.

20 E. A. Speiser, *Genesis*, Garden City, N. Y., 1964, XXV ff., and see also S. R. Driver, *Introduction* (above, n. 2), 156–157, who expresses the view that the phraseology of P "had formed gradually."

21 See A. Jolles, *Einfache Formen, Legende, Sage, Mythe, Rätsel, Spruch, Memorabile, Märchen, Witz²*, Darmstadt, 1956.

22 See M. D. Cassuto, *K^eneset*, 8 (1943–1944), 121 ff. (= U. Cassuto, *Biblical Literature and Canaanite Literatures*, Jerusalem, 1972, pp. 62–90) (Hebrew).

23 Cassuto, *ibid.*

24 22:28–30 is exceptional in this unit and is perhaps out of place; cf. the laws of the first-born in Ex. 34:19–20, there included in

the cultic section (Ex. 34:18–20), parallel to that in Ex. 23:10–19.

25 B. Landsberger, *Symbolae Koschaker*, Leiden, 1939, p. 223, compares this typology with the three categories in Mesopotamia: *dīnu* (civil law), *kibsu* (social and moral law), and *parṣu* (ritual).

26 This form, and in particular the instruction in the second person (singular or plural), is not unique to Israel, as A. Alt claimed (*Kleine Schriften*, I, 278 ff.). It is found in the ancient Near East and is embodied in the type of literature known as "Instructions," which were sets of legal imperatives issued by the Hittite king to his various officers and servants and affirmed by them by oath. These instructions are entitled "covenant" (*išḫiul*), as are the commandments in the Pentateuch. For this entire matter see Weinfeld, *VT*, 23 ((1973), 63–75.

27 See B. Gemser, *VTS*, 1 (1953), 50–66.

28 See U. Cassuto, *The Goddess Anath*, Jerusalem, 1971, pp. 50–51. The Ugaritic text cited by Cassuto is based on the completion: *ṭb[ḫ g]d bḥlb 'annḫ bḫm' at* (CTA 23:4 ff.), and see most recently, G. J. Botterweck, *gedī*, *ThWAT*, I, 922 ff.

29 For *nāśī'*, see Weinfeld, "Chieftain," *Enc. Judaica*, V, cols. 420–421.

30 See, for instance, the instructions to the temple staff (*ANET³* 207 ff.), some of which are included in the rules in the book of Numbers for guarding the Tabernacle. On the latter, see J. Milgrom, *JAOS*, 90 (1970), 204–209. On instructions to priests in Assyrian literature, see E. Ebeling, *Stiftungen und Vorschriften für assyrische Tempel*, Berlin, 1954, pp. 23 ff. For cultic instructions and in particular those connected to holiday rites, see A. Goetz, *Kleinasien²*, München, 1957, pp. 165 ff., and references there. For similar Assyrian descriptions or prescriptions, see G. van Driel, *The Cult of Aššur*, Assen, 1969, pp. 74 ff. On the interrelationship of descriptive and prescriptive ritual, see B. Levine, *JCS*, 17 (1963), 105–111; A. Rainey, *Biblica*, 51 (1970), 485 ff.

31 Cf. the articles of Levine and Rainey quoted in the previous note.

32 Th. Jacobsen, *The Sumerian King List*, Chicago, 1939.

33 A. Malamat, *JAOS*, 88 (1968), 163 ff.

34 I have especially in mind the book of Joshua, where we can find a Priestly redaction and also signs of JE. For this reason certain commentators use the term *Hexateuch*, grouping together the Pentateuch and the book of Joshua.

35 Joshua 24 and Judges 1:1–2:5, which contain very ancient material, are actually an appendix added after the Deuteronomic historiography was already crystallized and at the time when the material was divided into the presently existing books. In the Deuteronomic historiography, Joshua 23 ends the period of the Conquest and is followed immediately by a historical introduction to the period of the Judges (Judg. 2:6–3:4). However, the scribes who divided the material into books inserted after Joshua 23 the available material not used by the Deuteronomist because it did not suit his views (see Weinfeld, *VT*, 17 [1967], 93–113).

36 The concluding statement about the Southern Kingdom is included in the account of the reign of Manasseh, the king held responsible for the destruction (cf. also II Kings 24:3, Jer. 15:4).

37 In these orations we find entire verses borrowed from the book of Deuteronomy: cf., for example, Josh. 1:3–4 with Deut. 11:24–25; Josh. 1:6 with Deut. 31:7; Josh. 1:14–15 with Deut. 3:18–20; Josh. 23:15–16 with Deut. 11:16–17.

38 This technique is used extensively by the Greek historiographers Herodotus and Thucydides. The latter even explicitly states in his introduction to the *Peloponnesian Wars* that he has placed in the mouths of his principal figures the speeches which, in his opinion, they should have made under the circumstances. For all this, see Weinfeld, *Deut. and Deut. School*, p. 52.

39 *Ibid.*, pp. 35 ff.

[40] Even when the tradition violates such a central statute as cultic unification, the editor dares not change any part of the story. Rather, he adds sections at the end which are ancillary, as, for example, "to the place where He will choose" at the end of the story of the Gibeonites as Temple servants in Josh. 9:27.

[41] Even so, it must be pointed out that not all of these conquests can be attributed to Joshua himself. It seems that in the south, Joshua succeeded in dealing a decisive blow to the Amorite kings in the Valley of Ajalon, thereby terminating the war (see I. Eph'al, *The Military History of the Land of Israel in Biblical Times*, ed. J. Liver, Tel Aviv, 1964, pp. 79 ff., Hebrew). The story about the Cave in Makkedah and the conquest of the southern cities reflects a later conquest carried out at Judah's initiative. Concerning Debir and Hebron it is stated explicitly in Josh. 14: 6–15, 15:13–19, and Judg. 1:10–15 that Caleb and Othniel conquered them, visibly contradicting Josh. 10:36–39.

[42] H. Gressman, *Die Anfänge Israels*[2], Göttingen, 1922, pp. 14 ff.; A. Alt, *Kleine Schriften*, I, pp. 184 ff.; M. Noth, *Das Buch Joshua*[2], Tübingen, 1953, *passim*.

[43] B. S. Childs, *JBL*, 82 (1963), 279–292; I. E. Seeligmann, *Zion*, 26 (1961), 141–169 (Hebrew); J. Bright, *Early Israel in Recent History Writing*, London, 1956, pp. 79 ff.

[44] A. Alt, *Kleine Schriften*, II, pp. 276–288.

[45] J. Naveh, *IEJ*, 10 (1960), 12a ff.

[46] B. Mazar, *Yediot*, 27 (1963), 1 ff. (Hebrew).

[47] See Z. Kallai, *The Tribes of Israel*, Jerusalem, 1967 (Hebrew).

[48] For a recent exhaustive study of the period of the Judges, see A. Malamat, *Judges*, 1971, pp. 129–163.

[49] This extraordinary phenomenon should probably be equated with the anomalous and perhaps foreign nature of the tribe of Dan; see Y. Yadin, The Australian Journal of Biblical Archaeology 1 (1968), 9–23.

[50] The fall of Midian in the days of Gideon was still remembered centuries after the event. See Isa. 9:3, 10:26; cf. Ps. 83:10.

[51] See, for instance, Y. Kaufmann in his commentary to Judges, Jerusalem, 1962, pp. 191–193 (Hebrew).

[52] The fruit-bearing trees are not willing to accept the job of king and they therefore scorn it and present it as useless, Kaufmann's claim that according to this view the parable is incomplete since Gideon and his sons did rule over Israel is not convincing, for the following reasons: a) the parable and moral do not correspond in other details as well; b) Gideon in any case was not declared king.

[53] The stories about David's court start in II Sam. 9 and continue into Kings 2:46. However, in a later period, after the material was divided into books, Samuel alone and Kings alone, and the book of Kings began with the account of David's death, an appendix was added after II Sam. 20 which included a mixture of ancient material which was not integrated in the original Deuteronomic work.

[54] Following L. Rost, *Die Überlieferung von der Thronnachfolge Davids*, Stuttgart, 1926.

[55] See M. H. Segal, *The Books of Samuel*, Jerusalem, 1956 (Hebrew), 25.

[56] For a discussion of the various suggestions on this point, see Segal, *ibid.*, 25–26. He himself is of the opinion that Jehoshaphat son of Ahilud the *mazkīr* was the author.

[57] See E. A. Speiser, "Ancient Mesopotamia," in R. C. Dentan (ed.) *The Idea of History in the Ancient Near East*, New Haven, 1955, pp. 37–76.

[58] *Sefer* in Hebrew and Aramaic, as well as Akkadian *tuppu*, means anything that is written, including monumental writing on stone (cf. Job 19:23), a letter (I Kings 21:8, etc.), a bill of divorce (*sefer k^{e}rītūt*, Deut. 24:1), a bill of sale (= *sefer ha-miqnāh*, Jer. 32: 11 ff.), etc. Our case concerns a memorial pillar, cf. *yād* in v. 16, and see next note.

[59] For the meaning of *yād*, see II Sam. 18:18, and concerning the hendiadys *yād vāšēm*, as a memorial record on temple walls, see Isa. 56:5. For "establishing a name" as an expression for setting up a stele in Mesopotamia, see F. R. Kraus, *JNES*, 19 (1960), 128 ff.

60   See, for example, the Annals of Thutmose III, *ANET*[3], 234 ff.

61   See H. Tadmor, "Chronology," *Enc. Miqr.*, IV, col. 270 (Hebrew).

62   Cf. A. Rofé, *VTS*, 26 (1974), 143 ff.

63   See, for instance, the story of the two bears who tore up forty-two children (II Kings 2:23–24), which is of dubious moral character.

64   Cf. the test on Mount Carmel (I Kings 18), the flight to Mount Horeb (*ibid.* 19), and the incident of Naboth the Jezreelite (*ibid.* 21).

65   The passage about the "song" serving as a "witness" (vv. 16–22), which is an introduction to the Song of Moses along with the song itself, belongs to an ancient source (Elohistic in the opinion of many), which the author of Deuteronomy incorporated into his work and in a certain fashion is an archetype for his own work. Deuteronomy transfers the idea of the "witness," originally associated only with the Song, to "This Torah" (= Deuteronomy) in vv. 23–29 and thereby separates the introduction to the Song in vv. 16–22 from the Song itself (31:30–32, 43). Cf. M. Weinfeld, *Deut. and Deut. School*, p. 10, n. 2.

66   For *yph* as witness, see S. E. Loewenstamm, *Leshonenu*, 26 (1962), 205–208 (Hebrew).

67   See M. Streck, *Assurbanipal und die letzten assyrischen Könige bis zum Untergange Niniveh's*, Leipzig, 1916, p. 256:18: *kakku* (= *kanku*), *sakku ballu*, "hidden (= sealed) obscure and confused," see *CAD, B, balalu* 1 ff.

68   Cf. Streck, *Assurbanipal*, p. 362, 1, 3: *bârûtu pirišti šamê u erṣēti*.

69   *Pišru* in Akkadian is also connected to dream interpretation, signs, etc.

70   See Kaufmann, *Tol*[e]*dot*, III, p. 47, and cf. the prophecy of Neferti the Egyptian (see below), written down by the king at the dictation of the prophet.

71   For the prophet as an emissary in the Mari Documents, see A. Malamat, *Eretz-Israel*, 8 (1967), 237. It is especially significant to compare the sentence "now go, for I send you —*inanna alik aštaparka*—uttered by Dagan to his prophet (A. Malamat, *Eretz-Israel*, 4 [1956], 82, l. 32) with God's words to Moses "Go, therefore, I send you" (Ex. 3:10); and also compare "go . . . have I not sent you?" (Gideon, Judg. 6:14), "whom shall I send and who shall go for us (Isa. 6:8, comp. Jer. 1:7), see Weinfeld, forthcoming article in *VT* 27 (1977).

72   3:6–18 disturbs the smooth flow of the passage (note the address in the second-person feminine singular in 3:2–6 and the continuation of this style in v. 19) and is therefore an intrusion; see commentaries to Jeremiah.

73   For the *rîv* in prophetic literature, see most recently J. Harvey, *Le Plaidoyer prophétique contre Israël après la rupture de l'alliance*, Studia 22, Paris and Montreal, 1967. The pattern under investigation is not confined solely to passages where the word *rîv* actually appears and it cannot be exactly determined which sections belong to this pattern. It seems that the unique characteristic of this literary type is Israel's apostasy and breaking of the Covenant and God's warning expressed by *h'd b-*. See Ps. 50:7; 81:6, 9; cf. Deut. 4:26; 30:19; Jer. 6:10 (only *v*[e]*'a'îdāh*); 11:7; II Kings 17:13, etc.

74   Isa. 1:2; Micah 6:1–2; cf. Deut. 32:1; Ps. 50:4; see H. Huffman, *JBL*, 78 (1959), 286 ff.

75   See most recently J. Jeremias, *Kultprophetie und Gerichtsverkündigung in der späten Königszeit Israels*, Neukirchen, 1969.

76   This metaphor, which was developed in prophecy especially by Hosea, Jeremiah, and Ezekiel, occurs in a latent form in the Pentateuch; cf. Weinfeld, *Deut. and Deut. Sch.*, p. 81, n. 6.

77   See M. Weiss, *ha-Miqra ki-d*[e]*muto*, Jerusalem, 1962, pp. 126–128 (Hebrew).

78   This psalm belongs to the Elohistic Psalter in which the Tetragrammaton is replaced by the title *'Elohîm*, giving rise to strange combinations like *'Elohîm 'Elohēḵā* rather than *YHWH Elohēḵā*.

79   The Psalmist quotes chiastically and

therefore reverses the natural time sequence. For this mode of quoting, see M. Zeidel, *Sinai*, 1956, p. 150 (Hebrew).

[80] See the *Literature of Ancient Egypt* (ed. W. K. Simpson), New Haven, 1972, p. 55.

[81] M. Lichtheim, *Ancient Egyptian Literature*, I, Los Angeles, 1973, *ad loc.*

[82] See most recently G. Fecht, *Zeitschrift für Ägyptische Sprache und Altertumskunde*, 100 (1973), 6 ff.

[83] R. Borger, *Die Inschriften Asarhaddons Königs von Assyrien*, Graz, 1956, pp. 12–13.

[84] Compare Šurpu text II:59; Annals of Ashurbanipal (Streck, *Assurbanipal*, p. 28, III:80); Jer. 9:7; Ps. 55:22.

[85] Cf. Isa. 1:23.

[86] See Weinfeld, *Deuteronomy etc.*, 115–116.

[87] See, for example, *Tol^{e}dot* III, 8 ff.

[88] The "Day of the Lord" prophecies are not essentially different from the other prophecies which speak about "the day comes" or "that day." It would therefore be wrong to discuss the background of the "Day of the Lord" without considering prophecies which mention the other expressions.

[89] Translation according to the *Book of Psalms*, Jewish Publication Society, 1972.

[90] See S. E. Loewenstamm, *Sefer D. Ben-Gurion*, Jerusalem, 1964, pp. 508–520 (Hebrew).

[91] See J. Jeremias, *Theophanie*, Neukirchen, 1965.

[92] See W. W. Hallo–J. J. A. Van Dijk, *The Exaltation of Inanna*, New Haven, 1968, pp. 16 ff.

93 ní-m e-lám (line 21) equals Akkadian *pulḫu melammu*, which means "fear and splendor," actually the halo which surrounds the gods in Mesopotamia. This concept occurs as *pḥd wḥdr* in the theophany in Isa. 2:10, 19, 21. See Weinfeld in *Tarbiz*, 37 (1968), 231–232.

[94] Compare the divine appearance to Elijah on Mount Horeb (I Kings 19:11 ff.). The "fear and splendor" or "awe and glory" also accompany kings going out to do battle and it is therefore not surprising to find similar descriptions in the annals of the Assyrian kings (D. D. Luckenbill, *The Annals of Sennacherib*, Chicago, 1924, pp. 1–19, 23–24), and in inscriptions of Egyptians kings, *JEA*, 55 (1969), 88. In these descriptions the Assyrians run into caves like bats while in Isaiah men run into caves where bats are found (v. 9).

[95] E. Ebeling, *Akkadische Gebetserie "Handerhebung,"* Berlin, 1953, 104:33–34.

[86] See Weinfeld, *Deuteronomy etc.*, 115–116.

[97] Cf. Amos 9:13: "A time is coming . . . when the plowman shall follow the reaper, and he who treads the grapes (shall follow) the one who sows the seed," and Lev. 26:5: "Your threshing shall overtake the vintage and your vintage shall overtake the sowing."

[98] See *The Literature of Ancient Egypt* (ed. W. K. Simpson), New Haven and London, 1972, pp. 239 ff.; cf. M. Lichtheim, *Ancient Egyptian Literature*, I, Los Angeles, 1973, pp. 139 ff.

[99] See Y. Kaufmann, *Tol^{e}dot*, III, p. 160 ff.

[100] Note in particular Isa. 10:13–15, 14:3 ff., and Kaufmann, *ibid.*

[101] See Y. Kaufmann, *ibid.*, III, p. 244.

[102] See S. N. Kramer, *JAOS*, 88 (1968), 108 ff., and J. J. A. Van Dijk, *Orientalia* (1970), 205 ff.

[103] Cf. S. N. Kramer, *Hymn to Enlil*, lines 80 ff., *ANET^3*, 574.

[104] Cf. S. Langdon, *Die Neubabylonischen Königsinschriften*, Leipzig, 1912.

[105] This process had already occurred in the time of Hammurabi; see the most recent discussion of R. Borger, *BiOr*, 28 (1971), 22, n. 5.

[106] See M. Haran, *Between Ri'shonōt (Former Prophecies) and Ḥadashōt (New Prophecies)*, Jerusalem, 1963 (Hebrew).

[107] See Weinfeld, *JAOS*, 90 (1970), 190 ff.

[108] See H. Tadmor, *JCS*, 12 (1958), 12, 34.

[109] See W. W. Hallo, *JAOS*, 88 (1968), 71–89.

[110] H. Gunkel, *Die Psalmen*, Göttingen, 1929.

[111] See M. Weiss, *ha-Miqra ki-d^{e}muto*, Jerusalem, 1962, pp. 28 ff.

112 The Egyptian hymn to Aton is a parallel to this psalm; see *ANET*³, 365 ff.
113 *ANET*³, 365 ff.
114 RS 24.252, Ch. Virolleaud— C. F. A. Schaeffer, *Ugaritica*, V, 1968, 555 ff.
115 Cf. B. Margulis, *JBL*, 89 (1970), 302 ff.
116 Cf. Weinfeld, *Beth Mikra*, 57 (1974), 140–141 (Hebrew).
117 Cf. A. W. Sjöberg-E. Bergmann, *The Collection of the Sumerian Temple Hymns*, New York, 1969.
118 See Weinfeld, *Beth Mikra*, 57 (1974), 142–145.
119 Cf. S. Israelit-Groll, *IOS*, 4 (1974), 12–13.
120 W. H. Römer, *Sumerische Königshymnen der Isin Zeit*, Leiden, 1965.
121 *Ibid.*, 5–6.
122 *Beth Mikra*, 57 (1974), 151 ff.
123 S. Mowinckel, *The Psalms in Israel's Worship*, I–II, Oxford, 1962. His attempts to reconstruct the psalms' cultic background are extreme and should be approached with the utmost caution.
124 See Hallo, *JAOS*, 88 (1968), 80 ff.
125 See H. L. Ginsberg, *L. Ginzberg Jubilee Volume*, New York, 1954, pp. 159–171.
126 *Ibid.*
127 See S. Mowinckel, *VTS*, 3 (1955), 205–224.
128 See W. F. Albright, *Archaeology and Religion of Israel*², Baltimore, 1946, pp. 128 ff.; idem, *T. M. Robinson Festschrift*, Edinburgh, 1950, 6 ff.
129 For Egypt, compare the Instructions of Ptahhotep, Merikare, Amen-em-het, Ani, Amen-en-Opet, on the one hand, and "A Dispute over Suicide" and "The Protest of the Eloquent Peasant," on the other. For these texts, see *ANET*³, 405–410, 412–424. For Mesopotamia, cf. the various collections of proverbs in W. G. Lambert, *Babylonian Wisdom Literature*, Oxford 1959, 92-117, 150 ff., on the one hand, and *Ludlul bēl nēmēqi* ("I shall praise the Lord of Wisdom"), the "Theodicy," and the "Dialogue of a Master and his Servant" (*ibid.* 21–91,

139–149), and the "Sumerian Job" (S. N. Kramer, *VTS*, 3 [1955], 170–182), on the other.
130 Cf. the proverb, "Be not among wine-bibbers or among gluttonous eaters of flesh; for the drunkard and the glutton shall come to poverty and drowsiness shall clothe a man with rags" (Prov. 23:20-21). Verse 21 is a type of independent experential proverb which in the present case serves as a motive clause for the imperative which comes before it. See W. Zimmerli, *ZAW*, 51 (1933), 177–204.
131 See, for example, B. Landsberger in *City Invincible* (ed. C. M. Kraeling-R. M. Adams), Symposium on Urbanization and Cultural Development in the Ancient Near East, Chicago, 1960, pp. 95 ff.
132 See the comparative charts and the analysis of S. Aḥituv, *Enc. Miqr.*, IV, cols. 559–560, and I. Grumach, *Untersuchungen zur Lebenslehre des Amenope*, München, 1972.
133 Cf. e.g., 25:2–7 (*mlk*), 8–10 (*riv*), 18–20 ('*d*, *m'd*, '*dh*, etc.).
134 S. N. Kramer, *VTS*, 3 (1955), 170–182.
135 For references, see above, n. 129.
136 The Sumerian Job has a similar structure. It opens "Let a person always express the greatness of his god" (line 1) and ends in a similar manner: "[the man expressed] continuously the greatness of his god . . . and declared [it publicly]" (lines 130–131).
137 Compare as well the composition about the suffering righteous man found in Ugarit (*Ugaritica*, V, pp. 265 ff.), which is of a similar nature to *Ludlul*.
138 Cf. in particular Ps. 34, which begins, "I will bless the Lord at all times, His praise shall continually be in my mouth" (v. 2), goes on to describe the troubles from which he is saved (vv. 5–8), and returns to praise (9 ff.). As in the "Sumerian Job" (line 129), the psalmist speaks about the angel standing at his side and delivering him from trouble (v. 7); cf. also Ps. 31, 41, 69, 71, etc.

139   See especially the Prayer of Hannah, (I Sam. 2:1–10) and the Michtam of Hezekiah (Isa. 38:9–20), where we find praises reminiscent of those in *Ludlul*, tablet 4, lines 1–14, and of the Ugaritic composition cited above (n. 137), lines 34–45 (p. 268).

140   Cf., for example, *Ludlul* I, 82–92 with Ps. 31:11 ff.; 38:12 ff.; Job 19:13 ff. (social ostracism); *Ludlul* II, 58 ff. with Ps. 22:14 ff.; Job 16:13 ff. (physical pain); *Ludlul* II, 91–94 with Ps. 109:24; 102:4–5 (famine); cf. Lam. 4:8.

141   See N. Sarna, *JBL*, 76 (1957), 13:25.

142   Cf. S. Spiegel, *L. Ginzberg Jubilee Volume*, I, New York, 1945, pp. 305–355.

143   Note Baal's three daughters in the Ugaritic myth, whose names represent natural phenomena (*ṭly, arṣy, pdry*), as do the names of Job's three daughters (42:14), in contrast to the anonymity of the sons of Baal and Job alike.

144   See, for example, M. H. Segal (*Tarbiz*, 20 [1949], 35–48), who finds in Job many passages taken from earlier biblical books. Despite the numerous examples we are still not convinced that we are dealing with quotations. We are confronted with everyday expressions which the various sources used independently, giving each its own development.

145   H. L. Ginsberg, *VTS*, 17 (1968), 88–111.

146   A negative confession is also found in the Babylonian *Ludlul* (see n. 129), but there cultic sins are mentioned: negligence in sacrifice, prostration, and prayer; disregard of holidays, Festivals, and the like (table II, line 12 ff.), while Job 31 speaks about theft, adultery, oppression of servants, cheating the poor, the orphan, and the widow, and so on.

147   See M. Tsevat, *HUCA*, 37 (1966), 73–106.

148   See the commentaries to Song of Songs. It was K. Budde, *Preussische Jahrbücher*, 78 (1894), 92–117, who introduced this theory.

149   For the Egyptian songs, see the text in *ANET*², 467–469, and A. Herrmann, *Altägyptische Liebesdichtung*, 1959. For the Babylonian material, see M. Held, *JCS*, 15 (1961), 1–26; O. Loretz, *Biblische Zeitschrift*, 8 (1964), 191–216.

150   See Loretz's detailed list of motifs in his above-mentioned article and compare M. Held, *op. cit.* (see n. 149), col. II, 15–19; col. III, 6–7, 11, 20–21.

151   Some consider references to the king redactional (see most recently O. Loretz, *Das althebräische Liebeslied*, Neukirchen Vluyn, 1971), but even should we agree we still have no way of dating this redaction, which might even be that of the first author who gathered the collection of love songs in the book under discussion.

152   See, for example, S. N. Kramer, *The Sacred Marriage Rite*, Bloomington, Ind., 1969, pp. 85–106.

153   According to this opinion, we can say that the allegorical interpretation of the Second Temple period continues in this direction.

CHAPTER III

THE EMERGENCE OF CLASSICAL HEBREW

[1] The Tell el-Amarna letters, of the mid-14th century B.C.E., provide both in the mistakes in Akkadian made by the Canaanite scribes and in the several dozen glosses evidence that at the time a language was spoken in Palestine which resembles Hebrew so closely that it must be its ancestor (see H. L. Ginsberg, *Patriarchs*, p. 107). The question thus arises: since the Israelites came from outside Palestine, how did they come to speak a language that existed in Palestine before they arrived? This problem gave rise to the theory that Hebrew, as we know it, contains elements both of Canaanite (which the Israelites learnt from their neighbors) and of the original language of the Israelites, which also was a North-West Semitic dialect. Cf. on this, H. Bauer–P. Leander, *Historische Grammatik der hebräischen Sprache*, I, Halle, 1922, pp. 15–26; H. Bauer, *Zur Frage der Sprachmischung im Hebräischen*, Halle, 1924; G. Bergsträsser, *OLZ*, 26 (1923), 253–260, 477–481; G. R. Driver, *Problems of the Hebrew Verbal System*, Edinburgh, 1936; H. Birkeland, *Akzent und Vokalismus im Althebräischen*, Oslo, 1940; B. Landsberger, *OLZ*, 29 (1926), 967–976.

[2] Cf. W. F. Albright, *JBL*, 63 (1944), 207–234; *HUCA*, 23 (1950–1951), 1–40; *Studies... Th. H. Robinson*, New York, 1950, pp. 1–18; *Yahweh and the Gods of Canaan*, Baltimore, 1968; F. M. Cross-D. N. Freedman, *JBL*, 67 (1948), 191–210; 72 (1953), 15–34; *JNES*, 14 (1955), 237–255. The criticism by D. W. Goodwin, *Text-Restoration Methods in Contemporary U.S.A. Biblical Scholarship*, Naples, 1969, does not affect the basic principle that the texts are early. It is another question whether all or part of them go back to the time of the events they celebrate, or their composition dates from the time of King Saul, as has been maintained by the present writer in *'Iyyūnīm be-sēfer*

Shōfĕṭīm, Jerusalem, 1966, pp. 108–130; also whether their language was not actually much more archaic, but now obscured by spelling, as has been argued by the above-mentioned scholars.

[3] It is to be assumed that these forms were of the "jussive" type, and were distinct from the ordinary imperfect, but that this difference has been obscured for us by later phonetic developments introduced through the levelling effect of the 9th-cent. C.E. pointing.

[4] E.g., in the Song of Deborah, *yĕthannū*, v. 11, which would be *yĕšannū* in Hebrew, (cf. *Mishnah*), or *māḥăqāh*, v. 26, where also the Hebrew equivalent *māḥăṣāh* appears in parallelism. The question of Aramaic influences or traits in early Hebrew has been much discussed. Of older literature, note E. Kautzsch, *Die Aramaismen im Alten Testament*, Halle, 1902, and the criticism on this by Th. Noeldeke, *ZDMG*, 57 (1903), 412 ff. and R. D. Witson, *Princeton Theological Review*, 23 (1925), 234 ff. The material and views have been collected by M. Wagner, *Die lexikalischen und grammatikalischen Aramaismen im alttestamentlichen Hebräisch (BZAW* 96) Berlin, 1966. See also M. Wagner, *VTS*, 16 (1967), 355–371.

[5] It is quite a different question how this *ša-* is historically related to the same particle in Mishnaic Hebrew, in all probability a dialect of southern provenance. See, however, note 11.

[6] See, Part I, Chap. VII.

[7] True, ancient Ethiopic, a Semitic language, borrowed from Cushitic such words as *gaṣ*, "face," and *sakwanā*, "heel," and English borrowed from French words like *face* and *beef*, or from Danish words like *take*. But in all these cases the speakers of the lending language lived among and mingled with the native population. There is no indication

that in pre-exilic times Aramaic speakers lived among the Israelites.

[8] Cf. B. Mazar, "The Aramean Empire and its Relations with Israel," *BAr*, 25 (1962), 97–120.

[9] H.S. Nyberg, *Studien zum Hoseabuche*, Uppsala, 1952, is an interesting attempt to work out such connections.

[10] Or even words taken from adjacent languages for stylistic effect. In a commercial and sophisticated society of the kind Hosea describes, an ability to understand other languages was probably much more widespread than actual mentions of such matters in the Bible allow us to guess; cf. E. Ullendorff, "The Knowledge of Languages in the O.T.," *BJRL*, 44 (1962), 455–465. See, e.g., C. Rabin, *Studi sull'Oriente... G. Rinaldi*, Genova, 1967, pp. 303–309.

[11] This may, for instance, provide a rational explanation for the appearance of *še-* in Mishnaic Hebrew, which probably developed out of Judean urban dialects.

[12] An interesting case is found in I Kings 6:34, in the description of the doors made by Solomon for the Jerusalem Temple. What appear to be the wings of a double door are called once *ṣĕlāʿīm* and immediately afterwards *qĕlāʿīm*. The word *ṣĕlāʿ*, lit. "rib," represents Proto-Semitic **dilaʿ*, and **d* appears in Hebrew as *ṣ* but in Aramaic in the older stage as *q* and later as *ʿayin*. It is hardly thinkable that the word would be given first in Hebrew and then in Aramaic (with a Hebrew plural ending). The explanation be that this building term was northern Hebrew in origin (cf. *māḥăqāh* in n. 4) and current in normal speech in its northern form, but in official writing "corrected" the true Hebrew form with *ṣ*. In our text the corrector overlooked the second occurrence.

[13] W. v. Soden, *ZA*, 40 (132), 163–227; 41 (1933), 90–183.

[14] Cf. C. H. Gordon, *Ugaritic Textbook*, Roma, 1965, p. 68.

[15] Cf. *ibid.*, p. 1, §1, 3.

[16] Thus W. v. Soden, *Grundriss der akkadischen Grammatik*, Roma, 1952, p. 3.

[17] *Studi orientalistici... G. Levi della Vida*, Roma, 1956, 202–221.

[18] *Knesset*, 8 (1943–4), 121–142; *Yĕdiʿot ha-Universiṭah*, I, 3 (1950), 9–10; *Eretz-Israel*, 1 (1950–1), pp. 85–88; *Ha-Elah ʿAnath*, Jerusalem, 1951, pp. 30–36; I. L. Seeligmann, *BiOr*, 9 (1952), 198–200. The reasons for the "translation" from poetic form to prose are not clear. Among them may have been the wish to adapt the ideology to the needs of the Davidic dynasty, but also the fact that the old poetic language was no longer fully understood by the people at large.

[19] Collected by A. Hurvitz, *The Transition Period in Biblical Hebrew*, Jerusalem, 1972 (Hebrew).

[20] "Hebrew Poetic Diction," *VTS*, 1 (1953), 26–39, with special emphasis on Aramaisms.

[21] H. L. Ginsberg, *Orientalia*, 5 (1936), 171–172; M. Cassuto, *Tarbiz*, 13 (1941–1942), 197–212; 14 (1942–1943), 1–11; *Leshonenu*, 15 (1946–1947), 97–102; M. Held, *Leshonenu*, 18 (1947–1948), 144–160; M. D. Cassuto, *Ha-Elah ʿAnath*, Jerusalem, 1951, pp. 24–28; S. Gevirtz, *JNES*, 20 (1961), 41–46; S. A. Loewenstamm, *Tarbiz*, 25 (1955–1956), 470; 28 (1956–1957), 248–249; *Studies... M. H. Segal*, Jerusalem, 1965, pp. 180–187 (Hebrew); R. G. Boling, *JSS*, 5 (1960), 221–255; Y. Avishur, *Pairs of Words in Biblical Literature and Their Parallels in Semitic Literature, etc.* Ph. D. thesis, Jerusalem, 1974 (Hebrew).

[22] *Loc. cit.* Note that often the vocabulary of modern poets is much richer in the ends of the lines, because of the rhyme, than in in the text in general.

[23] This accounts for the many parallels in diction between Hebrew and Ugaritic poetry, as it is quite out of the question that Hebrew speakers should have known, or been able to read, Ugaritic tablets.

[24] Of course, even nations at war borrow from each other. Perhaps it is significant that, as the English language in World

War II borrowed *Blitz* from the German, so the Hebrews borrowed *qĕrāv*, "battle," from the Aramaic.

²⁵ See note 1.

²⁶ See the summary list in C. Rabin, *Enc. Miqr.*, IV, cols. 1076–1077; T. O. Lambdin, *JAOS*, 73 (1953), 145–155; M. Ellenbogen, *Foreign Words in the Old Testament*, London, 1962, *passim*. Scholars have not accepted the claims of A. S. Yahuda, *Die Sprache des Pentateuchs in ihren Beziehungen zum Ägyptischen*, I, Berlin, 1929; *The Language of the Pentateuch in its Relation to Egyptian*, London, 1933, that Hebrew borrowed a large number of Egyptian words in various spheres during the sojourn in Egypt.

²⁷ See Rabin, *ibid.*, cols. 1072–1074. The classic study by H. Zimmern, *Akkadische Fremdwörter als Beweis für babylonischen Kultureinfluss*, Leipzig, 1917, which also lists post-exilic and post-biblical borrowings, is to be used with caution because so many Akkadian words are now read or understood differently.

²⁸ The whole field is now covered in an unpublished Jerusalem doctoral thesis by B. Z. Eshel (1970).

²⁹ The more local character of the language of the Samaria Ostraca may be due to their being meant only for internal office use. We might perhaps compare the habit of Assyrian scribes in the 8th century onwards of putting their filing remarks on the cuneiform Akkadian documents in pen-written Aramaic, their own everyday language; cf. L. Delaporte, *Epigraphes araméens*, Paris, 1912. On the other hand, we cannot really say whether such official chronicles as the *Sēfer divrēy ha-yāmīm lĕ-malkhēy Yisrā'ēl* (II Kings 1:18 etc.) did or did not contain such forms as *šatt*, "year," and other northern features.

CHAPTER IV

RELIGION: STABILITY AND FERMENT

[1] On the historiography of the book of Kings, see M. Noth, *Überlieferungsgeschichtliche Studien*, Halle, 1942, pp. 87–110 (includes all of the deuteronomistic literature); on the religious standard of judgment, see G. von Rad, *Old Testament Theology*, I (transl. by D. Stalker), Edinburgh & London, 1962, pp. 334–346; F. M. Cross, *Canaanite Myth and Hebrew Epic*, Cambridge, 1973, pp. 274–290 ("The Themes of the Book of Kings and the Structure of the Deuteronomic History").

[2] J. Wellhausen's evaluation of the Chronicler's work in *Prolegomena to the History of Israel* (transl. by J. Black and A. Menzies), Edinburgh, 1885, pp. 171–227 is still worth careful study; the religious tendency of the book is characterized by Y. Kaufmann, *Tol^edot*, IV, Tel Aviv, 1957, 451–481. Sarah Japhet's *The Ideology of the Book of Chronicles and its Place in Biblical Thought* (Hebrew), Hebrew University doctoral dissertation, Jerusalem, 1973, a comprehensive and penetrating survey, devotes chapter 2 (pp. 209–255) to "Worship of God" (this major contribution is soon to be published).

[3] On the dating of the Latter Prophets, see the detailed analysis of Kaufmann, *Tol^edot*, III, 1–56 (English abridgement by M. Greenberg, *The Religion of Israel*, Chicago, 1960, pp. 347–356; hereafter, E); note the similar (though more cautious) conclusions of D. N. Freedman in "The Law and the Prophets," *VTS*, 9 (1963), 259–261.

Since throughout these chapters Kaufmann's *Tol^edot* is laid under heavy contribution, the reader may be interested in my assessment and critique of Kaufmann's biblical studies: "Kaufmann on the Bible: An Appreciation," *Judaism*, 13 (1964), 78–89.

[4] The particularly knotty problem raised by Ezekiel's testimony to the religion of the last age of Judah is a case in point; see my "Prolegomenon" to the *KTAV* re-issue of C. C. Torrey, *Pseudo-Ezekiel and the Original Prophecy* (with the rejoinder of S. Spiegel), in *The Library of Biblical Studies*, ed. H. H. Orlinsky, New York, 1970, pp. xviii–xxix.

[5] Linguistic criteria for the identification of late psalms are given in A. Hurvitz, *The Transition Period in Biblical Hebrew: A Study in Post-Exilic Hebrew and its Implications for the Dating of Psalms* (Hebrew), Jerusalem, 1972.

[6] Hazor: Y. Yadin, *Enc. Miqr.*, III, 1958, plate 7 (facing p. 257); Samaria: D. Diringer, *Le iscrizioni antico-ebraiche palestinesi*, Firenze, 1934, pp. 40–79; for dating, cf. N. Avigad, *Encyclopaedia of Archaeological Excavations in the Holy Land*, II (Hebrew), Jerusalem, 1971, pp. 531–532; Ophel: Diringer, 79; Lachish: N. H. Torczyner, *The Lachish Documents* (Hebrew), Jerusalem, 1940, pp. 230–231; Arad: Y. Aharoni, *Arad Inscriptions* (Hebrew, Jerusalem, 1975, pp. 163 f. (Index of Hebrew names).

[7] Hos. 2:18 assumes that YHWH is being called *ba'al;* cf. W. F. Albright, *Archaeology and the Religion of Israel*, Baltimore, 1946, pp. 160–161.

[8] Torczyner (n. 6), index, s. v. YHWH; on the oath formula, cf. M. Greenberg, "The Hebrew Oath Particle *ḥay / ḥe*," *JBL*, 76 (1957), 34–39.

[9] Aharoni (n. 6), no. 18 (pp. 37 ff.), and pp. 163 f.

[10] See the comprehensive survey of the question in B. Porten, *Archives from Elephantine*, Berkely, Los Angeles, 1968, pp. 103–179.

[11] Y. Aharoni, "The Israelite Sanctuary at Arad," in D. N. Freedman–J. C. Greenfield, eds., *New Directions in Biblical Archaeology*, New York, 1969, pp. 25–40; *idem*, "The Horned Altar of Beer-sheba," *BAr*, 37 (1974),

2–6; N. Avigad, "The Priest of Dor," *IEJ*, 25 (1975), 101–105).

[12] K. Kenyon, *Encyclopaedia of Archaeological Excavations* (see n. 6), I, 214 (and the facing illustration) (English, ed. M. Avi-Yonah, vol. II, Jerusalem, 1975, 596; illustr., p. 589, lower left). To such conjectured remains of cult installations must be added the cluster of about twenty tumuli discovered in western Jerusalem, which Ruth Amiran excavated and discussed in *Yediot*, 18 (1954), 45–59 (Hebrew). She surmised that these consisted of earth and stones piles artificially heaped upon *bāmōt* of the Judahite monarchy. Y. Elitzur followed with the suggestion that it was at the order of King Josiah that these heaps were raised during his purge of Judah's worship *(Proceedings of the Fifth World Congress of Jewish Studies* [Hebrew; n.d.] 92–97).

[13] On the meaning of such figurines, see W. F. Albright, "Astarte Plaques and Figurines from Tell Beit Mirsim," *Mélanges syriens . . . R. Dussaud*, Paris, 1939, I, pp. 107–120; *idem*, *Archaeology and the Religion of Israel*, pp. 114 f.

[14] A *maṣṣēbāh* of the Arad sanctuary is pictured in the *Enc. of Archaeological Excavations*, II, p. 475 (English, I, p. 84, lower left); outside Israel: the picture of the pillars symbolizing Ashtoret, standing on her throne (from the Hellenistic period), as interpreted by H. Danthime, *Mélanges . . . Dussaud*, II, 857–866.

[15] See the assessment of R. de Vaux, *Ancient Israel*, London, 1961, 278 f. W. B. Barrick challenges the supposed "funerary character" of the *bāmāh* in *VT*, 25 (1975), 565–595.

[15a] See E. Bickerman, "The Edict of Cyrus...," *JBL*, 65 (1946), 262–268 (reprinted with revisions in Bickerman, *Studies in Jewish and Christian History*, I [Leiden, 1976], pp. 91–103).

[16] The data on Israelite sanctuaries are conveniently summarized by M. Haran in the article "Sanctuaries" (*miqdāš*) *Enc. Miqr.* V, Jerusalem, 1968, cols. 322–328.

[17] In Ps. 99:5; 132:7; Lam. 2:1, the whole temple is, by extension, called God's footstool; by further extension the whole earth is so called in Isa. 66:1.

[18] For this interpretation of the golden calves, see Kaufmann, *Tol^edot*, II, pp. 259–261 (E 271); R. de Vaux, *The Bible and the Ancient Near East* (transl. by D. McHugh), London, 1972, pp. 100–103, regards the young bull as an embodiment of the divine attribute of strength and fecundity.

[19] On the regular incense offering in First Temple times, cf. M. Haran, "The uses of incense in the ancient Israelite ritual," *VT*, 10 (1960), 113–129.

[20] On the pilgrimage in early Israel, cf. M. Haran, *Ages and Institutions in the Bible* (Hebrew), Tel Aviv, 1973, pp. 77–88.

[21] So Mekilta, *Bo'* (*Pasḥa*, 7); Onkelos at Ex. 12:13; 23:27; Ibn Janaḥ in *The Book of Roots*, s. v. (comparing Isa. 31:5); cf. R. Weiss, *Leshonenu*, 27–28 (1965), 127–130, and S. Loewenstamm, *The Tradition of the Exodus and its Development* (Hebrew), Jerusalem, 1965 pp. 84–88. This interpretation is opposed by J. B. Segal, *The Hebrew Passover*, London, 1963, pp. 95–101.

[22] The anxiety is expressed through ascetic (purificatory) practices: eating unleavened bread, "bread of self-denial" (Deut. 16:3); the ban on eating any new produce until the first sheaf of the reaping was "lifted" (Lev. 23:14). The Jewish customs of counting the days between the festivals of *maṣṣōt* and Pentecost, and quasi-mourning during that interval also reflect the season's anxiety. "Some explain it. . . on the ground that the world is anxious between Passover and Weeks about the crops and the fruit trees . . . Therefore God commanded to count these days, to keep the anxiety of the world in mind and to turn to him in wholehearted repentance, to plead with him to have mercy upon us on mankind and on the land, so that the crops should turn out well, for they are our life" (*Abudarham haššālēm, s^efirat ha'omer* [ed. Jerusalem, 5719, p. 241]). See

M. P. Nilsson, *Greek Folk Religion* (New York, 1940), 27–29, for parallels, but especially L. H. Silberman, "The Sefirah Season," *HUCA*, 22 (1949), 226–232.

The origin of *pesaḥ* as a nomad festival (L. Rost) may be admitted without prejudicing its meaning for the settled Israelites, our present concern. In the land, *pesaḥ* and the *maṣṣōt* festivals were presumably celebrated as two parts of a single agricultural festival, even as they were fused into a single commemorative one. Neither is mentioned in the narrative between Josh. 5:10 f. and II Kings 23:21 ff., but this does not justify denying their existence during all that period (G. Fohrer, *History of Israelite Religion*, Nashville, 1972, 100 f.). No consensus on the origin of the Passover festival has emerged in recent investigations of it; see J. B. Segal, *The Hebrew Passover*, London, etc., 1963; J. Henninger, *Les fêtes de printemps chez les Sémites et la pâque israélite*, Paris, 1975.

23   Kaufmann, *Tolˁdot*, II, 496–498; H. J. Kraus, *Worship in Israel* (transl. by G. Buswell), Oxford, 1966, pp. 66 ff., doubts it.

24   For an analysis of the day's ritual, see J. Milgrom, "Day of Atonement," *Enc. Judaica*, V, Jerusalem, 1971, cols. 1384–1387. Milgrom judiciously weighs the doubts about the antiquity of this holyday.

25   Explicit testimony to the mixture of joy and anxiety that must have accompanied these festivals even in biblical times comes only much later. "R. Akiba (2nd century CE) said: The Torah enjoined you to make an offering of the first sheaf of the barley harvest at the Passover, when the barley ripens, in order that the crops may be blessed; to make an offering of the firstfruits of the wheat at Weeks, when the fruit-trees are ripe, so that the fruit may be blessed; to offer water libations at Tabernacles, so that the rain may be blessed" (Tosefta, Sukka, chap. 3, end). Although the cult laws of the Torah make no connection between the celebration of the festivals and fertility, such a connection is alluded to in Zechariah 14:17 f. "Whichever

of the families of the earth do not go up to Jerusalem [on the festival of Sukkot; vv. 16, 19] to worship the King, YHWH Sebaoth— no rain shall fall upon them."

A similar clustering of holy days during the spring is evident in Ezekiel 45:18–20; a two-day purgation of the uncleanness of the Temple (analogous to the Day of Atonement) on the first and seventh of the first (spring) month. See Kaufmann, *Tolˁdot*, pp. 492–496 (E, pp. 306–308).

26   A full reconstruction of Israel's festival celebration, combining data of diverse provenience with imagination, is found in Kraus, *Worship*, pp. 208–222.

27   Kraus, pp. 225 f.

28   A good account of the priestly and deuteronomic conceptions of the temple is given in M. Weinfeld, *Deuteronomy and the Deuteronomic School*, Oxford, 1972, pp. 191–209; Weinfeld develops the earlier treatment of G. von Rad, *Studies in Deuteronomy* (transl. by D. Stalker), Chicago, 1953, pp. 37–44.

29   Contrast the pagan view, expressed, for example, in the Egyptian adjuration of the gods threatening to stop their offerings: J. A. Wilson in *ANET*, 327 (b).

30   Such discrimination between types of sacrifice is not prophetic in spirit; it has nothing to do with the classical prophetic doctrine of the primacy of morality over cult; see my essay, "On the Refinement of the Conception of Prayer in Hebrew Scriptures," *Association for Jewish Studies review*, I (1976), pp. 57–92.

31   There is a theory that Zadok was the native Jebusite priest of pre-Israelite Jerusalem, and that David appointed him to promote syncretism with the conquered Canaanite population (for a brief statement and full bibliography of this theory see H. H. Rowley, *Worship in Ancient Israel*, London, 1967, pp. 72–75); cf. also S. Loewenstamm, "Zadok," in *Enc. Miqr*, VI, cols. 673–675. Haran, *Ages* (n. 21), 156, plausibly considers Zadok a Levite.

32   For a reconstruction of the history of

Israel's priesthood, see Kaufmann, *Tol^edot*, pp. 171–184 (E, pp. 193–200), on which cf. my critique in *JAOS*, 70 (1950), 41–47; for a comprehensive treatment, see A. Cody, *A History of Old Testament Priesthood*, Rome, 1969; cf. also Haran, *Ages* (above, n. 20), pp. 150–174.

[33] Written down during the united monarchy, according to the estimate of F. M. Cross, *Studies in Ancient Yahwistic Poetry*, Baltimore, 1950, p. 185 f., though he dates vv. 8–10 later (p. 220). O. Eissfeldt refrains from proposing a date for the Blessing, but regards it as early (*The Old Testament: An Introduction* [transl. by P. Ackroyd], Oxford, 1965, p. 228 f.); Cody (see preceding note) puts the latest elements in the Blessing of Levi (vv. 9[b]–10) no later than the 8th century (pp. 114–120).

[34] See the monograph of Jacob Milgrom, *Studies in Levitical Terminology, I: The Encroacher and the Levite*, Berkeley, Los Angeles, 1970.

[35] See W. F. Albright's discussion, with a parallel from ancient Egypt, "The Judicial Reform of Jehoshaphat," *Alexander Marx Jubilee Volume*, English Section, New York, 1950, p. 76 f.

[36] On the lower classes of Temple personnel, see R. de Vaux, *Ancient Israel*, pp. 382 ff.; Haran, *Ages*, 218–223; on Temple singers, S. Mowinckel, *The Psalms in Israel's Worship*, II, Oxford, 1962, pp. 79–84; on the evidence of names for dating these classes, W. F. Albright, *Archaeology and the Religion of Israel*. pp. 120–127. On the name *qrs* among the Arad ostraca, see B. Levine, *IEJ*, 19 (1969), 50 f.

[37] See the literature cited above in n. 32; the view of G. von Rad (*Studies in Deuteronomy*, 14, pp. 66 f.) that Levites served as teachers and preachers of *Torah* during the late monarchy (based in part on their post-exilic role, e.g., in Neh. 8) has no support in the sources, and is justly deprecated by Weinfeld, *Deuteronomy*, pp. 54 ff. The classical critical view that the inferior status of

the Levites came about as a result of the "demotion" of the *bāmōt* priests incidental to Josiah's reform is refuted by Kaufmann (citation in n. 32).

[38] On the pre-exilic dating of the passages dealing with the priestly dues, see Kaufmann, *Tol^edot*, I, pp. 143–159 (E, pp. 187–193); Haran offers a convenient summary of the question in the article *matnōt k^ehunnah* ("priestly dues"), *Enc. Miqr.*, IV, cols. 39–45; a comprehensive study of the tithe utilizing comparative material, and comparing royal with priestly custom, is M. Weinfeld's "The Tithe in the Bible—its State and Cultic Background" (Hebrew) in the annual, *Beer-Sheba*, 1 (1973), 122–131.

[39] See W. F. Albright, *Archaeology and the Religion of Israel*, pp. 121–125; M. Haran, "Studies in the Account of the Levitical Cities," *JBL*, 80 (1961), 45–54, 156–165; Y. Kaufmann, *Sefer Yehoshua'*, Jerusalem, 1959, pp. 270–282; B. Mazar, "The Cities of the Priests and the Levites," *VTS*, 7 (1960), 193–205.

[40] See J. M. Grintz, "Do not Eat on the Blood," *Annual of the Swedish Theological Institute*, 8 (1970–71), 78–105, where the prohibition is explained by pagan divination customs.

[41] See J. Licht, *mīlāh* ("circumcision"), *Enc. Miqr.*, IV, cols. 894–901; M. Fox examines the meaning of the rite as "the sign of the covenant," in *RB*, 81 (1974), 557–596; he concludes that the sign is to remind God to keep his promise of posterity to Abraham.

[42] "After the Babylonian Exile, the conception of marriage changed... According to Ezek. 16:8 and Mal. 2:13–16, the rite of marriage includes a covenant and an oath that obligates the two parties... God serves as witness and judge of violations of the covenant; the rite as a whole gains a religious dimension, and marriage itself acquires increased obligatoriness (Prov. 2:16 f.)"—so Z. Falk, *nissu'īm* ("marriage"), *Enc. Miqr.* V, col. 859. But the sense of the passages

cited is questionable. The Proverbs passage condemning the adulteress who "forgets the covenant of her God" (//"who forsakes the friend of her youth") recalls Ben Sira 23:37 (23): "For first she disdained the teaching of the Most High, next she betrayed her husband." Both passages take adultery as a violation of the divine injunction (in the "Tablets of the Covenant") "Thou shalt not commit adultery."

Mal. 2:14, condemning the betrayal of "the wife of your covenant" (or "your covenant-wife") must be understood in the light of verse 10: "Why should we be false to one another, thus profaning the covenant of our fathers." This in turn is illuminated by what follows immediately: "For Judah has profaned the holiness of God, which he loved, by taking to wife the daughter of a foreign god." The sanctity of Israel's line of descent from the covenant ancestors was "profaned" by intermarriage with gentile women. The gentile woman—"the daughter of an alien god"—is contrasted to "your companion and the wife of your covenant"—i.e., an Israelite woman, who might well be styled "daughter of your covenant" (viz. "the covenant of our fathers," through which the holy people came into being).

God's "attestation" in v. 14 recalls Gen. 31:50, in which Laban invokes God as witness against Jacob's ever maltreating his daughters or taking other wives besides them. The obscure situation in Mal. 2:11 ff. is perhaps analogous: the prophet denounces a current practice of some Jews who took gentile women besides their lawful Jewish wives, and thereby were false to them (since a time-honored view was that such a practice was heinous).

The allegory in Ezek. 16:8 is no sure ground for asserting that marriage involved a covenant and an oath. The prophet sometimes intrudes the referent into his allegory, e.g., in 17:9b. Since he allegorizing God's covenant with Israel, which, in his version, involved an oath (20:5 f.), it is altogether possible that his allegorical marriage is colored by the reality that God acquired Israel by a covenant oath.

43 T. H. Gaster, *Myth, Legend and Custom in the Old Testament*, New York, 1969, pp. 572; 590–602.

44 Kaufmann, *Tol^edot*, II, pp. 544–556 (E, pp. 311–316); Greenberg, "Resurrection," *Enc. Judaica*, XIV, cols. 96–98.

45 E. Neufeld, *Ancient Hebrew Marriage Laws*, London, 1944, pp. 23–49; R. Westbrook, "Redemption of Land," *Israel Law Review*, 6 (1971), 371–375.

46 H. L. Ginsberg, "Psalms and Inscriptions of Petition and Acknowledgment," *Louis Ginzberg Jubilee Volume*, English Section, New York, 1945, 159–171.

47 Kaufmann, *Tol^edot*, II, pp. 499–506 (E, pp. 309–311); A Wendel, *Das freie Laiengebet im vorexilischen Israel*, Leipzig, 1932, a comprehensive study of forms; J. Herrmann, "Prayer in the Old Testament," *Theological Dictionary of the New Testament*, II, Grand Rapids, 1964, pp. 785–800; A. Gonzalez, "Prière," *Supp. Dict. de la Bible*, fasc. 44 (1969), pp. 556–585.

48 Divine help in war is asked in several psalms; on Psalms 24, 20, 146, and 46, see S. D. Goitein, *Iyyunim ba-Miqra*, Tel Aviv, 1957, 239–247.

49 Concerning the trumpets, see Y. Yadin, *The Scroll of the War* . . . Oxford 1962, pp. 87 ff. 109 ff.

50 See A. Biram, *Mas 'oved, Tarbiz*, 23 (1953), 137–142; for the development of the ḥerem, see A. Malamat, "The Ban in Mari and the Bible," *Die Ou-Testamentiese Werkgemeenskap in Suid-Africa: Biblical Essays* (1966), pp. 40–49; Greenberg, "Ḥerem," *Enc. Judaica*, VIII, cols. 345–350.

51 W. F. Albright suggested that Samuel employed these enthusiasts in a "revival" movement: *Samuel and the Beginning of the Prophetic Movement*, Cincinnati, 1961.

52 A literary-evolutionary approach to the different depictions of prophetic miracles is found in A. Rofé's "The Classification of

the Prophetical Stories," *JBL*, 89 (1970), 427–440.

53 See the detailed account in F. Hesse, *Die Fürbitte im Alten Testament*, Hamburg, 1951; and Y. Muffs' essay, *Tefillatam šel Nevi'im* ("Prophetic Prayer"), *Molad*, 35–36 (5736), 204–210.

54 See A. Malamat, "Prophetic Revelations in . . . Mari and the Bible," *VTS*, 15 (1966), 207–227; J. F. Ross, "Prophecy in Hamath, Israel, and Mari," *HTR*, 63 (1970), 1–28.

54a On the distinction between Nathan's role as prophet and his role as advisor, see Kaufmann, *Mi-kivšonah šel ha-yeṣirah ha-miqra'it*, Tel Aviv, 1966, pp. 180–184; for the possibility that *ḥōzēh* = court prophet, see Z. Zevit, *VT*, 25 (1975), 786–789.

55 See S. R. Johnson, *The Cultic Prophet in Ancient Israel*, Cardiff, 1944.

56 "The essential meaning of this is: Within every community, even among idolaters, there are some pious, ascetical worshipers—such as, nowadays, the priesthood among the Hindus and the Christians—while the rest of the community are abandoned to licentiousness . . . Therefore God said, 'You must all be holy'; that is, 'Among you it must not be that some are pious and ascetical while others are abandoned to license and trangression . . .'" (Commentary to Ex. 19:6 of Abraham son of Maimonides).

57 See the discussion of the Ezekiel passage in the Talmud, *Menaḥot* 45a, and the forced interpretation rejected by Ibn Ezra in Lev. 22:8.

58 Comprehensive accounts of these theories are found in H. J. Kraus, *Worship in Israel* (transl. by G. Buswell), Oxford, 1966; W. Beyerlin, *Origins and History of the Oldest Sinaitic Traditions* (transl. by S. Rudman), Oxford, 1965.

59 See the full discussion by M. Haran, "The Ark and the Cherubs" (Hebrew), *Eretz-Israel*, 5 (1958), 83–90.

60 Kaufmann, in *Mi-kivshonah shel ha-yeṣirah ha-miqra'it*, Tel Aviv, 1966, pp. 205–207, understands the "wrath" as a reference to some magical effect of the actions of the king's priest-magicians.

61 Regarding the odd language of II Kings 10:25, see Y. Yadin's tentative proposal to place Jezebel's Baal temple somewhere in the territory, not the city, of Samaria (*Eretz Shomron* [Jerusalem, 1973], 56–58). As for Solomon, the 14th century commentator Gersonides notes a certain inconsequence in I Kings 11:4–8 (the mitigating clauses at the ends of vv. 4 and 6), indicating that Solomon's guilt was in allowing his wives to worship foreign gods (so explicitly v. 8) rather than in worshiping them himself.

62 On the ethnic heterogeneity implicit in the differing modes of designating the fiscal districts of Solomon, first suggested by Alt, see the concurring remarks of Z. Kallai, *The Tribes Israel* (Hebrew), Jerusalem, 1967, pp. 35–38.

63 See A. Soggin, "Der offiziell geforderte Synkretismus in Israel, etc.," *ZAW*, 78 (1966), 179–204; on Molech, M. Cogan, *Imperialism and Religion*, Missoula, Mont. (1974), pp. 77–84; M. Weinfeld, "The Worship of Molech, etc.," *Ugarit-Forschungen*, 4 (1972), 133–154 (criticized by M. Smith, *JAOS*, 95 [1975], 477–479). For Aramean influence on Israel's religion, see A. Malamat in D. J. Wiseman, ed., *Peoples of Old Testament Times*, Oxford, 1973, pp. 148–149.

64 The relation of the prose account of the dynastic oracle in II Sam. 7 to the poem in Ps. 89 is studied in N. M. Sarna, "Psalm 89: A study in Inner Biblical Exegesis," in A. Altmann, ed., *Biblical and Other Studies*, Cambridge, Mass., 1963, pp. 29–46. Several passages make the election of the Davidides conditional upon their observance of the covenant laws; e.g., I Kings 2:2–4; 5:25; 9:6. The relation of this to the unconditional promise is discussed by A. Šanda, *Die Bücher der Könige*, I, Münster, 1911, p. 224, and M. Weinfeld, "The Covenant of Grant in the OT and in the Ancient Near East," *JAOS*, 90 (1970), 189–196.

65   The contrasting ideologies of royal election in north and south are discussed by A. Alt, *Essays on OT History and Religion* (transl. by R. A. Wilson), Oxford, 1966, pp. 239–260. While the basis for later prophetic opposition to the Omrides is clear enough (see ahead), the reasons for the opposition ascribed to Ahijah (I Kings 14:9) and Jehu son of Hanani (16:2) seem to reflect the Judahite bias against Jeroboam's claves, rather than the true reason which moved these northern prophets to reject their dynasties (assuming, of course, that the author of Kings correctly depicts them as so doing). Noth conjectures that the northern prophets opposed supplanting Jerusalem, the seat of the ark (see his, *The Laws in the Pentateuch* (transl., R. Ap-Thomas) Philadelphia, 1967, 136–137).

66   Cf. S. Moscati, *The Face of the Ancient Orient*, Garden City, 1962, p. 221: ". . . the Aramaean pantheon has one characteristic feature—none the less significant for being negative—namely, the absence of any god that can definitely be considered as its own."

67   The argument for the separation of Hosea 1–3 from the rest of the book is set forth in Kaufmann, *Tol^edot*, III, pp. 93–107 (E, pp. 368–371); further in H. L. Ginsberg, "Hosea, book of," in *Enc. Judaica*, VIII, cols. 1010–1017. On the role of the desert cf. S. Talmon, "The Desert Motif, etc.," in A. Altmann, ed., *Biblical Motifs*, Cambridge, Mass., 1966, pp. 50–52.

68   M. Pope, "Rechab," *Interpreter's Dictionary of the Bible*, IV, pp. 14–16.

69   J. Gray, in his commentary to Kings, London, 1963, p. 523 f., identifies three sets of relationships in this covenant: God—king, God—people, and people—king. See further G. Fohrer, "Der Vertrag zwischen König und Volk in Israel," *ZAW*, 71 (1959), 1–22.

70   The positive and negative features of northern prophecy are assessed in W. Eichrodt, *Theology of the Old Testament*, I, London, 1961, pp. 328–338.

71   On early prophetic eschatology, see Kaufmann, *Tol^edot*, II, pp. 249–258, 287–293. (E, pp. 279–282).

72   Verse 6 notes that an asherah stood in Samaria during the reign of Jehoahaz son of Jehu. That neither Jehu nor Elisha took offense at this "heathen symbol" (as it is generally regarded), makes one suspect that its "heathenness" was of the same order as the calves of Jeroboam, to which no northern zealot took exception before Hosea. Deuteronomy 16:21, "You must not plant an asherah—any tree-beside the altar of YHWH your God which you shall make," reads like an equation of all sacred trees, perfectly legitimate through most of Israelite history [cf. Gen. 21:33; Josh. 24:26]), with the symbol of the pagan goddess Asherah. This agrees with Deuteronomy's novel, wholesale disqualification of many older usages which in neo-Assyrian times (see ahead) were associated by puritans with heathen worship (e.g. pillars and *bāmōt*). The deuteronomistic author of Kings shared this evaluation and anachronistically condemned earlier ages for committing those late-born sins. Jehoahaz' asherah probably belongs to this class of sin; Kings, looking for causes of trouble, found one in the sacred tree of Samaria, which he denigratingly (like Deuteronomy) calls an asherah.

73   Kaufmann, *Tol^edot*, III, pp. 56–92 (E, pp. 363–368); on the prophetic experience of Amos and his conception of God, see A. J. Heschel, *The Prophets*, New York, 1962, pp. 27–38.

74   Kaufmann, *ibid*. pp. 107–146 (E, pp. 372–377); H. L. Ginsberg, *Enc. Judaica*, VIII, cols. 1017–1022.

75   Kaufmann, *ibid*, pp. 147–256 (E, pp. 378–395); on the prophecies about the nations and on Assyria, see N. K. Gottwald, *All the Kingdoms of the Earth*, New York, 1964, pp. 147–208; for the interweaving of the story of the Assyrian invasion with Isaiah's specific prophecies about it, see B. S. Childs, *Isaiah and the Assyrian Crisis*, London, 1967;

see also H. L. Ginsberg, "Isaiah in the Light of History," *Conservative Judaism*, 22 (1967), 1–18, and idem, *Enc. Judaica*, IX, cols. 49–60.

76   On the asherah, see n. 72, above.

77   Some scholars connect Hezekiah's reforms with his rebellion, as though political subjection to Assyria implied some form of religious subjection as well; see, e.g., H. H. Rowley, *Men of God*, London, 1963, pp. 126–132; but Cogan (above, n. 63) has shown the error of this view with respect to Judah (*ibid*, 72–77). The dismantling and profane reuse of the Beersheba stone altar in the 8th century may have been in consequence of Hezekiah's reform (so Aharoni; see above, n. 11).

78   This interpretation of the religio-cultural situation of the reigns of Manasseh and Amon is developed by Cogan, *ibid*., pp. 65–96. An argument along similar lines was made earlier, by L. E. Fuller, *The Historical and Religious Significance of the Reign of Manasseh*, Leipzig, 1912.

79   For the reconstruction of events, see M. Weinfeld, "Josiah," *Enc. Judaica*, IX, cols. 290–292, and next note.

80   The relation of Deuteronomy to Josiah's reform is reviewed in E. W. Nicholson, *Deuteronomy and Tradition*, Oxford, 1967, pp. 1–12.

81   For a comprehensive survey of opinion on the northern origin of Deuteronomy, see H. Moler-Kodesh, "The Problem of the Northern Sources of Deuteronomy," (Hebrew), *Beth Mikra* 42 (1970), 264–297. The theory was first put forward by A. Alt, "Die Heimat des Deuteronomiums," *Kleine Schriften*, II, 250–275; on connections between Deuteronomy and Hosea, see M. Weinfeld, *Deuteronomy and the Deuteronomic School*, Oxford, 1972, pp. 366–370; H. L. Ginsberg, *Enc. Judaica*, VIII, cols. 1022–1025.

82   On the historical-religious significance of Deuteronomy, see Kaufmann, *Tol^edot*, I, pp. 109–111 (E, pp. 174–175); a rich, comprehensive presentation of Deuteronomic ideology and theology is found in Weinfeld (n. 81).

83   On the problem of the duration of Josiah's measures after his death, see M. Greenberg, "Prolegomenon" (*op.cit.*, n. 4), xviii–xxiii, xxxiii, and n. 47; criticized by M. Smith, "The Veracity of Ezekiel, the Sins of Manasseh, and Jeremiah 44:18," *ZAW*, 17 (1975), 11–16.

84   Kaufmann, *Tol^edot*, III, pp. 360–368 (E, pp. 398–400).

85   Jeremiah's trial is compared with the trial of Socrates by S. D. Goitein in *'Iyyunim ba-Mikra*, Tel Aviv, 1957, pp. 130–141.

86   The motives of Jeremiah's "Babylonian policy" have long exercised scholars: see Kaufmann, *Tol^edot*, III, pp. 456–459 (E, pp. 422–424); Goitein, *ibid*., pp. 142–155; A. C. Welch, *Jeremiah*, Oxford, 1955, pp. 195–212.

87   On the antiquity of the "covenant curses," see D. R. Hillers, *Treaty Curses and the Old Testament Prophets*, Rome, 1964, pp. 82–89.

CHAPTER V

THE STRUCTURE OF SOCIETY

[1] For the nature of the tribal organization and the patriarchal regime in Israel, see J. Liver, "The Israelite Tribes," *Judges*, pp. 183 ff., and its bibliography. Cf. R. de Vaux, *Ancient Israel, Its Life and Institutions*, London, 1961, *passim*; J. A. Soggin, *Das Königtum in Israel*, Berlin, 1967, pp. 149 ff. The two later works contain much bibliography. For a survey of the period of the Judges, cf. A. Malamat, "The Period of the Judges," *Judges*, pp. 129 ff. For the structure of Israelite society from the period of the Settlement onward, see M. Weber, *Ancient Judaism*, New York, 1952, *passim*.

[2] The scope and significance of intertribal descriptions and events was recently discussed (although with a different motivation) by R. Smend, *Yahwe War and Tribal Confederation*, Nashville, 1970, *passim*. For a discussion of the biblical passages dealing with the House of Joseph in general and the tribe of Benjamin in particular, and which supports the views of scholars concerning intertribal activity, cf. K. D. Schunk, *Benjamin*, Berlin, 1963, pp. 18 ff.

[3] For the significance of the geographical and tribal data of Saul's kingdom, see Y. Aharoni, *The Land of the Bible*, London, 1966; Z. Kallai, *The Settlement of the Israelite Tribes*, Jerusalem, 1967, pp. 26 ff. (Hebrew).

[4] For a description of the congregation and the community, with bibliography, see M. Weinfeld, "Congregation," *Encyclopaedia Judaica*, V, cols. 894 ff. See also A. Hurvitz, "Linguistic Observations on the Biblical Usage of the Term 'ēdāh," *Tarbiz*, 40 (1971), 261 ff. (Hebrew). An earlier work on the subject of the "congregation" is C. U. Wolf, "Traces of Primitive Democracy in Ancient Israel," *JNES*, 6 (1947), 98 ff. A serious question in the light of the above is the background for the use of "congregation" in II Kings 12:20, the last reference to this body. Possibly this too is an attempt to impart to the northern tribes the character of an inter-tribal assembly, thus reviving an ancient ceremony which suits the situation of re-electing a king in this particular instance.

On the subject of amphictiony, see M. Noth, *Das System der zwölf Stämme Israels*, Stuttgart, 1930; R. Smend, *op. cit.*, *passim*; G. Fohrer, "Altes Testament 'Amphictyonie' und 'Bund,'" *TLZ*, 91 (1966), 801 ff.; 893 ff.; G. M. Anderson, "Israel: Amphictiony, 'AM, KAHAL, 'EDAH," *Translating and Understanding the Old Testament* (Essays in honor of H. G. May), Nashville— N. Y., 1970, pp. 135 ff., R. de Vaux, "La thèse de l'Amphictionie' Israëlite," *HTR*, 64 (1971), 415 ff.

[5] For the political institutions, including the "men" of the tribe, particularly against the background of Absalom's rebellion, see H. Tadmor, "'The People,' and the Kingship in Ancient Israel: The role of Political Institutions in the Biblical Period," *Journal of World History*, 9 (1968), 3 ff. For the various uses of the above term see A. Besters, "'Israel' et 'Fils d'Israel' dans les livres historiques (Genése — II Rois)," *RB*, 74 (1967), 5 ff.

[6] Cf. n. 1 and also J. Pedersen, *Israel Its Life and Culture*, I, London–Copenhagen, 1926, pp. 26 ff., especially 46 ff.; C. U. Wolf, "Terminology of Israel's Tribal Organization," *JBL*, 65 (1947), 45 ff.; cf. M. Razin– S. Ben-Dor, *The Origin of the Monarchy in Israel*, 62 ff. (Hebrew).

[7] For the "elders" in Israel, see M. Weinfeld, "Elder," *Encyclopaedia Judaica*, VI, cols. 578 ff.; J. L. McKenzie, "The Elders in the Old Testament," *Biblica*, 40 (1959), 522 ff. For a different view, cf. J. Dus, "Die Ältesten Israels," *Communio Viatorum*, 3 (1960), 232 ff. See H. Reviv, "Types of Leadership

in the Period of the Judges," *Beer–Sheva Annual*, 1 (1973), 204 ff. (Hebrew). The elders mentioned in connection with Rehoboam's consultations (I Kings 12:6, 8) are not part of the traditional leadership, but a term for an age group among the king's advisers. However, see A. Malamat, "Kingship and Council in Israel and Sumer: A Parallel," *JNES*, 22 (1963), 247 ff.; G. E. Evans, "Rehoboam's Advisers at Shechem and Political Institutions in Israel and Sumer," *JNES*, 25 (1966), 273 ff. It appears that the various titles given to the Israelite leaders in the Song of Deborah, such as kings, princes (Judg. 5:3), governors of Israel (v. 9), nobles (v. 13), etc., also refer to the traditional tribal leadership.

8 For the interchange of congregation — elders, cf. for example, Ex. 12:3, 21; for the interchange of people ('*ām*) — elders, cf. 19:7–8.

9 On the subject of the elders and the Judges, concerning tribal leadership, see the article of the present author cited in n. 7.

10 For an attempt to give a general outline of early Israelite society in the spirit of historical materialism, cf. M. Lurje, *Studien zur Geschichte der wirtschaftlichen und sozialen Verhältnisse im israelitisch-jüdischen Reiche*, Giessen, 1927. For the biblical aspects, cf. A. Kuschke, "Arm und Reich im Alten Testament," *ZAW*, 57 (1939), 31 ff.; A. Menes, *Die vorexilischen Gesetze*, Giessen, 1928, *passim*. Cf. also n. 19.

11 For a discussion of this subject, cf. Reviv, *op. cit.*, 215 ff.

12 During the period of the Monarchy, a person of distinguished lineage, a holder of high office, or owner of extensive property was also termed "great" (II Kings 10:6, 11). For "a great woman," cf. II Kings 4:8; cf. J. van der Ploeg, "Les nobles israelites," *OTS*, 9 (1951), 49; cf. M. Razin–S. Ben-Dor, *op. cit.*, 218 ff.

13 Cf. A. Malamat, "*gᵉdūd*," *Enc. Miqr.*, II, cols. 432–433.

14 For the *ḥab/piru* in the ancient East, cf. M. Greenberg, "Ḥab/piru and Hebrews," *Patriarchs*, 188 ff., with additional bibliography. Cf. H. Cazelles "The Hebrews," *Peoples of Old Testament Times* (D. J. Wiseman, ed.), Oxford, 1973, pp. 1 ff. (with bibliography).

15 The connection between biblical law and the law of the ancient East has been extensively dealt with. For a selection of studies, see: S. E. Loewenstamm, "Law, Biblical Law," *Enc. Miqr.* IV, cols., 614 ff., with bibliography; *idem*, "Law," *Judges*, 231 ff.; P. Artzi, "Law," *Biblical Lexicon*, II, Tel Aviv, 1965, 518 ff. (Hebrew); R. de Vaux, (*op. cit.* n. 1), 143 ff. (with bibliography); M. David, "The Codex Hammurabi and its Relation to the Provisions of Law in Exodus," *OTS*, 7 (1950), 149 ff.; A. Alt, "Die Ursprünge des israelitischen Rechts," *Kleine Schriften*, II, 278 ff.; G. E. Mendenhall, "Law and Covenant in Israel and in the Ancient Near East," Pittsburgh, 1955.

16 Cf. for example: I. Mendelsohn, "The Conditional Sale of Free-born Daughters in Nuzi and the Law of Ex. 21: 7–11," *JAOS*, 55 (1935), 190 ff.; H. M. Weil, "Gage et cautionnement dans la Bible," *Archives d'histoire du droit oriental*, 12 (1938), 68 ff.; E. Neufeld, "The Prohibitions against Loans at Interest in Ancient Hebrew Laws," *HUCA*, 26 (1959), 355 ff.

17 For the "man of valor," cf. M. Weber (*op. cit.*, n. 1), *passim*; J. van der Ploeg, "Le sens de *gibbor hail*," *RB*, 50 (1941), 120 ff.; W. McKane, "The *Gibbor Ḥayil* in the Israelite Community," *Transactions of the Glasgow Oriental Society*, 17 (1957), 28 ff.

18 From now on called "township," which includes both towns and villages.

19 The Book of Genesis alludes to the early relations of the Israelites with the settled, non-Israelite population in the country. Cf. S. Yeivin, "The Patriarchs in the Land of Canaan," *Patriarchs*, 103 ff. For the complete integration of West Semitic elements originating in the tribal organization of the Hanaeans known from the Mari

Tablets, among the settled population of the Kingdom of Alalakh, cf. D. J. Wiseman, *The Alalakh Tablets*, London, 1953, esp. nos. 128 ff.; M. Dietrich – O. Loretz, "Die soziale Struktur von Alalah und Ugarit, II," *WO*, 5 (1969), 57 ff.

20 For a description of the development of urban society in Israel, cf. E. Neufeld, "The Emergence of Royal Urban Society in Ancient Israel," *HUCA*, 31 (1960), 31 ff.

21 For the genealogical chapters and their significance, cf. J. Liver, (*op. cit.*, n. 1), pp. 183 ff.; *idem*, "*yāḥas*," *Enc. Miqr.*, III, cols. 663 ff.

22 For the parallel urban institutions in Canaan, cf. H. Reviv, "On Urban Representative Institutions and Self-Government in Syria–Palestine in the Second Half of the Second Millennium B.C.," *JESHO*, 12 (1969), 283 ff. Cf. n. 23.

23 When the term "(free and permanent) citizens of the town" (*ba'ālēi ha-'īr*) refers to Israelite towns it defines the "men of the city." In a few contexts referring to non-Israelite towns, the elders are mentioned, because of an Israelite projection of an earlier situation. Cf. H. Reviv, "Urban Institutions, Personages and Problems of Terminology in Descriptions of non-Israelite Cities in the Bible," *Eretz-Israel*, 10 (1971), 258 ff. (Hebrew).

24 For examples of extradition clauses in treaties in the Ancient East, cf. *ANET*[3], 203, 204, 531.

25 Cf. A. Roifer, "The Breaking of the Heifer's Neck," *Tarbiz*, 31 (1962), 119 ff. (Hebrew). Cf. also H. Reviv (see above, n. 21).

26 See above, n. 7. See also H. Klengel, "Zu den *šibutum* in altbabylonischer Zeit," *Orientalia*, 29 (1960), 375 ff.; *idem.*, "Die Rolle der 'Ältesten' (LÚ^{meš}.ŠU.GI) im Kleinasien der Hethiterzeit," *ZA*, 57 (1965), 223–236. Cf. A. Walther, *Das altbabylonische Gerichtswesen*, Leipzig, 1917, *passim*.

27 For this division, cf. Yeivin in this volume, pp. 153–154.

28 For the use of the parallel term in Akka-

dian, cf. *CAD* A, II, 247 ff. Cf. R. de Vaux (see above, n. 1), 127 ff. Cf. J. van der Ploeg, "Les chefs du people d'Israël et leurs titres," *RB*, 57 (1950), 40 ff. For the formation of the above classes, cf. A. Alt, "Der Anteil des Königtums an der sozialen Entwicklung in den Reichen Israel und Juda," *Kleine Schriften*, III, pp. 348 ff.

29 For the relevant documents, cf. D. J. Wiseman (see above, n. 17); J. Nougayrol et alii, *Le palais royal d'Ugarit III*, Paris, 1955, *passim*.

30 On the *ḫupšu* in the Ancient East, cf. CAD H, 241 ff.; I. Mendelsohn, "The Canaanite Term for 'Free Proletarian,'" *BASOR*, 83 (1941), 36 ff.; *idem*, "New Light on the *ḫupšu*," *ibid.*, 139 (1955), 9 ff.; Dietrich-Loretz (see above, n. 17), *passim*.

31 For an agreement between the Manner of the King (*mišpaṭ ha-meleḵ*) and the Canaanite custom, cf. I. Mendelsohn, "Samuel's Denunciation of Kingship in the Light of the Akkadian Document from Ugarit," *BASOR*, 143 (1956), 17. Cf. also this volume, chap. I.

32 Cf. B. Maisler (Mazar), "The Scribe of King David and the Problem of the High Officials in the Ancient Kingdom of Israel," *BJPES*, 13 (1947), 105 ff. Cf. S. Yeivin, *p^eqīdūt*, *Enc. Miqr.*, VI, cols. 540 ff. (with bibliography). T. N. D. Mettinger, *Solomonic State Officials*, Lund, 1971.

33 For the Levites, cf. J. Liver, "Levites," *Enc. Miqr.*, IV, cols. 460 ff. (with bibliography). Cf. also R. de Vaux (see above, n. 1), 358 ff. (with bibliography).

34 B. Mazar, "The Cities of the Priests and Levites," *Studies in the Book of Joshua*, Jerusalem, 1960, pp.165 ff. (Hebrew). See also W. F. Albright, "The List of Levitic Cities," *L. Ginzberg Jubilee Volume*, I, New York, 1945, 49 ff.; A. Alt, "Festungen und Levitenorte im Lande Juda," *Kleine Schriften*, II, pp. 306 ff.; cf. *ibid.*, 289 ff. See also n. 3.

35 For the relations between the Monarchy and the non-Israelite population, cf. E. Neufeld, *op. cit.* (see above, n. 18), 37 ff.

36 It seems that the translation of *mišmāʿat* is misleading. The explanation of the term *mišmāʿat* as meaning the special obligations of towns and estates belonging to the king may become clearer from the following passages on the Mesha Stone: "And I rebuilt Bezer, for it was in ruins, with fifty men of Dibon, because all Dibon is *mišmāʿat* to me" (lines 27–28). The emphasis on the link between Mesha and Dibon as the king's estate (Mazar, "Mesha," *Enc. Miqr.* IV, col. 923) shows that the city was reconstructed by the special labor service of the citizens of the royal city-estate. Cf. II Sam. 23:23; I Chron. 11:25; cf. also I Sam. 22:14; Isa. 11:14.

37 Cf. A. Alt, (*op. cit.*; see above, n. 26), 369.

38 For the above-mentioned functions within the framework of the royal administration of the Kingdom of Mari, see A. Marzal, "The Provincial Governor at Mari: His Title and Appointment," *JNES*, 30 (1971), 186 ff. In documents from the Old Babylonian period the elders are frequently mentioned as performing the functions of royal representatives. Cf. n. 25.

39 For the character of the Monarchy and the political institutions — the basic problems for understanding the Kingdoms of Israel and Judah—see A. Alt, "Das Königtum in den Reichen Israel und Juda," *VT*, 1 (1951), 2 ff.; G. Buccellati, *Cities and Nations of Ancient Syria*, Rome, 1967, pp. 135 ff.; ff.; J. A. Soggin (see above, n. 1), 58 ff.; R. de Vaux (see above, n. 1), *passim*.

40 Concerning the fairly widespread assumption that guilds existed in the ancient East, including Israel, see I. Mendelsohn, "Guilds in Babylonia and Assyria," *JAOS*, 60 (1940), 68 ff.; idem., "Guilds in Ancient Palestine," *BASOR*, 80 (1940), 17 ff. For this phenomenon at a later period, cf. D. B. Weisberg, *Guild Structure and Political Allegiance in Early Achaemenid Mesopotamia*, New Haven and London, 1967.

41 For a different view, see W. F. Albright, "The Reform of Jehoshaphat," *Alexander Marx Jubilee Volume*, New York, 1950, pp. 61 ff.

42 Cf. H. Reviv, "Two Notes to Judges 8:4–17," *Tarbiz*, 38 (1969), 309 ff. (Hebrew). Cf. idem. (see above, n. 22), 262–263.

43 Cf. S. Yeivin, "Families and Factions in the Kingdom of Judah," *Studies in the History of Israel and Its Country*, Tel Aviv–Jerusalem, 1960, 250 ff. (Hebrew); idem. *pᵉqīdūt*, *Enc. Miqr.*, VI, cols. 540 ff.

44 Cf. H. Bardtke, "Die Latifundien in Juda während der zweiten Hälfte des achten Jahrhunderts v. Chr. (zum Verständnis von Jes. 5:8–10), *Homages à A. Dupont-Sommer*, Paris, 1971, pp. 235 ff.

45 For a different approach to the problem, see S. Talmon, "The History of 'Am ha-'āreṣ' in the Kingdom of Judah," *Beth Mikra*, 12 (1957), 57 ff. (Hebrew). For other studies, cf. de Vaux (see above, n. 1), 70 ff. (with bibliography).

This chapter was translated by Batya Rabin

CHAPTER VI

ADMINISTRATION

[1] The Sumerian King List, in *ANET*, p. 256.

[2] That is how this verb ($l^e\check{s}oft\bar{e}n\bar{u}$) is translated in all translations; but what the word really means in this context is "to lead us;" cf. the large number of articles on this subject in *Leshonenu*, 30 (1966), 243 ff.; 32 (1968), 272 ff.; 33 (1969), 3 ff. (Hebrew).

[3] Sh. Yeivin, *IEJ*, 25 (1971), 141 ff.

[4] On the suggestion for reading I Sam. 13:1 as: "[forty]-one years old was Saul when he began to reign, and two [and twenty] years he reigned over Israel" see *IEJ*, 21 (1971), 152.

[5] Undoubtedly a hypochoristicon of the one called elsewhere (cf., e.g., II Sam. 2:8) Ishbaal.

[6] This list seems to belong to the early days of Saul's reign, so that it does not include his youngest son Abinadab (cf. I Sam. 31:2) or his future sons-in-law.

[7] On the genealogy of this family see I Chron. 8:29 ff.; 9:35 ff.; cf. Sh. Yeivin, *Moznayim*, XXXVII/3–4 (1973), 210, and n. 22 (Hebrew).

[8] *Idem, Saul and David*, El Ha'ayin series, No. 15 (1969) (Hebrew).

[9] Sh. Yeivin, "David," *Enc. Miqr.*, II, cols. 629–643.

[10] Thus, e.g., S. Begrich, *ZDMG*, 86 (1933), 10* ff.; *idem, ZAW*, 58 (1940–41), 1 ff.

[11] Whether based on kingship, as in the majority of small Canaanite city-states (cf. Josh. 12), or a local "oligarchy," as, e.g., in the case of the Gibeonite tetrapolis.

[12] Cf. B. Mazar, *BJPES*, 13 (1947), 105 ff.; Sh. Yeivin, in A. Malamat (ed.), *The Kingdoms of Israel and Judah*, Jerusalem, 1961, pp. 47 ff. (both Hebrew).

[13] The adjective "Canaanite" is used here for the sake of convenience, without any definite ethnic linguistic connotations. It merely designates the pre-Israelite population of Canaan as a whole.

[14] Sh. Yeivin, "David," *Enc. Miqr.*, II, cols. 629–643.

[15] I Chron. 11:39–41, 46. It is true that most of these joined him when he was still an outlawed chief of a "marauding" unit.

[16] For a more detailed exposition, see Sh. Yeivin, *Did Jeroboam Intend to Overthrow the Davidides?* (to be published shortly).

[17] Cf. W. F. Albright, *BASOR*, 86 (1942), 28 ff.

[18] *Idem, ibid.*, 92 (1943), 21 ff.

[19] U. M. D. Cassuto, "Gezer, the Gezer Calender," *Enc. Miqr.*, II, cols. 471–474.

[20] On the names Meremoth ($mrmwt$), Korah (qrh), Keros ($hqrsy$), and Pashhur ($p\check{s}hr$) see now Y. Aharoni, *Arad Inscriptions*, Jerusalem 1975, 37–38, 82, 87–88 (Hebrew).

[21] On the proper interpretation of this term (q^ezoth) see Sh. Yeivin, *Korngrün Memorial Volume*, Tel Aviv, 1964, p. 84 (Hebrew).

[22] It is possible that this name indicates the man's affiliation, namely *Ben* (= son, in this case member of the family of) *Deker*, known since the days of King Solomon (cf. I Kings 4:9). This phenomenon of "sons of no name" (= no tribal notables) is blatantly contrary to the way of mentioning the Judahite officers of higher grades (cf. e.g., II Kings 18:18; 22:3, and several other examples); see also below, pp. 160, 163.

[23] About patronymics as a sign of noble descent (in tribal connections), or the omission of such as an indication of a "son of no name" (= the son of a "nobody"), of no "noble" descent, see Sh. Yeivin, *loc. cit.* (above, n. 12), p. 53; B. Z. Dinur, *Zion*, 35 (1970), p. 23 (Hebrew).

[24] Jerusalem had been "the town of the Jebusites" (cf. Judg. 19:12). Theoretically, it was considered tribal patrimony, with two claimants: Judah (Josh. 15:8, 63) and

Benjamin (Judg. 1:29). The later sages tried to accomplish a compromise between the contradictory traditions (*Bab. Yoma* 12, p. 2, and parallel texts); this was based on *Deut.* 33:12, Sh. Yeivin, "Benjamin," *Enc. Miqr.*, II, col. 277.

25 Thus the MT; the Targum reads here: *'Asheri* (i.e. the tribal allotment of Asher). It seems, however, much more plausible to read here with the Peshitta: *Geshuri* (i.e. the territory of Geshur), for this way the geographic contiguity is not disturbed (in the record): first Transjordania is enumerated (where his capital lay); Gilead and Geshur; then follow the Cisjordanian areas; furthermore, tribal areas are preceded by the preposition *'al* (= on, over), while geographic regions are preceded by the preposition *'el* (= to, over), as is the case (so also: Gilead, Jezreel).

26 Above, n. 14.

27 For details see Sh. Yeivin in A. Malamat (ed.), *op. cit.* (above, n. 12), pp. 51 ff.; 61 ff.; the idea, in general, had already been suggested by B. Mazar, "Eretz Israel," *Enc. Miqr.*, I, col. 709; cf. also the following note.

28 In Hebrew it includes the western part, commonly known in English as Esdraelon or (plain of) Megiddo.

29 Cf. Sh. Yeivin, *The Israelite Conquest of Canaan*, Leiden, 1971, pp. 115–116; on the extension of this province westwards, probably under Solomon, see B. Mazar, *IEJ*, 10 (1960), 65 f.

30 Possibly because it was really a pre-Israelite separate territorial unit; cf. *Proceedings of the 22nd International Congress of Orientalists*, II, Leiden, 1951, pp. 590–591; a similar case of a territorial unit dating to pre-Israelite times may have been the basis for the formation of the fifth province, cf. *ibid.*, pp. 595–597; for to be taken into account here was the integration of several Canaanite enclaves. It is also possible that the fourth province was really nothing but the old pre-Israelite state of Dor (of the *ṯkr/l*).

31 See above, n. 27.

32 There were several Canaanite city-states within the general region of the allotment of Asher and Zebulun (cf. Judg. 1:30–36), while Naphtali's tribal allotment comprised not only old Canaanite city-states, but included also the northern territory of Dan and the northern Canaanite city-states then recently conquered by David, to wit, Ijon and Abel-beth-maachah (previously Aramean; cf. the emphatic statement of "the wise woman" [II Sam. 20:19]).

33 On the suggestion that the number of Solomon's provinces had been thirteen, see above, n. 27.

34 On the details see Sh. Yeivin, *loc. cit.* (above, n. 21), p. 85, and n. 82 there (Hebrew); and the article cited in n. 16.

35 See Sh. Yeivin, *loc. cit.* (above, n. 34); Y, Aharoni, *The Land of the Bible*, London, 1967, 292.

36 Cf. II Chron. 11:6–10; it should be noted that Benjamin's allotment is not represented here; possibly because the northern boundary of the kingdom had not been stabilized by that time and therefore could not be fortified; but see below.

37 Thus, *Enc. Miqr.*, III, "Joshua, chapters 13–21" cols. 558–564; Y. Aharoni, *op. cit.*, pp. 297 ff.; but Z. Kallai, *The Tribes of Israel*, Jerusalem, 1967, pp. 254 ff. (Hebrew) attributes this list to the days of Hezekiah (cf. below, n. 40). At first this document had been attributed by A. Alt to the days of king Josiah (*Kleine Schriften*, II, op. 276 ff., first published in *PJB*, 21 [1925], 100 ff.); this view had already been disproved by Sh. Zemirin, *Josia and His Period*, Jerusalem, 1951, pp. 91 ff. (Hebrew).

38 Vv. 45–47 are an obvious interpolation (see preceding note), which hints at two conclusions: (a) the area included had been annexed to Judah; and (b) it had been turned into a royal domain and not made a separate province (cf. Sh. Yeivin, *R. Mahler Jubilee Volume*, Merhavia, 1974, pp. 1–28).

39 See, e.g., R. Kittel, *Biblia Hebraica*[3]; *ad loc.*

40   It seems that this fact also militates against the dating of the list of Josh. 15 to a period posterior to the days of king Uzziah; cf. above, references in n. 43.

41   B. Maisler (Mazar), *JPOS*, 21 (1948), 117 ff.

42   Detailed description of the ostraca in G. A. Reisner, C. S. Fisher and D. G. Lyon, *Harvard Excavations at Samaria*, Cambridge (Mass.), 1924, I: pp. 227–242.

43   Y. Yadin, *BASOR*, 163 (1961), 6 ff.

44   Sh. Yeivin, *The First Preliminary Report on the Excavations at Tel "Gat,"* Jerusalem, 1961, pp. 10–11 (of the English text).

45   H. L. Ginsberg, *BASOR*, 109 (1948), 20 ff.; for a full discussion of the problem of these impressions, see Y. Aharoni, *op. cit.* (above, n. 35), pp. 315–327, where also extensive bibliography (in notes).

46   Sh. Yeivin, *JEA*, 36 (1950), 51.

47   *Idem, BiOr*, 19 (1962), 6 ff.; *D. Ben Gurion Jubilee Volume*, Jerusalem, 1964, p. 380, 389, 399 (Hebrew).

48   Sh. Yeivin, *loc. cit.* (above, n. 12), pp. 53–54.

49   *Ibid.*, pp. 58 ff.

50   The genealogical chain is fragmentary here, and the intended one is probably to be restored as "Azariah ⟨the son of Ahimaz⟩ the son of Zadok;" there are similar examples in the Bible, such as the genealogy of Jehu, to which R. David Kimhi refers in his commentary on Kings.

51   In Kings 4:4 the two priests Zadok and Ebiathar are listed; this seems, however, to be an addition to the original record of the royal suite. Some of the traditional medieval commentators have already noted the fact; see the commentaries of R. Yesha'ayahu and R. David Kimhi, *ad loc.*

52   For details of the names cf. B. Maisler (Mazar), *BJPES* 13 (1947), 105 ff.; and Part I, chapter V.

53   Cf. Sh. Yeivin, *Meḥqārim beṭōleḏōt Yisra'el ve arṣō* (henceforth *Meḥqārim*), Tel-Aviv, 1960, pp. 250 ff. (Hebrew).

54   Thus the AV; the Chicago version translates slightly differently; but the MT reads " . . . to the officers of [= *sārēi*] Jezreel the elders [i.e., of the tribes, heads of the families] and those who bring up Ahab" (viz. Ahab and his family).

55   Sh. Yeivin, *Meḥqārim*, pp. 274 ff.

56   See, e.g., R. de Vaux, *Ancient Israel, Its Life and Institutions*, London, 1961, p. 132.

57   See, e.g., *idem, op. cit.*, p. 196, though there is no evidence for such an interpretation.

58   Septuagint: ὑπομνηματογράφος, ἐπὶ τῶν ὑπομνημάτων; Targum Jonathan: *mmn' 'l dkrny'*; Syriac Version: *m'hdn'*

59   R. de Vaux, *Ancient Israel*, p. 131.

60   Their names, Elihoreph and Ahiah, still reflect the ethnic mixture of their time; cf. *Enc. Miqr.*, I, 1950, s. v. Elihoreph.

61   Diringer, *Iscrizioni*, pp. 234–235, pl. XXI; *peqīḏūt*. cf. Sh. Yeivin, *Enc. Miqr.*, VI.

62   There is little doubt that this is the correct version, and not as in II Kings 25:19.

63   About the linguistics of the Hebrew terminology used here, see P. Arzi, in B. Z. Lurie (ed.) *Studies in the Books of Kings* (to appear shortly; Hebrew).

64   There, Shishak I (945–924 B.C.E.) meanwhile overthrew the last Pharaoh of the 21st dynasty, who had been Solomon's ally.

65   A literal translation; the AV translates: " . . . them that were near the king's person," while the Chicago version reads: " . . . the personal companions of the king;" the meaning is similar in all cases.

66   Cf. the similar standing of the *major domus* in Frankish France.

67   R. de Vaux, *RB*, 45 (1936), 96 ff.

68   Sh. Yeivin, *Meḥqārim*, p. 290, and the attached table.

69   The title, leader (= *nāgīd*) for the king, is still in use during the reign of Hezekiah (II Kings 20:5).

70   On their peculiar onomastic and gentilic association, see Sh. Yeivin, *op. cit.* (above, n. 29), pp. 19; 20; 72; 158 ff.; 226 ff.

71 Sh. Yeivin, "Joseph, the House of Joseph, the Tribe of Joseph." Cf. *Enc. Mirq.*, III.

72 The southern tribes, namely Judah and Simon, are not mentioned at all, as also Levi (cf. *op. cit.* [above, n. 33], pp. 133 ff.; 182 ff.); only the tribes settled in central and northern Cisjordania, as well as those of Transjordania, are enumerated.

73 True enough that the mention of Gaddites in the list of those who joined David before he became king (I Chron. 13:9–11) is rather difficult to square with such an assumption; however, the date of the composition of this list is still problematical.

74 In Transjordania; J. Weitz, *BJPES*, 6 (1939), 132 ff. (Hebrew).

75 B. Mazar, "Ahithophel." *Enc. Miqr.*, I, cols. 226–227.

76 If indeed one should read here invertedly: Benaiah the son of Jehoiada, as recorded in two versions of the MT, a version accepted by the majority of modern commentators; but even the ordinary MT version which omits Benaiahu and records here the name of his father(?) is not improbable (cf. II Sam. 23:20).

77 The mention of Abiathar alone points, too, to the early date of this list (in the reign of David).

78 For details, see Sh. Yeivin, *loc. cit.* (above, n. 12), pp. 62–3.

79 Sh. Yeivin, *p^eqīdūt*, *Enc. Miqr.*, VI, col. 552–553.

80 Sh. Yeivin, "son of the king," *Enc. Miqr.*, II, col. 160.

81 A. Gardiner, *Egypt of the Pharaohs*, Oxford, 1961, pp. 169–170.

82 A. F. Rainey, *Leshonenu*, 32 (1969), 304 ff.; cf. N. Avigad, *Eretz-Israel*, 9 (1969), p. 9, n. 78 (both Hebrew).

83 D. Diringer, *Iscrizioni*, pp. 232–233, pl. XXI, 9; probably of the eighth century B.C.E.

84 *Ibid.*, p. 341, pl. XIV, 12; probably of the beginning of the seventh century B.C.E.

85 N. Avigad, *IEJ*, 13 (1963), 133 ff., pl. 18, c.; of the first half of the eighth century

B.C.E.; see *Enc. Miqr.*, VI, 1971, col. s.v. *p^eqi-dūt*, h.

86 N. Avigad, *Eretz-Israel*, 9 (1969), 9, pl. II, 21, of the end of the seventh century B.C.E., (the owners of the last two seals actually bear names of known kings of Judah, see n. 85).

87 Diringer, *Iscrizioni*, pp. 126–127, pl. XIV, 11; Y. Aharoni, *Excavations at Ramat Raḥel, 1961 and 1962*, Roma, 1964, p. 33, pl. 40, 4.

88 This is a literal translation; the AV reads: "them that were in the king's presence;" the Chicago translation is: " . . . the personal companions of the king;" see below.

89 R. de Vaux, *Ancient Israel*, pp. 120–121.

90 For details, see Sh. Yeivin, *Eretz-Israel*, 7 (1969), 10–14 (Hebrew, with English summary, pp. ★165–★166).

91 N. Avigad, *IEJ*, 16 (1966), 50 ff., pl. 4, c.

92 Sh. Yeivin, *Memorial Volume for Benjamin de Vries*, Jerusalem, 1969, pp. 305 ff. (Hebrew).

93 See, e.g., N. Slouschz, *Thesaurus Inscriptorium Phoenicarum*, Jerusalem, 1942, pp. 2 ff. (Hebrew).

94 J. Naveh, *IEJ*, 12 (1962), 29 ff., pl. 6, A, C.

95 See now Sh. Yeivin, *Bulletin of the Museum Haaretz*, 14 (1972), Tel Aviv, pp. 84 ff., fig. 4 (on p. 95; English section).

96 Diringer, *Iscrizioni*, p. 231, pl. XXI, 8; p. 230, pl. XXI, 7; p. 229, pl. XXI, 6.

97 *Ibid.*, pp. 224–228, pl. XXI, 5.

98 Sh. Yeivin, *Eretz-Israel*, 6 (1960), 47 ff. (Hebrew); *idem*, *JNES*, 19 (1960), 205 ff.

99 Diringer, *Iscrizioni*, pp. 221–222, pl. XXI, 2.

100 *Ibid.*, pp. 223–224, pl. XXI, 4.

101 Moscati, *EEA*, p. 59 (no. 21), pl. XII, 9.

102 A. Reifenberg, *Ancient Hebrew Seals*, London, 1950, fig. 35 (on p. 42); G. R. Driver, *ADAJ*, 2 (1953), pl. VIII.

103 Diringer, *op. cit.*, pp. 233–234, pl. XXI, 10.

104 M. A. Levy, *Siegel und Gemmen*, Breslau, 1869, pp. 23–24, pl. II, 3.

105 E.g., R. de Vaux, *Ancient Israel*, pp. 129–131.

106 See now Sh. Yeivin, *Leshonenu*, 38 (1973), 33–37 (Hebrew).

CHAPTER VII

TRADE AND COMMERCE

1 Ex. 21:35–37; Lev. 19:35–36; Deut. 25:13–16; II Kings 4:7; 7:1; Hos. 12:8; Amos 8:4–6; Micah 6:10–12; Isa. 55:1–2; Prov. 31:24; Neh. 13:15–16.

2 When Amos condemned some residents of Samaria for oppressing their poorer countrymen by exploiting their affliction and tampering with the measures used in the sale of agricultural produce to the poor (Amos 8:4–6), it is possible that the reference is to the merchants, as is suggested by some commentators (J. L. Mays, *Amos*, London, 1969, pp. 142–145; H. W. Wolff, *Joel und Amos*, Neukirchen, 1969, pp. 375 ff.) It is possible, however, that Amos is referring to those landowners who acquired title to the holdings of poor farmers who could not make good their debts. What produce now remained to these poor farmers, after payment of rent, was not sufficient for their needs, and so they were forced to buy grain from their oppressors, who thus attempted to make additional profits from the produce which accumulated in their storehouses (see Amos 5:10–12).

The social polarization of the eighth-century northern kingdom is well illustrated by the remains of houses discovered at Tell el-Far'ah (biblical Tirzah). Level II, from the eighth century, contains one neighborhood with well-spaced and well-built houses, alongside of which is another neighborhood full of small houses densely crowded together. In level III (tenth–ninth centuries), in contrast, the styles and sizes of the dwellings are homogeneous. See R. de Vaux, "The Excavations at Tell el-Far'ah and the Site of Ancient Tirzah," *PEQ*, 88 (1956), 134. The eighth century saw the development of social polarization in Judah as well, due to the oppression of small farmers. Isaiah prophesied against "those who join house to house and add field to field" (5:8), and

Micah castigated Judah, "whose rich men are full of violence:" they have "the treasures of wickedness in the house of the wicked, and the scant measure ,that is accursed," they measure with "wicked scales," and in their pockets are "deceitful weights." It is clear that the merchandise and wealth here referred to stemmed from agriculture, for the prophesied punishment is the inability to realize agricultural profits any more: "You shall sow, but not reap; you shall tread olives, but not anoit yourselves with oil; you shall tread grapes, but not drink wine" (Micah 6:10–15).

3 See chapter IX by E. Stern in this volume pp. 240 f.

4 *Ibid.*, pp. 251 f.

5 B. Mazar, Trude Dothan, I. Dunayevsky, "En-gedi: The First and Second Seasons of Excavations, 1961–1963," *'Atiqot* (English series), 5 (1966), 20 ff.

6 E. Stern, *op. cit.*, pp. 249 f.

7 On the chemical tests, see R. B. Kallner (Amiran) and J. Vroman, "Petrographical Examination of Pottery," *BJPES*, 12 (1945/46), 10–15 (Hebrew); G. E. Wright, *BAr*, 12 (1949), 91–92. The chemical composition of the seals from *Mmšt* is different from the others; there is still no reasonable identification of this site. The fact that the composition of the two shards from Socoh is similar to that of the Hebron shard makes it clear that we are dealing with the Socoh in the mountains near Hebron (Josh. 15:48). On the problems related to the identification of the place-names on the *la-melek* seals, see D. Welten, *Die Königs-Stempel*, Wiesbaden, 1969, pp. 147 ff.; Welten's criticism of the conclusions drawn from petro-chemical investigations is not sufficiently substantiated (*ibid.* p. 48, n. 6; p. 130).

8 The name Tubal is derived from Tabal, a kingdom of Asia Minor which was famed

for its metal deposits and brass industry. There are some who claim that Tabal is derived from the Sumerian TIBIRA "metal worker;" see E. Dhorme, "Les peuples issus de Japhet d'après le chapître X de la Genèse," *Syria*, 13 (1932), 37–39.; G. A. Wainwright, "The Coming of Iron," *Antiquity*, 10 (1936), 16 ff.

9 For a parallel practise in Mesopotamian cities, see D. B. Weisberg, *Guild Structure and Political Allegiance in Early Achaemenid Mesopotamia*, New Haven, 1967, p. 93.

10 In Mesopotamia, there was in addition to the *kārum* (port, business district, etc.: see *CAD*, K, pp. 231 ff.), a market, called *maḫīru* (*AHw*, p. 584, s. v. *maḫīru*, 4; W. Röllig, "Der altmesopotamische Markt," *WO*, 8 [1976], 286–295). In Hittite, the term for market is *ḫappira*; see A. Goetze, *Muršilis Sprachlähmung*, København, 1934, p. 72.

11 Prov. 7:8; Cant. 3:2; Eccl. 12:4–5. The Akkadian *sūqu(m)* also has the meaning of street, alley, *AHw*, pp. 1061 ff., and this is also the meaning of *šūqā* in the Aramaic translations of the Bible; cf. J. Levy, *Chaldäisches Wörterbuch über die Targumim*, II, Leipzig, 1868, p. 463. It was only in the talmudic literature that *šūq* took on its modern meaning of market; cf. *idem*, *Wörterbuch über die Talmudim und Midraschim*, IV, Berlin 1924, pp. 523–524; M. Jastrow, *A Dictionary of the Targumim, the Talmud Babli and Yerushalmi, and the Midrashic Literature*, New York, 1903, p. 1541. In contrast to *šūq*, the biblical *reḥōv* referred to a courtyard or square, as in Ugaritic and Aramaic, parallel to the Akkadian *rebītu*; cf. C. Köhler and W. Baumgartner, *Lexicon in Verteris Testamenti Libros*, Leiden, 1953, p. 884; J. Levy, *Chaldäsches Wörterbuch*, II, p. 415; *AHw*, p. 964.

12 The ancient biblical translations also understood it thus: the Septuagint gives ἔξοδες (exodus-exit), and the Aramaic translations usually give *šūqā* (street); see above, n. 11.

13 Y. Yadin, A. Aharoni, I. Dunayevsky, J. Perrot, *Hazor*, I, Jerusalem, 1958, p. 17; II, Jerusalem, 1960, pp. 20, 29.

14 This meaning of *māḥōzīn* was pointed out by B. Mazar, *op. cit.* 1 (above, n. 5), p. 7, n. 22, and by E. Kutscher, "Ugaritica Marginalia," *Lĕšonénu*, 34 (1969/70), 9–10, (Hebrew).

15 E. g. II Kings 7; 1, 18. Transactions involving real estate were also negotiated at the city gate; cf. Gen. 23:10, 18. The city gate served the same purpose in ancient Mesopotamia; see, for example, M. Streck, *Assurbanipal und die letzten assyrischen Könige bis zum Untergang Ninivehs*, Leipzig, 1916, p. 76 col. IX, 49; p. 132 col. VIII, 11–12; p. 376 VAT 5600, col. II, 1–2. These passages refer to the delivery of camels, taken as war booty, as the *bāb maḫiri*, the "market gate;" it is clear that the reference is to one of the city gates.
Cf. L. A. Oppenheim, *Ancient Mesopotamia*, Chicago, 1964, p. 129; *CAD* B, 22, s. v. *bābu*.

16 Zeph. 1:10; II Chron. 33:14; Neh. 3:3; cf. Neh. 13:16.

17 Neh. 3:1, 32; 12:39. A gate of this name was also part of the city of Assur during the ancient kingdom; B. Landsberger-K. Balkan, "Die Inschriften des assyrischen Königs Irišum gefunden in Kültepe 1948," *Belleten*, 14 (1950), 224, and during the new kingdom, *ibid.* 236.

18 Jer. 19:2. In Assur there was also a "gate of the metal workers;" cf. Landsberger-Balkan, *op.cit.*, 236; B. Unger, *RLA*, I, 176, 15.

19 Y. Yadin, "Ancient Judaean Weights and the Date of the Samaria Ostraca," *Scripta Hierosolymitana*, 8 (1961), 9–17. For criticism regarding the reading of ciphers on these weights, see Y. Aharoni, "The Use of Hieratic Numerals in Hebrew Ostraca and the Shekel Weights," *BASOR*, 184 (1966), 13–19. For a description of all the weights and measures, see E. Stern, "Weights and Measures," *Enc. Miqr.*, IV, cols. 846–878.

[20] A. F. Rainey, "Royal Weights and Measures," *BASOR*, 179 (1965), 34–36; P. Welten, *op.cit.* (above, n. 7), pp. 131–133.

[21] On the merchant in the laws of Hammurabi, see the summary and analysis by W. F. Leemans, *The Old Babylonian Merchant*, Leiden, 1950, pp. 22–35. For other codices, see R. Yaron, *The Laws of Eshnuna*, Jerusalem, 1969, p. 26, sec. 15/10; G. R. Driver and J. C. Miles, *The Assyrian Laws*, Oxford, 1935, p. 378, II, R. 2; J. Friedrich, *Die Hethitischen Gesetze*, Leiden, 1959, p. 18, I, § 5.

[22] Samsi-Adad I (1813–1781): A. K. Grayson, *Assyrian Royal Inscriptions*, Wiesbaden, 1972, § 127; Assurbanipal (669–627): E. F. Weidner, "Segensgebet für Assurbanipal," *AfO*, 13 (1939/40), 210–211. For additional examples in royal Mesopotamian inscriptions and for discussion of their meaning, see Grayson, *ibid.*, p.20, n. 64, and Weidner, *ibid.*, p. 211, n. 38.

[23] Jeremiah's words about the Sabbath suggest some laxity in observance during the last generations of the First Temple period. Because Manasseh king of Judah generally conducted his policy to tally with the hegemony of the Assyrian empire, foreign cults intruded themselves and were adopted by the ministers of the kingdom and the courts. (Zeph. 1:5; 8:11; II Kings 21:1–7). This is possibly the reason for the weakening of Sabbath strictness, as expressed in Jeremiah. M. Greenberg, in "The Sabbath Portion of the Book of Jeremiah" *'Iyyunim b^esefer Yirmiahu*, II (Ed. B. Z. Lurie) Jerusalem, 1974, pp. 27–37 (Hebrew), disagrees with most scholars, who believe that these verses emerge from a religious concept that crystallized only at the time of the exile and are therefore not Jeremiah's.

On the origin of the Sabbath and the biblical literature dealing with it, see R. de Vaux, *Ancient Israel*, London, 1961, pp. 475–483; M. Greenberg, "Shabbat," *Enc. Judaica*, XIV, cols. 557–562.

[24] I am grateful to Prof. M. Greenberg for drawing my attention to this suggestion, made by G. A. Smith, *Jerusalem*, II (1877; reprinted by KTAV, New York, 1972).

[25] C. H. Gordon, "Abraham and the Merchants of Ura," *JNES*, 17 (1958), 28–31; *idem*, "Abraham of Ur," *Hebrew and Semitic Studies presented to G. R. Driver*, ed. D. W. Thomas and W. D. Hardy, Oxford, 1963, pp. 77–84; W. F. Albright, "Abraham the Hebrew," *BASOR*, 163 (1961), 44–54.

[26] W. H. F. Saggs, "Ur of the Chaldees; A Problem of Identification," *Iraq*, 22 (1960), 200–209; E. A. Speiser, "The Word $\check{SHR}$ in Genesis and Early Hebrew Movements," *BASOR*, 164 (1961), 23–28; T. L. Thompson; The Historicity of the Patriarchal Narratives," *BZAW*, 133 (1974), 172–186.

[27] B. Landsberger, "Akkadisch-Hebräische Wortgleichungen," *VTS*, 16 (1967) 189–190.

[28] Also Deut. 1:19 *contra* 8:15.

[29] The prophecy in Ezek. 17:1–10 deals with the fate of those exiled with Jehoiachin; cf. W. Zimmerli, *Ezechiel*, Neukirchen, 1969, p. 380. In 16:29 as well, Ezekiel identifies the land of Canaan with the land of the Chaldeans; cf. *ibid.*, p. 338.

[30] B. Maisler (Mazar), "Canaan and the Canaanites," *BASOR*, 102 (1946), 10.

[31] M. Haran, *Ages and Institutions in the Bible*, Tel Aviv, 1972, pp. 201 ff., esp. 218–226 (Hebrew); B. Levine, "The Nethinim," *JBL*, 82 (1963), 207–217; P. Weinberg, "N^etinim und Söhne der Sklaven Salomons im 6.–4. Yh. v.u.Z.," *ZAW*, 87 (1975), 355–371 (esp. 360–363).

[32] For example Landsberger, *op.cit.*, p. 187.

[33] Cf. F. Brown, S. R. Driver, C. A. Briggs, *A Hebrew and English Lexicon of the Old Testament*, Oxford, 1962, p. 1064; J. Gray, *I and II Kings*, London, 1964, p. 246.

[34] J. A. Knudtzon, *Die El-Amarna Tafeln*, Leipzig, 1915, 39:10–14.

[35] The term *roklim* in Ezek. 27 (vv. 13, 15, 17, 20, 22–24) appears in parallelism with *sōḥārīm* (Ezek. 27:12, 28, 21). For this reason, there does not seem to be force

to Landsberger's theory (see above, n. 30) that Solomon's *roklīm* were small-time merchants, as opposed to the *ta(ggā)rīm* who handled international commerce.

36 A similar historiographic tendency apparently lies behind Ezekiel's prophecy about Tyre (chap. 27). This prophecy is based upon an early Tyrian composition and, as in I Kings 10, the main theme is the glorification of the ruler through a detailed account of the various types of merchandise which were sent to his storehouses from lands near and far. (On the early Phoenician origin of Ezek. 27, see B. Mazar, "The Philistines and the Rise of Israel and Tyre," *Proceedings of the Israel Academy of Sciences and Humanities*, Vol. 1., No. 7, Jerusalem, 1964, p. 21. Mazar's conclusion was also accepted by Zimmerli, *op.cit.* (above, n. 28), 661; and in detailed treatment, M. Elat, *Economic Relations in the Lands of the Bible* (c. 1000–539), Jerusalem, 1977, pp. 153–159 (Hebrew).

37 In the period of the Israelite monarchy, see my book (*op. cit.*), pp. 99–102, and in Hellenistic and Roman times, see G. W. van Beek, "Frankincense and Myrrh," *BAr*, 23 (1960), 70 ff. These shrubs also grew in eastern Africa; see F. N. Herper, "Arabian and African Frankincense Trees," *JEA*, 55 (1969), 66 ff.

38 D. O. Edzard, "Die Beziehungen Babyloniens und "Ägyptens in der mittelbabylonischen Zeit und das Gold," *JESHO*, 3 (1960), 47–55.

39 In letters to kings of equal status: *Die El-Amarna Tafeln*, (see above, n. 33), 6:13–17; 7:33–36; 61–65; 16:32–35; 19:66–69; 37:8–18; 41:36–42. In letters sent by vassals to Pharaoh: *ibid.*, 43:29; 44:25–29. The Akkadian verb used for *hfs* in these letters is usually *ḫašāḫu*, occasionally *erēšu*; both verbs have the same meaning, since a scribe would even use them both in the same formula (19:68–69).

40 The geographic and political identification of the Queen of Sheba is very difficult. The biblical account portrays her as a great and sovereign ruler; for this reason, some scholars have held that she was a queen of the kingdom of Sheba southern Arabia. (See W. Phillips, *Qataban and Sheba*, London, 1955, pp. 104–110; W. F. Albright, "Was the Age of Solomon Without Monumental Art?", *Eretz-Israel*, 5 [1958], *7–*9). But no queens are mentioned in inscriptions from southern Arabia. Assyrian inscriptions, on the other hand, refer to queens among the Arabian tribes of the *northern* Syrian-Arabian desert; see N. Abbot, "Pre-Islamic Arab Queens," *AJSL*, 58 (1964), 1–22; R. Borger, "Assyriologische und altarabische Miszellen," *Orientalia*, N. S. 26 (1957), 8–11. For this reason, some believe that the queen of Sheba who visited Solomon was the ruler of one of the Sabaean tribes which brought merchandise from southern Arabia to the lands of the Fertile Crescent; this tribe may have settled in the oases of the northern peninsula. In the genealogy of Qeturah (Gen. 25:1–4), Sheba is listed with Dedan, Midian, and Ephah, which were tribes in the northern Arabian desert.

41 I Kings 9:26–28; 10:11, 22; II Chron. 8:17–18; 9:10, 21. The lastmentioned verse has Tarshish instead of Ophir, but this is merely a scribal error; the merchandise brought in that voyage was typical of Ophir. "Tarshish ships" were large and very strong Phoenician ships, according to R. D. Barnett, "Early shipping in the Near East," *Antiquity*, 32 (1958), 226 ff. Albright, on the other hand, thought that these were Phoenician ships built especially for the transport of metals (W. F. Albright, "The Role of the Canaanites in the History of Civilisation," *The Bible and the Ancient Near East, Essays in Honor of W. F. Albright* [ed. G. E. Wright], New York, 1961, p. 462). Also see J. Braslavy, "The Tarshish Ships, Ezion-geber, and the Ophir Sailings," in *Elath*, The 18th Archaeological Convention, Israel Exploration Society, Jerusalem, 1963, pp. 36–37 (Hebrew).

42 The Assyrians also forced the Sidonians

to build and launch for them ships when they wanted to set sail in the Persian Gulf; cf. D. D. Luckenbill, *The Annals of Sennacherib*, Chicago, 1924, p. 73:56–71; 86:23–24; *ABL*, 795, rev. 11–12; Diodorus II, xvi, 6–7.

43   B. Maisler (Mazar), *op. cit.*, above, n. 29.

44   See G. W. van Beek, "Ophir," *The Interpreter's Dictionary of the Bible*, III, New York, 1962, pp. 605–606; C. Rabin, "The Song of Songs and Tamil Poetry," *Studies in Religion*, 3 (1973/4), 205–209.

45   The reading in Chronicles is *'algumīm*, but this is merely a letter reversal. The *'almōg* is identical with the *elammaku* tree, which, according to cuneiform sources, grew in Syria. See H. Zimmern, *Wort- und Sachregister zu akkadische Fremdwörter als Beweis für babylonischen Kultureinfluss*, Leipzig, 1917, p. 215; J. Greenfield–N. Mayerhofer, "The Almuggim/Algummin Problem Reexamined," *VTS*, 16 (1967), 83.

46   H. von Wissmann, in O. Baumhauser (ed.), *Arabien, Dokumente zur Entdeckungsgeschichte*, I, Stuttgart, 1965, pp. 19–31.

47   J. H. Breasted, *Ancient Records of Egypt*, Chicago, 1906–1907, I, §161, 429; II, §265, 274, 276, 277, 321, 486; IV, §130, 407, 429.

48   For recent opinions on the location of Punt, see W. v. Bissing, "Pyene (Punt) und die Seefahrten der Ägypter," *WO*, 1 (1947/52), 146 ff.; M. Elliot, "Pount-Pwâne, l'Opôné de la géographie Ptolémée," *Revue d'Egyptologie*, 9 (1951), 1–7; W. L. Smith, "The Land of Punt," *Journal of the American Research Center in Egypt*, 1 (1962), 59 ff.; K. A. Kitchen, "Punt and How to Get There," *Orientalia*, N.S. 40 (1971), 188 ff.

49   Breasted, *op. cit.*, II, §255.

50   *Die El-Amarna Tafeln* (see above, n. 33), 8:14–15, 31–33; 34:39–54; 39:10 ff.; 40:16 ff., 34, 39 ff. See especially the description of the activities of Wenamun, who was sent by his king to purchase trees in Byblos: J. A. Wilson in *ANET*, 25–28. Cf. W. Helck, *Die Beziehungen Ägyptens zu Vorderasien im 3. und 2. Jahrtausend v. Chr.*, Wiesbaden, 1962, pp. 461–462; A. F. Rainey, "Business Agents at Ugarit," *IEJ*, 13 (1963), 314–316; Y. Lynn Holmes, "The Messengers of the Amarna Letters," *JAOS*, 95 (1975), 379–381.

51   N. Glueck, "Exploration in Eastern Palestine, II," *AASOR*, 15 (1935), 41–51; B. Rothenberg, *Illustrated London News*, 255 (1969), No. 6798, 32 ff.; No. 6800; 28 ff.; *idem*, *Timna Valley of the Biblical Copper Mines*, London, 1972, pp. 112–114; 127–129.

52   B. Maisler (Mazar), "The Excavations at Tell Qasile," *IEJ*, 1 (1950/51), 209 ff.; pl. 38A; *idem*, "Two Hebrew Ostraca from Tell Qasile," *JNES*, 10 (1951), 265–267.

53   See I Kings 9:28; 10:12, 14–15, and the parallel verses in Chronicles.

54   T. Save-Söderbergh, *Ägypten und Nubien*, Lund, 1941, pp. 86–89, 210 ff.; J. Vercoutter, "The Gold of Kush," *Kush*, 7 (1959), 120 ff.; R. J. Forbes, *Studies in Ancient Technology*, 8, Leiden, 1964, pp. 157–161.

55   *Die El Amarna Tafeln* (see above, n. 33), 3:13–22; 4:36–50; 7:64–72; 10:12–21; 14; 16:14; 19:34–70, esp. 61; 20:51–55, 71; 26:41–42; 27:21–31, 41–44, 50, 104–109, esp. 106; 29:34–42, 49–53, 136–165, esp. 146, 164; 31:30–31; 44:25–28.

56   F. C. Fensham, "The Treaty Between the Israelites and the Tyrians," *VTS*, 17 (1968), 71 ff.; according to Fensham, Hiram made a political treaty with David and Solomon.

57   For the background of the development of this tradition, see S. D. Waterhouse, "The Land of Milk and Honey," *Andrews University Seminary Studies*, 1 (1963), 161 ff.; F. C. Fensham, "An Ancient Tradition of the Fertility of Palestine," *PEQ*, 98 (1966), 166–168.

58   C. H. W. Johns, *Assyrian Deeds and Documents*, Cambridge, 1898, No. 148; J. Köhler and A. Ungnad, *Assyrische Rechtsurkunden*, Leipzig, 1913, No. 325. About the identification of the country named *Ya-ú-di* in this document, see H. Tadmor, "Azriyau of Yaudi," *Scripta Hierosolymitana*, 8 (1961), 236–239, esp. n. 13, and E. Lipiński, "Deux marchands de blé phéniciens

à Ninive," *Rivista di Studi Fenici*, 3 (1975), 1–6.

59 Z. Kallai, *The Tribes of Israel*, Jerusalem, 1967, p. 253 (Hebrew).

60 Egypt was particularly interested in trees from Lebanon, and paid high prices for them. As testimony for this, we have both the Wenamun letter and a document from the period of the declining middle kingdom; according to the letter, the Egyptians were no longer able to purchase these trees. See W. F. Albright, "Further Light on the History of the Middle Bronze Byblos," *BASOR*, 179 (1965), 41. An administrative document from the third quarter of the eighth century B.C.E. testifies that the kingdom of Tyre exported Lebanese trees to Egypt ND 2715, lines 1–29. H. W. F. Saggs, *Iraq*, 17 (1955), pl. XXX, p. 127; J. N. Postgate, *Taxation and Conscription in the Assyrian Empire*, Rome, 1974, pp. 390–391.

61 I Kings 9:11–13. On the sale of villages, both by kings and by private individuals, in Alalakh, see D. J. Wiseman, *The Alalakh Tablets*, London, 1953, No. 1, pp. 52–58; *idem*, "Abban and Alalakh," *JCS*, 12 (1958), 124–129; F. C. Fensham, "The Treaty between Solomon and Hiram and the Alalakh Tablets," *JBL*, 89 (1960), 59–60.

62 See Y. Aharoni, "Mount Carmel as Border," in *Archäologie und Altes Testament, Festschrift für K. Galling*, (ed. A. Kuschke – E. Kutsch), Tübingen, 1970, pp. 1–7.

63 So understood by most commentators; cf. A. Sanda, *Die Bücher der Könige*, I, Münster i. Westf., 1911, pp. 292–295; J. I. Montgomery, *The Book of Kings*, Edinburgh, 1951, pp. 226–228; J. Gray, *I & II Kings*, London, 1964, pp. 250–251; M. Noth, *Könige* I, Neukirchen, 1968, pp. 205, 234–237. For arguments supporting this opinion and a bibliography on the Muṣri problem, see Elat, *op. cit.* (above, n. 35), pp. 198–201.

64 For quotations of these inscriptions and documents, see Elat, *op. cit.*, pp. 73–81.

65 G. Davies and R. O. Faulkner, "A Syrian Trading Venture to Egypt," *JEA*, 33 (1947), 44–46, pl. 8.

66 A. Evans, *The Palace of Minos at Knossos*, IV/2, New York, 1964, p. 827. fig. 805.

67 *ABL* 336: 5–7: an official informs Esarhaddon that emissaries of the ruler of Bit-Dakūri (a Chaldean kingdom in southern Babylonia) have asked to buy horses.

68 L. W. King, *Babylonian Boundary Stones and Memorial Tablets*, London, 1912, vii, 39, 15–16.

69 Some have understood this verse as spoken entirely by Ben Hadad, reflecting his own actions only. A. Jepsen, "Berith," *W. Rudolph Festschrift*, Tübingen, 1961, pp. 164 ff.; Y. Van der Woude, "I Reg. 20, 34," *ZAW*, 76 (1964), 188 ff.; see Driver's analysis, which convincingly disproves their thesis: G. R. Driver, "Forgotten Hebrew Idioms," *ZAW*, 78 (1966), 1 ff.

70 See above, p. 175. It is possible that in other biblical passages as well the word *ḥuṣōt* has a double meaning: streets—market; Mazar believes that the *ḥuṣōt* of Ashkelon mentioned in David's lament (II Sam. 1:20) were the bazaars of that city (above, n. 33), *op. cit.*, p. 5. Similarly, when Ezekiel prophesies against Tyre, warning that Nebuchadnezzar would "trample all your streets [*ḥuṣōteḵā*]. . . make a spoil of your riches and a prey of your merchandise and break down your walls" (26:11–12), it is possible that the "merchandise" referred to was regularly exchanged in the city's *ḥuṣōt*.

71 To appoint to a position: Gen. 45:9; Ex. 2:14; I. Sam. 8:12; II Sam. 8:14, etc. To set up, establish: Jer. 49:38, and in a parallel meaning in religious contexts: I Kings 12:29; II Kings 21:7; II Chron. 33:7, etc. To impose a legal or political obligation: II Kings 18:14; Est. 10:1, and in a parallel legal-religious sense (e.g., "to set up a law for Israel"): Gen. 47:26; Ex. 15:25; Deut. 4:44, etc.).

72 For a summary of the status of this institution in this period in Cappadocia, see P. Garelli, *Les Assyriens en Cappadoce*, Paris, 1963, pp. 171–230; L. L. Orlin, *As-*

syrian Colonies in Cappadocia, The Hague – Paris, 1970, pp. 139–183, esp. pp. 169, 183; M. T. Larsen, "The Old Assyrian Colonies in Anatolia," *JAOS*, 94 (1974), 468–475; in Babylonia: W. F. Leemans, *Foreign Trade in the Old Babylonian Period*, Leiden, 1960, pp. 74, 88, 108, 135.

73 For a comparison of the *ḫūṣōt* with the status of the merchants from Ura, see C. H. Gordon, *op. cit.* (above, n. 24), p. 29, n. 4; on the legal status of those merchants in Ugarit, see W. H. F. Saggs, *op. cit.* (above, n. 25), pp. 202–205; R. Yaron, "Foreign Merchants in Ugarit," *Israel Law Review*, 4 (1969), 70–78.

74 For this meaning of *kāru* in this document, see *CAD* K, p. 232 b, §1, c. H. Hirschberg claims that the document originates from the end of Esarhaddon's reign: *Studien zur Geschichte Esarhaddons, Königs von Assyrien* (681–669), Ohlau in Schlesien, 1932, p. 64, and his arguments are convincing against those of B. Meissner, who ascribes the document to the beginning of Assurbanipal's reign: "Jakinlu von Arpad," *OLZ*, 17 (1914), 422 ff.

75 The cooperation between Israel and Tyre in the building of a fleet is defined by a word stemming from the root *ḥbr*, which refers to cooperation in an economic endeavor; see B. Mazar, *op. cit.* (above, n. 29; above, n. 33), p. 3.

76 G. A. Reisner, C. S. Fischer, D. C. Lyon, *Harvard Excavation at Samaria*, Cambridge, Mass., 1926, I, p. 247; II, pl. 58.

77 Josephus, *Against Apion*, 1, 60.

CHAPTER VIII
THE ARCHAEOLOGICAL SOURCES FOR THE PERIOD OF THE MONARCHY

[1] A. Biran, *IEJ*, 20 (1970), 118; *ibid.*, 22 (1972), 165; *ibid.*, 24 (1974), 262 ff.; *BAr*, 37 (1974), 27 ff.

[2] *IEJ*, 16 (1966), 145; *ibid.*, 19 (1969), 239.

[3] *IEJ*, 22 (1972), 165.

[4] *IEJ*, 19 (1969), 239.

[5] Y. Yadin, *Hazor*, Schweich Lectures, London, 1972 (henceforth Yadin, *Hazor*).

[6] In addition to the entry "Megiddo" in the *Encyclopaedia of Archaeological Excavations*, II, pp. 474–495 (English), and bibliography there, see *IEJ*, 22 (1972), 161 ff., and also Yadin, *Hazor*, pp. 150 ff.

[7] See Y. Aharoni, *Eretz-Israel*, 10 (1971), 53 ff. (Hebrew); *idem, JNES*, 31 (1972), 302 ff.

[8] *AASOR*, 21–22 (1943), 29 ff.; *BASOR*, 155 (1959), 14.

[9] Y. Aharoni, *BASOR*, 154 (1959), 35 ff.

[10] Aharoni later changed his mind and accepted Pritchard's opinion that those buildings were not stables but storehouses. Thus he himself destroyed the basis for his assumption. See below.

[11] On this problem, see Y. Shiloh, *IEJ*, 20 (1970), 184 ff., and especially Figs. 3, 4.

[12] On a similar suggestion to explain the plan of palace 1723, see D. Ussishkin, *IEJ*, 16 (1966), 174 ff.

[13] *BASOR*, 124 (1951), 21 ff. (following Albright's first suggestion).

[14] The attempt made lately to ignore this stratigraphical fact (*Eretz-Israel*, 10, above, n. 7) or to attribute the palace and its casemates to a second phase of stratum VB (*JNES*, 31 [1972], 307) absolutely contradicts the stratigraphical facts. See Y. Yadin, *JNES*, 32 (1973), 330.

[15] On the various possibilities of explaining the situation, see, for the time being, Yadin, *Hazor*, p. 160.

[16] N. Avigad, *Encyclopaedia of Archaeological Excavations*, II, pp. 527 ff. (Hebrew).

[17] *Ibid.*, p. 530.

[18] *Ibid.*, p. 531.

[19] *Eretz Shomron*, the 30th Archaeological Convention of the Israel Exploration Society Jerusalem, 1973, pp. 52 ff. (Hebrew). See also my article in the *Kathleen Kenyon Festschrift*, London (1977).

[20] See R. de Vaux, *Encyclopaedia of Archaeological Excavations*, II, pp. 395 ff. (Hebrew), and bibliography there; also *idem*, in *Archaeology and Old Testament Study* (ed. D. Winton Thomas), Oxford, 1967, pp. 371 ff.

[21] On the plan of this town and the incorporation of the four-room buildings into the line of fortifications, see Y. Shiloh, *IEJ*, 20 (1970), Fig. 5. An important proof for the existence of this wall in the area of the gates can be found in the walls C—C shown in *Tell en-Naṣbeh*, I, Fig. 57.

[22] See the article by G. E. Wright in the *Encyclopaedia of Archaeological Excavations* I, pp. 248 ff. (English), and bibliography there.

[23] For a similar phenomenon at Gezer during Solomon's reign, see below.

[24] See *Qadmoniot*, 10 (1970), 57 ff. (Hebrew), and W. G. Dever, H. Darrell Lance, G. Ernest Wright, *Gezer*, I, *Annual of the Hebrew Union College Biblical Archaeology School*, I, Jerusalem, 1970; *Gezer*, II, *Annual of the Hebrew Union College Biblical Archaeology School*, II, Jerusalem, 1974.

[25] For details, see Yadin, *Hazor*, pp. 147 ff.; *IEJ*, 8 (1958), 80 ff.

[26] See *Encyclopaedia of Archaeological Excavations*, I, pp. 580 ff. (English); *Jerusalem Revealed*, Jerusalem, 1975, and the bibliography for this chapter.

[27] See N. Avigad, *IEJ*, 20 (1970), 130 ff.

[28] First conducted by B. Mazar and M. Ste-

kelis (1931); later and mainly by Y. Aharoni (1954–1962). Y. Aharoni, *Excavations at Ramat Raḥel, Seasons 1959 and 1960*, Rome, 1962, pp. 1–60; idem, *Excavations at Ramat Raḥel, Seasons 1961 and 1962*, Rome, 1964, pp. 13–63.

29 See Y. Yadin, in *The Kingdoms of Israel and Judah* (ed. A. Malamat), Jerusalem, 1961, p. 108, n. 90 (Hebrew).

30 The subject is discussed by me in detail in *Eretz Shomron*, Jerusalem, 1973 (Hebrew). See also my article in the forthcoming *Kathleen Kenyon Festschrift*, London, 1976 (in press).

31 See in particular N. Avigad, in *Enc. Miqr.*, IV, cols. 504 ff. (Hebrew); Olga Tufnell, *Encyclopaedia of Archaeological Excavations*, I, pp. 290 ff. (Hebrew).

32 H. Darrel Lance, "The Royal Stamps and the Kingdom of Josiah," *HTR*, 64 (1971), 315 ff.

33 After the above was prepared for the press, the "clinching" discussions of Ussishkin's recent excavations on the site were published (*IEJ*, 24 [1974], 272 ff.). In a clear-cut "stratum III," a locus was found with complete jars bearing the *la-melek* stamps—both of the four-winged (class I) and the two-winged (class III). To quote his words: "These finds prove conclusively that. . . : (b) storage jars with royal stamps of classes I and III were used contemporaneously; (c) storage jars with royal stamps of class III were in use in (Starkey's) Level III" (p. 273). These finds completely bear out Lance's point of view. Since all scholars agreed that the stamps of "class III" belonged to the seventh century, the new finds seem to prove that Lachish III existed until the seventh century, or else that this class of stamp had already appeared in the eighth century—a less probable assumption from epigraphical and stratigraphical points of view.

34 In Ussishkin's (*ibid.*) excavations a definite six-chamber gate was found (p. 273). The exact position and plan of the exterior towers (if existing) have not yet been cleared. See further below.

35 See *IEJ*, 18 (1968), 157 ff.

36 Y. Aharoni, *Yediot*, 31 (1967), 80 ff. (Hebrew).

37 See recently article, *ZDPV*, and especially D. Schlumberger, *L'Orient Hellénisé*, Paris, 1970, and the photograph on p. 31, depicting the base of the column from Ai Khanoum in Afghanistan from the Hellenistic period, which is absolutely identical with the column bases from Lachish. This similarity has been confirmed by D. Schlumberger in his letter to me of 6 December, 1971. See also E. Stern's detailed analysis in *The Material Culture of Palestine in the Persian Period*, Jerusalem, 1973, pp. 59 ff. (Hebrew). D. Ussishkin's latest excavations also seem to confirm the excavators' conclusions (see *Hadashot Arkhiologiyot*, 48–49 [1974], 73 [Hebrew]). A vital stratigraphical fact, ignored by Aharoni, shows clearly that the building was constructed on the Babylonian destruction, where it is stated that the building was partially constructed *over* the destroyed stratum II buildings. See *Lachish* III, p. 131.

38 See now a summing-up article by M. Dothan, head of the expedition, in *Qadmoniot*, 17 (1972), 2 ff. (Hebrew), and the further bibliography there.

39 For the latest summaries, see Y. Aharoni, *Encyclopaedia of Archaeological Excavations*, I, pp. 74 ff. (English); idem, "Ancient Arad," *Catalogue of the Israel Museum*, No. 25, Jerusalem, 1967, pp. 24 ff. (henceforth *Catalogue*).

40 The small settlement of the early stratum XII, out of seven strata, is attributed to "the first half of the tenth century," in the *Encyclopaedia of Archaeological Excavations* (English), and in the above-mentioned *Catalogue* to "approximately the eleventh century." In the *Encyclopaedia of Archaeological Excavations* (English), its date is fixed in the 12th–11th centuries.

41 *Catalogue*, p. 24.

42 At first this wall was also attributed to stratum VII (*Encyclopaedia of Archaeological Excavations*, II [Hebrew], p. 473), and see below.

43 Thus the reports state that Josiah abolished the temple, since "the casemate wall of the last citadel, built during his reign (stratum VI), cut through the sanctuary (*hēkāl*), apparently intentionally, in order to abolish it. It can be assumed that this was done by Josiah in the framework of the great religious reforms carried out in order to centralize worship in Jerusalem" (*Catalogue*, p. 30). In an earlier publication, this development was explained differently: "After the destruction (of the sanctuary) at the end of stratum VIII (apparently at the time of Ahaz, in 734), it was not rebuilt, but the casemate wall of stratum VIII, which was apparently changed by Hezekiah, passes through its center. This is an instructive confirmation of the biblical story about Hezekiah, who was the first king of Judah to remove the high places and the altars (II Kings 18, 4:22)." *Encyclopaedia of Archaeological Excavations*, p. 476 (Hebrew); on this see the statement of the excavator, in *Eretz-Israel*, 8 (1967), 102, n. 8 (Hebrew): "It became clear that the casemate wall which put an end to the existence of the sanctuary was built at the time of stratum VI, and not at the time of stratum VII." See also the following note of the excavator: " . . .in this report [on the second season—Y. Y.] we dated stratum VII too early; the stratum was not destroyed earlier than the middle of the seventh century," Aharoni, *ibid.*, 101, n. 2. Furthermore, on the basis of the lines of the above walls (see below) and their attribution to the various strata, the excavator reached the conclusion that in the last phase of the existence of the citadel the altar went out of use because of the wall built by Hezekiah, although the "sanctuary" itself was still used for cult purposes; *Catalogue*, p. 27.

44 A check on the spot proved that often even the inner sides of the stones were dressed.

45 See C. Nylander, *IEJ*, 17 (1967), 56 ff.; Y. Yadin, *IEJ*, 15 (1965), 180.

46 *Encyclopaedia of Archaeological Excavations*, I, p. 88 (English).

47 My attention was drawn to this discovery at the time of the excavations by the late I. Dunayevsky, who during that season was the architect of the expedition.

48 *Eretz-Israel*, 8 (1967), 101 (Hebrew).

49 The excavator, who admits that "this fact is very surprising," is compelled to suggest that the owner of the seals was "one of the ancestors" of the man mentioned in the ostraca, and that either the functions of the officials in the citadel were hereditary or—his latest opinion—that Elyashiv, after the destruction of citadel VII, "returned to his previous duties when the new citadel was being built. The room of the ostraca lies not very far [in fact very near—Y. Y.] from the room of the seals and it seems, therefore, that Elyashiv's office stayed on the same spot and only the shape of the rooms *was changed a little* [my italics—Y. Y.] because of the alteration in the wall.

50 *Ibid.*, p. 103.

51 It should be mentioned here that the absolute dates of the phases of the "temple" and the altar are also not clear. Not only were they partly fixed on the basis of the dates of the late walls, but furthermore the finds discovered there seem sometimes to be later than the date suggested by Aharoni; thus, for instance, he attributes two pottery bowls to stratum X (ninth century), because they were found in this level. However, not only do the bowls look much later (see their photographs in "Inscriptions Reveal," *Catalogue of the Israel Museum*, No. 100, 1973, p. 79), but one of the two letters engraved in them—ש—belongs to the type of the seventh to sixth centuries. The excavator therefore interprets the first letter as p (*q*), and the ש as "a sign similar to the early צ which is apparently a symbol;" *Catalogue*, p. 29, and "Inscriptions Reveal." In the final publication of the Arad inscriptions (Y. Aharoni, *Arad Inscriptions*, Jerusalem, 1975 [Hebrew], p. 117), Aharoni equates the sign to the one scratched on the Herodian vessel found by Mazar. However, it is clear that the alleged sign in the

Jerusalem vessel is nothing but the leg of the bird!

52 *Encyclopaedia of Archaeological Excavations*, I, p. 85 (English).

53 *Beer-Sheba*, I, p. 110 f.

54 *Ibid.*, pp. 9, 106.

55 *Ibid.*, pp. 4, 9 ff.

56 *Ibid.*, pp. 9, 86.

57 The connection between the wall attributed to stratum V and the buildings of this stratum is also not at all clear. From the plan (Pl. 88), the walls of the buildings seem to have been cut by the foundation trench of the city wall. From the photography of the section (Pl. 7), the foundations of the city wall seem also to have intruded into the levels of this stratum.

58 *IEJ*, 19 (1969), 246.

59 *IEJ*, 22 (1972), 169.

60 *Beer-Sheba*, I, p. 10, n. 2.

61 *Beer-Sheba*, I, p. 107. Previously, in the volume *Excavations and Studies in Honor of Prof. Sh. Yeivin*, Tel Aviv, 1973, p. 19 (Hebrew), Aharoni dated the period of stratum II to the seventh century.

62 On the problem of the dating of stratum III at Lachish, see above.

63 *Hadashot Arkhiologiyot*, 44 (1972), 27; *IEJ*, 24 (1974), 13 ff.

64 *Ibid.*, *IEJ*, p. 15. See above the discussion of the gate at Dan, from which it follows clearly that this gate cannot have been built before the end of the tenth century or the beginning of the ninth. See also below, the discussion of the fortifications.

65 *Beer-Sheba*, I, p. 16.

66 Now (*Beer-Sheba*, I, p. 17) they are attributed to the Hellenistic period. See also *Qadmoniot*, 23–24 (1973), 83 (Hebrew).

67 See *Beer-Sheba*, I, pp. 61 ff.

68 *Qadmoniot*, 23–24 (1973), back cover photo. See also a vessel with a similar inscription from Hazor: Yadin, *Hazor*, pl. XXXV, c.

69 On this altar, see *Qadmoniot*, 23–24 (1973), 84, and color plate B; *BAr*, 37 (1974), 2 ff. This altar raises interesting problems in terms, for example, of its measurements (size)

and the fact that it is built of ashlar. The conclusion that it is an altar for the offering of sacrifices in a temple still needs proof. The discovery of this altar is, according to Aharoni, a final proof "that a temple had existed at Beersheba during the period of the monarchy" (*IEJ*, 24 [1974], 271). Nevertheless, it is a fact that by the end of the seventh season (1975) no such temple had been discovered. Aharoni's suggestion that the area of the alleged temple "was dug out and the temple had been torn down and removed stone by stone," (*ibid.*), is at best based on an *ex silentio* proof. Evidence for attributing the altar to a "high-place" in the times of Josiah see Y. Yadin, *BASOR* 222 (1976), 5–17.

70 *S͏ᵉfunōt Negev*, Tel Aviv, 1967, pp. 59 ff. (Hebrew), and the bibliography there.

71 *BIES*, 25 (1961), 157–159; *Eretz-Israel*, 12 (1975), p. 49–56 (both in Hebrew).

72 *BAr*, 28 (1965), 70 ff.; *Encyclopaedia of Archaeological Excavations*, II, p. 581 (Hebrew).

73 The time of Jehoshaphat, in Glueck's opinion, based on I Kings 22:49; II Chron. 20:36–37.

74 The suggestion that Ezion-geber be identified with Jazirat Far'un—see B. Rothenberg, *S͏ᵉfunōt Negev*, Tel Aviv, 1967, pp. 207 ff.—has not yet been archaeologically confirmed. In a test excavation on the site, carried out by R. Cohen on behalf of the Israel Department of Antiquities, only late pottery was discovered in the "casemate" wall. Further excavations are required in order to verify the dating of the buildings on the site.

75 See below, in the discussion of the fortifications.

76 See B. Mazar, Trude Dothan, I. Dunayevsky, "En-gedi," *'Atiqot* (English series), 5 (1966); B. Mazar, *Encyclopaedia of Archaeological Excavations*, II, pp. 370 ff. (English).

77 Clark Collection, YMCA, Jerusalem; and see above, n. 76.

78 Cf. Ezra 5:8 and especially 6:4.

79 This subject is now exhaustively treated by Y. Shiloh in his *Foreign Influences*

on the Masonry of Palestine in the 10th–9th *Centuries B.C.E.* (PhD Dissertation), Jerusalem, 1974 (Hebrew).

[80] Including other architectural elements which will be detailed below, and also for historical reasons.

[81] For instance, during the reign of Athaliah, and see above, n. 30.

[82] In his attempt—*Yediot*, 31 (1967), 89—to contest this fact, Y. Aharoni did not succeed in pointing to a single instance which could be dated to this period. His proposal to date the "Residency" at Lachish to the period of the Monarchy is nothing more than an improbable suggestion; for reasons against accepting it, see the literature in n. 37. The fact mentioned in Aharoni's article—p. 90, n. 45—that in some Assyrian reliefs signs of similar dressing are recognizable is not exact. In the Assyrian reliefs the tool in question is a fine one used for smoothing the stones. There is no similarity whatsoever between this and the dressing of the ashlar stones in question; in any case, whether a similar tool was used in the Assyrian reliefs or not, the fact remains that no ashlar stone of this kind has been found among the building stones themselves. As already mentioned, the above dressing has not been found in other sites and even the one case, Ramat Raḥel, where there are signs of similar dressing, was thus defined at the time by Aharoni himself (before his excavation at Arad): "There is a small section of combed stonecutting which *is unknown before Roman times* [my italics—Y. Y.]. But it is precisely this section that testifies to the stone's having been cut in an earlier period. Apparently, an attempt was subsequently made in the Roman or Byzantine periods to put it to some secondary use ..." (*Excavations at Ramat Raḥel*, 1959–1960, Rome, 1962, p. 15, n. 46). It is hard to assume that only in distant Arad were the stone dressers of the seventh century in need of a dressing technique for ashlar that was not introduced into general use until several hundred years later. As long

as the excavator maintains his opinion, it is impossible to accept his dating of the destruction periods of the various phases of the sanctuary (see above and also below).

[83] N. Glueck, *BASOR*, 51 (1933), 13, Fig. 2; *AASOR*, 14 (1934), 67 ff., Fig. 26.

[84] Y. Shiloh (*op. cit.*, above, n. 80) believes that the actual use of proto-Ionian capitals in *stone* is an Israelite invention.

[85] Since the above was written, a casemate complex of fortifications was finally found in Beersheba too, under the solid wall (*IEJ*, 24 [1974], 270). Its date, according to the present writer, is in the 11th–10th century B.C.E. This is another proof that the sequence of fortifications in Beersheba is the same as in other places, and that the solid wall is post-10th century.

[86] Here a large shaft was discovered, which, without doubt, was intended for water works of this kind. The conclusion of the excavators was that the work had not been completed, but it should be pointed out that the shaft has not yet been completely excavated, so that for the time being this conclusion should be treated with reservations.

[87] It is difficult to know exactly when this water system was quarried; on the different opinions, see *BAr*, 32 (1969), 71 ff.

[88] In the northeastern corner of the mound, part of a shaft with descending steps has been discovered. Until this spot is excavated, it is difficult to state exactly to which type of water system it should be attributed: if indeed this was a water system that exploits the groundwater or exterior water sources—of the type of Hazor and Megiddo, as is the opinion of the excavator—or a cistern for the collection of rain water.

[89] See Y. Yadin, *IEJ*, 19 (1969), 18.

[90] For a comprehensive discussion of the problems of these and similar buildings, which will be dealt with below, see Y. Shiloh, *Eretz-Israel*, 11 (1973), 277 ff. (Hebrew); *idem*, *IEJ*, 20 (1970), 180 ff., and schematic drawings of the various types there, and full bibliography. See also the discoveries at Tel

Masos, A. Kempinski, *Qadmoniot*, 23–24 (1973), 105 (Hebrew).

[91]   See Yadin, *Hazor*, p. 183, Fig. 49.

[92]   *IEJ*, 20 (1970), 190.

[93]   Yadin, *Hazor*, p. 170, Fig. 45.

[94]   Yadin, *Hazor*, p. 186, Fig. 50.

[95]   See Shiloh, *IEJ* (above, n. 90), p. 181, Fig. 1; see also Z. Herzog, *Beer-Sheba*, I, pp. 23 ff.

[96]   See J. B. Pritchard, "The Megiddo Stables: A Re-assessment," *Near Eastern Archaeology in the Twentieth Century, Essays in honor of Nelson Glueck*, (ed. James A. Sanders), Garden City, N. Y., 1970, pp. 268 ff.

[97]   See my article on this subject in the *G. E. Wright Festschrift* (forthcoming), and also *Eretz-Israel*, 12 (1975), pp. 57 ff. (Hebrew).

[98]   It is difficult to accept the assumption that the buildings in Beersheba served as storehouses, but contained troughs for the animals' use during unloading (Z. Herzog, above, n. 95). The "mixture" of manure and "good-ies" in the same building certainly did not add to the quality of the foodstuffs. On the other hand, the unloading itself was a quick process and the animals could have been fed afterwards, outside the building. It is possible that the Beersheba structures were originally built as stalls, only to be used as storehouses in their last phase. See my articles, above, n. 97.

[99]   *Megiddo*, II, p. 45, Figs. 100–102, Locus 2081: Fig. 388.

[100]   See also the plan in Fig. 388; the reconstruction in Fig. 100 is—even in the opinion of the excavators — only hypothetical and not founded on definite architectural data.

[101]   On the problems of dating the building, see above, the discussion of Arad.

[102]   See the recent justified criticisms of P. Welten, "Kulthöhe and Jahwetempel," *ZDPV*, 88 (1972), 19 ff.

[103]   *Proceedings of the American Academy of Jewish Research*, 34 (1962), 152 ff.

CHAPTER IX

CRAFT AND INDUSTRY

1 S. Abramsky, *Eretz-Israel*, 3 (1952), 116–124 (Hebrew).

2 I. Mendelsohn, *BASOR*, 80 (1940), 17–21; see also: A. F. Rainey, *A Social Structure of Ugarit*, Jerusalem, 1967, 83–95 (Hebrew).

3 A. Demsky, *IEJ*, 16 (1966), 211–215; Y. Aharoni, *Lachish*, V, Tel Aviv, 1975.

4 Y. Aharoni, *IEJ*, 18 (1968), 164–169.

5 D. Diringer, *Le iscrizioni antico ebraiche palestinesi*, Firenze, 1934, p. 259; N. Avigad, *IEJ*, 16 (1966), 50–53.

6 For examples of Iron Age mortars and pestles, see *Hazor*, I, pl. 149; *Megiddo*, I, pls. 106, 112–113; B. Mazar, *IEJ*, 14 (1964), pls. 12b, 14b; cf. R. K. Amiran, *Enc. Miqr.*, IV, cols. 120 ff., "Tools, Stone Implements" (includes bibliography) (Hebrew).

7 R. Amiran, *Eretz-Israel*, 4 (1956), 46–47 (includes bibliography) (Hebrew).

8 Cf., for example, *Tell en-Naṣbeh*, I, fig. 91:1, 2, 4; *Megiddo*, I, pl. 114:11.

9 See *Samaria, Harvard*, I, p. 338, fig. 212.

10 Y. Aharoni, *IEJ*, 16 (1966), 3.

11 Pritchard, *ANEP*, No. 152.

12 J. B. Pritchard, *Expedition*, 6 (1964), 6. For a typical example of an Israelite oven, see *Tell en-Naṣbeh*, I, pl. 93:3–4.

13 For Iron Age baking trays, see *Hazor*, I, pls. 146:15; 148; 22; *Tell en-Nasbeh*, I, pl. 93: 2; *Lachish*, III, pl. 104:682.

14 Cf. A. M. Honeyman, *PEQ* 71 (1939), 76–90.

15 On the Iron Age cooking pot and its development, see Amiran, *Pottery*, pp. 227–232; Honeyman, *ibid.*

16 See N. Avigad, *Yediot*, 30 (1966), 209–212 (Hebrew); B. Mazar *et alii.*, *IEJ*, 14 (1964), 27, pl. 13.

17 Cf. Jer. 2:22; I Mal. 3:2; and *Enc. Miqr.* II, Col. 347, "*Borit;*" IV, cols. 1010–1012 ("crafts; washing").

18 For the various techniques of spinning practiced in antiquity, see *Enc. Miqr.*, IV, cols. 998–1003, ("Crafts, spinning").

19 Cf., for example, the forms of the numerous Iron Age whorls from Megiddo in *Megiddo*, I, pls. 93–95; another large collection of 11th century B.C.E. whorls at Megiddo were found in a woman's handbag.
    See also Y. Yadin, *BAr*, 33 (1970), 77.

20 T. Dothan, *IEJ*, 13 (1963), 97–112, pls. 14–16 (includes additional biography).

21 *Idem, ibid.*

22 See also *HT*, I, 424–425 (includes bibliography).

23 Clear traces of the weaving craft have been uncovered in many Iron Age houses at Shechem, Lachish, Tell Beit Mirsim, etc., and see H. Keith-Beebe, *BAr*, 31 (1968), 49–58; J. B. Pritchard, *Expedition*, 6 (1964), 6.

24 On the biblical use of the terms *būṣ* and *šēš*, see A. Hurvitz, *HTR*, 60 (1967), 117–121.

25 *Enc. Miqr.*, cols. 1003–1008 ("Crafts, weaving"); and also cf. G. M. Crowfoot, *PEQ* 73 (1941), 141–151; 76 (1944), 121–130; *MAB*, I, 460–475.

26 Y. Yadin, *Eretz-Israel*, 4 (1956), 68–73 (Hebrew).

27 C. L. Starkey, *PEF QSt*, 1936, 188 ff.

28 G. Edelstein, "Weavers' Settlements from the Time of the United Monarchy," *Guide* of the Archaeological Museum at Nir David; *idem*, *Qadmoniot*, 4 (1972), 84–85 (both Hebrew).

29 For examples of loom weights of different periods, see B. Maisler, *IEJ*, 1 (1951), pl. 39b; 14 (1964), pl. 14a; J. B. Pritchard, *Expedition*, 6 (1964), 7; *Samaria*, III, 398–402.

30 Cf., for example, *Megiddo*, I, pls. 95–96.

31 For examples of animals' horns, see *Megiddo*, I, pl. 98:3–20. For a case filled with needles from the Late Bronze Age, see *Hazor*, III–IV, pl. 343: 1–15.

[32] A woman's cloth bag of personal articles from the 11th century B.C.E. was recently discovered at Megiddo. Some of the cloth has been preserved but a full description has not yet been published. See Y. Yadin, *BAr*, 33 (1970), 78. A small piece of cloth from the 12th century B.C.E. has also survived at Tell es-Saʿidiyeh: see J. B. Pritchard, *Expedition*, 6 (1964), 7.

[33] Y. Yadin, *Finds From the Bar-Kokhba Period in the Cave of the Letters*, Jerusalem, 1963, pp. 177–278 (Hebrew).

[34] See II Chron. 2:6, 13; and cf. *Enc. Miqr.*, IV, cols. 1008–1010. ("Crafts, dyeing").

[35] See C. B. Jensen, *JNES*, 22 (1963), 104–118.

[36] The installation was excavated by the writer in 1959 during the expedition to Tel Mor led by Prof. M. Dothan. It is not yet published; the photo of the murex snails found there appears in *Enc. Miqr.*, VI, cols. 465–466.

[37] See W. F. Albright, *AASOR*, 21–22 (1943), 55–62; *idem*, *Archaeology of Palestine and the Bible*, New York, 1932, pp. 119–121; *Ain-Shems*, IV, pls. 19:5; 20:4; 21:1; V, 73, 75–77; *Tell en-Naṣbeh*, I, 256–257; pl. 97; J. C. Kelso, *AASOR*, 39 (1968), pl. 12b; the installation from Gezer has not yet been published.

Thanks are due to Mr. S. Gitin for this information.

[38] Cf. G. Edelstein, *Qadmoniot*, 4 (1972), 84–85 (Hebrew).

[39] Cf. Yadin, *op. cit.* (above, n. 33), 278–288 (includes bibliography).

[40] J. Naveh, *IEJ*, 10 (1960), 129–139; 14 (1964), 158–159.

[41] For the Bronze Age belts of bronze from Jericho and Tell el-Farʿah (north), see *Jericho*, I, 312, fig. 117; Iron Age belts were found at Tell ʿAitun in excavations directed by Trude Dothan: *Qadmoniot*, 4 (1972), 87 (Hebrew).

[42] See Pritchard, *ANEP*, Nos. 355, 366, 369, 372–373.

[43] Aharoni, *Ramat Raḥel*, I, 42–43, pl. 28, fig. 30:1; B. Mazar, *IEJ*, 17 (1967), pl. 31:5.

[44] See especially J. W. Crowfoot-G. M. Crowfoot, *Early Ivories from Samaria*, London, 1938.

[45] *Enc. Miqr.*, IV, cols. 1034 ff., ("Clothing"), and also *MAB*, I, 460–475; G. E. Wright, *Biblical Archaeology*, London, 1957, pp. 187–190; A Rubens, *History of Jewish Costume*, London, 1967. pp. 5–14.

[46] See, for example, *Megiddo*, I, pl. 102: 14–18; 20.

[47] For examples of Iron Age toggle pins, see *Megiddo*, I, pls. 71, 72, 78–79.

[48] H. Keith-Beebe, *BAr*, 31 (1968), 49–58.

[49] See Amiran, *Pottery*.

[50] Vronwy Hankey, *PEQ*, 110 (1968), 27–32; Robert H. Johnston, *BAr*, 37 (1974), 86–106.

[51] *Lachish*, IV, 291–293; pls. 8, 49, 92. A similar workshop from the Late Bronze Age was found at Hazor; *Hazor*, I, 95–96, pl. 179.

[52] R. de Vaux, *RB*, 62 (1955), 558–563, figs. 8–10, pl. IX; M. Kochavi, *Yediot*, 27 (1963), 288 (Hebrew).

[53] *Megiddo*, I, pl. 114:1–3; II, pl. 268; *Ancient Gaza*, IV, pl. XV.

[54] Cf., for example, R. Amiran, *Eretz-Israel*, 4 (1956), 46–49, pls. 5–6; *idem*, *Yediot*, 30 (1966), 85–87 (both Hebrew).

[55] For the latest discussions, see P. W. Lapp, *BASOR*, 158 (1960), 11–22; Y. Yadin, *ibid.*, 163 (1961), 6–12; Aharoni, *Ramat Raḥel*, I, 51–56; A. F. Rainey, *BASOR*, 179 (1965), 34–36; F. M. Cross, *Eretz-Israel*, 9 (1969), 20–27; H. Darnell Lance, *HTR*, 64 (1971), 315–332.

[56] This is attested by an ostracon from Tell Qasileh which confirms that gold was imported from Ophir; and see B. Maisler (Mazar), *IEJ*, 1 (1951), 208–210, fig. 13F, pl. 38A.

[57] See especially R. J. Forbes, *Studies in Ancient Technology*, Leiden, 1964; "Metals." *Enc. Miqr.*, V. cols. 644 ff.,

[58] N. Glueck, *AASOR*, 14 (1935), 1–114; *idem*, *BASOR*, 71 (1938), 3 ff.; 75 (1939), 8–22; 79 (1940), 2–4; 131 (1953); *BAr*, 145 (1957), 11 ff.; B. Rothenberg, *Timna—Valley*

of the Biblical Copper Mines, London 1972.

59 See S. Abramsky, *Eretz-Israel*, 3 (1954), 116–124 (Hebrew).

60 On metal-working at Tel Zeror and Tell Deir 'Alla, see M. Kochavi, *Qadmoniot*, I (1969), 128–131 (Hebrew), on the crucible at Tell Qasileh, see B. Maisler (Mazar), *IEJ*, I (1951), 74–76; on the crucible at Tel Harashim, Y. Aharoni, *Settlement of the Israelite Tribes in Upper Galilee*, Jerusalem, 1957, pp. 19–21 (Hebrew); on the crucibles at Gezer, Beth-shemesh, Tell el-Ḥesi, Tell el-Far'ah (south), and Tell Jemmeh, see G. E. Wright, *AJA*, 42 (1939), 458–463.

61 See *Hazor*, III–IV, pl. 342:1–2; *Megiddo*, I, pl. 105; W. F. Albright, *AASOR*, 17 (1938), pl. 43; E. Sellin, *ZDPV*, 50 (1927), 210, pl. 21.

62 Cf. *MAB*, I, 362–402 (includes bibliography).

63 G. E. Wright, *op. cit.* (above, n. 60).

64 *Enc. Miqr.*, IV, cols. 1012 ff. ("Crafts, tools").

65 For examples of blades of plows, scythes, hoes, sickles, spades, and pitchforks from the Iron Age, see, for example, *Megiddo*, I, pls. 82–83; *Lachish*, III, pls. 40:7, 61.

66 For examples of Iron Age implements, including various knives, see *Lachish*, III, pl. 59.

67 Y. Yadin "Weapons," *Enc. Miqr.*, V, cols. 931–970, and also *The Art of Warfare in the Near East in the Light of Archaeology*, Ramat-Gan, 1967 (includes bibliography); for examples of Iron Age weapons, see *Lachish*, III, pls. 39, 60; *Megiddo*, I, pls. 80–81; J. P. Pritchard, *Expedition*, 6 (1964), 7.

68 A particularly fine group of bronze objects including a tripod from the beginning of the Iron Age was discovered at Tell es-Sa'idiyeh, and see Pritchard, *op. cit.* (above, n. 67).

69 *MAB*, I, 398–402 (includes bibliography).

70 J. H. Iliffe, *QDAP*, 5 (1935), 61–68.

71 H. Beinart, "Wine" *Enc. Miqr.*, III, cols. 675–682.

72 Cf. Isa. 5:2; 16:10; 63:2–3; Jer. 48:32, etc.

73 Cf., for example, N. de G. Davies, *The Tomb of Nakht at Thebes*, New York, 1917, pp. 69–70, pls. 23b, 26. For wine presses in Israel, see *MAB*, I, 327–332; *Hazor* II, 22, pls. 2:1, 10:1; *Shechem*, 165–166; figs. 89–90, 202; *Ain Shems*, IV, pls. 18:2–4, 19:1–2, 20:1.

74 J. B. Pritchard, *Winery, Defenses and Soundings at Gibeon*, Philadelphia, 1961, pp. 1–27.

75 Y. Aharoni, *Beer-Sheba*, I, Tel-Aviv, 1973, pl. 32:1.

76 N. Glueck, *BASOR*, 80 (1940), 3–10; J. Naveh, *ibid.*, 203 (1971), 31, n. 30.

77 Y. Aharoni, *IEJ*, 16 (1966), 2–3.

78 *Hazor*, II, 69–71, pls. 171–172; and M. Altbauer, *Eretz-Israel*, 10 (1971), 64–66 (Hebrew); and cf. also Cant. 2:13, 15; 7:13.

79 Aharoni, *op. cit.* (above, n. 77).

80 Cf. *Orlah*, I, 8, etc., and see E. L. Sukenik, *Qedem*, I (1942), 20–23 (Hebrew).

81 Hos. 14:8; Ezek. 27:18; and cf. A. Cowley, *Aramaic Papyri of the Fifth Century B.C.*, Oxford, 1923, no. 72, lines 4, 10, 17.

82 I Chron. 27:27; and cf. also Chron. 11:11, 32:23.

83 N. Avigad, *IEJ*, 22 (1972), 1–9.

84 J. B. Pritchard, *Hebrew Inscriptions and Stamps from Gibeon*, Philadelphia, 1959; N. Avigad, *IEJ*, 9 (1959), 130–133; F. M. Cross, *BASOR*, 168 (1962), 18–32; A. Demsky, *ibid.*, 202 (1971), 16–23.

85 F. M. Cross, *Eretz-Israel*, 9 (1969), 20–32 (includes bibliography).

86 N. Avigad, *BJPES*, 13 (1947), 129–132; *idem*, "Seals," "Yehud" *Enc. Miqr.*, III, cols 82–86, 484–487; E. Stern, *Material Culture of the Holy Land in the Persian Period*, Jerusalem, 1973, pp. 195–212 (Hebrew); N. Avigad, *IEJ*, 8 (1958), 113–119; P. W. Lapp, *BASOR*, 172 (1963), 22–35; F. M. Cross, *IEJ*, 18 (1968), 226–233; A. N. Richardson, *BASOR*, 192 (1968), 12–16; N. Avigad, *IEJ*, 24 (1974), 52–58.

87 Cross, *op. cit.* (above, n. 85).

88   E. Stern, *Qadmoniot*, 6 (1973), 15–17 (Hebrew).

89   N. Glueck, *BASOR*, 80 (1940), 7–9.

90   Y. Elgavish, *Shiqmona*, I, Haifa, 1968, pl. 61; nos. 147–148.

91   Cf. Ezek. 27:17; Hos. 12:2; II Chron. 11:11, etc., and see also M. Avi-Yonah, *Essays and Studies in the Lore of the Holy Land*, Tel Aviv, 1968, 137–151 (Hebrew).

92   Ex. 27:20; Lev. 8:2; Deut. 35:25; I Kings 5:25; II Kings 2:13; Ps. 92:11; Est. 2:12.

93   M. Dothan, *IEJ*, 15 (1965), 141, 151, figs. 7, 13, Y. Aharoni, *Qadmoniot*, 1 (1968), 103 (Hebrew); B. Maisler (Mazar), *IEJ*, 1 (1951), 208–209.

94   See, for example, Y. Elgavish, *Qadmoniot*, 3 (1970), 93 (Hebrew); *Gezer*, II, 48–67; W. F. Albright, *AASOR*, 21–22 (1943), 62–63.

95   Z. Yeivin, *'Atiqot*, 3 (1966), 52–63 (includes bibliography) (Hebrew).

96   R. Hestrin–Z. Yeivin, *Qadmoniot*, 4 (1972), 92–95 (Hebrew).

97   M. Zohary *Enc. Miqr.*, II, cols. 371–375, "Spices."

98   For the latest discussions of this inscription, see Y. Aharoni, *Qadmoniot*, 2 (1970), 32 (Hebrew); F. M. Cross, *BASOR*, 193 (1969), 21–24; J. Naveh, *ibid.*, 203 (1971), 29–30.

99   See E. Stern, in *Beer-Sheba*, I, Tel-Aviv, 1973, pp. 52–53 (includes bibliography).

100   Amiran, *Pottery*, 320–306.

101   See Cant. 1:13 and Isa. 3:20.

102   See Ex. 30:22–25, 34–38; I Chron. 9:30.

103   On the growing and marketing of perfumes, see Gen. 43:11; I Kings 10:2; Isa. 6:6; Jer. 6:20, 8:22; Ezek. 27:17, 22.

104   On the cultivation and processing of perfumes at En-gedi, see B. Mazar *et alii*, *'Atiqot*, 5 (English series) (1966), 1–12.

CHAPTER X

DWELLINGS AND GRAVES

1 For the main studies of Iron Age houses, see M. Avi-Yonah - S. Yeivin, *Qadmoniot Arṣenu*, Tel Aviv, 1955, 89–105; *Enc. Miqr.*, II, cols. 179 ff., "Building" (both Hebrew); *MAB*, I, 265–270; H. Keith-Beebe, *BAr*, 31 (1968), 49–58; Y. Shiloh, *IEJ*, 20 (1970), 180–190; idem, *Eretz-Israel*, 11 (1973), 277–285 (Hebrew).

2 See W. F. Albright, *AASOR*, 21–22 (1943), 55; B. Maisler (Mazar), *IEJ*, 1 (1951), 137 ff.; R. de Vaux, *PEQ*, 88 (1956), 133; J. B. Pritchard, *BAr*, 28 (1963), 10–17.

3 See above, n. 1, for references to each of these sites, and now also Y. Aharoni (ed.), *Beer-Sheba*, I, Ramat Gan, 1973, 23–37; *IEJ*, 14 (1974), 264–265 (for Tell esh-Shariʿah); 267 (for Tel Mevorakh); 268–269 (for Tel Masos).

4 See proposed reconstruction of this type of building in G. E. Wright, *Shechem, A Biography of a Biblical City*, New York, 1965, fig. 79.

5 Clear traces of such activities were discovered in buildings of this type at Tell Beit Mirsim, Tell el-Farʿah, Shechem, and many other sites. See also Keith-Beebe (above, n. 1).

6 J. B. Pritchard, *Expedition*, 6 (1964), 5–6; Aharoni, *op. cit.* (above, n. 3).

7 Aharoni, *op. cit.* (above, n. 3).

8 Y. Shiloh, *Eretz-Israel*, 11 (1973), 277–285 (Hebrew); Y. Yadin, *Qadmoniot*, 3 (1970), 38–56 (Hebrew); Aharoni, *op. cit.* (above, n. 3); K. Braningan, *IEJ*, 16 (1966), 206–208.

9 D. Ussishkin, *IEJ*, 16 (1966), 174–186; idem, ibid., 20 (1970), 213–215; idem, *BAr*, 36 (1973), 78–105; K. M. Kenyon, *Royal Cities of the Old Testament*, London, 1971.

10 For this type of building, see Avi-Yonah - Yeivin, *op. cit.* (above, n. 1), 95–103.

11 The excavators attribute the earliest capitals at Megiddo to stratum VI. Aharoni dates the capitals from Ramat Raḥel to the end of the Judean kingdom.

12 R. Amiran - I. Dunayevsky, *BASOR*, 149 (1958), 25–32; R. Amiran in A. U. Pope (ed.), *A Survey of Persian Art*, XIV, Oxford, 1967, pp. 3017–3023.

13 On this matter, see E. Stern, *Qadmoniot*, 5 (1973), 7–8 (Hebrew).

14 See E. Stern, *The Material Culture of the Land of the Bible in the Persian Period*, Jerusalem, 1973, pp. 51–64 (Hebrew).

15 See Aharoni, *op. cit.* (above, n. 3), 19–22; Y. Shiloh and A. Hurwitz, *Qadmoniot*, 8 (1975), 68–71 (Hebrew).

16 J. B. Pritchard, *Expedition*, 6 (1964), 2–9; Wright, *op. cit.* (above, n. 4), fig. 80.

17 Aharoni, *op. cit.* (above, n. 3), 97–103.

18 See, for example, *Megiddo*, I, pl. 114:9–10.

19 See, for example, Aharoni, *op. cit.* (above, n. 3), pl. 9:2.

20 Z. Kallai, in M. Kochavi (ed.), *Judea, Samaria and the Golan, Archaeological Survey 1968*, Jerusalem, 1972, p. 154 (Hebrew); R. Gophna - Y. Porat, ibid., 197–198.

21 Cf. *Enc. Miqr.* I, cols. 40–45 "Mourning" (includes bibliography).

22 M. Haran, *IEJ*, 8 (1958), 15–25; T. Dothan, *Eretz-Israel*, 9 (1969), 42–46; idem, ibid., 11 (1973), 120–121 (both Hebrew).

23 See, for example, *Enc. Miqr.*, I, cols. 41–42 (Hebrew).

24 Cf. A. Biran - R. Gophna, *IEJ*, 20 (1970), 151–169 (contains additional bibliography).

25 E. Stern, *op. cit.* (above, n. 14), 83–86.

26 See D. Ussishkin, *Excavations and Studies, Essays in Honor of Prof. Sh. Yeivin*, Tel Aviv, 1973, pp. 31–47 (Hebrew); J. Naveh, *IEJ*, 13 (1963), 74–92; W. G. Dever, *HUCA*, 40–41 (1969–70), 139–204; D. Barag, *IEJ*, 20 (1970), 216–218; F. M. Cross, in James A. Sanders (ed.), *Near Eastern Archaeology in the Twentieth Century, Essays in Honor of Nelson Glueck*, Garden City, New York, 1970, pp. 299–306.

27 E. L. Sukenik, in *Samaria-Sebaste*, I: *The Buildings*, London, 1942, pp. 23–24.

28   Cf. N. Avigad, in M. Avi-Yonah (ed.), *Sefer Yerushalayim*, Jerusalem, 1956, pp. 150–153 (contains additional bibliography) (Hebrew); also, B. Mazar, *Qadmoniot*, 1 (1968), 11–12 (Hebrew); about a new tomb area situated at the northern site of Jerusalem, see now, G. Barkai *et alii*, *Qadmoniot*, 8 (1975), 71–76 (Hebrew).

29   B. Mazar, *Eretz-Israel*, 10 (1971), 32 (Hebrew).

30   See N. Avigad, *Ancient Monuments in Naḥal Kidron*, Jerusalem, 1954, pp. 18–36 (includes bibliography) (Hebrew); *idem*, *IEJ*, 3 (1953), 137–152; *idem*, *ibid.*, 5 (1955), 163–166; D. Ussishkin, *BASOR*, 196 (1969), 16–22; *idem*, *BAr*, 33 (1970), 34–46.

31   The only inscribed tombstone connected with the burial of the kings of Judah found thus far dates from the Second Temple period. It tells of transferring the bones of Uzziah king of Judah from their original resting-place (in the tombs of the kings) to another place (apparently outside the city on the Mount of Olives). The tombstone is exhibited at the Israel Museum, Jerusalem.

32   B. Mazar, *op. cit.* (above, n. 29); D. Ussishkin, *PEQ*, 103 (1971), 101–102.

33   G. Lankester-Harding, *QDAP*, 11 (1945), 67–74; 13 (1948), 92–102; 14 (1950), 44–48; *idem*, *ADAJ*, 1 (1951), 37–40; *idem*, *Palestine Exploration Fund Annual*, 6 (1953), 49–65; R. W. Dajani, *ADAJ*, 11 (1966), 41–47.

34   J. C. Waldbaum, *AJA*, 70 (1966), 331–340.

35   For this subject in detail, see T. Dothan, *The Philistines and Their Material Culture*, Jerusalem, 32–35; 211–246 (includes bibliography) (Hebrew); also *idem*, *IEJ*, 23 (1973), 130–151.

36   See Pritchard, *ANEP*, nos. 851–853. The problem of the nationality of the owners of these 9th- to 7th-century B.C.E. coffins has not yet been solved; see E. Stern, *Qadmoniot*, 6 (1974), 132–133 (Hebrew).

37   G. Edelstein, *Qadmoniot*, 4 (1972), 86–87 (Hebrew).

38   See R. Amiran, *'Atiqot*, 2 (1957–58), 116–118; E. Stern, *Qadmoniot*, 6 (1973), 8–9 (both Hebrew); *Megiddo*, I, pls. 18:91; 54:91; J. P. Free, *BASOR*, 156 (1959), 27.

39   C. N. Johns, *QDAP*, 2 (1933), 41–104; *idem*, *ibid.*, 6 (1938), 121–152; *Beth-Pelet*, I, 12–13; W Culican, *The Australian Journal of Biblical Archaeology*, 2 (1973), 66–105. The tombs from Achzib have not yet been published. I am grateful to Dr. M. Prausnitz for this information.

40   G. R. Driver, *ADAJ*, 2 (1953), 63–64.

BIBLIOGRAPHY

CHAPTER I

KINGSHIP AND THE IDEOLOGY OF THE STATE

Alt, A., "The Monarchy in the Kingdoms of Judah and Israel," *Essays on Old Testament History and Religion*, Oxford, 1966, pp. (= *Kleine Schriften*, II, pp. 116–134)

Buber, M., *Kingship of God*, London, 1967

Engnell, I., *Studies in Divine Kingship in the Ancient Near East*[2], Oxford, 1967

Frankfort, H., *Kingship and the Gods*, Chicago, 1948

Liver, J., "King, Kingship," *Enc. Miqr.*, IV, cols. 1080–1112

Moran, W. L., "A Kingdom of Priests," in *The Bible in Current Catholic Thought* (ed. J. L. McKenzie), New York, 1962, pp. 7–20

Noth, M., "God, King and Nation in the Old Testament," *The Laws in the Pentateuch and Other Essays* (transl. D. R. Ap-Thomas), Edinburgh-London, 1966, pp. 145–178

Soggin, J. A., *Das Königtum in Israel* (= *BZAW* 104), 1967

de Vaux, R., *Ancient Israel: Its Life and Institutions* (transl. J. McHugh), London, 1961, pp. 91–114, 525–527

Widengren, G., *Sakrales Königtum im Alten Testament und in Judentum*, Stuttgart, 1955 "King and Covenant," *JSS*, 2 (1957), 1–32

CHAPTER II

LITERARY CREATIVITY

Eissfeldt, O., *The Old Testament, An Introduction* (transl. P. R. Ackroyd), Oxford, 1965

Gunkel, H., *The Legends of Genesis:* The Biblical Saga and History (transl. Gunkel-Begrich). Introduction by W. F. Albright, New York, 1964

Hallo, W. W., "Individual Prayer in Sumerian: The Continuity of a Tradition," Essays in Memory of E. A. Speiser (= *JAOS*, 88 [1968]), 72–79

Jepsen, A., *Die Quellen des Königsbuches*[2], Halle a/S, 1956

Kaufmann, Y., *Tol^edot*, I, part 1

Kramer, S. N., *The Sacred Marriage Rite*, London, 1969

Loewenstamm, S. E., "Law, Biblical Law," *Enc. Miqr.*, V, cols. 614–637

Mowinckel, S., *The Psalms in Israel's Worship* (transl. D. R. Ap-Thomas), I–II, Oxford, 1962

Noth, M., *Überlieferungsgeschichtliche Studien*, Halle a/S, 1953

Pope, M. H., *Job, The Anchor Bible*, New York, 1965, pp. XIII–LXXVIII

Scott, R. B. Y., *Proverbs-Ecclesiastes, The Anchor Bible*, New York, 1965, pp. XV–LIII, 3–30

Weinfeld, M., "Ancient Near Eastern Patterns in Prophetic Literature," *VT*, 27 (1976), pp. 178–195

Wellhausen, J., *Prolegomena to the History of Ancient Israel* (transl. Black-Menzies), New York, 1957

Würthwein, E., *Das Hohelied*, Gütersloh, 1969, pp. 25–37

CHAPTER III

THE EMERGENCE OF CLASSICAL HEBREW

Beyer, K., *Althebräische Grammatik*, Göttingen, 1969

Chase, Mary Ellen, *Life and Language in the Old Testament*, New York, 1955

Chomsky, W., *Hebrew: The Eternal Language*, Philadelphia, 1957

Cross, F. M. – Freedman, D. N., *Early Hebrew Orthography*, New Haven, 1952

Harris, Z. S., *Development of the Canaanite Dialects*, New Haven, 1939 "Linguistic Structure of Hebrew," *JAOS*, 61 (1941), 143–167.

Rabin, C., "Hebrew," *Current Trends in Linguistics*, VI, 1970, pp. 304–346; *A Short History of the Hebrew Language*, Jerusalem, 1974.

Schulte, H., *Die Entstehung der Geschichtsschreibung in Israel* (*BZAW*, 128), 1972, Chapter C: "*Die hebräische Sprache des zehnten Jahrhunderts*," pp. 181–202.

Sperber, A., *Historical Grammar of Hebrew*, Leiden, 1966

CHAPTER IV

RELIGION: STABILITY AND FERMENT

Albright, W. F., *Archaeology and the Religion of Israel*[2], Baltimore, 1946, chaps. iv–v

Cogan, M., *Imperialism and Religion: Assyria, Judah and Israel in the Eighth and Seventh Centuries B.C.E.*, Missoula, 1974

Cross, F. M., *Canaanite Myth and Hebrew Epic*, Cambridge, 1973, chaps. iii–iv

Eichrodt, W., *Theology of the Old Testament* (Eng. transl. J. A. Baker), I–II, Philadelphia, 1961, 1967

Fohrer, G., *History of Israelite Religion* (Eng. transl. D. E. Green), Nashville, 1972

Gaster, Th., *Myth, Legend, and Custom in the Old Testament*, New York – Evanston, 1969

Haran, M., *Ages and Institutions in the Bible*, Tel Aviv, 1972 (Hebrew)

Heschel, A. J., *The Prophets*, New York, 1962

Kaufmann, Y., *The Religion of Israel: From Its Beginnings to the Babylonian Exile* (Eng. transl. M. Greenberg), Chicago, 1960

Kraus, H.-J., *Worship in Israel* (Eng. transl. G. Buswell), Oxford, 1966

Lindblom, J., *Prophecy in Ancient Israel*, Philadelphia, 1962

Milgrom, J., *Cult and Conscience*, Leiden, 1976

Uffenheimer, B., *Ancient Prophecy in Israel*, Jerusalem, 1973, chaps. v–vii (Hebrew)

de Vaux, R., *Ancient Israel: Its Life and Institutions* (Eng. transl. J. McHugh), London, 1961

von Rad, G., *Old Testament Theology* (Eng. transl. D. Stalker), I–II, Edinburgh – London, 1963, 1965

CHAPTER V

THE STRUCTURE OF SOCIETY

Anderson, G. M., "Israel: Amphictyony: 'Am; Ḳāhāl; 'Edāh," in H. T. Frank – W. L. Reed (eds.), *Translating and Understanding the Old Testament* (H. G. May Volume), Nashville, New York, 1970, pp. 135–151.

Liver, J., "The Israelite Tribes," *Judges*, pp. 183–211, 326–331

Lurje, M., *Studien zur Geschichte der wirtschaftlichen und sozialen Verhältnisse im israelitisch-judischen Reiche*, Giessen, 1927

McKenzie, J. L., "The Elders in the Old Testament," *Analecta Biblica*, 10 (1959), 388–406

Neufeld, E., "The Emergence of a Royal-Urban Society in Ancient Israel," *HUCA*, 31 (1960), 31–53

Pedersen, J., *Israel, Its Life and Culture*, I–IV, London – Copenhagen, 1926–1940

Reviv, H., "Types of Leadership in the Period of the Judges," *Beer-sheva Annual*, 1 (1973), 204–221 (Hebrew)

Tadmor, H., "'The People' and the Kingship in Ancient Israel," *Journal of World History*, 11 (1968), 46–68

de Vaux, R., *Ancient Israel, Its Life and Institutions* (Eng. transl. J. McHugh), London, 1961

Weber, M., *Ancient Judaism* (Eng. transl. and eds. H. H. Gerth and D. Martindale), New York, 1952

CHAPTER VI

ADMINISTRATION

Maisler (Mazar), B., "The Scribe of King David and the Problem of the High Officials in the Ancient Kingdom of Israel," *BJPES*, 13 (1946–1947), 105–114 (Hebrew)

Mettinger, T. N. D., *Solomonic State Officials*, Lund, 1971

de Vaux, R., *Ancient Israel* (transl. J. McHugh), London, 1961, pp. 127–138, 152–155, 213–225, 376–379

Yeivin, Sh., "The Administration in Ancient Israel (under David)," in A. Malamat (ed.), *The Kingdoms of Israel and Judah*, Jerusalem, 1961, pp. 47–65 (Hebrew); "Families and Parties in the Kingdom of Judah," *Studies in the History of Israel and His Country*, Tel Aviv – Jerusalem, 1960, pp. 250–293 (Hebrew)

CHAPTER VII

TRADE AND COMMERCE

Aharoni, Y., *The Land of the Bible*, London, 1966

Albright, W. F., "The Role of the Canaanites in the History of Civilization," *The Bible and the Ancient Near East: Essays in Honor of W. F. Albright* (ed. G. E. Wright), New York, 1961

Archaeology and the Religion of Israel, Baltimore, 1942, pp. 95–175

Barnett, R. D., "Phoenicia and the Ivory Trade," *Archaeology*, 9 (1956)

Diakonoff, M., "Main Features of the Economy in the Monarchies of Ancient Western Asia," *Third International Conference of Economic History*, III, Munich, 1965; Paris, 1969, pp. 13–32

Elat, M., *Economic Relations in the Bible Lands (c. 1000–539 B.C.E.)*, Jerusalem, 1977 (Hebrew)

Eph'al, I., *The Nomads on the Borders of Palestine during the Periods of the Assyrian, Babylonian and Persian Empires* (Ph. D. Dissertation, Jerusalem, 1971 [Hebrew])

Grohmann, A., *Südarabien als Wirtschaftsgebiet*, I, Wien, 1922; II, Prag, 1933

Helck, W., *Die Beziehungen Ägyptens zu*

Vorderasien im 2. und 3. Jahrtausend v. Chr., Wiesbaden, 1962

Herzfeld, L., *Handelsgeschichte der Juden des Altertums*, Braunschweig, 1879

Leemans, W. F., *Foreign Trade in the Old Babylonian Period*, Leiden, 1960
"Old Babylonian Letters and Economic History," *JESHO*, 11 (1968), 171–226

Meissner, B., "*Warenpreise in Babylonien*," Abhundlungen der Preussischen Akademie der Wissenschaften, Philosophisch-Historische Klasse, Berlin, 1936

Oppenheim, A. L., "Essays on Overland Trade in the First Millennium B.C.," *JCS*, 21 (1969), 236–254
"Trade in the Ancient Near East," *Fifth International Congress of Economic History, Leningrad, 1970*, Moscow, 1970, pp. 1–37

Rathjens, C., "Die Weihrauchstrasse in Arabien," *Tribus des Linden Museum*, Stuttgart, N. F., II/III (1952–53)

Van Beek, G. W., "Frankincense and Myrrh," *BAr*, 23 (1960), 69–95 (= *BAR*, 2, 1964, pp. 99–126)

Vercoutter, J., "The Gold of Kush," *Kush*, 7 (1959), 120–153

CHAPTER VIII

See Archaeological Reports cited in the notes
to this chapter.

CHAPTER IX–X

CRAFT AND INDUSTRY/DWELLINGS AND GRAVES

Avitsur, Sh., *Man and his Work*, Historical Atlas of Tools and Workshops in the Holy Land, Jerusalem, 1976

Barrois, A. G., *Manuel d'archéologie biblique*, I–II, Paris, 1939–1953

Forbes, R. J., *Studies in Ancient Technology*, III–V, VIII–IX, Leiden, 1964–1966

Paul, S. M.—Dever, W. G. (eds.), *Biblical Archaeology*, Jerusalem, 1973

Pritchard, J. B., *The Ancient Near East in Pictures*, Princeton, 1954, 1969[2]

Singer, C. – Holmyard, E. J. – Hall, A. R. (eds.), *A History of Technology*, I: From Early Times to Fall of Ancient Empires, Oxford, 1954

de Vaux, R., *Ancient Israel, Its Life and Institutions* (Eng. transl. J. McHugh), London, 1961, pp. 56–61, 76–78

Wright, G. E., *Biblical Archaeology*, Philadelphia – London, 1957, pp. 183–201.

INDEX OF NAMES AND PLACES